Discourses of Service in Shakespeare's England

David Evett

First published in 2005 by
PALGRAVE MACMILLAN™
175 Fifth Avenue, New York, N.Y. 10010 and
Houndmills, Basingstoke, Hampshire, England RG21 6XS
Companies and representatives throughout the world.

PALGRAVE MACMILLAN is the global academic imprint of the Palgrave Macmillan division of St. Martin's Press, LLC and of Palgrave Macmillan Ltd. Macmillan® is a registered trademark in the United States, United Kingdom and other countries. Palgrave is a registered trademark in the European Union and other countries.

ISBN 1–4039–6815–2

Library of Congress Cataloging-in-Publication Data

Evett, David.
  Discourses of service in Shakespeare's England / David Evett.
    p. cm.
  Includes bibliographical references and index.
  ISBN 1–4039–6815–2
    1. Shakespeare, William, 1564–1616—Characters—Servants.
  2. Master and servant—England—History—16th century.
  3. Master and servant—England—History—17th century.
  4. Domestics—England—History—16th century. 5. Domestics—England—History—17th century. 6. Master and servant in literature. 7. Domestics in literature . 8. Servants in literature.
    I. Title.

PR2992.S47E97 2005
822.3′3—dc22   2004059777

A catalogue record for this book is available from the British Library.

Design by Newgen Imaging Systems (P) Ltd., Chennai, India.

First edition: April 2005

10 9 8 7 6 5 4 3 2 1

Printed in the United States of America.

CONTENTS

Acknowledgments   vii

Chapter 1   The Paradox of Service and Freedom   1

Chapter 2   The Hop and the Pole: The Limits of Materialism   17

Chapter 3   "Surprising Confrontations": Discourses of
             Service in *The Taming of the Shrew*   35

Chapter 4   "Monsieur, We Are Not Lettered":
             Classical Influences and the Early Modern
             Marketplace   55

Chapter 5   "Clubs, Bills, and Partisans":
             Retainer Violence and Male Bonding   81

Chapter 6   *Fidelis Servus* . . . : Good Service
             and the Obligations of Obedience   109

Chapter 7   . . . *Perpetuus Asinus*: Bad Service and
             the Primacy of the Will   133

Chapter 8   "A Place in the Story": Gender,
             Commodity, Alienation, and Service   159

Chapter 9   "As Willing as Bondage E'er of Freedom":
             The Vindication of Willing Service in *The Tempest*   183

Notes   213
Works Cited   263
Index   279

ACKNOWLEDGMENTS

This book has been long in the making, and the list of my debts is correspondingly long. Most of the research and writing was done while I was still an active member of the Department of English at Cleveland State University, and I received steady support from my department and college. A sabbatical term at the Folger Shakespeare Library allowed me to explore early modern writings on service; another freed me from teaching and administration in order to write. I found the books I needed and the staff support I hoped for at the CSU library, at the Folger, and at the libraries of Case Western Reserve University, Harvard University, and Tufts University. Early versions of various chapters were presented to the Southeast Renaissance Conference, the Ohio Shakespeare Conference, the Citadel Conference, the Guild of Episcopal Scholars, and several meetings of the Shakespeare Association of America; the reactions encouraged me to continue the work and helped shape it. My worldwide associates in SHAKSPER, the ongoing international internet conference, have provoked and responded to statements and restatements of many of the book's ideas and points, and all of us owe thanks to SHAKSPER's indefatigable manager, Hardy Cook.

Everyone now working on Shakespeare and service must honor the trailblazers, who moved a previously marginalized topic toward the center of our field. I feel special obligations to Richard Strier, who not only helped lead the way but has encouraged many others to follow, and to Mark Thornton Burnett, with whom I often disagree but never without having to improve my own understanding first. The book was read in various manuscript stages by T. G. Bishop (who has also contributed by way of dozens of conversations and emails), John Cox (whose advocacy over several decades of a Christian reading of essentially Christian texts has been exemplary), Lars Engle (whose own brilliant book on early modern intellectual exchange gave me my title and whose challenges I can only hope to have met), Stuart Evett, Whit Hieatt, Carol Chillington Rutter, and Debora Shuger; all of them made many useful suggestions, and none of them led me astray. More recently, David Schalkwyk has materialized as companion and guide. I got detailed comments on parts of the book on the way to publication as articles from Daniel Doerksen, Christopher Hodgkins, and Michael Neill. To Michael, whose own writing on early modern service is rich, subtle, humane, and wise, I owe special thanks for encouraging me at a dark hour. My editors at Palgrave Macmillan have been consistently supportive and helpful.

My largest tribute must go to my wife, Marianne. For more than four decades her acumen as a reader and editor of early modern dramatic texts, and of writing about them, has fostered my better understanding and curbed my vagaries. Her deeply informed sympathy with actors and audiences as one of America's most distinguished drama critics has enriched my sensitivity to the plays in performance. I argue here that action more than language truly informs the servant–master relationship. I owe that insight mainly to my experience of Shakespeare on the stage, and my duties as her chauffeur and baggage-handler have enabled me to see significant professional productions of every single one of the Shakespeare plays mentioned in this book, in the United States, Canada, and Great Britain, most of them over and over again. For what Marianne has taught me and many others about service in the widest, warmest sense of that word, to family, community, world—and the wonderful freedoms that follow from it—I can find no words.

David Evett
Arlington, Massachusetts
November 2004

CHAPTER 1
THE PARADOX OF SERVICE
AND FREEDOM

This book takes its inspiration from a magically paradoxical phrase in the Tudor Book of Common Prayer, "service is perfect freedom." The book explores this concept in early modern English culture, with special attention to the various kinds of people we can label as servants, and to such people as they are represented in the plays of William Shakespeare. It carries out this exploration in the larger context of the complex and dynamic understandings of service in England as they evolved through the sixteenth and early seventeenth centuries. Such relationships patently involved people who were deeply dependent on other, wealthier, more powerful people for their livelihoods, and whose orders they took. It is essential to realize at the outset, however, that the ideals and practices of service came at one point or another to inform the attitudes and lives of women and men at every level of society, so that even people at the highest economic and political levels sometimes felt, thought, and acted as servants. And all these people were explicitly called to an ideal of service by the central doctrines of the Christianity to which they subscribed.

The book thus has an ethical, even spiritual agenda. Initially, the focus is historical, working through the several ideologies of service that were active in early modern English society, both from the idealist and from the materialist points of view. Later, the book takes a political and psychological turn, as specifically postmodern ideas increasingly come into play. The agenda operates both within and against the overwhelmingly pragmatic and materialist ethos of late-twentieth- and early-twenty-first-century critical practice, especially in connection with a psychological concept I call *volitional primacy*. The servants in the Shakespeare plays, like their counterparts in early modern society outside the drama, have lately attracted critical and historical attention after centuries in which they were almost entirely ignored. Much of that attention is informed by sensitivity to issues of power, and my argument tries to take account of the real force of this work. Still, the book tries to show that the idea and the praxis of service invoked and enacted the motives of love and sacrifice that make social life not only possible but also desirable. It thus contends that a full response to these plays—and by implication to many other early modern cultural artifacts—requires a fuller awareness of service than has generally been achieved. And it contends that the ideals of service have important twenty-first-century applications.

The exploration begins with a brief history of the great paradox of freedom in service. The paradox stands at the center of the Collect for Peace of the Anglican Prayer Book's service of Morning Prayer:

> O God, which art author of peace, and lover of concorde, in knowledge of whome standeth oure eternall life, whose *service is perfect fredome*: defende us, thy humble servauntes, in al assaultes of our enemies, that wee surely trustyng in thy defence, maye not feare the power of any adversaries: through the myght of Jesu Christ our lorde. Amen. (1549; emphasis added)

In assembling the 1549 version of the Prayer Book, Thomas Cranmer took this collect from the *postcommunio* of the *Missa pro pace* in the Sacramentary of Gregory the Great, as found in the Sarum rites followed in English churches and which Cranmer himself had heard and used through almost all of his 60 years as layman, priest, and bishop.[1] The Latin version, which had been a constant feature of the missal from the twelfth century onward, reads as follows:

> Deus autor pacis et amator caritatis quem nosse uiuere cui servire regnare est. protege ab omnibus impugnacionibus supplices tuos. ut cui in defensione tua confidimus. nullius hostilitatis arma timeamus. (Legge 396)[2]

The rubric in the Sarum Missal states that the *Missa pro pace* was routinely used on the eighteenth Sunday in Trinity, and exceptionally whenever war threatened. Many versions of the missal, however, include five other prayers under the heading *pro pace*, and twenty-seven more under the heading *tempore belli*; none of them exhibits anything similar to *servire regnare*, making Cranmer's choice even more striking.

In the Sarum Primer, on which the daily offices of the Prayer Book are largely based, a different Collect for Peace had appeared at the end of the second morning office, Lauds, the service on which Morning

Prayer was modeled:

> O God, from whome all holy desyres, all good counsels, and all iust works do procede, geue vnto thy seruantes that same peace which the world cannot geue: that oure heartes beyng obedient to thy commaundementes, and the feare of our enemyes taken awaye, oure time may be peaceable by thy protection. Through Christ our lorde. Amen.[3]

By substituting the collect from the *Missa pro pace* for this one, Cranmer saw to it that a prayer formerly heard once or twice a year was now placed where it would be said or heard every day by every conscientious Anglican priest, heard almost every Sunday by every churchgoer, and said or heard almost every day by the masters and servants of pious conforming households (Brightman 148; Legge 395).[4] The original collect called attention to servants, and to obedience; in promoting the new one from occasional to incessant use, however, Cranmer laid the emphasis of repetition and of Establishment on the paradox of "perfect freedom" in service. And in adapting the prayer, he made changes that strengthen the features of the prayer most germane to a consideration of service as a social practice. For Cranmer promotes the idea from an infinitive phrase, *servire regnare*, to a clause, "whose service is perfect freedom," and replaces the essentially political term "to reign" with a word, "freedom," that not only explicitly invokes liberty within constraints of all kinds, but also has a much more generally social, psychological, and situational emphasis. Cranmer then goes on to domesticate the quasi-military "assailants" and "attackers" of the Latin prayer (*omnibus impugnationibus, hostilitatis arma*) into more general "enemies" and "adversaries," so that they could be cruel masters or pitiless creditors as well as besieging armies. Cranmer's translation of *caritas* as "concord" foregrounds social or domestic harmony rather than the top-down solicitude for the less fortunate that operates in the Bible in things like the story of the rich man and the beggar and that had generally characterized medieval Christian thought.[5] And Cranmer turns Sarum's *supplices*, "supplicants," into "servants," reiterating, more sharply than the Latin rite, the theological concept invoked by the service–freedom paradox, but also on phenomenological grounds rendering the prayer particularly relevant to any auditors who already think of themselves as servants in nontheological contexts.

We can certainly situate this development in a familiar materialist history in which rulers and their spin doctors exploit the elements of religious belief and practice to sustain their power and privilege. Such an analysis rests on the demonstrable instabilities wrought on the model of service operating in England around the accession of Henry VII. This model was quasi-military. In it, mainly male servants, bound by vows of lifetime service and compensated for it by their lodging, clothing, and food plus occasional gifts, did most of the household chores, but also stood ready to accompany their master to war; similar patterns of exchange governed households in which the military dimension was less significant. In Tudor times, an increasingly centralized royal authority reduced the power of the magnates by reducing the size of their retainer bands. The feudal household gave place to a more obviously capitalistic model in which women as well as men were hired by the quarter or year for maintenance plus cash wages. Driven by enclosure and drawn by the growth of commerce and industry, thousands of men and women, former tenants, beholden to their landlords, but also in significant ways independent, became the hirelings of better-to-do farmers, or left the land altogether and moved to cities and towns to become dependents in the households of merchants and crafters as apprentices, journeymen, or domestics. The closing of the monasteries, by redistributing ecclesiastical wealth and turning many former monastics to seek a living for themselves, together with the first groups of Protestant refugees from the Continent, generated economic uncertainty and enlarged the number of people for whom domestic service represented a possible livelihood.[6] Later in the period, soldiers discharged back into civilian life after English military activities in France, the Low Countries, and Ireland returned in significant numbers to look for work in the cities or in the large households of agrarian magnates.

For these and other reasons, the dominant model of service became increasingly domestic rather than military. Over the same period, the economic developments of an emerging capitalism shifted the standard service relationship from long-term affiliations grounded in neighborhood and custom to short-term arrangements for cash wages. The shift gave servants much greater mobility—even as it made the social system less stable. The increase in the population of dependents no longer fixed in customary places for life aroused anxiety. Civil strife, especially the Peasants' Revolt (which fed the conservative reaction against the initial success of radical Protestant thought across Europe) and the Catholic uprisings of 1536–37 in England itself, a largely popular movement, shook the seats of the mighty. Thus, the anxiety of rulers about subjects blended into the anxiety of masters about servants; this anxiety provoked legal and conceptual strategies of control and containment. The notion of "ideological misrepresentation" developed by Jonathan

Dollimore and Alan Sinfield suggests the possibility that Cranmer's work on the Prayer Book (which also includes prayers for the monarch and other magistrates) made part of the general strategy of hegemonic legitimation undertaken by the supporters of Henry VIII, Edward VI, and Elizabeth, of which the *Book of Homilies*—including the homilies against disobedience and rebellion—is a familiar instance (Dollimore and Sinfield 206–27). A reading of the collect might plausibly see in it an appeal to subordinated persons to remain contentedly in the stations to which God had called them—a call that, indeed, only echoes significant strains in the Bible, and especially the Pauline epistles. Such a view has dominated the materialist treatments of service that we examine more closely in chapter 2.

An examination of the history of the paradox, however, suggests that by the time Cranmer boosted its liturgical visibility, it had not only sustained its ability to inspire anew each generation of Christian idealists, but had also come over time to have a more general and intrinsic claim, independent of the interests of the privileged few. Indeed, foregrounding the paradox only amplifies a leveling strain present in Christian theology and polity from the earliest days, when members of the brand new church repeatedly invoked Christ and his followers by the title of servant (Acts 2:18, 27; 3:13, 26; 4:25, 27, 29, 30, and passim). There is a solid Old Testament basis for this in the periods spent in servile roles by Jacob and Joseph, Samuel's service of Eli and David and David's service of Saul, and the national service of the Israelites during both the Egyptian and the Babylonian exiles. Christ takes this further, turning models into prescriptions: "If anie man desire to be first, the same shalbe last of all, and seruant vnto all" (Mark 9:35; see also Mark 10:43–44; Matt. 20:26–27; 23:11–12; Luke 9:48; 22:26).[7]

In Scripture, the notion as incorporated in the collect emerges most fully in Galatians 4–5. Here, Paul constructs an elaborate allegory of bondage and freedom (citing the relationships among Abraham, Sarah, Hagar, and their children), in which the law of the old covenant is required by the bondage of the body, but the freedom of the new covenant is enabled by the new freedom of the spirit, which comes to a focus in an injunction obviously relevant to our present purposes: "For brethren, ye haue been called vnto libertie: only vse not *your* libertie as an occasion vnto the flesh, but by loue serue one another. For all the Law is fulfilled in one worde, which is this, Thou shalt loue thy neighbour as thy selfe" (5:13–14). (It is on this text that Luther and other Protestant theologians primarily found their understanding of service.) There is no question that even in the early Christian period, the words are used in a primarily spiritual sense; relief from literal slavery, always a perquisite of Greek and Roman masters, might come somewhat more often for the bond servants of Christians than for those of pagans, but most born or sold into the servant class could expect to spend their lives there, only looking forward to freedom, even the reversal of roles (as in the story of the rich man and Lazarus) in the afterlife. Yet the argument has the effect of blurring the distinction between Law and law, service to an ideal and service to a man, for only rarely do the biblical texts make social distinctions, and when they are made in the context of a particular situation or story, they tend to get lost when the statement is cited by itself. Either way, then, the life of service is extrinsically bound and hence extrinsically undesirable, intrinsically free and hence intrinsically valuable. The ultimate argument is the life of Christ, who "*chose* a laborious and painful life. . . . So that if thou be his disciple and servant, thou must not disdaine that which thy Master chose" (Fosset 1612, 13; emphasis added). And Paul himself, as he tells his Christian brothers and sisters in Corinth, is striving to live this argument: "For thogh I be fre from all men, yet haue I made myself seruant vnto all men, that I might winne the mo" (1 Cor. 9:19).[8] Or, as he puts it more generally, in a verse repeatedly cited by Tudor commentators, "For he that is called in the Lord *being* a seruant, is the Lords freman: likewise also he that is called *being* fre, is Christs seruant" (1 Cor. 7:22).[9]

Christian emphasis on service, and its paradoxical association with freedom, passes over from the Bible into the writings of the Church Fathers and thence into the practice of the church. From early on, the popes call themselves *servus servorum Dei*, servant of the servants of God (that the proposition looks remarkably hypocritical in connection with somebody like Alexander VI does not invalidate it theologically). The paradox of freedom in service is particularly marked by St. John Chrysostom. Indeed, Chrysostom develops the theme of service more fully than any other of the early fathers, with a specifically domestic, practical emphasis, particularly in his commentary on Ephesians (of which an English translation was published in 1581, popular enough to deserve a second printing). The condition and institution of servitude in the world is without question a direct consequence of the Fall (303). But taken aright, this is the Fortunate Fall; adducing the example of Christ washing the disciples' feet, Chrysostom argues that "It were better, that both Maisters and servants, would serve one another. Much better were it thus to be servant, than to be otherwise a free man" (255). The theme is that other paradox of the last being first: in the world to come, faithful servants will occupy "the last [i.e., highest] place in worthinesse" (298).

Of servants serving, he writes that "it is not a basenesse so to doe, but it is the greatest nobilitie that can be, for men to knowe howe to submitte themselues, and to keepe a meane, and to yielde to their neighbour" (299–300). Of particular importance is the way Chrysostom amplifies the importance of the will, invoking the turning of the other cheek: "for, he that is readie to suffer more iniurie than is already offered him, hath made that to be his owne, which was not his owne" (300–1), that is, by *willingly allowing* rather than merely *enduring* the injury, the Christian has, in effect, made the transition from child to adult and servant to master outlined in Galatians 4.[10]

I will call this process, whereby one treats as self-imposed various conditions and actions that are in fact imposed from outside, *volitional primacy* (see chapter 7 for a detailed treatment). Aquinas would subsequently connect such a process with the concept of Christian charity, and put it on an Aristotelian footing, in a way that gives servants responsibility for all that they do, even when following a master's orders: ". . . men who are slaves [*servi*] or subjects in any sense, are moved by the commands of others in such a way that they move themselves by their free-will; wherefore some kind of rectitude of government is required in them . . ." (2–2 q.50 A2, 2.48).

Augustine, who wrote a commentary on Galatians, repeatedly invokes the ideal; writing when the institution of slavery is still normative for Mediterranean societies, he edges toward, if he cannot quite endorse, a notion of the spiritual equality of masters and servants:

> Moreover, if [a] slave is receiving from you, his master, a better moral training or a guidance more correct and better adapted to the worship of God than can be given him by the man who wants to take him away, I doubt whether anyone would venture to say that this slave—like a garment—ought to receive no consideration. For, as subsequent pronouncements reveal, a man ought to love a man [note the absence of social discriminators] as he loves himself, because the Lord commands him to love even his enemies. (*Mount* 86–87)

Augustine did not necessarily initiate the service–freedom paradox itself; he certainly used it, however, if in a less concentrated form than the collect: "This is the true, perfect, and only religion, through which it becomes a property of the greatness of the soul, which we are studying now, to be reconciled to God, and by which it makes itself worthy of freedom. For He whom it is most useful for all to serve, and to delight in whose service is the only perfect freedom, frees all things" (*De quantitatae animis* 78).[11] Augustine speaks here of service to God. But from the first Pentecost onward, the church has always understood that people serve God by serving their neighbors, that is, subordinating their own interests to others'. Service to God means service to man. And Augustine's immense subsequent authority authorized the recurrence of the idea.

Augustine's movement is usually away from the actual toward the spiritual, however, and unlike Chrysostom, he does not develop his thinking about service in terms of quotidian human life. His monastic rule, the basis for all the subsequent orders, does not emphasize service, though it does insist that the leader of a monastic house, even when honored by all the other residents, should nevertheless think of himself as their servant (*Rule*, ch. 10).[12] The ideal of service takes a more fully practical and experiential form in later manifestations of the monastic impulse. In the Benedictine Rule, mutual service is clearly a condition of the monastic vocation from the Abbot to the lowest novice:

> Let the brethren serve each other so that no one be excused from the work in the kitchen, except on account of sickness or more necessary work, because greater merit and more charity is thereby acquired. . . . or if, as we have said, any are engaged in more urgent work; let the rest serve each other in charity. (ch. 35)

> Before and above all things, care must be taken of the sick, that they be served in very truth as Christ is served; because He hath said, "I was sick and you visited Me" (Matt. 25:36). (ch. 36)

> But when the Abbot hath been elected let him bear in mind how great a burden he hath taken upon himself, and to whom he must give an account of his stewardship [cf. Luke 16:2]; and let him be convinced that it becometh him better to serve than to rule. (ch. 64)

Note that in the last sentence the idea though not originally the actual language of the paradox appears.[13] A similar ideal appears in the constitutions of the mendicant orders; thus the Rule of St. Francis repeatedly calls the leaders of these monks "ministers and servants" of the others (*Writings* 36, 38, and passim).

Monastic devotion to service reappears in the writings of Martin Luther, an Augustinian monk, who scatters dozens of appeals to service, including several extensive treatments of the idea, across dozens of works over the whole course of his career.[14] He follows Chrysostom in emphasizing in *The Freedom of a Christian Man* (1520) the element of absolutely free choice: "a Christian is a servant of all and made subject to all. Insofar as he is free he does no works, but insofar as he is a servant he does all kinds of works. . . . it is his one occupation to serve God [which means serving other people] joyfully and without thought of gain, in love that is not constrained" (*Works* 31.358–59). Luther enumerates the various meanings of the term *servant* using the traditional exegetical paradigm. In the moral and typological senses, he says, somewhat opaquely, it refers to "every person by himself and for himself"— presumably under the compelling universality of the Golden Rule. In the allegorical sense, it is "a person for others and over others and for the sake of others." The latter sense signifies "dignity and honor," and the former "complete submission and humility" (*Comm. Romans, Works* 25.140–41). The latter is "worth more": in this passage, Luther was writing with an eye to clerical ministry, the "servants" of the faithful who nevertheless enjoy the people's honor and esteem, like the popes and abbots of the Augustinian–Franciscan monastic tradition invoked above. The former meaning, applicable to "every person," however base, is "more salutary." It is this first, wider sense that most influences and informs subsequent commentators. And it takes special force within the Lutheran context because of Luther's pervasive insistence on the importance of individual Christians' need to identify themselves with Christ. Christ lived a life of service, and in every moment of that life, he saw and responded to the needs of others, at whatever cost to himself, including the ultimate cost of death on the Cross. A Christian trying to live a Christian life could try to do no less.

Incorporated in these definitions is the duality of body and soul: physical bondage, spiritual freedom. Phenomenologically, all of us are enslaved by our bodies and the laws of nature. We have to eat, drink, and sleep; we are inescapably subject to gravity, time, and death— St. Paul calls these constraints "the elements of the world" (Gal. 4:3; Geneva and Bishops' "rudiments of the world," but Vulgate "*elementis mundi*," Authorized Version "elements of the world"). Psychologically and theologically, all people are enslaved by their passions. True freedom can be found only in the motions of the spirit. Thus, Luther's English follower William Whately treats servitude as an equation of dichotomies: bond is to flesh as freedom is to spirit (1640, 1.156). The Scottish commentator Robert Rollock argues that if it is a vice in a servant to be disobedient (i.e., free) in body, it is equally a vice to be submissive (i.e., bound) in spirit to anyone but God (361). It is on this ground that servants are encouraged to resist and even to disobey the wicked orders of their masters, a crucial component of fully faithful service, as we shall see.

In any event, Luther pays a lot of attention to service, in strikingly practical and quotidian terms. A commonplace of his writing is that sixteenth-century servants are conspicuously less conscientious and faithful than their biblical counterparts. (It is, indeed, a marked feature of the Bible that servants are by and large represented as faithful and hard working.[15]) Thus, in his lectures on Genesis, he comments on the readiness of the servants of Abraham to leave the country of their birth to follow their master to Canaan: "The servants and maids surprise me; for if they had been like ours, they would never have lifted up a foot" (2.280). But they are only reflecting the spirit of their master; though Abraham was Lot's uncle, his elder, his superior in wealth and dignity, he nevertheless yielded his own rights to the younger man (Gen. 13:7): "Is this not what Christ commands in John 13:15 ff., that he who is the greater should be as the lesser and as the servant of others," reiterating the injunctions to popes and abbots in Augustine and the monastic rules (2.336–37).[16] The service of Jacob to Laban and Joseph to Pharaoh is likewise exemplary: "Today, how sad and all too common the complaints of all fathers of households are regarding the treachery and dishonesty of servants!" (*Works* 6.67).

Indeed, the reiterated burden of Luther's treatment of service is the need for servants to be faithful and obedient. What though a man be formally dependent on another man? " 'God loves me, and I believe that my master, too, shares in all the blessings of God that I enjoy.' Therefore you should consider in what a favorable position you are. To be sure, you are in a slavery of the body, but you are equals in spirit. When a servant thinks this way, he serves gladly" (*Comm. 1 Timothy, Works* 28.363).[17] There is a certain sense of strain in this and other similar passages: Luther himself by this time had left the monastery, married, set up housekeeping, and so was now himself presumably an employer of servants, as worried as any other early modern master about his employees' reliability.[18] So he repeatedly urges the spiritual superiority of social and economic inferiority—and in the process comes close to, though he never explicitly reaches, the oxymoron of service and freedom. "How much better is the kind of life when a man is servant to another man, promising fidelity and the duties of a servant! Here there is a voluntary fidelity [*fides voluntaria*]"—note again the Augustinian and Thomistic emphasis on the will (*Comm. Titus, Works* 29.60).[19] More to the purpose, then, is the general spirit of Lutheran teaching, with its powerful endorsement of personal identification with the life and death of Christ, and its reiteration of the notion that true freedom arises from eager obedience to God.[20] And the crucially important consequence of these writings is to blur the distinction between servants, in the familiar economic and social sense, and other people. Christianity calls all people to a life of service; it is only that some are more fully (or merely) servants than others. As we shall see in chapters 2 and 3, however, that line was also blurred in the social practices of early modern England, inasmuch as most people spent at least part of their lives in formally servile roles, including members of the economic and social elite.

Almost as soon as he had formulated these ideas, Luther was driven to repudiate them. When some of his early followers began to act out a program to obliterate social hierarchy, the beneficiaries of the hierarchy responded ferociously. Hence, Luther retreated almost desperately from his own early socialism (in which we may see the egalitarian ideals of the monastic tradition extended into secular life) into the ancient distinction between earthly and heavenly justice. Stephen Greenblatt has forcibly reminded us that Luther's response to the Peasants' Revolt of 1523–24 was first (May 5, 1525) a letter in which he tells his "dear friends" that the Bible marks a distinction between spiritual and social or economic freedom; then a pamphlet, "Against the Robbing and Murdering Hordes of Peasants," which sees the rebels as agents of the Devil and encourages good Christian people to put the rebellion down with all necessary violence (*Learning* 105–06). If he was moved by the furious charges of betrayal from the peasants he had inspired, he did not show it, and in time, the institutionalized Lutheran church became "an established church, predominantly an aristocratic and middle class party of vested interest and privilege" (P. Smith 86).

As ideas do, however, these, once articulated, took on a life of their own, and it seems certain that all these influences bore on Thomas Cranmer at the point where he was assembling the materials for the Prayer Book. The Bible he knew intimately. St. John Chrysostom was an important source for his thought and writing throughout his career; a prayer identified as Chrysostom's closes the service of Morning Prayer.[21] Chrysostom, along with Augustine, was the patristic wellhead for justification by faith, the core concept of Cranmer's reforming theology; the two provided sources on which Cranmer could safely call for support while avoiding explicit debts to that more dangerous Augustinian, Luther. As layman, don, and archbishop, Cranmer had extensive knowledge of English monastics; his sister Alice was a Cistercian nun and prioress of her convent, and although he came to share the general reformation view of the monasteries as pustules of popish corruption, he did seek at the time of the Dissolution to protect individual monastics whom he knew and admired. Lutheran writings and practice inspired English reformists of the 1520s and 1530s, including many in Cambridge where Cranmer lived and worked at that time as a Fellow of Jesus College. During this period, Cranmer followed an essentially Lutheran line on the highly vexed question of the Real Presence, until the influence of Martin Bucer and others moved him toward the views of the Schmalkaldic League (MacCullough *Cranmer* 380). Indeed, after he took orders, traveling as Ambassador to the Emperor through Germany early in 1532, he met some Lutheran divines, and very quietly married the niece of one of them—by marriage acting out one element of Lutheran reform—and was deeply involved in the unsuccessful negotiations of 1538 seeking common ground between Lutherans and Henrician Anglicans (Ridley 163–64).[22] In 1548, while he was working on the Prayer Book, he might well have seen this translation from one of Luther's commentaries: "in the Christianite, there are the iuste and righteous, euery man doeth, as he oughte to do wyllyngly, and gladly, there is no power of dominion of the one, ouer the other, but there are they al brethren, and the one serueth the other, helpeth hym, deliuereth hym, and careth for his neyghboure, as for hys brother, yea euen as for hym self" (*Frutefull* Eiir).

Under a king, Henry VIII, who wanted political and economic but not theological separation from Rome, even the reforming wing of the English ecclesiastical establishment saw the early manifestations of Lutheranism as socially subversive as well as heretical, and generally rejected it in favor of the Zwinglian Reform movement of Simon Grynaeus, Martin Bucer, and Pietro Martire—Peter Martyr—who became Cranmer's correspondents, colleagues, and friends. Even the more radical developments under Edward, although they gave relatively extreme Lutheran partisans like Latimer a fuller and freer voice in the discussion, retained a strong socially conservative element. One of Cranmer's own contributions to the famous *Homilies*, oddly enough, the *Homelie of the Salvacion of Mankynd*, puts a strong if diffuse emphasis on freedom, by using the word and its expanded forms 13 times in 6 pages (79–85). But as many materialist and new historicist scholars have observed, the central call of those texts, including Cranmer's, is to obedience, to both secular and sacred powers, as "the very roote of all vertues, and the cause of all felicitie" (209).[23]

For all that, emergent Lutheran thought suffuses Cranmer's work.[24] Luther's ideals of service, of staying—rejoicing—in the place to which God has called you, informed Cranmer's life as well as his writing. From Belloc and Hutchinson to MacCullough, his biographers emphasize the largely unquestioning fidelity he offered to the two kings he served, Henry VIII and Edward VI, a fidelity that repeatedly linked God and King on a rhetorical footing that only places God higher by placing his name first (Ridley 257): "complete obedience [to the monarch] had been Cranmer's consistent policy" (MacCullough *Cranmer* 559), or, as Ridley puts it in more assertively materialist terms: "the weakness which Cranmer always showed toward the established order"—the papacy excluded (156).[25] The political aspect of his fall, his conviction of treason for his part in the short-lived attempt to put Jane Grey on the throne instead of Mary, can be in part explained by the fact that the plan was Edward's as much as anyone's (MacCullough 540).

Cranmer's commitment to service, and its conscious intellectual and emotional ground, are summarized in a proposition from a note on Ceremonies in the 1552 Prayer Book that echoes the freedom/service paradox: "Christes Gospell is not a Ceremonial lawe (as much of Moses lawe was) but it is a religion to serve God, not in bondage of the figure or shadowe but in the fredome of spirite."[26] The frame of reference here is spiritual, of course, but the same kind of diffusion of the concept from the spiritual realm into the social that we saw in Luther occurs in and around Cranmer and his successors. We can trace the development, and the Christian ideal of service more widely conceived and applied, through the sermons and treatises of four succeeding generations of both conforming and dissenting clergy, and through them into the lives of a people whose culture, as Susan Dwyer Amussen has argued, was "rooted in the Church of England" (35).[27] The ultimate argument is the life of Christ, who "*chose* a laborious and painful life. . . . So that if thou be his disciple and servant, thou must not disdaine that which thy Master chose" (Fosset 1612, 13; emphasis added). In Christ's service, all persons are justified. Being justified, they become free (Althouse *Theology* 266; Verkamp 26). "Art thou a servant? Care not for it, thou art Christ's freeman" (Byfield 135). Page-heading: *A servant fearing God, the Lords Freeman* (Elton 571).

That being the case, as Thomas Fosset states, the servant should willingly and cheerfully answer the call

> . . . to obey, and to be in subjection, to have no will of his owne, nor power over him selfe, but wholly to resigne himselfe to the will of his Master . . . *Spontaneum & rationabile voluntatis propriae sacrificium*, a voluntarie and reasonable sacrificing of a mans owne will, voluntarily, freely, and without any constraints: and reasonably, that is, according to reason and religion, in the obedience, and feare of God. (Fosset 22)

For my purposes, therefore, it is crucial to note those statements and images that find in cheerful, willing obedience, the conscious and voluntary subordination of one's own immediate interests to those of another, not only the hope of future bliss but also the experience of present satisfaction. Before the Fall, Luther had said, carrying out God's will had given Adam joy; if attaining a similar joy in the postlapsarian world can only be accomplished through Christ, it is nonetheless still accessible (Althouse *Theology* 253). As noted earlier, in his homily, Cranmer uses the words "free" and "freely" 14 times in 6 pages, mostly in connection with the word "faith" (*Homilies* 79–85). Hence, William Perkins's insistence that "wee must be *voluntaries, Psalm* 110.4, without constraint, freely yeelding subiection to the will of God" (256; emphasis in original), and Daniel Touteville's stress on Paul's requirement of single-minded servants, serving *"freely, from their heart* . . . when the heart not onely desires to doe it, but withall rejoyceth, and is much delighted in the doing of it" (349). According to William Gouge (citing Augustine *Civ. Dei* l.19 c. 15), "let there be cheerefulness in a seruants minde, and he is as free as his master: for such a seruant is the *Lords freeman* (1 *Cor.* 7.22), and when he cannot be made free of his master, he doth after a manner make his seruice free" (*Domesticall Duties* 619). George Downame's formulation is particularly interesting because of its explicit invocation of "outward things"—that is, quotidian life rather than some purely spiritual future—and its quotation of Luther:

> The right vse of Christian libertie in outward things is, when it is vsed to a free and cheerefull seruing, both one of another in charitie, and of the superiour in obedience and loyaltie; that being free from all, we make our selues seruants unto al, for their good.
>
> For as *Luther* saith, *A Christian in respect of the inner man is free, but in respect of the outer man hee is, through charitie, the seruant of all.* (98, emphasis in original)

John Denison tells us that "[Christ's] yoke is light and sweet indeed, whom to serue is to raign as King" (123).[28] A pure echo of the phrase in the Anglican collect comes from Paul Baynes, who distinguishes between servants as "more slavish, or else more free and liberal"; the latter category is the one "schooled by the Holy Ghost" (365). In heaven, he says, we have "this perfect good will; our service shall be perfect freedom" (369). Another, perhaps the most striking and moving, is from George Herbert, who had himself put the temptations of secular greatness behind him to accept the clerical collar, and a life of service to his rural congregation. On his deathbed, says Izaak Walton, he sent a copy of *The Temple* to Nicholas Ferrars, with these instructions: ". . . tell him, he shall find in it a picture of the many spiritual Conflicts that have past betwixt God and my Soul, before I could subject mine to the will of *Jesus my master*: in whose service I have found perfect freedom" (417).[29]

It is not my intention to argue in what follows that Shakespeare endorsed in a creedal way any specifically Christian practice as the only way to freedom. The concept of willing service to God but also to man was active around him, his fellows, and his audience. Expressions of that concept threw plenty of emphasis on servants in the narrow modern sense of the term, but all the commentators insist that the concept applied to people of every rank, and assumed greater force than it might have for us given the fact that people of every rank sometimes found or placed themselves in servant roles. The demotic theatrical tradition of the mystery cycles and many of their humanistic derivatives, the moralities, had set a high value on the *potentia humilatatis* (Cox *Dramaturgy* 26). Shakespeare and his fellows belonged to a social group whose legal subordination and marginality must have made these ideas appealing.[30] It is the ubiquity of the concept in the discourses of the society that encourages me to argue that it applies in practical as well as spiritual ways.[31]

Materialist reading tends to treat people as atoms in a deterministic universe. Individual people themselves, however, want to make sense of their lives, believe that they count, are more than steel balls on the ends of strings on some executive's desk. Even postmodern people, with the Marxian formulae available to them, will not normally accept that their consciousness is false. Beyond that, however, lies the real possibility of something for which *spiritual* is as good a word as any, that actions and speeches and ideas that generate the greatest good for the greatest number truly express some underlying or supervenient reality. Whatever Shakespeare's own doctrinal views, I believe that the concept of freedom in service directs our attention to a moral if not a theological ideal that he enacts so repeatedly and effectively that it seems to me to become finally the cornerstone of his ethical vision.[32]

The operative term is *enacts*. Shakespearean texts do not very often or very explicitly discuss these issues. Instead, they repeatedly ask their audiences to watch characters performing acts of freely elected service. These acts sometimes lead to rewards for the characters themselves (especially in the comedies and romances), in the form of social and economic gains in status, wealth, the emotional security of stable married love. Sometimes (especially in the tragedies), they bring characters such as Kent in *King Lear* and Enobarbus in *Antony and Cleopatra* not gain but bitter loss. Even these outcomes, however, offer heuristic rewards to the audience, in the form of feelings of satisfaction (perhaps in that word's etymological sense of completion). These actions, of course, are carried out in terms of conceptions and expressions of service, practical as well as ideal, that were current in Elizabethan and Jacobean society, and in order to evaluate such actions, we need to learn more about early modern English servants and service. This inquiry will entail attention to the Marxist–materialist treatments of the subject that have dominated recent scholarly and critical discourse. Subsequent chapters will continue to invoke both the idealist and the materialist treatments as they look at various models of service, in an order that generally follows the historical line of development of the institutions of service.

CHAPTER 2
THE HOP AND THE POLE
THE LIMITS OF MATERIALISM

In dramatic moments that construct the idea that the fullest state of human freedom can be found in the freely chosen service of God and others, we find early modern ideals of service at work. Such ideals are not those to which most early-twenty-first-century critics will comfortably assent: our understandings of service and freedom are too radically conditioned by materialist political assumptions and argument. Foucaultian emphasis on power dominated English studies in the last quarter of the twentieth century, and hence animated much of the recent published work on Shakespearean service.[1] Indeed, the Marxian and Foucaultian analyses of early modern service carried out by literary scholars, such as Mark Thornton Burnett and Michael Neill, and by a whole host of social historians, will materially assist us in anatomizing Shakespearean service. But an argument that wants to respect both the past and the present must try to open and sustain a dialogue between those materialist analyses and the more idealistic one we have developed to this point. I have already suggested that emphasis on power distorts our view of service, especially the phenomenon of willing submission implied in the Christian paradox.[2] The hierarchical structures of early modern society, even more than our own, placed large groups of people in subordinate roles on account of the accidents of birth. Most of the members of those groups had little or no real opportunity to change the material conditions of their lives. Nor did they have access to the Marxist analysis of power, and the political mechanisms to which it gave rise. They did have an opportunity to choose whether to live in a perpetual state of *ressentiment*, or to find a way to ascribe value to the work they did. And they did have access to an orthodox psychology that placed a powerful emphasis on the role of the will in human behavior. The voluntary acceptance of subordination was a value that Shakespeare sometimes challenged, but often seems to endorse. Such a view of service, moreover, is not just historically appropriate, but can continue to have heuristic value for us.

We can find a fulcrum for our investigation in *King Lear*, at that point during the blinding of Gloucester where one of Cornwall's servants, appalled by the recklessness, viciousness, and high-handedness of his master's actions, calls on Cornwall to desist (*TLr.* 3.7; *HLr.* 14).[3] When his verbal protestations fail, the servant draws his sword and attacks his lord; in the fight that ensues, he mortally wounds Cornwall, but is himself stabbed in the back by Regan, and killed, and the other servants are ordered to fling his body on the dunghill.

Lear, by overriding his feudal liegeman Kent's similar (though less strenuous) resistance to his own disastrous decisions in the opening scene, has deeply destabilized the social order. As the competition for power he has initiated becomes increasingly selfish and violent, not only in his own family but also in Gloucester's, all the relationships, including those of masters and servants, lose their footing, and through the first half of the play, further acts of service are trivial (Kent's tripping up of Oswald), futile (Kent's resistance to Oswald and Cornwall at Gloucester's gates, the Fool's sensible counsels to Lear), or unsociable (Oswald's indifference to Lear). Empowered by the division of the kingdom and the disinheritance of Cordelia, the antagonistic characters— Goneril, Regan, Cornwall, Edmund—have had their way, almost without resistance. After Cornwall's servant challenges his master's wrongful act with force, however, the antagonists' hold on power begins to slip, and within a short time, all of them are dead (not, of course, without taking Gloucester, Lear, and Cordelia with them).[4] The passing of all these great ones is explicitly marked. The servant whose generous intrusion has initiated effective resistance to the darker powers in the play dies nameless and apparently unmourned.

Indeed, it has generally been the fate of servants, in literature and in life, to be cast unnamed on the dunghill of history. Until quite recently, political and even social historians have peered over and around and through the subordinates who were attending to the basic needs of the kings and barons and knights, the landowners and commercial magnates, the scientists and artists, whose interests historians themselves have mostly served; if observed at all, the servants were distinctly peripheral figures, just as in early modern pictorial representations of European life servant figures are rarely at the center. Literary critics and literary historians have likewise tended to pass by on the other side both servants as a class, and servants as individual characters, unless, like Sancho Panza or the Fool in *Lear*, they are simply too assertive to overlook.[5]

Yet, throughout the history of the world, servants have been crucially important in the maintenance of complex societies. Until modern technology brought water, heat, and light into the house at the turn of a switch or tap, encouraged most of us to cook for ourselves in an hour or so a day, allowed people to communicate easily at a distance, it was the servants who hewed the wood and drew the water, built and maintained the fires, cooked the meals and washed the clothes, carried the messages and ran the errands, groomed the horses and drove the carts, who literally made it possible for governors to govern, generals to fight, merchants to trade—and for playwrights, poets, even critics and historians, to write.

More recently, to be sure, attention has been paid. Social historians such as Peter Laslett and his associates and successors have told us that in early modern England, at any given time, at least 15 percent of the population was in service, in a totally dependent role, as agricultural laborer, domestic laborer, or apprentice. Close to half were servants (in this limited sense) during some part of their lives.[6] The clergy took oaths of service when they took orders, and were dependent on individual bishops and the gentry for their places. So were those secretaries and clerks and other agents of what would subsequently become the civil service, which continued to be comprised, through the early modern period, of the households of its officials. Many members of the privileged class spent time during their childhood as pages and ladies in waiting, and some went on to take at least nominally servile roles in the households of the monarchs and the great magnates. In time of war or insurrection, traditional obligations of military service put yeomen, country squires, knights, and earls under the authority of their traditional seigneurs. And virtually everyone had lived in a household in which servants served—as Kevin Sharpe puts it, this was a society "organized around service relationships" (13).[7] Michael Neill cogently summarizes it: when service is broadly conceived, early modern society "consisted of an unbroken chain of service that stretched from the humblest peasant to the monarch who owed service only to God" (8).

Some decades have passed since literary scholars, including Arthur Dale Barnes and Ralph Berry, began to look at these relationships in terms of individualistic concepts of class.[8] Postmodern political historiography has redirected emphasis from individuals to groups, and servants, a very large group, could hardly escape notice. In literary studies, Marxian and Foucaltian concentration on the themes of dominance and subordination has brought service, among other previously marginalized topics, under much fuller scrutiny. Indeed, Bruce Robbins observed some years back that the exclusion of servants and other laborers from fiction and history is by now such a familiar fact that it may be thought to have lost its interest (x). He went on, however, to write a fine book, *The Servant's Hand*, which supplies both a subtle, thoughtful theoretical basis, and an exemplary application of that theory, to other students of the subject. But the servants whom Robbins studies mainly go about their business in and between the households of nineteenth-century novels. More recently yet, some important studies have analyzed particular aspects of the servant problem in early modern England.[9] In a hatful of articles, and in his *Masters and Servants in English Renaissance Drama and Culture*, Mark Thornton Burnett has brought together a great deal of information about the ideology of service in early modern England, drawing not only on published treatises and handbooks, but also on archival materials of various kinds, and has applied his findings to servant characters and relationships to the early modern drama, from Shakespeare (whom he does not treat in detail, however) to Broome. Most recently, in the opening chapters of *Putting History to the Question*, Michael Neill has produced a subtle, dense, and elegant survey of the important place of service in early modern society and culture, which anticipates in many ways the emphases of this book.

The present study means to continue to give servants and service "a place in the story."[10] It intends to augment and balance the previous analyses in two ways. The first is substantive: to carry out a detailed investigation of servants and service in the single most admired body of early modern writing: the works of Shakespeare. This enterprise seems well worthwhile because on close study, servant relationships, the ideologies they represent, the discourses by which they are constructed, and the ideals that can be discerned in them are, like servants themselves in early modern English society, discreet but crucial elements in the Shakespearean plays. Characters in obvious servant roles appear in all the plays of the canon; they participate in the action and discussion in significant ways in all but a few.[11] Hence detailed attention to them will genuinely enrich our understanding of those plays, and through them not only of the culture that produced them, but also of our own culture as we reflect upon them. The present argument, furthermore, will pay much fuller attention than Burnett and Neill do to some important elements in the literary and social traditions that the plays incorporate or adapt, such as the literary and educational heritage of classical comedy, and the fading but still significant social model of the feudal retinue

with its disposition toward violence. Finally, and perhaps most important-
antly, this book will take a much fuller account than any of the earlier
studies do except Neill's, and much more fully than he can in his
relatively short treatment, of the ways in which ideals and attitudes of
service apply to the behavior of social superiors as well as social inferiors, so that almost any Shakespearean character may act at some point
in a service role, just as did the upper-class men and women of his time.
Since the texts devote far more stage time to members of the elite than
to commoners, the change in emphasis means that many elements of the
plays can be newly considered.

The second departure is methodological. As I have indicated, recent
criticism has tended to view relationships between masters and servants
pretty exclusively as relationships of power, of the kind that materialist
and new historicist critics have found so absorbing.[12] This emphasis is
patent in the subtitles of both Burnett (*Authority and Obedience*) and
Neill (*Power, Politics, and Society in English Renaissance Drama*). The
assumption—and it runs very deep in most published Shakespearean
scholarship and criticism of the past three decades—is that master–
servant relationships are so essentially determined by factors of economic
and political coercion and exchange that no other ways of looking at
them are either relevant or informative.[13] That masters had power over
servants is not in question; yet, the actual nature of this power is still
unclear. One question concerns the relative importance of physical and
economic constraints. Ralph Houlbrooke has investigated the records of
early modern Essex and observes that many more men were accused of
murdering their servants than their children, and were very rarely convicted; if true, and if true for the country as a whole, the fact implies that
violent treatment of servants was condoned. Fran Dolan traces a more
complex pattern, citing Houlbrooke and many others, but the upshot is
that both masters and mistresses were authorized by custom and law
to use physical force in disciplining their subordinates ("Gender").
Maurice Hunt, reacting against the tendency among modernist critics to
regard the abusive treatment of servants in *The Comedy of Errors* and
other plays as merely a custom of the genre, has tried to argue that the
play inscribes the "de facto enslavement" that did occur in early modern
Britain. He cites Patricia Fumerton's recent work on fosterage, and the
evidence (mostly scattered and anecdotal) that some social historians
have uncovered revealing widespread abuse of servants by their masters
("Slavery" 5–9). Carolyn Prager argues, however, that although the
English were able to accept the idea of slavery as compatible with
Christianity because of the ubiquity of the institution in the Bible, so

that the moral issues and theological issues per se were not extensively debated until the Enlightenment, the thing itself was incompatible with British law and custom; she cites an assertion in William Harrison's *Description* (1577) that people who were slaves in other countries became free when they came to England (111–12).[14] The crucial point is that true slavery is at its root an involuntary status; almost all early modern English servants, however, entered service on their own or on their parents' initiative, served for set terms only, not for life, and were legally, if not always practically free to leave service at the end of the term.

Indeed, it is difficult even to find the boundary that divides early modern servants from their masters, and hence generate the kinds of distinction among socioeconomic groups with which materialist criticism is comfortable. Whereas classical masters and servants belonged to clearly differentiated legal and social classes, Daphne Simon observes that most of the relevant English laws after the development of capitalism did not, strictly speaking, assign *groups* of people to the status of master or servant; all the distinction rested on the particular economic situation of particular individuals, and on contracts between particular masters and servants, and the decisive factor, the ownership of land or a certain sum of money, was notoriously fluid and unstable and susceptible to accident. The point carries methodological weight because of the materialist commitment to the primacy of groups over individuals as the subject of analysis (and the concomitant concern for the individual as a touchstone of classical liberalism). The same laws did give special recognition to those servants whose relationships with their masters were governed by a legal document, an indenture, and applied much more loosely to those thousands of others serving only under verbal agreements (Daphne Simon 160). One crucially important statute, to be sure, the Statute of Artificers, and the important social practices based on it, insisted that, at any given time, nearly everybody had to be either a master or a servant—had either to own enough land or cash money to be economically independent, or to be a dependent member of the household of such an independent person. But the categories were not fixed by the circumstances of birth or race—while young, eventual masters (and their children in their turn) routinely became servants; former servants routinely became masters, especially as they grew older. "Service," says Keith Wrightson, "was part of the child's preparation for an independent existence in an adult world" (*English Society* 113).[15]

Whatever the nature of the agreement governing the servant–master relationship, this relationship was pervasive and close. The decisive factor was membership in a household, a "family," linked by bonds even closer than blood. The Greek word used by Matthew (8:6) in the story of the centurion's servant, παῖσ, can be translated "child or son" (Luke 7:2 uses δοῦλοσ, a term more unequivocally meaning "servant"); the hugely important prescriptions for the behavior of servants in Ephesians 6:5–8 and Colossians 4:22–25 (which also use δοῦλοσ) immediately follow similar prescriptions for parents and children. Bartolemeus Anglicus, writing "De seruo" around 1250, distinguishes three kinds of servants: those born into bondage, those made bondmen by war or other external forces, and those who have freely entered into bondage. These last he calls *famuli*, "and have the name of 'famulando,' serving," so that the root of the word *family* is a word for "servant" (Trevisa 6.15). For practical purposes only this third group existed in England in the period with which we are concerned. In most cases, the relationship meant that the servant ate meals cooked in the same kitchen as those of the people she or he served, and slept within the same walls if not necessarily under the same roof. And if the master no longer had power of life and death, the "family" connection extended to the point where the head of the household effectively stood *in loco parentis* to its servants, controlling their behavior even in such personal matters as whether, when, and whom to marry. Increasingly, however, servants working for cash wages had the chance to accumulate by their willing service the necessary condition of their independence.

The conditions of service for these people rested on a body of law initially articulated in the Statute of Labourers in the middle of the fourteenth century and focused, for our purposes, in the Statute of Artificers of 1563. Without exactly saying so, this act did, in fact, try to identify nearly everybody in England as either a master or a servant.[16] It sought to compel all persons under 60 years of age who did not have income from £40 worth of real property or merchandise to work for some master for "customary wages" as set by the justices of each county. The act sharply restricted the grounds on which a servant could legally decline to work or leave a master's service; but it did at least concede the possibility, and so gave English servants a freedom classical servants did not have, to negotiate with one or more masters on the terms of their employment (Simon 195–97).[17] Because acting (then as now) was a hand-to-mouth profession, in which most individual actors found it difficult to accumulate wealth and property, it was the enforcement of this law, at least initially, that required Shakespeare and his fellow actors to become the "servants" of Lord Strange or the Lord Chamberlain or eventually the King.[18] The statute was supported by propaganda, such as the *Homily Against Idleness*. It was grounded on the command to

Adam to live by the sweat of his brow—whence the name of Oliver's and Orlando's servant in *As You Like It*.

We can divide these people into two principal sets. Indentured servants (including apprentices) were bound by a written contract to perform specified tasks for a master during some specified extended period (usually seven years), in exchange for food, clothing, lodging, general sustenance, usually some kind of lump-sum severance pay, and little if any cash payment during the term of service. Wage earners, the other group, were hired at a stipulated rate of pay (in addition to their bed, board, and sometimes clothing) for a quarter, a half-year, or a year, the agreement to be newly negotiated (and occasionally canceled altogether) at the end of each period.[19] Wages were normally set by the local justices or borough councils. Domestic and commercial servants of all kinds were sometimes able to augment their wages by means of *vails* (more or less equivalent to modern tips) and bribes.[20] Such an agreement seems to bond Lancelot Gobbo to Shylock. He tells us that he longs to quit his master, but feels guilty about it. Soon, however, we learn that he has evidently worked for Shylock long enough that his master is ready to see him go. The grounds for Lancelot's transfer are not clear; Bassanio tells him that "Shylock thy master . . . hath preferred thee" (2.2.140–41), but the language could imply either that Shylock has transferred Lancelot's indenture to his new master, or that because Lancelot's term of service has expired, he is legally if not psychologically free to move, and Shylock has recommended him. Shylock's readiness to release a "huge feeder" who "sleeps by day / More than the wildcat" (2.5.45–47) implies that such separations could be mutually satisfactory.[21]

The actual texture of servants' lives varied. Whether indentured or working for wages, many agricultural workers seem to have known the hard and narrow existence invoked by Henry V on the eve of Agincourt:

> . . . the wretched slave
> Who with a body filled and vacant mind
> Gets him to rest, crammed with distressful bread;
> Never sees horrid night, the child of hell,
> But like a lackey from the rise to set
> Sweats in the eye of Phoebus. . . . (*H5* 4.2.265–70)

Domestics and apprentices might live hard, too. But many were more comfortable. Through much of the period, such servants shared their masters' houses and diets, sleeping and eating in the common hall or sometimes in their master's chamber. The anonymous author of "The Seruingmans Comfort" invokes such a life, with a reference to the blue coat that was a common indicator of service:

> When Countreys causes did require
> Each Nobleman to keep his house,
> Then Blewcoates had what they desyre,
> Good chear, with many a full carouse:
> But not now as it was wont to be,
> For dead is liberalitie.[22]

We get a sense of this tradition in those scenes of *King Lear* involving Lear's band of retainers, well-enough habituated to good living that they can count on the old king's support when they complain of inattention from the resident servants.[23] Indeed, the conflict between Oswald and his fellows on the one hand, and Lear's followers on the other, may be interpreted as an evolutionary clash between two types of household. Lear's, like the Lord's in *The Taming of the Shrew*, is an old-fashioned one in which social distinctions tend to be submerged in shared military or agricultural or commercial or social activities. Of these, the most distinctive is the household dinner, with everyone from master to potboy gathered in the hall, sharing whatever food, drink, and entertainment is available. Though the master, his or her children and relations and guests, and some of the senior servants sit raised above the others on the dais, the social gradient is not necessarily all that steep. So Lear demands neither sycophancy nor gentility from his "new" servant Caius (the banished Earl of Kent in disguise).[24] The fact that Goneril and Albany are not in the room with Lear and his followers suggests that theirs might well be one of those new-model households, reflecting real changes in Elizabethan patterns of domesticity, full of "silly-ducking observants / That stretch their duties nicely" (*TLr.* 96–97), in which social distinctions were very sharply marked by the master's retiring with a few friends and upper servants to a private dining room, leaving the lower servants only to eat in the hall—perhaps a different, less sumptuous meal.[25] In great households, the upper servants were likely to be of gentle birth themselves, younger sons or daughters of their masters' relatives and friends. And while the scullion or kitchen maid doubtless slept less soft and perhaps ate less well than the steward who was also the master's nephew, both types would have spent their days living and working under the same roof and by and large sharing the same living conditions. Yet, whether treated like beasts or living in much the same comfort as their masters, servants at all levels were at least nominally at their masters' beck and call 24 hours a day, seven days a week, for the whole period of their service, were subject to summary punishment and discharge, and largely forfeited control over much they did and said when they entered into service.

For all that, the relationships, in practice and in literary representation, were never confined to a mere vertical binary. A noted materialist scholar and theorist, Frederic Jameson, has explained how ideology informs fictive texts by deploying "real social contradictions, insurmountable in their own terms," so that they "find a purely formal resolution in the aesthetic realms" (79). But the contradictions are intellectual and moral and emotional as well as economic.[26] Burnett has recognized the degree to which masters become dependent on their servants. Multiple roles, which placed servants like Malvolio in charge of other servants, or made a master like Edmund at least temporarily the servant of Cornwall, challenge any merely binary reading of master–servant relationships. Jamesonian contradictions between and among pairs of desires, needs, wills, inhabit every element of every master–service situation.[27] Servant figures make especially effective foci for such inquiries because most of them are relatively minor characters, and, as M. M. Mahood has said, bit parts "shift attention to social groups rather than central figures" (7)—perhaps she means rather to those social groups that were marginalized in previous criticism.[28] Hence every time a servant strains at the limitations on his or her behavior, he or she pushes for all servants. And there are certainly many places in the plays where servants at every social level pick at the knots of their bondage, and where masters, galled by awareness of their profound practical and emotional dependency on their servants, reassert their social dominance with a word or a blow.[29] Judicious readers can learn much from these scholars, and their influence will be apparent in what follows.

There are some other issues, however, that still go largely unexplored and unexplained. Of these, the most salient stands adjacent to the one we have just been considering: the question of compliant submission. In many societies, such as those depicted in the Homeric epics or experienced by the ancestors of many African and Latin Americans, servitude follows warfare; the surviving men, women, and children on the losing side are carried off to the victors' tents, houses, and farms to become their captors' slaves, to do their work and bear some of their children. In some of these societies—notably, for our purposes, those of classical Greece and Rome—the relationships so established are carried beyond the military moment and rigidified by the social structure, so that the descendants of slaves remain slaves unless they are explicitly freed by their masters.[30] Later on, however, military force and caste relationships yield place to economic forces; people go more or less voluntarily into service in order to exchange their labor and fidelity for food, shelter, clothing, and protection against violence.[31] In all these cases, I believe, we need to wonder why those whom fortune has placed in the subordinate position are content to stay there, largely unresisting, largely uncomplaining—more, why so many of them, like the traditional wives who have also sometimes been those servants' masters, not only tolerate but also—at least outwardly—embrace their subordinated state. And to wonder whether the Marxian explanations for submission are indeed adequate to explain the phenomenon in all its manifest variety of forms.

It is true that most hegemonies are initially (and perhaps finally) sustained by force, and later on by customary institutions of education, ritual, and law. The materialists whose voices have dominated critical discussion of these questions for a couple of decades have persuaded academic students of plays and other texts that the illusory subjectivity of individual subordinates, constructed as it is by the discourses of social relationship, whose nature is in turn dominated and determined by their masters, includes elements of passivity and helplessness that keep them in their place. Not only common sense (also illusory, of course, according to theory), however, but also a revised understanding of subjectivity in relationship to experience, replies that such explanations seem inadequate all by themselves to account for the ability of the few to control the many in place after place, society after society, generation after generation.[32] The question urges itself whether biological, psychological, perhaps even spiritual factors enter the nexus, whether there is not something in or beyond many people that makes them ready to welcome another's mastery. It will be one of the important enterprises of this book to explore the significant matter of willing service.

One part of that exploration, the pervasive social influence of the Christian paradox of service, has already been sketched. A second proposes a novel concept with an ungainly name, volitional primacy. This idea is developed more fully in chapters 6 and 7. In outline, however, it offers an essentially psychological solution to the problem posed by the social and economic imperatives that caused individual people to take service. Let me emphasize *individual*. Marxist social analysis has insisted on looking at people in groups, partly because materialism sees even highly dominant individuals as only expressing the ineluctable dynamics of impersonal social forces, and partly because it is only by acting as a group that subjugated individuals can force the privileged elite toward a more just distribution of the world's goods. Even within a modern or postmodern society, however, individuals have to find ways to make sense of their world. Following Marx, Antonio Gramsci argues that the worker, even in obeying some master's orders, "imparts a purpose of his own . . . to which he must subordinate his will" (Hoffman 113). This means in effect that if the subaltern (to use a Marxist term) carries out a master's order, it is only because the subaltern has freely directed his or her will to accede to the will of the master. And this is the case in a modern society in which the Marxist analysis has wide currency. From within early modern society, in the experience of people to whom the modern analysis of dominance and subordination is not yet available, the imperatives of service appear so profoundly woven into the structure and texture of the world as to be as natural as gravity or death. Except for the elder sons of men of property, everybody they know, almost everybody they have heard or read about, occupies at birth a situation in which they are obliged by custom and law to accept a servant's position. Faced with these inescapabilities, some people exhibit mere dull passivity. Some act out the mostly covert resistance of Nietzschean *ressentiment*. Others, however, treat the existential conditions of their lives as a challenge, not as a burden. They treat death as a potential lover, to be studied, teased, and courted. They enlist gravity as an accomplice in the building of a tower or the execution of a *grand jeté*. They treat their service (as, legally, it was in early modern England) as the conscious acts of an uncoerced agent only selecting among competing options. The essential thing here is the sense of *choice*, and behind choice, of *will*. If I act as if by an act of will (hence *volitional*) I have initiated the artistic or social relationship (hence *primacy*), I make myself at least psychologically free, and therefore able to find in the obduracy of my medium, or my master, pleasure as well as pain, satisfaction as well as frustration. The process seems to be one that can occur in any historical context, but of which Shakespeare's generation ought to have been particularly aware, because of the emergence in this period of the more or less modern conception of the individual self, and of the centrality in that period's dominant psychological theory of the active, assertive will. As I have already suggested, it also seems to me a process to which the artist—and perhaps above all artists the dramatist—should be peculiarly alert.

I investigate these issues more fully later. For now, let us look at a traditional emblem of the servant–master relationship, bequeathed to us by a Jacobean gentleman, Sir John Holles, advising his son and heir to pay suit to some magnate: "Be sure you always keep some great man to your friend but trouble him not for trifles, compliment him often, present him with many yet small gifts, and of little charge; and if you have cause to bestow any great gratuity on him, then let it be some such thing as may be daily in sight; for otherwise you shall live like a hop without a pole, live in obscurity and be made a football for every insulting companion to spurn at."[33] Significantly, the relationship operates at the top, not the bottom, of the economic table. Significantly, it is described as mediated primarily by commodities, and hence recognizes a general movement in the ideology of service toward a cash basis. It would nevertheless have included a whole repertory of customary speeches and gestures, and a certain amount of action—dancing attendance and what not—as well, invoking early patterns of exchange in which money per se was less important. Holles's is an ingenious reminder that in early modern England the concept of service was not confined to the lower orders. Many of the greatest men in the kingdom were formally and, in some ways, practically members of the royal household—the monarch's secretary, chamberlain, captain of horse; their offices and land were theirs by royal gift, and in the long run, only continuing faithful service guaranteed continuing enjoyment of their lofty status. Just so, Holles says, his son needs to make his way into the patronage of some greater man than he if he wishes to thrive.[34]

Still, the image of the hop and the pole invokes the master–servant relationship at all social levels. The hop is fruitful. But all by itself the hop is lowly—a mere vine, crawling along the ground. And on the ground, its very fruitfulness is diminished; the wet soil rots even such meager fruit as the hop has been able to produce while competing with taller plants for light. The pole stands tall. But by itself the pole is fruitless, a mere dry stick. By lifting the hop above the ground and sustaining it, the pole raises both the status and the productivity of the hop. By depending from the pole, the hop makes the pole productive, meaningful, and valuable. The relationship is therefore mutually useful. A cogent statement of the interdependence appears in an anonymous pamphlet of 1567, *A Lettere Sent by the Maydens of London*, defending the maidservants of the city against the misogynistic effusions of Edward Hake: "For as ye are that care and provide for our meat, drinke, and wages, so we are they that labor and take paines for you: so that your care for us, and our labor for you is so requisite, that they cannot be separated: so needful that they may not be severed" (Fehrenbach 38).[35] Either member of the linkage without the other is radically lessened. It is nonetheless appropriate to observe that in terms of intrinsic worth, the hop is more valuable than the pole: even lying on the ground, it is productive whereas the pole is not.[36] The irony here, given the relative social value of mastering poles and subordinate hops, energizes much of the treatment of the relationship in plays and other fictions, not least because they tended to be written by people who were hops rather than poles themselves.[37] In real hop fields, indeed, poles not only elevate hops, but they also draw them together; a single pole may support several vines. Allegorically, then, the master derives some of his value from the fact that he becomes the occasion and focus for that kind of social organization and specialization that enhances individual productivity, that submerges individuals into groups.

Some elements in the complex relationships of hops and poles, as they appear in the work of William Shakespeare and others, supply the materials for this book. I confine my attention almost entirely to literal master–servant relationships, though those will be of many kinds, involving the service performed by earls as well as kitchen maids. The troping of such relationships—men as servants of Petrarchan mistresses, money, the passions—is pervasive and significant, and will occasionally enter this discussion. But for reasons of economy—a full treatment would be a long book in itself—I only touch such tropes incidentally, not systematically. I should concede that to some readers the concept of service as it appears in ruling-class people "serving" their ruling-class superiors may itself appear as a kind of trope: a set of aristocratic attitudes and behaviors referred to in language adapted from that originally applied to their subordinates, verbally but not essentially the same. But I have already shown how hard it is to draw the lines of demarcation. (Among other things, the fact makes it difficult and perhaps inappropriate to apply the Marxian insistence on group over individual.) Hence I have decided to treat service at all social levels as, in many respects, intrinsically the same.[38] This does not mean that there are not important differences between earls and kitchen maids, and I should also concede that when I use the term *servant* without some modifier, it will most often refer to a person or character relatively far down the social hierarchy.

A word about the concentration on drama. From a historical point of view, it makes sense because in no other genre are master–servant relationships so fully and variously explored. They get some treatment in prose fiction, to be sure. Thomas Nashe took a servant as the observing consciousness of *The Unfortunate Traveller*; servants also appear in the Boccaccian tales (mostly translated or adapted from Continental originals), of Painter, Pettie, and others, while apprentices and household servants make an inescapable part of the social landscape in Deloney's bourgeois fictions.[39] The aristocratic bias of romance and history, and the pastoral bias of Ovidian epyllion, mean that servants do not for the most part have substantial places in *The Faerie Queene* (except perhaps for Artegall's enforcer, Talus) nor in the pastoral

romances of Greene and others, the historical narratives of Drayton and
Daniel, and the erotic versions of classical tales like *Hero and Leander*.[40]
Both Nashe's raffish traveler and Deloney's romanticized Londoners
have their counterparts in the drama, however, while many other kinds
and styles of servants appear in the plays of Dekker, Heywood, Jonson,
Middleton, and the rest. Still, for the purposes of the present study, a
further concentration on Shakespeare also makes sense. To be sure, servants are not more numerous or more important in Shakespeare than in
the other Elizabethan and Jacobean playwrights. An important group,
the apprentices and household servants of the city merchants, goes
largely unrepresented in Shakespearean drama; for theatrical treatment
of these people, we need to turn to the writers of city comedy. The agricultural servants who still comprised a large fraction of all the servants
in the nation (although many of them, displaced by enclosure, had
sought other kinds of service in the rapidly growing cities) likewise make
infrequent and generally very modest appearances. A highly important
type of dramatic servant, the so-called tool villain of revenge tragedy, is
more fully developed by Heywood, Middleton, and Webster than by
Shakespeare, whose examples of this type are usually minor figures. But
no other playwright treats service itself, the concept as well as the practice, in so many different kinds of relationship, from the humble water-
carriers of *Romeo and Juliet* to the king's counselors of *King Lear*. And
no one explores the ethical as well as the social and economic aspects of
these relationships with such subtlety, complexity, tenacity, and vigor.
For those reasons I have not hesitated to put the works of Shakespeare
at the center of this study, and to relegate his peers, for the most part, to
the illustratory periphery.

The immediate difficulty in preparing to write such a study grows
from the variety, in both literature and life, of relationships among
masters and servants, on which I have already insisted.[41] William Cecil,
second in power only to the Queen in the latter part of the sixteenth
century, spoke and perhaps thought of himself as servant; he was formally a member of her household as secretary and then treasurer—roles
that in more modest establishments were usually filled by gentlemen
with little or no independent means. In the mid-1550s, he listed among
the 35 servants of his own still relatively modest household his son
Thomas, his sister-in-law, and a gently born ward (Barnett 9). Still, the
distance from Lord Burghley in his closet to the scullion in his kitchen
was physically small but socially, economically, educationally, and emotionally great; so is that from the Kent who serves Lear as Burghley
served Elizabeth, to the Kent who does him "service / Improper for

a slave" (*HLr.* 27.217–18). These four all differ in their own ways from
Launce and Speed in *Two Gentlemen of Verona* or Lancelot Gobbo in
Merchant of Venice, and these in turn from Aaron in *Titus Andronicus* or
the Nurse in *Romeo and Juliet*, and Aaron and the Nurse from the
Waiting Gentlewoman in *Macbeth*, who is appalled by her mistress's
bizarre behavior. The binary hierarchy of master and servant, moreover,
is very often only one element of a hierarchical range or register, so that
when Oswald, who seems to be Goneril's household steward, encounters Kent, apparently a mere footman, he expects the latter to defer to
him, and is seconded by the master he does not formally serve, Cornwall,
in regarding Kent's boldness as insolence.[42]

It is furthermore the case that master–servant roles collide and elide
with other social determinants. Of these—and not only because it has
thrust forward with such urgency in recent scholarship and criticism—
the most inescapable is gender, and I hope to illuminate the question of
willing subordination so as to enrich our understanding of relationships
between men and women as well as between masters and servants. In
any case, in law, ideology, and custom, women, like servants, occupy
formally subordinate stations, and although women could be masters of
servants, as Goneril masters Oswald, they nevertheless shared the experience of inferiority within the patriarchal system.[43] But family relationships also intrude—Gobbo is the servant he is for being the son he is
(Shakespeare's mingling of the two roles at Gobbo's first entrance is both
delightful and informative). So do considerations of place and time—
servants behave differently with each other than with their masters (we
can see this especially in *Romeo and Juliet*), differently at home than
abroad, differently in private places than in public. All this means that
in working with this topic it is difficult to keep it clearly in focus; consideration of one aspect of it tends to slide off into another.

A useful conceptual model with which to bring the complexity under
some conceptual control is Lars Engle's pragmatic version of the idea of
competing and otherwise interacting *discourses*, as they were derived
partly from their constructions in both nonfictional and fictional texts,
and partly from actual early modern English practices as those developed over time. To accept Engle's lead here is at least partially to accept
the linguistic and cultural bias of the postmodern theoretical project,
which it is part of my intention to resist. The choice concedes that to a
very great extent, what we can understand about a topic like service is
what we can read and say about it. One of my points, however, will be
that we can observe and respond emotively, psychologically, as well as
intellectually to gestures and actions, as distinct from words, and it is in

the gestures and actions implied by the words of the plays, as well as some of the words linked to those actions, that I will look for verification of my particular contentions.[44] As it happens, by looking closely at a single early play, *The Taming of the Shrew*, we can set up most of the categories that we will then consider more extensively later, as we go on to survey the whole canon in a variety of relationships to the society around it.[45] There are five of these:

(1) The biblical discourse, not only from the sacred book itself but also from the liturgy, and from thousands of sermons, commentaries, devotional manuals, moral treatises, polemics, and other writings, in which the economy is primarily emotional and spiritual; this undergirds and infuses treatments of service relationships among the gentry, and those that ignore or elide differences in social hierarchy (we have already looked in some detail at this one).

(2) The classical discourse, which Shakespeare and his contemporaries encountered in Greek and Roman texts (especially the drama of Plautus and Terence) and in early modern imitations and derivations of those texts.

(3) The discourse of retaining, harking back to feudal times.

(4) The discourse of traditional household or domestic service as practiced or at least articulated in the fifteenth and earlier sixteenth centuries, mediated by in-kind exchange, drawing its ideology though not all its practical features from the classical and Christian models, and involving somewhat distinct subsystems for men and women.

(5) The discourse of late Elizabethan household service, mediated by cash and characterized by relatively impermanent bonds between master and servant.

More often than not these appear all mixed and mingled in both life and drama; individual masters and servants and writers called on one or another of them according to time, place, and temperament. In *The Taming of the Shrew* (not uniquely, of course, but usefully) all these discourses are in complex and fascinating dialogue with one another, and with the ideologies or discourses of service of the play's readers and audiences. It is with this play, therefore, that we will begin. Subsequent chapters will investigate the various discourses further, with emphasis on plays in which a given discourse is particularly active. The final chapter uses an analysis of *The Tempest* to draw all the strands of the argument together.

CHAPTER 3

"SURPRISING CONFRONTATIONS"

DISCOURSES OF SERVICE IN
THE TAMING OF THE SHREW

The complexities sketched at the end of chapter 2 are only particular versions of a more general complexity. Given the reductive disposition of all critical writing, it is useful to be reminded that Shakespeare plays construct and reconstruct, present and represent a dialectic among histories, "at once formal, institutional, social, and vocational" (Engle 72). Such histories, moreover, are the histories of the characters and situations in the plays, yet also to some greater or lesser extent of all the people who had a hand in the making of the plays. Preeminently this was its primary author—the person who first wrote most of the words that constitute the text. But it must also include all those others involved in the process by which an early modern dramatic text made its way into print—secondary writers, who might be full-fledged collaborators, as Fletcher collaborated with Beaumont and (in *Henry VIII*) with Shakespeare, or might just contribute a song or a scene; members of the acting company and others whose opinions and suggestions made their way into the text as it was being prepared for performance; patrons and censors whose expectations or prohibitions encouraged or repressed particular words, actions, or ideas; printers and booksellers who undertook to produce books from scripts; scribes and typesetters who converted drafts and promptbooks into fair copies and printed pages. And that does not include the earlier authors and performers in dramatic and nondramatic texts and activities whose plots, characters, themes, ideas, uses of language, bits of stage business, and modes of organization had prepared the ground and pointed the way.

Postmodern theory and criticism have accustomed us to believe that such histories are determined and constituted by language. In its most rigorous form, the theory holds that the determination is absolute—that not only all we can express but all we can know is what language allows us to express and know. This theory thus holds that language is in effect generated by language. The language generated, moreover, is the decisive component of a feedback loop in which the representation of experience so shapes the perception of experience as to determine the extension of experience in the form of actions. In effect, we do the things we have been taught how to do by the things we have heard and read. Thus, in the end, all patterns of social behavior are culturally determined, to the point where language and the discourses into which it flows are seen as the *only* determinant, to the point where the ancient idea of some essential human nature has been explicitly and unqualifiedly repudiated.

This strictly linguistic theory of human society has, however, been challenged. A vigorous qualification has been offered by the work in evolutionary sociobiology initially championed by E. O. Wilson, and brought to a wide public by Robert Wright, Matt Ridley, and others. These investigators insist that there is, indeed, a specific human nature, in the biological sense, that is, the nature of the human species, those animals and only those animals that can breed with each other to produce more of their kind. This nature, genetically determined, like the nature of cats or planarian worms, takes a variety of particular forms within which ubiquitous, and profoundly important, similarities can nevertheless be discerned. Among human beings, these forms are powerfully affected by culture—by the operation of the linguistic determinants described by postmodern theory. But the natural elements abide under and through the cultural ones. These proposals remain vigorously contested within the social scientific disciplines, and have been further problematized by developments in cognitive science that have begun to uncover the extraordinary complexity of human mental activity at the most literally material level, and the difficulty of accounting adequately for the nature and function of fundamental processes like consciousness and decision making. It will be long, I think, before we can call on these disciplines with any confidence to assist us in settling literary quarrels. For all that, however, the hue and cry raised by some simplistic features of Wilson's early arguments has given way to an increased level of respect, and the challenge posed to a reflexive cultural materialism remains.

A second, relatively familiar, and relatively long-standing alternative is offered by the psychoanalytical critics, mostly working along the line that passes from Sigmund Freud to Melanie Klein and beyond; conspicuous Shakespearean performers in this kind are Norman O. Holland, Janet Adelman, and Kirby Farrell. These scholars have their methodological disagreements, but they share a conviction that because virtually all humans who survive to maturity undergo profoundly similar experiences in their relationships with their mothers and other caregivers, there develop fundamental patterns of human behavior that precede and underlie the culturally diverse behavior in particular times and places. Writers, they argue, represent these patterns, and readers and spectators know how to respond to them. Such experiences are primarily tactile, olfactory, gustatory, rather than visual; they arise from immediate body-to-body contact. Debora Shuger has reminded me that modern and postmodern Western philosophy "depends heavily on visual and semi-otic paradigms, and both sight and language require the fissure of object from object, signifier from signified" (personal communication, May 21, 1997). The insight helps explain the resistance in post-structuralist criticism to psychological approaches. But the physicality and tactility of these approaches consort well with my own emphasis on gesture and action.

With respect to the idea of history, E. O. Thompson uttered a different but related challenge by insisting that physical objects as well as linguistic objects have histories, that these histories give rise to experiences, and that when these experiences, individual or social, encounter other experiences, they can change each other. In other words, linguistic experiences, including those codified by Althusser as "ideological 'facts' " (and, by extension, those codified by Foucault as discourses), are tested and sometimes modified by their encounters with material facts (7).[1] If the Emperor parades about in the buff long enough, however skilful his press secretary, almost all of us will eventually admit that he's naked. A further correction is supplied by Harry Berger, Jr., who observes that viewing dramatic speakers in terms merely of "the more or less corporate, more or less institutional, structure of roles and relationships" by which we commonly label both people and characters—for instance, *servant* or *master*— "freezes and personifies what in textual perspective are dynamic and interactive discourses; role is detextualization and allegorization of discourse" (xv). He thus explores a set of discourses that are psychosocial and literary rather than economic—the sinner's, the victim's, the revenger's, the hero's, and the donor's (note the moral disposition of these terms); the drama's interest in differences rather than similarities among its characters means that two or more versions of each type typically occur in the same play. Another way of saying this is to note that a dramatic figure, such as Cornwall's nameless assailant, can be at once servant, hero, revenger, donor, and victim. But heroes and donors and servants define themselves by what they do more than by what they say about it.[2]

Lars Engle likens the encounter of experiences and discourses to the activity of a market. In the discursive market place, the value of the systematic patterns of ideals and ideologies is constantly being determined and then modified in a pragmatic economics of investigation and exchange. The energies of the process were increased in the period when the Shakespearean texts were being produced, Engle says, as emerging capitalism made the marketplace in its more familiar sense increasingly important as a model for other relationships. Engle also argues that within the cultural as within the commercial marketplace, the various exchanges are carried on by individual agents, not in the traditional bourgeois sense of the completely free and self-defining subject, but of subjects powerfully determined by the prevailing discourses, yet nevertheless obliged always to negotiate among and assign value to those discourses as they compete among themselves—and, in the process, change themselves. On that ground, he is led to resist the tendency in Althusserian and Foucaultian historicism to emphasize "ideological fissures," intransigent divisions between discourses and the agents they construct, "overstating the power of structure over subject" (198). Observing that the preeminent cultural marketplace in early modern England was the popular theater, always engaged in "an active evaluation of ideas" (55), he concludes that the "unified dramatic effect" toward which early modern plays typically strive represents not "mystified social idealization," whose primary purpose is to serve the ideology of the dominant class, but "demystified social understanding" (108).[3]

Early modern service can, I think, be usefully approached within such a pragmatic understanding of competing discourses and the agents negotiating among them. Prevailing ways of talking and writing about service there certainly were; the behavior and the language of masters and servants, both actual and fictive, were certainly to some large extent determined by them. Yet, within particular situations, we can often observe that two or more discourses are, indeed, in competition, with now one, now another claiming greater value. We can also observe, following E. O. Thompson, that as discourses or ideologies are tested by the material world, they are modified. And although at the end of a play a particular discourse may be given (literally) the last words, the understanding that any reader or spectator has of it, as one agent in a cultural negotiation, may well have been changed, revalued, by the experience gained of the play.

The Taming of the Shrew constitutes such a negotiation. In this play, almost everybody is at some point servant to someone else. Indeed, Shakespeare seems to have gone out of his way to foreground master–servant relationships and issues. Doubling the plot, by increasing the number of masters, increased the number of master–servant situations. Adding the Induction increased them even more. In the source play, George Gascoigne's *Supposes* (1566), much of the fun centers on that socially ambiguous type, the parasite Pasiphilo, not quite a gentleman (no independent means), not quite a servant (no formal obligation to stay with a particular master), entrepreneurially moving from patron to patron like a flea in a pack of hounds. Shakespeare is elsewhere very interested in these ambiguous types—Gratiano and perhaps Lorenzo in *Merchant of Venice*, Sir Toby Belch in *Twelfth Night*, Parolles in *All's Well*, Falstaff. But Shakespeare dropped the parasite from *Shrew*, so that everybody begins unequivocally as either servant or master. Even more striking is his abandonment of the romantic twist (in which *Supposes* imitates a device common in Plautus and Terence) whereby it is revealed that a supposed servant Dulippo—in fact, a slave, purchased as a boy for four-and-twenty ducats—is actually a gentleman's son. That this servant can successfully behave like a master thus comes as no surprise. Shakespeare's counterpart, Tranio, however, has humble origins. His father was a sailmaker in Bergamo, insists his master, Vincentio, as he threatens condign punishment to this uppity underling (5.1.70).[4]

If Shakespeare begins by clearing away confusion about which characters are born to master, which to serve, he almost at once introduces new complexities. Bruce Robbins observes that on the mimetic or inventive ground of fiction, the play of language can produce "surprising confrontations" (9). To amplify the surprise, Shakespeare makes some of the relationships in *Shrew* doubly or triply or even quadruply fictional. Within the main body of the play, we find a servant pretending to be a master (Tranio), and two masters pretending to be servants (Hortensio and Lucentio). Although the servant characters are fictitious, the actors who first played them—and the playwright who wrote their lines—were legally and to some degree practically the "servants" of some great man. The Statute of Artisans (1563) had required all persons to have independent means, either land or money, and the fixed habitation that came with it, or to be formally in the service of such a person of means. Because most actors lacked such means, and because until the late 1580s their lives made them itinerant, the Puritans and city fathers and others hostile to the professional drama used poverty and vagabondage as grounds for their attempts to squelch the development of the theater. The actors countered the ploy by becoming official members of the households of magnates who, for whatever reasons, wished theatrical production to continue. Thus, the men who first performed *Shrew* might have had as their nominal master the Earl of Pembroke,[5] Thomas Howard the Lord Admiral, George Carey the Lord Chamberlain, or Ferdinando Stanley, Lord Strange, all patrons of troupes of actors in the late 1580s and early 1590s.[6] Many of the players had passed through some form of apprenticeship, to become freemen of one or the other of the livery companies, though whether most of them ever actually worked as goldsmiths or grocers is open to question. Some of these, indeed, were masters, in the bourgeois sense, within the business enterprise of the company of actors, in which others, such as the boy-apprentices, were technically and practically servants.[7] Thus, a spectator at the inaugural performance of the play might have seen at one point a discussion between a master who was also a servant playing a servant playing a master, and a servant who was also a master playing a master playing a servant. "Surprising confrontations," indeed.

The play opens with a framing scene in which it seems as if Shakespeare, right at the beginning of his career, wished to offer a paradigm for the various ideologies of early modern service—and then to interrogate it. In this Induction, Christopher Sly, a tinker (about as low class as you could get, but still, notoriously, his own man) staggers out of a country tavern and falls into a drunken sleep. He is discovered by a noble lord who has apparently been out with his followers in the countryside near Stratford.[8] This group can be said to represent the discourse of *retaining*, based on the feudal and prefeudal *comitatus*—the male-bonded group of the war-leader and his fighting men, here engaged in the other customary activity of such groups, hunting. And their opening exchange, a lively discussion of the qualities of the various hounds in their pack, exhibits the camaraderie that yet does not amount to equality typical of that relationship (Ind. 1.14–28). This discourse, as we see in chapter 5, was rapidly losing currency in the England of the 1580s and 1590s. Mahood calls attention to striking differences in diction between the members of this household, who all speak "richly Ovidian verse"—like that used by Tranio in the play proper—and Petruchio's servants, whose country coarseness appears in their demotic prose (47–48).[9] That contrast might well also involve the shift, mentioned earlier, toward commercial service for cash wages. (Both contrasts would be heightened if the same actors took both sets of roles.) We learn from J. M.'s little book on service, *A Health to the Gentlemanly Profession of Serving-Men* (1598), which laments the emergence of the new order, that the willingness of "Robin Roushe, gaffer russet-coats seconde sonne," to serve for wages is driving the more accomplished men of the previous age, "chosen men of witte, discretion, gouernment, and goode bringing up," out of service (B2v, B3r).[10] But the same contrast exists between the lord's meynie and Sly, so that the discourse of retaining, for late Elizabethan spectators now derived as largely from literary records as from experience, and the discourse of service for wages, becoming dominant in both society and the drama, are crossed and invaded by a contrast between the discourses of courtly and bucolic writing.

Back in Warwickshire, the Lord has his retainers carry the unconscious Sly to his nearby country house, where they trick the drunken tinker into thinking that *he* is the Lord, just coming to his senses after a long period of insanity. The stratagem involves presenting the real Lord as some sort of upper servant, a steward or chamberlain, and disguising his page as Sly's supposed lady—in the original London theater, a boy-servant playing a boy-servant playing a woman-master. Some speeches in this scene incorporate important components of the discourse of *household* or *domestic* service.[11] This mode had largely replaced the discourse of retaining (though here placed in dialogue with it) during the couple of centuries preceding the writing of the play, and was itself in the process of giving way to service for cash. Its underlying principle is mutual loyalty and responsibility, the servants pledged to take care of the master by doing most of the work, the master to take care of the servants by supplying their food and clothing and housing. Its survival into late Elizabethan times is both indicated and contested by the fact that many girls were indentured, like their brothers, but to housewifery rather than to carpentry or shoemaking.[12] It is patriarchal rather than fraternal, domestic rather than military, ideologically rooted in the Bible rather than in heroic texts and summarized in familiar passages from the Epistles to the Ephesians and Colossians:

> Seruants, be obedient vnto them that are *your* masters according to the flesh in all things, not with eye service as men pleasers, but in singleness of heart. . . . Ye masters, do vnto your seruants, that which is iuste, and equal. . . . (Col. 3:22, 4:1)

The servant's duty can be reduced to one word: *obey*; and we can clearly hear this word echoing in the Lord's instructions to the page:

> Tell him from me, as he will *win my love*,
> He bear himself with *honourable* action,
> Such as he hath observ'd in noble ladies
> *Unto their lords*, by them *accomplished*.
> Such *duty* to the drunkard let him do,
> With *soft low* tongue and *lowly courtesy*,

And say, "What is't your *honour* will *command*,
Wherein your lady and your humble wife,
May show her *duty* and *make known her love*." (Ind. 1.105–13;
emphasis added)[13]

For of course St. Paul's instructions to servants follow and closely parallel his instructions to wives: "be subject to your husbands"—and, for that matter, to children: "obey your parents in everything" (Col. 3:18, 20); and Bartholomew, the page, for the moment falls into all three categories.[14] But he learns his lesson, and so does Sly. Yet, note how the new stress on formality and hierarchy struggles in Sly's language with the demotic familiarity of the plebeian home where he is more normally (if perhaps only nominally) master:

> *Sly.*   Are you my wife, and will not call me husband?
>   My men should call me "lord", I am your *goodman*.
> *Page.* My husband and my lord, my lord and husband;
>   I am your wife in all *obedience*. (Ind. 2.101–04; emphasis added)[15]

This emphasis on obedience to the patriarch recurs in Petruchio's treatment of his servant Grumio, in Baptista's treatment of his daughters, and of course in the taming of Katherine, her transformation from a woman who bears a martyr's name (and that of a recent queen) into a Kate—spelled with a *c*, a mere dainty morsel, a consumable object on a plate.

Cate, however, with a *c*, directs attention to signs of an important factor in the historical shift from *comitatus* to household, from a master–servant relationship predicated on defense and survival toward one predicated on conspicuous display and physical comfort. This transition shows up in the Induction's emphasis on the opulence of the lord's country house—a place like Montacute, perhaps—with its "wanton pictures," its musicians, its trio of attendants bearing rose water, ewer, and towel. We see the same ideology struggling into view at Petruchio's house, no doubt smaller and cruder and darker and older, where his rustic meynie does its clumsy best to adapt to (or parody) the newer modes. And it reappears in Baptista's discreet boast: "I have many servants" (4.4.51).[16]

When the traveling actors begin to perform the play proper for Sly and the others, they open first the subplot, borrowed from George Gascoigne's English adaptation of Ariosto's *I Suppositi*, and centered on the competition among several suitors for the hand of Katherine's apparently docile younger sister Bianca. The master–servant relationships in this plot—which is highly romantic—are more strongly affected than the Induction by images of service of a *literary* kind, based on drama and fiction rather than on the Bible and social tradition, and especially on the classical New Comedy of Menander, Plautus, and Terence, which Ariosto was very self-consciously imitating. As Bruce Robbins tells us, literary servants are not so much an occupational group as the result of the conjunction of such a group with "a certain body of aesthetic functions, a repertory of gags and tags" (41). In this discourse, the central element is the profound practical and psychological dependency of the *master upon the servant*, the pole upon the hop. In life this dependency must go largely unstated, or if stated, stated only in comic terms: "I swear, I don't know what I'd do without Mrs. Higgins." In literature, as distinct from life, it can be more fully inscribed in merely mimetic relationships, where it can be contemplated without being endorsed, relationships in which masters are more likely to request, even to negotiate, even to plead, than to command.[17] And the purely theatrical articulation of this dependency involves a small set of highly stable conventional roles—the young man, the old father or rival, the braggart, the parasite, and of course, centrally for our purposes, three types of servants. It is fully within this discourse that Shakespeare's *iuventus* figure Lucentio relies on his wily servant Tranio first for advice, then, more radically, for a role in their campaign to woo Bianca that literalizes the inversion: Tranio becomes the master by pretending to be Lucentio, Lucentio the servant by pretending to be a tutor. (The inversion echoes the inversion along lines more clearly of *class* presented in the Induction.) In this connection, indeed, it must be said that in *Shrew*, as in most works in the tradition from Menander on, a complementary relationship, here between Lucentio and his boy-servant Biondello, but especially between Petruchio and his servant Grumio, balances the potentially subversive image with an orthodox representation of master dominating servant. We will more fully investigate these classically inspired relationships in chapter 4.

In this same set of relationships, we get glimpses of what was, in the actual culture of Elizabethan England, the *commercial* discourse of service that governed the behavior of an increasingly large proportion of late-sixteenth-century servants and their masters. Our category of household service was extensively and explicitly idealized in a number of early modern texts, most notably J. M.'s *Health* and the household manuals of Cleaver and Dod and Gouge; the formal ideology is easy to recover, and its expression in the discourse of service easy to recognize.

By contrast, reconstruction of actual social ideas and actions in the commercialized sphere is very difficult, even impossible. Most of the readily accessible records we have were produced by masters, not servants, mostly within the constraints of highly conventional, highly idealized, and highly systematic media, whether sermons, legal briefs, letters, or Elizabethan imitations of Italian imitations of Roman imitations of Greek New Comedy.[18] On the rare occasions when the servants spoke for themselves, their words were often recorded by a master, or by another servant of the same or a different master; and even those servants able (because they could write) to put their own words into writing usually did so in the presence of, if not directly to, their masters. Those servants able to write for themselves were typically upper servants, likely to be the sons of gentlemen—people in whom the discourse of service necessarily negotiated with the discourse of mastery.[19] Moreover, the circumstances that provoked such utterance were likely to be extraordinary. Hence, even the most plausible representations need to be studied very skeptically.

Nevertheless, as Burnett and others have illustrated, it is possible to develop some feeling for the range of feelings and attitudes actually present in early modern English society, and to look at the plays through that filter. In the master–servant relationships of *Shrew*, including that between Grumio and the other servants of Petruchio, we see how complex the practical ideology becomes, for Grumio and Tranio dominate Biondello and the other under-servants as they are dominated by Petruchio and by Lucentio's father Vincentio, the real head of that household.[20] Grumio and Tranio presumably share similar social origins, and each lives in terms of some intimacy with his boss. They are temperamentally very different, however, and to the degree that Grumio's antecedents are literary, he descends from the second group of classical slaves, the faithful curmudgeons, more usually affiliated with the *senex* than the *juventus*, and in Plautus and Terence, as here in *Shrew*, likely to have rural associations as the wily slave has urban ones.[21]

Having invoked these discourses in his opening scenes, Shakespeare is then free to play with them. We get various glimpses of the practical concerns of Elizabethan servanthood. Baptista sends a nameless servant to carry a message to his daughters (2.1.106–08), and asks him to tell them to use their new tutors well. The message seems to imply some anxiety about the girls' obedience, which will indeed be ratified by Katherine's breaking a lute over Hortensio's head, and Bianca's insolence to him later on. Such behavior runs counter to the modest demeanor prescribed for gentlewomen, and presumably Baptista would prefer that people outside the family not know of it. But the servants *would* know of it, and be in a position to tell others. Over and over again, Elizabethan and Jacobean commentators on the master–servant relationship express fear that servants will reveal the household secrets; the concern emerges when we hear Baptista asking the supposed Lucentio and his supposed father to negotiate the wedding contract at their lodging, not his:

> Not in my house, Lucentio, for you know
> Pitchers have ears, and I have many servants. (4.4.50–51)

That the concern is conventional and habitual becomes clear when we notice that there seems to be no practical ground for the anxiety, no enemy to whom revelation of the details of the arrangement would convey an advantage.[22]

By an odd kind of elision, those "many servants" are mostly conspicuous by their absence from the text—a few supernumeraries may appear for Katherine's wedding in the middle of the play and the wedding feast at the end, but none of them speaks or is given a name. It is the servants of the wooers coming into the house who are developed. Tranio and Biondello, the two servants of Lucentio and Vincentio, use the traditional discourse of service, implying a pattern in which domestics first took service as young boys, like Biondello, and then served for many years on a customary basis, without any formal contract—Tranio and Lucentio seem to have grown up and been educated together, for the former speaks familiarly of Ovid, Aristotle, and the other subjects of a typical Renaissance education, training that presumably helps him take his master's place (1.1.30–40).[23] In the interaction between the Genoese and the Paduans, however, we see a new pattern beginning to emerge. When Baptista auctions Bianca to Gremio and Tranio/Lucentio (2.1.336–89), an essential feature of the increasingly capitalistic nature of service arises from their bourgeois privileging of chattels (plate, ships, and especially coffers full of crowns) over land as the determinant of wealth. It expresses itself here when Baptista takes the disguised Lucentio and Hortensio into his service as tutors; we do not actually witness the fiscal negotiations—indeed, it initially appears that Baptista himself will not be obliged to spend a penny, for Petruchio and Gremio both offer the two supposed servants as gifts, to enhance their status as suitors for the two girls. But then we hear Gremio assure Lucentio that

> Over and beside
> Signor Baptista's liberality
> I'll mend it with a largesse. (1.2.142–44)

The speech suggests that Baptista will in fact pay customary sums for the tutors' services, while the final phrase refers to the kind of tips or vails with which servants augmented their wages.

On the other hand, there is no talk of wages among Petruchio's servants, but there is a jovial familiarity—an echo of the camaraderie of the Induction—that implies long service together, of the kind envisaged in the old retainer model; it emerges especially in Grumio's willingness to second Petruchio's efforts to tame Katherine, even if it costs him a beating (4.3.1–32 and s.d., 117–57). And there are further echoes of the discourse of retaining in Petruchio's call to Grumio to defend Katherine with his sword as they are leaving the wedding (3.3.106–10), and in the final scene, where a group of men that includes the servant Tranio uses its womenfolk as tokens in a struggle for dominance.

All these discourses are historically situated, although those histories are complex and their margins blurred. Within and across all of them, generated by them yet denying that generation as a son may deny a father, we can observe those counter-discourses that express *ressentiment*, the alienated reversal of orthodox attitudes in master–servant relations, remarked by Marx and Nietzsche, and explored in many subsequent studies.[24] The play explores various inversions or denials of normal power relationships, involving various hierarchies. At their first appearance, Grumio offers an apparently unmotivated resistance to the orders of his master, in language that contains an actual threat of a kind of physical violence by servant on master that would, if carried out, subject him to far more violent reprisals[25]—an effect all the more striking if he is, as he suggests later (4.1.1–25), an uncommonly small man:

> Hear, sirrah Grumio, knock, I say.
> *Grumio.* Knock, sir? Whom should I knock? Is there any man has rebused your worship?
> *Petruchio.* Villain, I say, knock me here soundly.
> *Grumio.* Knock you here, sir? Why, what am I, sir, that I should knock you here? (1.2.5–8)

The episode foregrounds what Frances E. Dolan perceives as one of the most urgent of early modern social anxieties. Crudely, this involved the fear that the beaten dog might eventually bite back. But within the household, "in which relations are less clearly or stably dialectical [than between governor and governed], violence takes on a subtler set of meanings, and the line between acceptable and unacceptable, everyday and transgressive violence must constantly be negotiated and redrawn" ("Chastisements" 204).[26] Such a negotiation is represented before

Hortensio's door. The dispute need not be violent, however. Petruchio, who ought to be submissively grateful to his "father," Baptista, for the large dowry that will evidently save him from acute pecuniary distress, refuses to observe the usual marital ceremonies by wearing his best suit and eating the wedding banquet. Katherine beats her sister and Grumio, and strikes Petruchio once, early in his wooing (2.1.217 s.d.), but her resistance to her father and Petruchio after the wedding is verbal and attitudinal. Tranio enthusiastically takes Lucentio's rightful place, and goes so far as to attempt to defeat Vincentio by having him imprisoned. In the end, however, Grumio carries out the rest of Petruchio's orders, Katherine is apparently submissive to her husband (if not her father), Lucentio is master again and Tranio servant, and Vincentio is at least formally reinstated as the head of his household—he marks his return by scolding and then beating Biondello (5.1.35–46): customary order is restored.

Or is it? Terry Eagleton, following Althusser and Foucault, sees in the ending of *Shrew* Shakespeare almost desperately returning to the orthodox patriarchy that provides the ideological baseline for these plays, but only managing to paper over the fissures that have appeared between essentially incompatible discourses (23). More theoretically, Jonathan Dollimore, following Gramsci, insists that alternative ideologies once presented do not go away: "closure could never guarantee ideological erasure of what, for a while, existed prior to and so independently of it" (61).[27] The fissures remain, and the paper joints are weaker than the originary structure. The point corresponds to Engle's belief in the possibility of demystified understanding leading toward a modification of discourse.

In *Shrew*, the outcome is certainly ambiguous. In the framing text of the play as we have it, the potential for a full overturn of normal hierarchy remains, unrealized, because the situation developed in the Induction in effect disappears without being resolved.[28] Christopher Sly is still a lord, forever, and the Lord his servant. Patriarchy and hierarchy seem to be endorsed by Katherine's obedient retrieval of Bianca and the widow, and her long speech accepting Petruchio's domination that follows. The closing lines of the play are oddly inconclusive, however, and imply a question whether Kate's transformation is for real:

> *Hortensio.* Now go thy ways, thou hast tam'd a curst shrew.
> *Lucentio.* 'Tis a wonder, by your leave, she will be tam'd so. (5.2.192–93)

At this point recall that we have seen Tranio as master, in his fine clothes, lording it all over Padua, and Lucentio, in his servant's clothes, being rather surprised at how well Tranio is carrying it off (1.2.245). When discovered by Vincentio, Tranio is threatened with having his nose slit— a punishment customarily inflicted on disobedient servants that, by visibly and irremediably marking him as disloyal with a highly visible scar, would make it difficult for him to find other employment (5.1.112). When we see him next, however, he seems to participate in the final scene on close to an equal footing with the gentlemen; though he does tactfully concede that he has only been Lucentio's "greyhound," he goes on in his next speech to break a witticism upon Petruchio (5.2.52–60), as if to insist that his time in grade as gentleman has raised his real status. It may just be, as the imagery of the hunt suggests, that Shakespeare here returns to the discourse of retaining initiated in the Induction, with its relatively egalitarian rhetoric; this is especially plausible because the women are absent. On the other hand, the dominant discourse in both wooing plots has been that of patriarchal domesticity, strongly reasserted by Vincentio when he roars his fury at the audacity and insolence of his servant. It would be gratifying to know whether the Elizabethan production left Tranio in those magisterial clothes or returned him to his servant's blue coat; Albert Memmi and others have written about the importance of the *signs* of status—costume, gesture, modes of address (156; see also Fumerton and Jones and Stallybrass)—and we remember the Lord teaching Sly how to talk to his lady, and especially how important in Petruchio's schooling of Katherine are the scenes in which he denies her the visual and gestural signifiers of her rank as a lady, her right to be served food of her choice, to sleep soft and warm, to wear her fashionable gown and hat—even while he and his servants allow her the merely verbal accoutrements. Action here, not language, is decisive.

It is, of course, not only in inversions of the master–servant relationship that the play figures a profound threat to patriarchal hegemony. I observed earlier that negotiations among the discourses of service tend to bring in other negotiations, especially those of gender. It is important to recall here that in the parallel sections of the epistles to the Ephesians and Galatians, those crucial source-texts for the ideology of early modern service, the duties of wives, children, and servants are successively discussed, all three groups being linked as subordinate sets within the patriarchal system.[29] *The Taming of the Shrew* entangles the roles of servants and women in a complex web of interaction; it is almost impossible to consider one set without looking at the other. Others have noted that the women resist patriarchal domination. The dreadful specter of female revolt appears most obviously in Katherine, more subtly but more surprisingly in Bianca, who seems to me, in the present context, the most interesting character in the play. I say this first because it is Bianca through whom Shakespeare gives us most fully the primal image and name of servant, representing the oldest discourse of all, the discourse of slavery, carried forward from the Homeric epics and the Pentateuch, a veritable type of Joseph, when her sister hales her onto the stage, with her hands tied, remonstrating:

> Bianca. Good sister, wrong me not, nor wrong yourself
> To make a bondmaid and a slave of me. (2.1.1–2)[30]

Even this image is equivocal, for her "master" is a woman (though both roles, of course, were initially played by men), albeit a woman visiting on Bianca the identical patriarchal control, based on superior physical strength and social custom, which she resists being imposed on herself.[31] The positioning of the scene, indeed, helps to prepare Katherine and us for her subsequent resistance of her father and Petruchio. Whether the sexual ambiguity amplifies or subdues the inversion will, I think, depend on the spectator. At any rate, when Bianca goes on to offer to divest herself of her signs of rank—"all my raiment, to my petticoat"—and to articulate the core concept of the dominant ideology—"so well I know my duty"—it seems impossible that this meek thing should turn into the defiant bride of 5.2. Bianca here radically accepts the position assigned her by her father and her suitors, as well as her sister, as a creature without will of her own whose behavior will be determined by those higher up the scale of authority. The absence in the play of female servants, moreover, and of menservants in Baptista's household other than the two gentlemen-tutors (whose particular servant role, in principle if not in practice, gives them authority over her at least in the classroom), means that she has no one over whom to exercise socially authorized authority.

Yet a closer look reveals that Bianca cloaks self-assertion under a guise of submissiveness throughout the play—a kind of White Devil, ultimately more dangerous than her sister because her rebellion is covert.[32] Katherine seems to think Bianca has been encouraging suitors despite the older sister's rightful priority. Bianca's demeanor to her father is invariably submissive, but out of his sight she escapes his control by accepting the underhanded advances of Lucentio and Hortensio. She explicitly opposes her will to that of her tutors (and explicitly throws off her subordinate role as child as well as that as woman):

> Bianca. I am no breeching scholar in the schools,
> I'll not be tied to hours nor 'pointed times,
> But learn my lessons as I please myself. . . . (3.1.18–20)

She teases both Hortensio and Lucentio by appearing to prefer the wooing of the other. The most telling point is that Bianca tolerates, even encourages, the sexual advances of social inferiors—a point that energizes another of the reiterated anxieties of masters about their servants.[33] It is made twice. The first time Hortensio only expresses his discomfort that she appears so willing to break out of the hegemony by responding to advances from a mere servant (the Folio puts Lucentio "in the habit of a mean man," to emphasize the apparent social distance [2.1.38 s.d.]):

> *Hortensio.* Yet if thy thoughts, Bianca, be so humble
> To cast thy wandering eyes on every stale,
> Seize thee that list. If once I find thee ranging,
> Hortensio will be quit with thee by changing. (3.1.87–90)

The comment is ironized by the servant's costume he is wearing himself, which recognizes the hard fact that upper class Tudor women had far more social intercourse with the male servants of their own household than with the gently born members of other establishments. Later, in 4.2, the disgusted wooer carries his verbal threat into action. But it is a pitiful gesture; Bianca has already successfully exploited patriarchal customs and attitudes in order to get her way, and Hortensio must perforce be satisfied with his rich widow, herself a member of a class accustomed to control and obedience in their own households and hence disposed to the resistance of patriarchal authority illustrated in her denial of his summons at the wedding feast.

Similar points have been made in other recent treatments of the play, and I do not wish to make too much of this. I do not, however, think that the underlying affiliation between servants and women has been heretofore so fully grounded in both ideology and social practice. Nor have the risks the resistant servants run (especially Tranio) been so explicitly remarked. The destabilizing threats they pose are serious. They are also more or less dissipated; at the end, the discourse of patriarchal hegemony dominates this play as it did the society to which it was addressed. But the alienation of Katherine and Bianca, so repeatedly expressed and enacted in the play, is inscribed as well in the enthusiasm with which Sly enters into the magical new life proposed to him, in the affectation of stupidity with which Grumio responds to the very first direct order the extremely dominant Petruchio gives him in the play (1.2.1–19), in Tranio's attack on the real Vincentio as "a madman" who must be arrested and jailed, that is, brought to the very depths of subordination (5.1.56–85). Kenneth Burke calls alienation, in the

Marxist sense, a "psycho-dynamic concept" synonymous with "the need to reject reigning symbols" (quoted in Lentriccia 77). The dynamic is mostly only implicit in *Shrew*; we as discerning agents must read it out of actions and gestures, for at no point in the play is there any explicit examination of the discourses of service. As we will see, even in his adaptations of the New Comic treatment of service and servanthood, already distanced from contemporary English life by their sources, and their nominal placement in Italy, not England, Shakespeare deals very gingerly with issues of dominance and subordination. But he is interested. Indeed, early in his career, in *Comedy of Errors*, *Titus Andronicus*, and *Shrew*, he gives frequent expression to speeches and gestures of *ressentiment*; he will explore this dynamic further in *Twelfth Night*, in the figure of that shrewd loner Feste, who (like the players) has chosen to wear motley and so quibble for his livelihood a coin at a time rather than submit to the secure subservience of the liveried servant's blue coat.[34] He will explore it in Lear's Fool, whose dependence on his master seems less economic than psychological and moral, while his master depends on him not for protection or physical service but for the kind of advice and counsel he cannot accept from social near-equals like Kent and France. He will give it very full expression in Iago and Edmund. And through Viola and Lear's daughters, of course, Shakespeare will take an even richer and subtler look at the underside of Elizabethan patriarchal hierarchy.

I find a second marginal discourse in *Shrew*, however, one of those that satisfy Bruce Robbins's criterion for interest by not being "self-evident" (11). This one complements the first one by reversing the dominant ideology in a peculiarly subversive way, that is, not by rejecting it but by co-opting it, reasserting it but on a different basis—the discourse of freedom and service discussed at the beginning of this book, what Frank Lentriccia calls "the gospel of service" (79), with its insistence on the *privilege* of duty and submission. As we have seen, articulating that view may only amplify the insistence on magisterial responsibility in those seminal verses from Colossians and Ephesians; in many instances it will cost masters little or nothing, mere gestures—and it was masters, members of the gentry, who wrote those early modern prayers and sermons and treatises. If the servants can claim the ideology and its concomitant discourse as theirs, however, can take the moral high ground, seize the psychological initiative in the very act of refusing it, the masters who decline to enter the covenant themselves become like Petruchio's falcons "That bate and beat, and will not be obedient" (4.1.177). Whether this kind of *ressentiment*, where the reversal is internal, not external, asserted in the name of psychological rather than material advantage, appears in *Shrew* is certainly debatable. I think we get glimpses of it in Katherine's fellow-feelings for the persecuted Grumio—"how he beat me because her horse stumbled, how she waded through the mud to pluck him off me" (4.1.64–66)—and in the admiration for Katherine's heroic recalcitrance implied in Tranio's image of Petruchio as a dog held at bay by a deer (5.2.57).

The contrast between patriarchal hegemony and mutual service can be summarized as the contrast between *resolution* and *dissolution*. Dissolution is implicit in an important speech in which Petruchio states the rationale of his scheme for taming Katherine:

> And where two raging fires meet together
> They do consume the thing that feeds their fury.
> Though little fire grows great with little wind,
> Yet extreme gusts will blow out fire and all.
> So I to her, and so she yields to me. . . . (2.1.130–34)

I am especially interested in the syntax of the last line. *To her* can refer back to the image of wind blowing out fire that precedes it, and thus be construed as anticipating Petruchio's victory in the contest. But there are two fires, and the phrase *to her* is grammatically parallel with *to me*: if the egocentricity that "feeds their fury" can be consumed, each can then yield, dissolving in the other as blaze in blaze, allowing them to move into a new relationship predicated on mutual service. I think I see some fertile ground ready to accept the seed of "the gospel of service" in Petruchio's constant ironizing, by exaggeration, of his own macho patriarchy. At the outset, to be sure, assorted elements assign him an ego as big as Katherine's—his insistence on Grumio's implicit obedience, Grumio's own statements confirming his toughness (1.2.103–10), the recurrent Marlovian hyperbole of his rhetoric:

> Have I not in my time heard lions roar?
> Have I not heard the sea, puffed up with winds,
> Rage like an angry boar chafèd with sweat?
> Have I not heard great ordnance in the field,
> And heaven's artillery thunder in the skies? (1.2.195–99)

But two soliloquies assure the audience that his treatment of Katherine is a calculated campaign, not merely the expression of a naturally bellicose nature (2.1.166–78, 4.1.169–92). His wedding equipage parodies the familiar image of the down-at-heels braggart warrior; it is, however, quite at odds with the reasonable civility of most of his speeches:

> To me she's married, not unto my clothes.
> Could I repair what she will wear in me
> As I can change these poor accoutrements
> 'Twere well for Kate *and better for myself.* (3.2.110–13)

As the added emphasis suggests, these lines anticipate a change in behavior. The bullyboy emerges again, of course, in Petruchio's coarse behavior during the wedding ceremony, is again replaced by the reasonable gentleman as he takes his early leave from the wedding festivities, emerges once more when Katherine joins her father in resisting this, and remains onstage (in two senses of the term) through the trip back to the country house and the well-known scenes (during which he also physically and verbally abuses his servants) in which Katherine is denied food, sleep, and decent clothing. Yet, Petruchio shares much of her discomfort; it can be argued that he sacrifices his own reputation, appearance, dinner, and night's sleep to the cause of persuading her to a life of mutual service. And once she has put on service to him with a stated willingness nowhere explicitly contradicted by the text, he behaves to her and to others with courtesy and restraint—indeed, leaves it to her to instruct the other brides—and the audience—in the marital version of the gospel of service, of which a totally non-ironic reading of her climactic speech constitutes one of the fullest expressions in the canon. It does not come out of nowhere, however. It arises from a ground prepared in the play by the readiness of Lucentio and Hortensio to assume servile roles, by Tranio's readiness to return to his own original identity, by the way Grumio and the others in Petruchio's household make his enterprise their own, even by the service rendered by the Lord and his men to Sly in the Induction. And, as I have argued in chapter 1, it is ground prepared by the ideal of service developed over 15 previous centuries, articulated by Cranmer and others, and diffused throughout all levels of early modern British society.[35]

Within the critical community, this is still awkward ground. Feminist readers, and others resistant to the institutionalization of traditional hegemony, may be forgiven for seeing such an approach to life and texts as, at best, co-optative if not positively reactionary. Althusserian readers will argue that this fissure cannot truly be closed, and that the appearance of reconciliation is only another instance of the mystification of control. Engels, Nietzsche, and their followers warn of the trap of false consciousness or bad conscience. Still, it can be argued that the willingly accepted subordination of one's own desires and needs to those of others—family and friends and neighbors, students and colleagues, strangers in need—generates a life more satisfying than one based on self-service. It is, at the very least, economical—it spares the locally dominant person the energy needed to insist, the locally subordinate the energy spent in resistance—to say nothing of energies devoted to frustration and resentment, and involving other members of the household or neighborhood. When such relationships are working, they seem to me to generate pleasure and profit on both sides—to produce the kind of freedom invoked in the Cranmerian paradox.

My immediate purposes, however, are explanatory, not persuasive. I think that when we look closely and extensively at images of and statements about servants and service in all of Shakespeare's works, within all of the several ideologies of service, in a discursive context reconstructed as best we can from other early modern documents, we will find that willing subordination is frequently enacted and rewarded, and that the concept I call *volitional primacy* helps account for its power. As we investigate these issues in the other plays, we will move from the lowest to the highest levels of society, and back, from England to Illyria, from gender to gender. The discourses sketched in this brief look at *Shrew* will organize but not circumscribe the inquiry. Along the way, we can expect many "strange confrontations"—but many familiar ones, as well, only now being seen from below, from the perspective of the servants, on their knees, or on their pallets at the foot of their masters' beds, or at the back of the hall looking up to the dais, but also looking down, at a master or mistress rendered vulnerable and yet lovable, like a child or a lover, by sleep or sex, anxiety, fear, solitude, childbirth, disease, despair, or death.

CHAPTER 4

"MONSIEUR, WE ARE NOT LETTERED"

CLASSICAL INFLUENCES AND THE EARLY MODERN MARKETPLACE

In all likelihood, Shakespeare's first exposure to formal comedy occurred in the schoolhouse, not the playhouse, when he and his fellow students read the texts of Plautus and Terence that constituted an important part of the grammar school syllabus.[1] Indeed, it is not hard to imagine this young writer from Stratford arriving in London from the country with drafts of a comedy adapted from Plautus's *Menaechmi* and *Amphitruo* (*Comedy of Errors*), and a tragedy strongly influenced by Seneca (*Titus Andronicus*) already in his briefcase. Shakespeare was English, and his own man, from the start, but classical influences dominate many of the plays we suppose him to have written early in his career.[2] And the dominance is natural, for this was the time in his theatrical life when his school-day experiences, as a student and perhaps even as a teacher (if there be truth in the suggestion that he did time in that role before coming to London to join the players), would have been freshest and strongest, and before extensive exposure to the works of other dramatists in the theater and to nonacademic influences of various kinds supplied alternative models for constructing plots, developing characters, and using language.[3] Analysis of Shakespeare's relationships to his classical predecessors is nothing new, of course; there have been admirable studies by T. W. Baldwin, Madeleine Doran, John Velz, Robert Miola, and many others. But I hope that we can find fresh interest in the topic by exploring fully the dialectical interactions between the literary discourse of classical service and the other discourses of actual early modern life.[4] For although in some of the early plays the classical influence on the treatment of service is strong, from the beginning, it is also affected by specifically early modern understandings of service.

The Shakespearean treatment of the classical *topoi* of service grows ever more complex as he explores the possibilities, just as did the institutions of service in early modern society itself. Those institutions, and the plays that derive in part from them, drew particular energy from the fact that unlike their classical models, they could increasingly treat service not as a status forced on an individual by an accident of war or birth, but as a freely chosen *role*—a role not fundamentally incompatible with a well-developed sense of individual identity and competence. The evangelists and St. Paul had incorporated classical expectations about service into the gospels and epistles, into the Christian paradox. Obligations freely accepted as expressions of the will of God were to be more than compensated by the enjoyment of freedom in the afterlife: service was, or at least was becoming, freedom. Christians, and especially Protestants, highlighted the workings of divine grace—freedom granted, not earned. In some of the religious writings, but especially in secular texts such as popular plays, however, the rewards of free service could be seen to be potentially available in this world as well as the next. And there is something at work in the classical model, the model of Plautus and Terence, that is, indeed, analogous to Christian grace, a kind of secular grace: New Comic masters who are well-pleased by their servants sometimes, though not always, set them free, not because they have *deserved* it by carrying out some prior set of obligations, but because their masters choose to be generous, to love them in this way.[5] And even within the constraints of service, at least some classical servants move freely enough.

In Shakespeare's earlier plays, relationships between servants and masters of a classical kind are among the most vigorous elements. Such relationships are staple elements of New Comedy, of course, both Greek and Roman. Terence for sure and Plautus quite probably were servants themselves; following Menander and the other Greek New Comic dramatists the Romans were imitating, servants have prominent roles in almost all their works. Servants' names often supply the title of the play—for example, *Pseudolus, Phormio.* New Comic servants display stock features, but their characters and plot functions are by no means uniform. We find stolid blockheads who serve mostly as whipping posts; we also find the wily schemers who undertake to solve the fiscal and amatory problems of their masters' sons and advance their own interests in the process. Most of these relationships, however, are finally colored by the absolute formal subordination of servant to master. That is because in classical life most servants were slaves, sold like livestock at the market, literally the property of their masters, who held over them the power of life and death. This does not mean that classical servants, in life or in literature, were cringing dogs; from Homer's Eumaios (as princely born as Telemakhos, to be sure) onward to Plautus's Pseudolus, we get images of servants who have made for themselves a place in their masters' lives in which they can stand relatively tall. But the successful slave is the slave who becomes legally free. And such slaves know, and let their masters know, who's boss; that is, they acknowledge and accept their subservient position. By the same token, from Homer's Melanthios to Shakespeare's Malvolio, literature gives us images of servants who try to stand too tall, and suffer for it (though Malvolio is punished rather by his peers than his superiors). Malvolio, to be sure, pays for his presumption with a few hours in the cellar and the fleers and gibes of the other dependents, whereas Melanthios pays with ignominious death.[6] For Elizabethan servants were not slaves, nor did their masters any longer hold over them the legal power of life and death. And it is this element of freedom that Shakespeare particularly explores and exploits in all his deeper treatments of service relationships.

Not surprisingly, the classical connection is clearest and fullest in *Comedy of Errors*.[7] The two Dromios, we are told, are slaves:

> . . . twins both alike.
> Those, for their parents were exceeding poor,
> I bought. . . . (1.1.55–57)[8]

In many ways, they seem at least as bright, energetic, and otherwise competent as their masters—more so, perhaps, for we do not need the *commedia*-based whizzing around of the Dromios in some recent productions to see that the physical and practical demands on the two servants are much greater than on their masters.[9] But their lives are hard; and the very first speech we hear either of them utter sets Shakespeare's baseline position on service (which, indeed, is the one most commonly implied by the treatment of service in treatises and sermons), that is, resentment of the situation, but a kind of resigned willingness to see it out:

Antipholus S. (*to Dromio*)	Get thee away.
Dromio S.	Many a man would take you at your word,
	And go indeed, having so good a mean.
	(1.2.16–18)

He does not "go indeed," but rather trudges about Ephesus, very responsibly, safeguarding large sums of money and quantities of baggage, arranging for lodgings, carrying messages, worrying about schedules—and suffering, in the process. He is beaten on at least one and perhaps another occasion, having given no offense except that of defending himself against false accusations. And the beatings are, to be sure, resented.

> I have some marks of yours upon my pate,
> Some of my mistress' marks upon my shoulders,
> But not a thousand marks between you both.
> If I should pay your worship those again,
> Perchance you will not bear them patiently. (1.2.82–86)

Maurice Hunt hears these remarks as "ominously subversive" (32), invoking the materialist concept of *ressentiment*. A lengthening string of critics has documented the early modern master's customary and legal right to administer corporal punishment to disobedient or otherwise unruly servants (Beier, Burnett, Dolan, Moisan), as parents and teachers had and evidently used their right to "chastise" (the term used by Cleaver and Dod, by distinction from merely verbal "rebuke") their children and pupils (D1r). As Michael Neill states, reasonably enough, "the routine violence" inflicted on these servants cannot be explained away merely by referring to New Comic antecedents: theatrical convention does not operate in "a social vacuum" (41).

We can observe that in Shakespeare, the incidence of servant-beating declines markedly after the two early comedies most directly dependent on classical models, *Comedy of Errors* and *Taming of the Shrew*. Ordinary servants are unreasonably punished in two late classical tragedies, *Antony and Cleopatra* (2.5.60–74, 3.13.85–154) and *Coriolanus* (4.6.48–57); all are messengers, who are punished or threatened with punishment merely to give vent to the feelings aroused by their messages. Cleopatra repents and gives a compensatory reward, Enobarbus condemns Antony's irrationality, and Menenius persuades the other Roman counselors to heed the messenger. Otherwise, the pattern of punishment for actual presumption holds. The punching bags continue to be clowns, fools, and scoundrels: Thersites, the Clown of Rossilian, Lear's Fool, Autolycus—all punished or threatened with punishment for presumption, not for disobedience or incompetence. All occupy roles much closer to the classical parasite (of which more later) than to either the wily or the clownish slave. And in all these cases except perhaps the Duchess's threats to the Clown, the action says more about the distressed and distracted state of the master than about the resentment of the servant—after all, most people have been unfairly abused by their parents, siblings, teachers, supervisors, friends, and spouses simply for being a convenient object on which to unload psychic or physical distress.[10] There is one more complex case: Oswald, an upper servant and probably a gentleman by birth, who would not normally be disciplined by corporal punishment. He too, however, has ambiguous status. Twice he is physically abused by Kent, in the latter's character as Lear's servant Caius; whether Kent can be supposed to see the punishment of insolent or unruly servants as his magisterial right (as Cornwall clearly supposes he has a right to discipline Kent-Caius), or whether this is one of those cases within the retainer tradition where the servants of warring masters make war on each other, as in *Romeo and Juliet,* is not easy to discern. The latter explanation does fit Edgar's mortal chastisement when Oswald tries to capture Gloucester.[11]

In any event, Dromio's "ominously subversive" remarks are never translated into action. Indeed, when his Ephesian brother, who gets it even worse, being beaten at least three times, perhaps more, is bound and imprisoned for being as mad as his master, putting the servant in a position to take some revenge, he remains faithful in a way that reinforces a crucial emphasis in traditional treatments of the master–servant relationship, both classical and feudal: that in important ways the bondage is mutual. For Dromio of Ephesus and Antipholus of Ephesus are literally tied up, one to the other. It is the master who first frees the servant, physically, by chewing through the cords. And though the servant could take advantage of the opportunity to run away, Dromio unties Antipholus and remains to support and defend his master. Practically, the action allows the two of them to reach the stage in time for the appearance of the Abbess and the cutting of the other knots in this complex plot. Its larger import, however, is ambiguous. At the end of classical comedies, productive servants are often rewarded with their freedom. Rather than seeing the loosing of the cords as symbolic prelude to liberty, however, Dromio apparently reconfirms his servitude:

> Within this hour I was his bondman, sir,
> But he, I thank him, gnawed in two my cords.
> Now I am Dromio, *and his man,* unbound.
> (5.1.289–91; emphasis added)

It is quite possible, of course, that in the last line lurks an appeal for fuller freedom. The master's response is equally unclear; Antipholus of Ephesus does not take the hint, if there is one, nor the one afforded later on when the Abbess and Dromio of Syracuse both recognize Egeon:

> *Dromio S.*   My old master, who hath bound him here?
> *Abbess.*   Whoever bound him, I will loose his bonds. . . . (339–40)

Nor the one afforded by the various references to the chain. The issue emerges obscurely from the uncertain grammar of an exchange near the end:

> *Antipholus E.* Dromio, what stuff of mine hast thou embarked?
> *Dromio S.* Your goods that lay at host, sir, in the Centaur.
> *Antipholus E.* He speaks [i.e., should be speaking] to me—I am your
>   master, Dromio.
>   Come, go with us. We'll look to that anon.
>   Embrace thy brother there; rejoice with him. (411–15)[12]

Here the *that* in the fourth line could refer to the matter of the goods deposited at the Centaur,[13] or to the matter of the freeing of servants; the latter possibility seems reinforced by "rejoice with him," and by the image of equality with which the play ends: "Now let's go hand in hand, not one before another" (a line given extra emphasis by an extra iamb). Yet in striking contrast to many classical works, these long-suffering yet useful slaves remain officially bound to their masters. It may be that just at the point where the classical world of the play is about to dissolve, and the spectators—including a good many servants, if the old ideas about the groundlings have any validity—are about to be returned to the quotidian actualities of late Elizabethan London, the classical discourse is already giving way to one or another of the contemporary ones. Under any of these, servants serve until some stipulated point in time, to a point in their service that corresponds to this point in the play. Phenomenologically, the end of the play might signal the end of the Dromio's period of service. The question remains, however, why these faithful servitors—especially the one to whom his master owes his own, literal, freedom—are not materially as well as emotionally rewarded, at least in the text. We will consider later the possibility that Shakespeare ascribes to service full satisfaction, psychological and spiritual if not economic. For the moment, what we can say is that a materialist reading sees here an ironic reaffirmation of masters' ineluctable economic and social control over their dependents, and an idealist reading places value on service per se.

In another early play, *Titus Andronicus,* apparently conventional service likewise leads to ends that do not satisfy classical conventions. Right at the outset of his career, Shakespeare exhibits his gift for innovation by transferring the type of the wily servant from comedy to tragedy, with results that may affront good taste but make good theater.[14] Aaron, an African slave, schemes on behalf not of his master's son but of his mistress (usually a blocking character, not one whose fortunes are to be improved), to gain her the mate she wants, in opposition to a *senex*, Titus, who in contrast with most instances of the type (such as Baptista in *Shrew*) is almost ludicrously insensitive to his own material interests. Aaron strives also on behalf of a pair of *juventus* characters, Chiron and Demetrius, in particular by helping them trap and rape Lavinia; it was a standard device of classical comedy for the wily slave to get the youth and the girl in a situation where he could rape her and thus ultimately claim her as wife by sexual conquest—apparently quite free there of moral or social stigma, though the change in attitudes toward rape helps make the episode tragic in *Titus* (see Duckworth 289–90). Of course, Aaron "serves" his mistress in the stockbreeder's sense, as well. When she fails to reciprocate his fidelity, by asking him to kill their child, he abandons her, but keeps the child, for whom he exhibits a laudable degree of parental care. This image is variously distanced from early modern social practice—by the classical setting, Tamara's explicit barbarian status, Aaron's racial difference at a time when the few black servants visible on London streets mostly accompanied foreign masters. Only on one ground is it obviously resonant with Elizabethan social concerns, in the anxiety, so often expressed as to appear routine, about the sexual vulnerability of women to aggressively male servants—an anxiety that *Shrew* also addresses, though around the corner, as it were, by having the successfully seductive servant be an actual master. Mark Thornton Burnett has examined this phenomenon in detail (*Masters* ch. 4); he does not list either play as one of the conspicuous exhibits.[15]

Classical images of servitude also appear in *Shrew*, but with more fully developed early modern elements. Like *Comedy of Errors,* this play offers substantial roles for two servants, Tranio in the subplot and Grumio in the main plot. (Biondello and Curtis, the other servants in the play to whom the text gives more than a name, are not fully enough developed to merit discussion here.) Like the Dromii, they are sometimes beaten and otherwise (especially Grumio) abused. But, not being twins, nor the servants of twin masters, they are also more fully differentiated. It is worth observing that they never officially meet (though brought onstage together for some scenes of most productions), because sometimes in New Comedy, the blockhead is an ally of the blocking character against the wily servant and his young man, and there are scenes between the opposing servants in which now one, now another has the upper hand.[16] Here, however, since Grumio's young man, Petruchio, is wily himself, the blockhead becomes an ally on his side of the double plot, arrayed not against an old man but a young woman—herself, to be sure, another displaced New Comic type, analogue to the shrewish wife in *Menaechmi* (the model for Adriana in *Comedy of Errors*). Another surprising confrontation. It is impossible to say whether theatrical exigencies, the appeal of the contrasting types in conjunction with the transfer of wiliness to a *juventus* figure, the competition and conflict among the well-to-do suitors and between Petruchio and Katherine, making additional conflict among servants unnecessary, or the doubling of plots, putting them in different households, contributed more to the play's suppression of this traditional rivalry.

In any event, Grumio, who serves the wily and vigorous Petruchio, is the laborious endurer, whose role is always to be at fault; he contrives to get his ears wrung within a few lines of his first entrance. He has apparently served for a long time—"your ancient, trusty, pleasant servant Grumio" Hortensio calls him (1.2.46); it was common enough in Elizabethan as in classical times for a servant to be assigned as a young man to serve a child, and to age along with his young master. He also seems to represent the rural rather than the urban servant—one of those of which the otherwise unidentifiable J. M. speaks, in a book whose main theme is a complaint that in great households, servants of gentle or yeomen breeding are being replaced by "Robin Roughe my gaffer russet-coats seconde sonne" (B3r).[17] But he has followed his master to the city, not come there on his own to look for work, for in overall design (by beginning in Warwickshire and ending in Padua) and in the movements of Petruchio, the play inscribes another important social and economic development, the increasing tendency of the rural gentry, drawn by the Court and the courts, to spend most of their time in London, returning to their country seats only to hunt and look after necessary business.

And for our purposes, Grumio carries forward from the classical tradition another significant dimension. Within certain limits, he insists on remaining volubly his own person. The slaves of Roman comedy— and their early modern descendants—are not very free with regard to action. In that realm, their self-assertion is mostly negative, *not* carrying out their orders, or doing so slowly, or badly, all typical expressions of Nietzschean *ressentiment*, which can not enact itself directly by overt resistance or disobedience. Like Staphyla in *Aulularia*, whose way is to hobble and stall, Grumio's first response to his first command from Petruchio, to knock on Hortensio's door, is to deflect it. And he does so through language, by willful misprision.

Petruchio. Here, sirrah Grumio, knock, I say.
Grumio. Knock, sir? Whom should I knock? Is there any man has rebused your worship?

Petruchio.	Villain, I say, knock me here soundly.
Grumio.	Knock you here, sir? Why, sir, what am I, sir, that I should knock you here, sir?
Petruchio.	Villain, I say, knock me at this gate, And knock me well or I'll knock your knave's pate.
Grumio.	My master is grown quarrelsome. I should knock you first, And then I know after who comes by the worst.

Here is a clear echo of Dromio's comment on corporal chastisement.

Petruchio.	Will it not be? Faith, sirrah, an you'll not knock, I'll ring it, I'll try how you can sol-fa and sing it. *He wrings him by the ears.*[18]
Grumio.	Help, masters, help! My master is mad! (1.2.5–17)

Grumio's responses are superficially deferential; he repeatedly marks his master's dominant status (*sir, your worship,* then *sir* three times in one line), asks questions rather than makes statements, disallows his own valid agency ("Why what am I . . . ?"). But at least for a time he asserts his command of the discourse: he it is who will define *knock*, invent words,[19] appeal to the audience for their sympathy (I take "My master is grown quarrelsome" to be a de facto aside, though most editors have not marked it as such, addressed to the world in general, not to Petruchio). That is made explicit in "Help, masters" (including those in the audience) which also has the effect, if short-lived, of giving Grumio the social superiority of any sane man to any lunatic. (If the *you/thou* distinction is as important as Neill argues it is [6–7, 64], there is a sign in line 17 that Petruchio himself is extending him a certain respect.) All this while, it is he who is controlling the tempo of the conversation— and deferring his execution of the order. Indeed, in the absence of a stage direction to that purpose, we are at liberty to suppose that he never does knock at that door. Nor do these verbal exercises stop when Hortensio enters, having evidently heard the commotion. To him, Grumio plays the lawyer: "If this not be lawful cause for me to leave his service—look you sir: he bid me knock him and rap him soundly, sir. . . . Well, was it fit for a servant to use his master so, being perhaps, for aught I see, two-and-thirty, a pip out?" (27–31).[20] And his final question shows that within his construction of the term he has the best of the argument: "Knock at the gate? Oh heavens"—the appeal is now cosmic—"spake you not these words plain? 'Sirrah, knock me here, rap me here, knock me well, and knock me soundly'? And come you now with knocking at the gate?" (37–40).

There may be a further consideration here. As he equivocates and stalls, he is aware of his risk: "I know after who comes by the worst"; he is presumably not surprised when Petruchio reasserts his own linguistic authority by first punning on *ring–wring,* and then turning word into deed.[21] Even here, Grumio sustains a kind of covert authority (a psychologist might call it passive-aggressive): he knows how to push Petruchio's buttons; he does push Petruchio's buttons; Petruchio reacts exactly as expected. There may be enough psychic satisfaction in this concealed control to make the pain of the wrung ears worthwhile. Indeed, he can subtly claim responsible agency:

> ... would to God I had well knocked at first,
> Then had not Grumio come by the worst. (32–33)

We will revisit this issue later, in considering volitional primacy (see below, ch. 7).

In any event, Grumio's freedom of speech has plenty of New Comic antecedents. "Almost all the slaves have one characteristic in common—talkativeness; from this stems their boastfulness and self-glorification, their impudence and insolence, their inquisitiveness, indiscretion, and love of gossip" (Duckworth 249). Loquacity, to the point of insolence, is also a quality of all Shakespeare's comic servants, from Speed and Lance in *The Two Gentlemen of Verona* through Lear's fool. And while masters may eventually tire of it, they mostly tolerate it, even, in the case of the professional fool, pay for it. Masters and servants, especially personal man- and maid-servants like Grumio, spent a lot of time alone together; they were familiar, in several senses of that word, and all other things being equal, a servant who could be amusing and stimulating, even if a little outrageous, would be to most masters more agreeable than somebody glum or silent. (We do need to note here the value of lively talk in amusing theatrical audiences.) Jonson's Count Ferneze says of his Grumioesque servant, Onion, that

> He'll bandy with me word for word; nay more,
> Put me to silence, strike me perfect dumb;
> And so amaze me, that oftentimes I know not
> Whether to check or cherish his presumption.... (*Case* 1.7.60–63)

We can see this even more clearly in the other important servant in *Shrew,* Tranio. He is as much Lucentio's companion as his man. According to Vincentio, Lucentio's father, he has urban rather than peasant origins.[22] Like Grumio, he has served his master for some time, for he was brought into the household as a boy of three (5.2.70–76). He seems then to have grown up with Lucentio, sharing enough of the latter's training to enable him to carry off the masquerade—he talks familiarly of Aristotle, Ovid, and "the metaphysics" (1.1.25–40), and speaks mainly verse where Grumio speaks mainly prose. He is Shakespeare's fullest straightforward development of the New Comic wily servant, the *servus callidus,* whose cunning, resourcefulness, and familiarity with the details of his master's world, energized partly by self interest, partly by the sheer pleasure of the enterprise, allow him to help his master overcome the obstacles raised by assorted *senex* figures (Baptista, Gremio, and Vincentio) to get the girl and the money. As Madeleine Doran has observed, in English comedy, the intriguer is more likely to be a master than a servant (155). That is and is not true of *Shrew.* First, note that the intrigues of Lucentio and Tranio cannot proceed until the intrigues of a wily master, Petruchio, have preceded them. Then note that the idea of disguising Lucentio as a tutor (i.e., a servant, for Lucentio says that he will "be a slave t'achieve that maid" [1.1.213]) occurs to both master and servant at the same moment, though it is Lucentio who verbally proposes that Tranio should take his place.[23]

Lucentio.	Ah, Tranio, what a cruel father's he!
	But art thou not advised he took some care
	To get her cunning schoolmasters to instruct her?
Tranio.	Ay, marry am I, sir, *and now 'tis plotted.*
Lucentio.	*I have it, Tranio.*
Tranio.	Master, for my hand,
	Both our inventions meet and jump in one.
	. . .
Lucentio.	. . . Thou shalt be master, Tranio, in my stead. . . .
	(1.1.179–96; emphasis added)

Once in disguise, however, Tranio must take the initiative, most markedly by duping the old pedant to pass himself off as Lucentio's father—without consulting Lucentio first, at least not in the text, for we first hear Tranio explain the scheme to his master, whom he then pushes offstage without waiting for his reply, as Biondello is bringing the old guy on (4.2.60–72). And it is Tranio alone who brazens it out so well— Doran calls him an "impudent slave" (156)—that he seems to have achieved at least a temporary triumph over his old master, the true Vincentio, for he persuades Baptista to command the officer to cart Vincentio off to jail. Were it not that at this point Lucentio arrives, reveals the subterfuge, and pleads for forgiveness (5.1.52–118).

Tranio's response here is most intriguing (in more than one sense), especially in conjunction with the typical loquacity of the New Comic underling: at a point where common sense seems to demand appeals for mercy even more abject than those being made by Lucentio, this voluble rogue remains silent (anticipating that terrible mutation of the wily servant type, Iago, at a similar moment in his masquerade). It is as though, by continually talking in the master's vein to other masters (including Lucentio), he had become so fully committed to the exchange that he could not abandon it, resolved to face down even threats of being defaced:

> *Vincentio.* I'll slit the villain's nose that would have sent me to the jail. . . . Go to, but I will in to be revenged for this villainy. (5.1.112–17)

Whether, and if so how, the patriarch carries out his threat we never learn. Phenomenologically, the rich father has been put down. He speaks but one more line in the play: " 'Tis a good hearing when children are toward" (5.2.186). And while in that line he continues to affirm patriarchal privileges, the affirmation is unassertive—*toward* is glossed as "promising," "apt," and so on, with strong connotations of docility and obedience (*OED* A.3–4), reinforced by the contrast in Lucentio's line that follows: "But a harsh hearing when women are froward."[24] The implication is that his son's behavior has been examined and found satisfying. Tranio—as toward as his young master, but also much more froward—seems undismayed, however, and it seems likely that he escapes punishment because the outcome of his plottings has been so satisfactory.[25] The stage direction at the beginning of the last scene places him among but not of the group of servants ("*the servingmen with Tranio bringing in a banquet*") from where he jests with Petruchio in familiar terms, responding to Petruchio's canine insult with one of his own—which Petruchio, addressing him as "Signor" (perhaps a mildly ironic recollection of Tranio's changes of status), then deflects at Lucentio and Hortensio, leaving him and Tranio as equals and both, for the moment, superior to them:[26]

> *Petruchio.* She hath prevented me here, Signor Tranio.
> This bird you aimed at, though you hit her not.
> Therefore a health to all [including Tranio?] that shot and missed.
> *Tranio.* O sir, Lucentio slipped me like his greyhound,
> Which runs himself and catches for his master.

Petruchio.	A good swift simile, but something currish.
Tranio.	'Tis well, sir, that you hunted for yourself.
	'Tis thought your deer does hold you at the bay [like a dog].
Baptista.	O, O, Petruchio, Tranio hits you now.
Lucentio.	I thank you for that gird, good Tranio.
Hortensio.	Confess, confess, hath he not hit you here?
Petruchio.	A has a little galled me, I confess,
	And, as the jest did glance away from me,
	'Tis ten to one it maimed you two outright. (5.2.50–63)

This is not the behavior of someone who has been effectively punished—certainly not of someone who has undergone the terrible humiliation of the slit nose. If we read the scene naturalistically, it seems most probable that Vincentio, his attention mainly drawn to his son's achievement of the heiress Bianca, has vented his anger in the verbal threats, to the point where Tranio's explicit resumption of the servant's role can avert more condign penalties, just as Grumio's early capitulation, with Hortenio's pleading in support, restores him to Petruchio's favor. If we read it generically, we can suppose that Tranio is included in the general comic benediction. Psychologically, we can interpret the passage as Tranio's successful attempt to instate himself as the household's allowed fool. But the political reading remains highly ambiguous—as much so, and for many of the same reasons, as the political reading of the behavior of Bianca, treated in the previous chapter, and of Katherine, subject of so much recent critical attention.

In any event, the ambiguities in the position of Tranio, at the end and in the shift in inventive priority from servant to master and then back, bear consideration. As we saw earlier, Shakespeare, in adapting Gascoigne, augmented and clarified the opportunities for masters and servants to struggle for control. In the process, he suppressed some New Comic conventions—the parasite, the revelation of the servant's gentle birth—just as in *Comedy of Errors* he had suppressed the customary award of freedom to faithful slaves. Why should Shakespeare, who adapts the classical pattern pretty closely in the basic situation, in the character of Grumio, in the definition and development of the *senex* figures, and in other ways, diverge from it here?

The answer seems to me to lie in the social circumstances of the theater. Plautus and Terence, servants themselves, nevertheless wrote for the rough-and-tumble popular audience of the marketplace, *platea sine sedibus* (the terms are Robert Weimann's, *platea* for the ground-level occupied by the common people and *sedibus* the raised seats of the mighty), where Bakhtinian carnival mirth prevailed, and where the audience included many servants.[27] While they did not go so far as to promote absolute violations of the master–slave ordinance, the New Comic writers, working through actors whose grotesque masks, costumes, postures, and gestures alienated them visually, and in a highly artificial language that alienated them verbally, were free to explore modifications in the normative master–servant relationship in relatively direct and unequivocal terms.[28] Shakespeare, though also a "servant," was writing for the permanent playhouse, a privileged space, to be sure, but in its bourgeois substantiality nevertheless vulnerable to social pressure in a way the trestles and planks of the Roman actors never were, writing for actors whose faces were visible and whose costumes and gestures identified them with the society outside the theater doors, and who could only continue in their craft as long as they were formally the servants of some great personage themselves, writing for an audience that included many masters and mistresses whose six-penny or shilling seats (*sedes*), placed physically above the one-penny ground (*platea*) where their servants stood, offered a constant visual reminder of normal hierarchy. In the 1590s, moreover, as Burnett and others have shown, recent episodes of unruly behavior by husbandmen, apprentices, and other servants, perhaps reflected in the Jack Cade episode of *2 Henry VI*, had alarmed both city and court, provoking a spate of legal, political, and military attempts to insure control of masters over subordinates. Finally, mere legal freedom from the categorical servitude of classical slaves was not enough; under the Statute of Artificers, escape from the obligation to serve came only with the acquisition of 40 marks in property or cash; a servant (Dromio or Tranio) released from obligations to a particular master (Antipholus or Vincentio) without a very handsome parting gift might well be "free," like Lancelot Gobbo, only to seek another master.

Recognizing changes in the social structure also might have led Shakespeare to extend the range of his classical models. Consider what it would mean in practical terms for an early modern master like Vincentio or Lucentio to have a personal servant such as Tranio— educated, articulate, confident, and clever enough to carry off an extended masquerade as his young master and to flout the authority of his older one in that master's face. Such a servant might well be useful. Indeed, there were such servants well up the social tree—men like Lord Burghley himself, servant of the Queen, or those upper servants in Burghley's household studied by Richard C. Barnett and Alan G. R. Smith, who routinely associated and worked with the greatest men and women of the country, and sometimes rose to positions of independent authority. But such men did not usually have sailmakers from Shrewsbury for fathers. (That pattern was more common in the earlier Tudor period, when the Church advanced a butcher's son, Wolsey, to became a cardinal; later in the period, after it became customary to give aristocrats academic educations, opportunities for commoners to rise to the top were substantially curtailed.) Yet they could sometimes serve for a quarter or a year or even a contractual seven years, and then be free to hire themselves to some other master—and to take with them whatever they knew in the way of insider secrets and whatever they had by way of insider contacts. Barnett's study of the Cecil servants makes it clear that the family went to considerable lengths to keep in their employ those in the household who were admitted to their masters' confidences.

In other words, although the classical model remains active in Shakespeare's writings, its activity is less and less overt. In the plays written after 1595 or so, there are no servants as directly and fully in the New Comic mode as those we have considered so far. Costard brings to *Love's Labour's Lost* a variant of the rustic type we saw in Grumio, and Lancelot Gobbo in *Merchant of Venice* adds a touch of another traditional New Comic type, the parasite. But neither of these models develops very far; the Costard and Gobbo we remember, of the hilarious speeches and unflappable composure, surely owe as much to the personality and experience of that consummate professional entertainer Will Kempe as to any literary source, and the same is true for Peter (*Romeo and Juliet*) and Dogberry (*Much Ado*), the latter no servant at all but a burgher.[29] The development becomes explicit in Feste and Touchstone, after Robert Armin replaced Kempe, and the Plautine link was largely snapped, for Touchstone, Feste, Lavatch, the Fool in *King Lear* become figures very much like actors themselves, birds of passage, marginalized but independent men who may be in but are never really of a household. If they have New Comic origins, it is in the classical parasite, one of whose modes of pleasing is to entertain, and who are sometimes insolent, though also sometimes merely fawning.[30]

Indeed, I would argue, with Robert Miola, that Shakespeare's most stimulating developments in this area generated characters whose New Comic origins are scarcely visible. We have already noted some of the striking ways in which Aaron, in *Titus Andronicus,* plays variations on the wily servant. The relationship of Juliet's nurse to the Plautine *lena* has, indeed, been frequently noted (Velz 115); such a character, called Bromia, appears in *Amphitruo,* frequently identified as a source for *Comedy of Errors,* and like the Nurse, she is garrulous and full of complaints.[31] But Shakespeare's Nurse is given a far more extensive and complex development than any surviving classical *lena,* and neither Plautus nor Terence uses such characters as *loci* for the subtle exploration of the crucial master–servant issues of obedience and loyalty that we find in *Romeo and Juliet*—which we explore ourselves in chapter 6. The Nurse's eagerness to get her young charge into some man's bed—whether Romeo or Paris is all one to her—does remind us that many of the *lenae* in Plautus and Terence are bawds. Shakespeare returns to a relatively classical treatment of this New Comic type in Mistress Quickly, who serves Falstaff's turn in a variety of ways, then, in the traditional English manner, marries his former servant Pistol. The type also appears, doubled, in *Measure for Measure,* where Pompey Bum (a variant on the Grumio type of servant), observes that his Mistress Overdone has "worn [her] eyes almost out in the service" (1.2.90–91).[32] But Pompey himself takes on some of the traditional qualities of the *lena.* Like the Nurse (and Grumio), he talks volubly, but rarely to the purpose: "As I say, this Mistress Elbow, being, as I say, with child, and being great-bellied, and longing, as I said, for prunes; and having but two in the dish, as I said, Master Froth here, this very man, having eaten the rest, as I said, and, as I say, paying for them very honestly; for, as you know, Master Froth, I could not give you threepence again . . ." (2.1.90–95). He accepts if he does not initiate Elbow's malaproposterous use of the word *respect.* And he retains an essential integrity in the face of the oppressive law of Vienna:

> Whip me? No, no; let carman whip his jade.
> The valiant heart's not whipped out of his trade. (2.1.226–27)[33]

Having bent the *lena* in inventive ways, Shakespeare plays an especially inventive set of developments on the type of the parasite.[34] It is perhaps a bit easier to assign servant status to these characters in early modern than in classical drama, because, as we have seen, in early modern society, service was not strictly a function of social status. The playwright initiates his innovations in this role in *Merchant of Venice,* with that curious personage, Graziano. He appears first as Bassanio's friend, Mercutio to Bassanio's Romeo. But without being in any way formally recruited, he then becomes part of the entourage whose apparel, transportation, and lodging Bassanio is presumably supplying with Antonio's 3,000 ducats. Within that entourage, he has no practical responsibilities—we do not see him looking after the horses or paying the bills or running errands, or even carrying out the quasi-military functions of the traditional retainer. His responsibilities seem to be to keep Bassanio company, offer generalized moral and social support, and, most notably, to be amusing, in the mocking, irreverent, sometimes nearly insolent way of parasites in both classical and early modern comedy. At the end of the play, it seems to be understood that he will continue in that role indefinitely—there is certainly no talk of his returning to Venice with Nerissa once the nuptial ceremonies are complete.

Graziano is echoed or anticipated at a lower social level by someone who is formally a servant, but who acts like a parasite, Lancelot Gobbo. Having some qualities of the traditional rural servant type, like Grumio, his relations with his original master, Shylock, and his eventual master, Bassanio, yet reflect the early modern development of cash-based servitude organized by quarterly or annual contract—appropriate for a play energized by money. Gobbo does not suffer actual ill treatment from his master Shylock. He complains, to be sure, of a lack of food. But then Shylock, on his part, complains of Gobbo's huge appetite (the near homonymy with *gobble* is unmistakable), and since the likelihood is that the actor Will Kempe, who presumably played Lancelot for Shakespeare's company, was rather corpulent than otherwise, the visual evidence would have supported the master. In fact, Gobbo, arguing with himself in terms of the old familial ideology, indicates that he has no legitimate grounds for a departure he repeatedly calls running away (*Mer.* 2.2.5, 7, 10). His conscience calls for the traditional fidelity of servant to master irrespective of the master's treatment; it is the devil who suggests flight. Gobbo wrestles with this problem through a delightful soliloquy (2.2.1–25) and resolves it on emotional rather than rational grounds (though his stance is, in fact, acceptable within the emerging cash-nexus ideology if the quarter or year for which he contracted to serve is nearing its end): "The fiend gives the more friendly counsel. I will run, fiend" (24). And having teased his sand-blind father in a way that also at least temporarily inverts the customary father–son hierarchy, he persuades the old fellow to sue to Bassanio for a place in his new retinue. As it turns out, his contract has already been transferred by agreement between his old and new masters:

> I know thee well. Thou hast obtained thy suit.
> Shylock thy master spoke with me this day,
> And hath preferred thee, if it be preferment
> To leave a rich Jew's service to become
> The follower of so poor a gentleman. (2.2.128–33)[35]

The effect is to bleed off most of whatever moral urgency Gobbo's comic language has not already appropriated, placing at comic distance a kind of conflict that must have produced real strains in many early modern households. In his new livery at Belmont, he continues his parasitic ways—he gets a fellow servant pregnant, trades words with the temporary steward Lorenzo, and seems generally tolerated more for his entertainment value than his practical use.

A more various figure is Sir Toby Belch in *Twelfth Night*; like Graziano and Falstaff, his New Comic antecedents are partially obscured by his gentility.[36] His parasitism is complex: he depends upon his kinswoman, Olivia, for food and shelter, but for cash money on the gullible Sir Andrew Aguecheek, to whom he claims a superiority of experience and perhaps age even if he is economically subordinate. He proposes to serve Sir Andrew in the wily servant way by helping this bumbling *juventus* win the girl. In his readiness to quarrel, we can also discern something of the braggart warrior, although he is willing to fight, not just talk. It is noteworthy that within the household, his associates are not so much his kinswoman Olivia as the upper servants, Fabian and Maria. Only in the never–never world of Illyria, I suppose, could he marry Maria without any apparent income of his own, without her mistress Olivia's permission, and without any discussion of the place in the household the couple could then be expected to occupy.[37] But there is not in the text itself any sense that he struggles against his circumstances—the presence of Malvolio, who does hanker for higher status, underscores this fact. Sir Toby seems to have identified a place in Olivia's household and Illyrian society that he can comfortably occupy, and to have claimed it and made it his own. But the place as we observe it is curiously unstable, with a kind of instability otherwise to be discerned in Illyria, and which we might perceive as deriving in part from friction between the play's classical models and the actual patterns of early modern social life. For while there were probably Elizabethan and early Stuart uncles and brothers whose nieces and siblings gave them homes, the strong insistence on steady work articulated in the Statute of Artificers meant that when we come across such relationships in the household rosters of the period, the dependent kinsperson almost always has an office, as steward or secretary or waiting gentlewoman, with regular duties implied if not specified.

Parolles, too, combines features of both *thraso* and parasite; in his case, the Shakespearean innovation lies in what happens to him after he is unmasked and discomfited, his striking, even amazing restoration to grace by the judicious Lafeu. There is an implication that somebody like Parolles offers a valuable service, not in leading young men away from their duties but in being available as a constant monitory emblem—and constant source of amusement. Thersites, in *Troilus and Cressida,* is parasite through and through, but distinctly different from most of his classical progenitors in that he rails at his patrons rather than flatters them, thus taking on qualities of the licensed fool: he is quite willing to accept a series of blows from Ajax in exchange for the privilege of showering insults on that blockheaded prince. He apparently depends on Achilles and Ajax for food, lodging, and transportation. But much more than Grumio, he insists on his essential independence:

> *Ajax.* I bade the vile owl go learn me the tenor of the proclamation,
> and he rails on me.
> *Thersites.* I serve thee not.
> *Ajax.* Well, go to, go to.
> *Thersites.* I serve here voluntary. (2.1.88–91)

Falstaff, the amusing glutton, is commonly treated as a *thraso,* a bragging but vainglorious warrior (a more fully New Comic instance of the type is Pistol; I would add Achilles in *Troilus and Cressida,* whose assault on the unarmed Hector is grimly reminiscent of an episode in Terence's *Eunuchus* in which the *thraso* comes to carry off the *puella* with an armed retinue, which he commands from the rear).[38] Translated into late feudal terms, his thrasonical character as a military man entails actual military service, however ambiguous his actions in that role may be. But Falstaff's economic dependence on Hal (and in Hal's absence, on Mistress Quickly) marks him as a parasite.

In all these cases, however, Shakespeare treats the social and psychological dynamics of this mode of dependency in a far more complex way than his Roman predecessors, if only because all of Shakespeare's parasites clearly occupy the same social class as their patrons, though at lower levels. That is, they are men who could be masters themselves had they independent incomes to support them.[39] And all of them, but especially Falstaff, constitute extended parodies of the sort of upper-class service—like that of Cecil and Cecil's own upper servants—which was a real feature of early modern English society. That is, had Falstaff's service been true—had he placed his master Hal's interests ahead of his own—he could indeed have earned the rewards—the manors or guardianships or monopolies—that he expects to receive from Hal for having been merely entertaining. The issue comes to a focus in Falstaff's assessment of the rural household of Justice Shallow (another instance of the old retaining model): "It is a wonderful thing to see the semblable coherence of his men's spirits and his. They, by observing him, do bear themselves like foolish justices; he, by conversing with them, is turned into a justice-like servingman" (*2H4* 5.1.54–58). Falstaff's own corrupt understanding of service, which drives him to his discomfiture in the streets of Westminster a few scenes later, leads him here to propose to make of the Gloucestershire group a mere source of amusement for the Prince: "I will devise matter enough out of this Shallow to keep Prince Harry in continual laughter the wearing out of six fashions . . ." (66–68). There are things wrong with the Gloucestershire household. Shallow's steward, Davy, uses his influential position to sidestep the law, just as Falstaff does: ". . . a knave should have some countenance at his friend's request. . . . I have served your worship truly, sir, this eight years. An I cannot once or twice in a quarter bear out a knave against an honest man, I have little credit with your worship." Shallow assents—but then he has himself a few lines before urged Davy to use Falstaff's men well, not according to their real deserts but according to expediency: "for they are arrant knaves, and will backbite," so that we are not surprised when Davy takes the opportunity to prefer his own knavish friend (5.1.27–45). For all that, the earlier part of the dialogue that opens this scene suggests that Davy is a conscientious and competent manager, attentive to detail, whose service has presumably contributed to Shallow's prosperity. And the comfortable geniality of the Gloucestershire ménage contrasts sharply with the rapacious violence of Eastcheap (especially in Part Two), as represented by Pistol, Doll Tearsheet, and Falstaff himself.

Still, Falstaff, Parolles, and Thersites all manage to seem more than mere parasites because they are more complex than that. The essence of that complexity, I would argue, is a *self-conscious assumption* of the dependent role that goes well beyond mere acceptance of economic and social accidents. This emerges most clearly, perhaps, at the moment where Parolles proposes to remake himself—in New Comic terms, from *thraso* to parasite:

> Captain I'll be no more,
> But I will eat and drink and sleep as soft
> As captain shall. Simply the thing I am—
> Shall make me live . . .
> . . . being fooled, by fool'ry thrive. (4.3.308–15)

I read "fooled" as more fundamental than the idiom "being made a fool of" (ed. Hunter) normally implies; here, as meaning something like, "having been transformed from one who makes fools of others into one who is himself a fool," a truly ontological change. Here, however, "fool" carries the sense it has in *Lear*, of the professional entertainer. And the passage as a whole suggests that Parolles is actively willing this change, not merely accepting it passively as something thrust upon him.[40]

King Lear works as a kind of summary of these developments, by offering comi-tragic variants of several New Comic types. Thus, the disguised Kent has affinities with the rustic servant of the Grumio type ("This is some fellow / Who, having been praised for bluntness, doth affect / A saucy roughness" [*TLr.* 2.2.88–90]); like Grumio, Caius suffers for his insolence. As is common in Plautus and Terence and as Shakespeare had done with Grumio and Tranio, this type is contrasted with one smoother and more urbane, Oswald, with whom he comes in conflict. Oswald in turn derives his function in the plot (though not necessarily his style) from another New Comic type, the dependent— often a bailiff or steward—of the *senex* or *thraso* or other blocking character, who struggles for his older master's interest against the intriguing of the younger master's servant.[41] But Kent also has features of the trickster, as well—his "saucy roughness," although of a piece with the forthright resistance he offers to Lear in his proper noble self in the opening scene, is nevertheless part of his disguise, behind which he plots but especially improvises to help his master.

And in the disguised Edgar we may discern a very provocative elaboration of the *servus callidus,* a servant so wily that he can also sometimes appear to be a *servus rusticus.* Here, a structuralist approach calls attention to the fact that the social inversion from *juventus* to *servus* effected by Edgar's fall entrains other inversions as well. For this servant, who initially presents himself as a crazed sophisticate, an *habitué* of brothels and moneylenders' establishments who "curled my hair, wore gloves in my cap, served the lust of my mistress' heart and did the act of darkness with her" (*TLr.* 3.4.79–82—all acts or at least desires we can readily impute to Oswald), then modulates himself into a rustic like Grumio to scheme on behalf not of a youth but a pair of *senex* figures (Gloucester and Lear) and a *puella* (Cordelia). Is there a suggestion here that when the improvisational activities of traditional comedy are called forth by the needs of the old rather than the young, they take a necessarily tragic turn—are doomed to fail because the opportunities for second chances and new lives inherent in youthful comedy are closed off by the imperatives of age? Such a recognition by an audience much more deeply familiar with classical dramatic conventions than ours would have deepened the ironic pathos of Gloucester's death.

A similar idea also seems to emerge from consideration of Iago, who, as Michael Neill has noted, may be usefully regarded as Shakespeare's most dazzlingly perverse and dazzlingly successful improvisation on the type of the wily servant (32 ff.).[42] As with the *lena* and the parasite, Shakespeare has already played interesting variations on the wily servant type. Here, too, from early in the canon, he shifts genders and inverts hierarchies. We have already glimpsed the possibilities in Aaron the Moor and the boy servant-as-wife of the Induction to *Shrew*. It goes further in *Two Gentlemen of Verona*, when Julia disguises herself as a boy to serve and follow Proteus. But her only service is to carry a letter to Sylvia and get a picture in return; in the process she does rather less than nothing to advance her master's suit, only reports as someone else's her own feelings of betrayal. In *Twelfth Night*, Viola carries out the typical activities of the *servus callidus* much more fully.[43] I think it matters that Viola enters Orsino's household as a musician, like the disguised Hortensio going to work for Baptista. Possession of a particular skill, as an entertainer, relates her to Feste inside the play, and to the actors who are performing it, as she is performing her own play within. The effect, like the situations of Tranio and Lucentio, is to call attention to the ways in which the social dimensions of all servant–master relationships are performative rather than essential, and depend for their success on the willingness of the individuals involved to accept their roles, to act as though the circumstances that have placed them where they are were indeed produced by their own agency: as Thersites puts it, to "serve . . . voluntary" (2.1.91). It is thus important that even more than Julia, Viola undertakes the gender reversal and the position as servant on her own initiative (indeed, her motives for doing so are not satisfactorily explained). She carries out very fully the type's function to be witty and interesting, especially in her conversations with Malvolio and Feste. Most significantly, like any truly faithful servant, she strains her wits, in the customary wily servant way, to satisfy her/his master's sexual desires, even if the undertaking runs counter to her own best interests, as though, as the Christian tradition teaches, service was in some real way an end in itself, not a means. And she insists on her readiness to serve her lord and master even unto death, if it will do him ease:

> And I most jocund, apt, and willingly
> To do you rest a thousand deaths would die. (*TN* 5.1.128–29)

That is, like Tranio, she will not sacrifice some notion of personal integrity to avoid pain.

Iago retains his sex, of course, but in him the various elements of classical service are even more fully explored. He fulfills the Plautine and

Terentian model quite directly in his game with Roderigo, pretending to help a *juventus* figure (who has far more of that type's characteristic helpless inanity than Lucentio) outwit the *senes* Brabantio and Othello, in order to gain a material reward. He offers similar services, on a much smaller scale, to Cassio and Desdemona. What Shakespeare does with the type in the main plot is far more venturesome. Iago strongly insists on his role as Othello's servant in the opening lines of the play, though of course with a deeply subversive twist—"I follow him to serve my turn upon him" (1.1.42)—that replaces mutual with sequential dependency, Iago serving Othello only until he has managed to make Othello serve him in turn.[44] And in many ways he does give service—of Othello's ten direct commands to Iago (mostly domestic rather than military) the ensign carries out all but the last—to which he responds with an imperative of his own that Othello in turn obeys (4.1.197–202). His scheming, however, is designed to separate his master from the beloved that master has won without his help, not to win her, or if to win her, to take her permanently away from the rival, Cassio, who has, he says, stepped in between Othello and his hopes. (Indeed, in the courtship of Desdemona, it is apparently an even smoother and more urbane servant, Cassio, who has been Othello's confidant and go-between.) It is important to recognize that the relationship is not hierarchically inverted, even in play, as it could be in *Shrew*. Iago sustains the rhetoric of submission all the way to the end, to that command of his own just cited, and beyond it, until that point where Othello is forced by Emilia's testimony to confront Iago's betrayal of the ideal of master–servant relationship, and by a gesture ironically complementary to that of the nameless servant in *King Lear* attempts to end or rebalance the relationship by a blow of his sword. The element of obedience is marked by Emilia's refusal to satisfy her wifely obligation:

> *Iago.*   . . . I charge you, get you home.
> *Emilia.*   Good gentlemen, let me have leave to speak.
>   'Tis proper I obey him, but not now. (5.2.201–03)[45]

But if not exactly inverted, the hierarchy is temporally reversed: Iago starts as servant and ends, in a way, as master; the masterful Othello is mastered and reduced.

In all of this, a crucial element is the element of *play*. Early modern ideologies of service were articulated by writers at all levels, and of all political and religious persuasions, who had nonetheless shared an education with Plautus and Terence at its center. That is, the literary images of service they encountered as they themselves passed through that part of the educational landscape where ideology first becomes conscious and articulate had at their bases something fundamentally ludic. Service appeared as a form of play. There is a strong sense in New Comedy that the servants (not just the wily ones, but the blockheads and old women as well) do what they do not just to entertain the audience but to entertain themselves: running around Athens trying to prevent some soldier from carrying off the courtesan your young master loves is a lot more fun than polishing the doorknobs. That ludic spirit informs a great deal of the service behavior in Shakespeare, too. It is obvious in the high spirits of the early clowns—Lance relishing the misbehavior of his dog Crab, or the Nurse teasing Juliet by withholding her message from Romeo. (We may recognize the element of play with a shock when we consider the very different effect the same strategy of deferral has when Juliet's question is, who died in the duel?) But we notice that even Malvolio and Oswald play, at being masters; while Lucentio, Edgar, Kent, and Iago in their very different ways play at being servants. Grumio's willing service through most of *Shrew* is highlighted by the way he plays at stupidity and incomprehension at his first appearance. Something in the situation of the parasite seems to require a self-conscious assumption of the role: Parolles, in his deepest shame, resolves that he will "being fooled, by fool'ry thrive" (4.3.315); Lafeu picks this up: "poor, decayed, ingenious, foolish, rascally knave. . . . Wherein have you *played* the knave with Fortune . . . ?" (5.2.19–26, emphasis added). Falstaff, Feste, Touchstone, and Lear's Fool all put on their different sorts of motley in ways that clearly suggest some alienation between inner self and outer role, although in Falstaff's case, the role eventually takes over entirely enough to set him up for his disastrous repudiation by his erstwhile master, Hal. We recognize that the dominant New Comic function of the parasite, though he might occasionally run an errand or do other small domestic services, is to entertain his host (Duckworth 265–66). But because the parasite is in some ways the dependent *par excellence,* the question urges itself whether the *role* of servant—how often do we use that metaphor without consciousness of its theatrical origin?—necessarily entails some kind of playacting, some initial moment of self-definition to which subsequent moments more or less consciously approximate. "Circumstances have made me a servant," says a Dromio. "I know that servants gripe and grumble. Notwithstanding, they also stand and wait, fetch and carry, lie at the foot of their master's bed. I will do those things. But I will do so in such a way as to sustain some fundamental distinction between my outside and my inside, my blue coat and my red blood." That such attitudes may affect behavior in other roles is not to be gainsaid; we will consider the issue more largely in connection with what I call volitional primacy later on. But our concern is with this role, and the importance of playacting may, I think, be greater for subordinates than for superiors, as Kent and Edgar are *forced* by circumstance to playact when they have lost their aristocratic status.

In any case, because the whole notion of playing a part implies a conscious choice, even requires a conscious choice, it connects very fully and suggestively with the paradox of freedom and service, with the fundamental notion that when service is freely offered, the freedom spreads all through the service relationship, and fundamentally alters its nature, in just the way, in Christian theology, that the free choice to love and serve God produces a brand new man or woman.

New Comedy influenced Shakespeare's treatment of masters and servants strongly, from the beginning, and whether drawing directly on classical models such as Plautus's *Menaechmi,* on earlier Renaissance imitations such as Gascoigne's *Supposes,* or on such derivatives as *commedia del arte*, the early comedies flaunt their Roman antecedents proudly. From the beginning, however, the classical influences interact with early modern experience to produce servant–master relationships that are more complex and ambiguous than their New Comic prototypes. As early as *Titus Andronicus*, Shakespeare the innovator begins to transfer the conventional attributes of New Comedy across genres, as some elements among many, in tonally and psychologically complicated situations and characters rather than as stereotypes. In particular, from *Comedy of Errors* on, these plays interrogate the ideologies of service, using the provisionalities of fiction to test and stretch the boundaries of admissible behavior. And from the beginning, these plays analyze the psychology of both service and mastery—the freedoms that come with subordination, the constraints imposed by responsibility, the dynamics of mutual dependence. Such dependence, in which the master and the servant are united by their need for one another in a struggle for life itself, had characterized the oldest indigenous English form of service, that of the retainer band. Although retainer relationships had been giving way to other modes of service for a long time when Shakespeare began to write, the model retained enough vitality to have a substantial effect on the construction of many Shakespearean texts, including *Romeo and Juliet, King Lear,* and *Antony and Cleopatra*. Because of the centrality in it of peculiarly masculine relationships, especially in connection with issues of aggression and sexuality, this model has much in it of interest to postmodern criticism. To it, therefore, let us now turn.

Chapter 5
"Clubs, Bills, and Partisans"
Retainer Violence and Male Bonding

If the theatrical discourse of service had some of its roots in the classical drama, others grew in the discourse of retaining (more deeply affiliated to the epic), which arose from feudal and prefeudal sources in the Germanic north, and carried on with relatively modest changes until capitalism and the other modern -isms began to dismantle all the old social arrangements. Retainer relationships are based in the male bonded group. Such groups are disposed toward a rough equality from which a relatively simple hierarchy of leader and follower will emerge, mediated by contests of will, intelligence, courage, and physical prowess. These qualities might seem to keep retaining aloof from the service/freedom paradigm. As the premodern retainer band imaged in *Beowulf* or *The Wanderer* developed into a feudal institution, it did not yet amount to the kind of freely chosen service invoked by the Christian paradigm. The element of custom and expectation in it was too strong for that, so that a Justice Shallow would supply soldiers for the king's wars because the Shallows had always supplied soldiers for their king; indeed, if a Shallow declined to serve in this way, it was altogether possible that the king would send six or eight other retainers to explain why Shallows would be better advised to do so.

For all that, when the nobles lined up to swear their oaths of fidelity to a newly crowned king, or the neighbors gathered to offer their allegiance to a manorial heir who had just come into his majority, they mostly seem to have done so willingly enough (James 56). And elements of free choice do appear, linked on the one hand to the familial and clan relationships that foster service in all societies and thus seem to spring from human biology itself, and on the other to the ideological and economic relationships that sometimes come to override the familial bonds. We can see these competing claims at work in the two Henriads.

where a father can unwittingly kill his son and a son his father because, not given an opportunity to choose their side, they have the bad luck to be retainers of opposing leaders (*3H6* 2.5.55–122), but where, too, a Stanley can come close to sacrificing his beloved son and heir to express in military ways his moral disgust at the murderous tyranny of Richard III, or the members of the Percy affiliation risk death and economic loss to follow the leaders of the clan into rebellion first against Richard II, then, largely on grounds of self-interest and wounded pride, against their erstwhile patron Henry IV.[1]

Whatever the grounds, retaining carried a strong commitment to self-sacrifice on behalf of the group that not only links it with Cranmerian service but in actual ways helped prepare the social ground for more complex, more subtle, more psychological understandings of service. And it is particularly important for the argument of this study because it supplies a necessary element in a full understanding of service at the upper levels of society, although, to be sure, a study of Elizabethan and Jacobean retaining uncovers the same elasticities and obscurities we have found in looking at other modes of service.

How retaining survived into Shakespeare's England is illustrated by an episode that illustrates most of its salient characteristics. On Friday, October 4, 1594, two prominent young Elizabethan aristocrats, Sir Charles and Sir Henry Danvers, with a band of their followers numbering 17 or 18 men, rode up to an inn at Cosham, in Hampshire. Inside the inn, another pair of Wiltshire gentlemen, Sir Walter Long and his brother Henry, were dining with some friends. The Danvers Boys burst in on the party, and Charles Danvers attacked Henry Long with a club, beat him, and turned to leave. Long counterattacked with a sword, wounding Danvers in the hand and elsewhere; coming to his brother's defense, Henry Danvers shot Long through the body, killing him instantly. The Danvers and their friends fled toward Southampton, and, after managing to evade for several days the officers sent to arrest them, escaped to France.[2]

Trouble had been building between the Danvers and the Longs for a long time.[3] Sir John Danvers, the head of that clan, had in his capacity as Justice of the Peace indicted servants of the Longs for two robberies and a murder; servants of the Longs had murdered one of Sir John's men, wounded another, and thrown beer in the face of a third. Insulting letters were exchanged; in one of them, according to the Danvers's mother, Henry Long told Charles Danvers, then about 25 and recently knighted by Lord Willoughby for his military service on the Continent, that "Wheresover he mett him, he would untye his points & whip his etc with a Rodd: calling him Asse, Puppie, ffoole & Boy" (Akrigg "Shakespeare" 42). It was apparently in response to this insult that the Danvers mounted the Cosham assault.

Although the family lawyers eventually got the original indictment of murder against Sir Henry Danvers quashed on a technicality (Coke 3.246–50), the Danvers's flight violated an order of the Privy Council for their arrest, and they lived as exiles in France and Italy until 1598, when a combination of their good behavior while abroad, the assiduous efforts at court of their family and friends, and payment of a £2,000 fine to the Crown, and £1,200 in damages to Long's brother, Sir Walter, earned them pardons. Sir Henry lived on to do notable service in the Irish wars and eventually became Earl of Danby. Sir Charles got himself involved in Essex's rebellion and died on the block. The Longs remained a quietly important Wiltshire family.

Several scholars have suggested connections between these events and Shakespeare's *Romeo and Juliet*. The common elements between the slaying of Long and the slaying of Tybalt are obvious: the feuding families, the earlier violence, the insults, the escalation of the episode from a quarrel between two men into the killing of one of them by a close associate of the other.[4] The Danvers's flight to France finds a parallel in Romeo's exile to Padua. According to Lady Danvers, grief over his sons' exile killed their father, Sir John, just like Lady Montague in the play (Rowse 102).[5] The connection has seemed particularly probable because after the killing the Danvers sought refuge with their friend Henry Wriothesley, Earl of Southampton, perhaps Shakespeare's patron, perhaps his intimate friend. Southampton's mother had been born Elizabeth Montague.[6] And the timing is right, late 1594, when the closing of the theaters had thrown Shakespeare onto Southampton's patronage (to which the poet appeals in the dedications of *Venus and Adonis* and *The Rape of Lucrece*), and just before the widely accepted date for the composition of the play.

In marking the connection, however, previous writers have focused on the earl, not the tragedy. Nor have they looked at the wider social and literary implications of this outbreak of aristocratic violence. Nor have most scholars even accepted the link. G. V. P. Akrigg is dismissive: "No references to Southampton are to be found in *Romeo and Juliet*" ("Shakespeare" 224).[7] Brian Gibbons is cautious: "the suggestion of some allusion to the Earl of Southampton seems possible, though scarcely indicating that the play owed its genesis to the Southampton–Danvers incident" (ed. 30–31n.). A. L. Rowse, to be sure, has no hesitation about surmising that "it all made its impression on the Earl's poet. . . . And so, placed safely in its Italian setting and with its Italian atmosphere, next year we have *Romeo and Juliet*," though he makes no particular critical use of the statement (102); he is followed by J. H. Forse. In Shakespearean academic circles, one does not impulsively align oneself with A. L. Rowse.[8] But he is correct in assuming that playwrights often choose the subjects they choose rather than some other subjects because things happen in the world immediately around them to bring those subjects to the fore.[9] Even were there no probable connection between Shakespeare and Southampton, the Danvers–Long episode was enough of a *cause célèbre* to have shocked him and his company into considering and then dramatizing the phenomenon of Elizabethan clan violence— a phenomenon that was, in any case and on several grounds, taking on special importance in the mid-1590s.

For the purposes of the present study, the main point of interest is that both the Danvers–Long murder and the violence in the play involve not just a few hotheaded young aristocrats but their servants as well. There are a lot of them, in both history and drama. At the beginning, there were the Long servants prosecuted by Sir John Danvers and the Danvers servants killed and wounded and insulted by the Longs. Then there were those 17 or 18 men who accompanied Sir Charles and Sir Henry to Cosham. Many of them—about a dozen according to evidence presented to the commission that investigated the affair—accompanied the Danvers to the Earl of Southampton's lodge at Whitley, not far from Cosham, then to Calshot Castle at the mouth of Southampton Roads, then back to Whitley. During this period of flight and hiding, servants of both the Danvers and Southampton households carried messages, looked after the horses and the meals, and concealed the evidence after the party had left. When John Florio, the translator, then in Southampton's service, and Humphrey Drewell, another of Southampton's followers, met the Sheriff of Southampton on one of the local ferries, they threatened to throw him overboard for daring to meddle with their friends.[10] Some of them, doubtless, accompanied the Danvers to France. In contrast with Southampton and the other aristocrats, many of the servants also paid a price for their involvement. At the very least, they had to stand up under the various inquiries into the affair, in which the testimony of servants comprises all the recorded evidence—there is no sign that Southampton, for instance, was ever interrogated.[11] And while the actual killer was escaping with a fine and the inconvenience of having to live in Paris, some of the servants paid with their lives—at least according to Aubrey, reporting on his grandfather Ralph's involvement, apparently as one of the Danvers retainers, in the Cosham fracas: "His servants were hanged and so Long of Linets" (42).[12]

These facts remind us that in Shakespeare's play the action is initiated not by the gentlemen, but by the servants—first of the Capulets, then of the Montagues.[13] As Gregory puts it, "The quarrel is between our masters and us their men" (1.1.17), but the servants start the trouble; the first master present, Benvolio, tries but fails to prevent the brawl, and the arrival of Tybalt only brings on a skilled swordsman, whose ferocity perhaps turns a comic knockabout into a real fight in which blood is shed.[14]

The tradition according to which the retainers of substantial households foment, carry on, and carry out the animosities arising between their masters is an old one. I use the term *retainer* in both its strict and its looser senses.[15] Strictly, it is used to refer to those men, independent householders and usually gentlemen, bound to the essentially military service of a greater man by a long-standing feudal obligation—like the thanes of *Macbeth*, bound by their oaths, and their obligations, to defend the overlord. The retainer in such a relationship could be a great man himself, as William Baron Hastings served Edward Plantagenet when the latter was Earl of March, then Duke of York, then King Edward IV. But in a looser usage, it came to refer to those male members of the household staffs of great men who at any point bore arms on their masters' behalf, and even to other adherents bound only by ties of neighborliness or political affiliation. Relationships of that kind tacitly undergird all the alliances and conflicts of the history plays, so profoundly a part of the ethos and praxis of feudalism that they only call for notice when somebody breaks an oath and switches sides. A salient instance is the Bastard Falconbridge, in *King John*, the dominant figure in most recent criticism of that play, but not, to my knowledge, treated anywhere as a servant figure. Yet at his first appearance, he swears formal fealty to his grandmother, Eleanor of Aquitaine: "Madam, I'll follow you unto the death" (1.1.154), and from that moment to the end of the play his service—military, political, and personal—to her and to her son is unquestioning, untiring, and effective. (The point seems particularly significant in view of the fact that the character is almost entirely Shakespeare's invention.) In the present connection, it is worth noting that Kent, disguised as Caius, is taken on in company with Lear's "hundred knights," not as a household servant with specific tasks; there is no talk of compensation, and although he serves by carrying messages and supplying support in trying circumstances, he begins his service by doing physical violence to a man he perceives as his master's enemy.

Edgar serving his father in disguise likewise defends his master against the much more overt assault of that same enemy, Oswald. And the enemy, in both cases, is somebody who seems to represent a new, cash-based attitude toward service.[16] In any case, the tradition has roots running all the way back to *Beowulf* and beyond. Shakespeare's names for the retainers in *Romeo and Juliet*—Samson, Abraham, Balthasar—invoke an even more ancient world of essentially tribal allegiances. The pattern appears in many cultures, even in modern times. Those of us who spent the Saturday mornings of their childhood watching B Westerns will recognize it in that group of horsemen to whom the arrogant owner of the Double Bar Z cried, "C'mon boys, let's ride!" Younger readers can see it in urban gangs, Balkan militia bands, or Al Quaeda cells.

The psychological structure of such groups deserves consideration. They are, first and foremost, composed of men—if there are female counterparts they are hard to find. (We consider matters of gender more fully in chapter 8.) They have a hierarchy, but it is a simple one: leader, and followers. The model is thus fundamentally patriarchal: retainers might be described as men who are temporarily offering the obedience and honor that would naturally go to their fathers to some other man. The leader offers leadership and sometimes gifts in exchange for the service of the followers. As we have seen, that service may include essentially domestic activities, or the peacetime practice for warfare that was hunting. But at its core is a readiness for violence, and it is from the shared willingness to face wounds, even death, that its energies arise. This means that it tends to define itself in opposition to some designated Other—Grendel, the Longs, the Montagues. And it will always want to realize itself fully by finding and assailing that Other—always looking for a fight.

As we have just seen, violent groups of masters and servants did break the peace of Elizabethan England.[17] In the city, says Lawrence Stone, brawls between feuding nobles and their followers were common.[18] In the country, armed men rustled cattle, broke down hedges, arrived at assizes and quarter-sessions to intimidate judges and juries.[19] A major element in the London riots of the later Elizabethan period was resentment by skilled and unskilled workers of competition from immigrants, mostly Protestant refugees from France and the Low Countries; apprentices took the lead (and most of the ensuing punishment), but their masters were as deeply interested as they. How common violence of this kind actually was is hard to know. Alan Macfarlane analyzes a historiographical commitment in the earlier twentieth century to a pattern of social development from feudalism to capitalism by way of a transitional period of great social upheaval. Historians in this group, he says, were ready to perceive violence as the natural expression of the economic and social dislocation, and they found support for their ideas in the rioting—both agrarian and urban—of the 1590s.[20] MacFarlane goes on to argue, however, that more recent detailed studies of court records and other local sources reveal a surprising lack of physical violence. There were plenty of crimes against property, he writes, but relatively few against persons. By contrast with preindustrial communities in China, France, and Italy, the English did not commonly engage in class warfare, banditry, rape, arson, casual assault, or even actual vagabondage (as distinct from anxiety about it), and were far more likely to settle disputes in court through negotiation or law than through bloodshed (*Justice* 1–23, 173–99).

Retainer violence, of the kind exhibited in the Danvers–Long episode, can, nevertheless, be documented. In Wiltshire, we find a history of attack and counterattack among several great families—Danvers and Long but also Thynne and Knyvett—over a period of 40 years, in which the Cosham murder was only one among many violent episodes as the parties struggled for local supremacy (A. Wall). The feud between Thomas Knyvett and the Earl of Oxford, which began with a duel between the two men themselves, eventually produced at least four deaths in as many incidents (Stone, *Crisis* 233–34). In 1593, as part of a long-lived feud between the Talbot–Cavendish clan and the Stanhopes, several Talbot servants lay in wait in the Three Tuns until John Stanhope came by with four men, attacked, knocked an old servant down, and hacked at him as he lay in the street (Stone 225). The servants of James I's son Henry expressed their master's rivalry with his father by tossing the King's Fool, Archie Edwards, in a blanket (Kernan 152). These developments qualify, if they do not contradict, the position taken by A. L. Beier and Linda Boose and implicitly endorsed by Burnett and Neill, that, by the end of the sixteenth century, Elizabethans shared "a social anxiety that came to locate the source of all disorder in society in its marginal and subordinate groups" (Boose 195); the proclamations, statutes, and ordinances by which the monarch, Parliament, the Council, and various local governments sought to control retaining and its disposition toward public violence were addressed to masters who were very much part of the political center.

Indeed, whatever the actual prevalence of retainer violence, there can be no doubt that the centralizing institutions of early modern England viewed it as a problem that demanded to be brought under control.[21] William Huse Dunham has documented an ongoing political and judicial enterprise from the mid-fifteenth until the mid-seventeenth century in which both the Crown and the city corporations sought to bring the quasi-military retainer groups to heel.[22] I find it comfortable to suggest that *Romeo and Juliet* reflects that enterprise, and the anxieties that drove it, on both hands. The central authority, in the person of the Prince, works from the top, striking at the aristocratic leaders with fines and threats: "If ever you disturb our streets again / Your lives shall pay the forfeit of the peace" (1.1.89–90; see also 3.1.184–85). The citizens of Verona—read London—go after the servants in vigorously physical terms: "Clubs, bills and partisans! Strike! Beat them down! Down with the Capulets! Down with the Montagues!" (1.1.66–67). Indeed, the play also mirrors the results of the process by which English civil authority gradually succeeded in bringing retainer violence under control. In the first brawl, several servants and several masters; in the second one, several masters only; in the third, two masters, Romeo and Paris, alone—the latter no party to the feud, but a lamentable testimony to the way violence unleashed by the insensate patriarchs has spread to assail the lifeblood of the city, its young men.[23]

Retainer violence is, in fact, a recurrent theme in Shakespeare's work. It appears in *1 Henry VI*, when the Duke of Gloucester's men in blue coats and the Bishop of Winchester's in tawny battle for control of the Tower; as in *Romeo and Juliet*, the skirmish ends with the arrival of the Mayor and city officers, the disarming of the combatants, and the invocation of the Riot Act (1.4). But, again as in *Romeo*, it starts up anew several scenes later; lacking true weapons, the retainers throw stones, and are calmed this time by the young king himself (3.1). These men are denominated "servingmen" by the Folio text (3.1.78 s.d.). Later on, however, the gentlemen Basset and Vernon ask the king for permission to fight, explicitly as servants of York and Somerset (4.1.78–136).[24] In *Troilus and Cressida*, the faceless, nameless, speechless Myrmidons of Achilles become his murderous surrogates in the slaughter of Hector: "Strike, fellows, strike!" (5.9.10). Violence is only threatened, not achieved, when Brabantio raises an apparently mixed pack of "all my people" (i.e., household servants, 1.1.142), "kindred" (168), neighbors ("At every house I'll call; / I may command at most" 181–82), and "special officers of night" (183) to help him seek private vengeance on the Moor. Since Othello has his supporters as well (perhaps better armed and trained), his disinclination to fight saves Venice the kind of bloody brawl that later flares up in Cyprus, and offers a telling image of the moral and civic preferability of law over private vengeance.

The most extensive Shakespearean exploration of retaining occurs in *King Lear*. Lear explicitly demands that he be accompanied in his retirement by "an hundred knights" (*TLr.* 1.1.131); stipulating "knights" rather than "followers" or "servants" invokes the old feudal meaning of "retainer" as defined by Dunham, appropriate to a play set in a distant English past. (We have already observed that the play is not historically coherent on this point, and that chronologically subsequent models of service seem to inflect the representations of Oswald and Edgar-as-ex-servant.) Lear's decline is imaged by the progressive reduction of this train, from the hundred who follow him at the outset— a hundred and one, if we add Kent as Caius—to the rag-tag trio of Kent, the Fool, and Edgar during the scenes on the heath. We subsequently hear of "five or six and thirty" accompanying him to meet Cordelia (3.7.14); there is an interesting proportion in this falling off, one-third of his men faithful as are one-third of his daughters. Oswald's rise in favor and authority is likewise marked when Goneril assigns him a "retinue" (etymologically identical with "retainer") for his embassage to Regan (*HLr.* 4. 308),[25] though the others are not there to defend him in his encounter with Kent. Lear seems to be thinking of this kind of private army in his madness: "To have a thousand with red burning spits / Come hissing in upon them" (*TLr.* 3.6.14).

It is, needless to say, the real if sometimes exaggerated unruliness of Lear's meynie (a word actually applied to the retinue of Cornwall and Goneril [*TLr.* 2.2.205]), that gives occasion for Goneril's demand that he abate his train—having 100 semi-professional soldiers living in your house, with nothing in particular to do, does seem a troublesome burden. Here, as it had been in both *1 Henry VI* and *Romeo and Juliet*, the ideological enterprise involves testing and hence defining authority by means of resistance to authority, by gentlemen and servants alike. Whatever its source, public violence dismays the pacific looker-on. Hence, retainer violence represents the same threat to an increasingly centralized and authoritarian monarchy, or to increasingly populous and wealthy cities like London, Bristol, and York, as unruly domestic servants represented to individual householders. As we have seen, the issue had been given political prominence by the urban and rural rioting of the later Elizabethan period. But politics and history only summarize the impulses and actions of individuals, and in his study of some psychological aspects of *Romeo and Juliet*, Kirby Farrell offers a provocative analysis of a development within individual personalities that helps account for the prevalence and recurrence of retainer violence. He proposes that Tybalt's violent animosity toward Romeo is a "reaction formation." Himself resentful of the constraints of patriarchal authority—exhibited first by the Prince in suppressing the brawl, then by old Capulet in restraining him at the ball—Tybalt unconsciously sees himself as a potential "devilish enemy" to that authority. Rather than admitting such taboo sentiments, he projects them onto a youth from another family, whom he can then in good conscience assail, in the process assuming the patriarchal authority he longs to enjoy to the full (90).[26]

It is tempting to read this argument back into the quarrel of Danvers and Long. Notably, the fatal dispute was not between Charles Danvers and Walter Long, the elder sons, both at this point heads of their families (if the *DNB* date for the death of Sir John Danvers is correct) and hence secure in their enjoyment of patriarchal authority, but the younger, Henry Danvers and Henry Long, who from birth had perforce looked forward to marginal, subordinate status as long as their older brothers were alive to enjoy the privileges of primogeniture. (On the other hand, Charles's rebelliousness continued into his association with another resister of authority, Essex, and traitor's death; Henry Danvers subsequently led a long and apparently responsible life.) Thus, men whose social rank might well entail freedom, but whose actual status meant some sort of servitude, unable to express their resentment freely to its true objects, referred it instead to the Others within their retainer frame of reference. And the argument would apply as well to those somewhat lower on the social scale than Charles Long or Tybalt— to the servants who apparently entered eagerly enough into the Long–Danvers quarrel, to Abraham and Samson.

Farrell's ideas are susceptible of an even more interesting and complex development in *King Lear*. Edmund, too—though consciously rather than unconsciously—projects his own resistance to patriarchal authority onto another, his innocent brother Edgar, then subsequently overgoes Tybalt by contriving to have his resentment acted out in repulsive violence by Cornwall, whose almost parodically intemperate insistence on his own patriarchal authority makes him a peculiarly appropriate agent. And Lear's own frantic demand for a large and potentially violent retinue develops at the point where he has, as the Fool insists, childed himself by making his daughters his mothers (1.4.53). At the same stage, the former magnate Kent, acting outside the law it was formerly his task to enforce, and reduced in status to a common retainer, is picking fights with Mercutio's insistence and much of his gift for insult. Within the freedom/service paradigm, the energies that might otherwise go into resisting or resenting subordination turn in some more constructive direction. But none of these men—even the suddenly fallen Kent—is able to embrace the subordination forced on them by circumstance as something so freely chosen that it absorbs contention rather than acting it out.

Commoners act out, as well. Bruce Robbins takes off from Robert Weimann's contrast between *locus* and *platea*, the ruler's *sedes* on its dais versus the amorphous space around and below it, to see that in medieval and early modern cities, and in the drama written for their inhabitants, the public spaces—piazzas, streets, wharves—really belonged to the servants (54–57). In these spaces, armed mostly with makeshift weapons—sticks, rocks, pitchforks—unruly apprentices and farm workers managed to do a lot of damage, and to give the constabulary—both urban and rural—all they could handle. One component of the civic as well as the royal anxiety about retaining may well have been that the servant armed with actual weapons—even the legitimate retainer with his master's badge authorizing his sword—represented an even greater threat to hierarchy. We get a flash of this in the stychomythic exchange between Samson and Gregory that opens *Romeo and Juliet*, when a series of puns—coal, collier, choler—culminates in Gregory's exhortation, "draw your neck out of collar" (1.1.1–4). Editors gloss this as a proverbial expression meaning to avoid the hangman's noose (Gibbons 82). In the context, however, I suggest that it refers as well to the collar with its household badge that would have been in the Elizabethan marketplace the most visible sign of Gregory's servitude. To take military initiative is the prerogative of the knight, not the hind; just so these socially marginalized men announce their intention to marginalize others, to claim the center, and while Samson's aggression must be displaced from the masters who dominate him to his fellow-servants in the other family, it is not surprising when he shortly proposes to "show myself a tyrant" (1.1.18)—perhaps with an echo of Tamburlaine, another base fellow who became a king.[27] The same energies show up in the leveling implications of the citizens' war cry: "Down with the Montagues! Down with the Capulets!"—that is, the whole aristocratic households, not just the belligerent servants.

This development does not go far; within a few minutes, the hegemonic power, in the person of the Prince, brings the city back to a semblance of order, and for the remainder of the play servants are, by and large, kept in their places. But on the larger scale, the assertion of patriarchal authority does not endure, suggesting that Farrell's insight, though informative, is also flawed. For one striking feature of the plays in which retainers figure prominently—not just *Romeo and Juliet* but also *1 Henry VI, 1* and *2 Henry IV*, and *King Lear*—is the inefficacy of patriarchy.[28] The three parts of *Henry VI* can be usefully considered as an exploration of the ways in which retaining becomes self-destructive when there is division within the household.[29] The problems start at the top, of course, in the young Henry's inability to control, first, the great nobles who are nominally his retainers—who have sworn to give him moral, political, and military support against his enemies—and, later, more fully and merely within the household in the domestic sense, his ambitious wife Margaret. Henry IV's vassals, the Percies, revolt against his rule, and his heir consorts with rogues and vagabonds—a kind of comic parody of the retainer band with a curiously divided leadership, taking its tone and many of its initiatives from Falstaff, but ultimately centered on the Prince, who alone affords the sheltering protection, and the hope of economic reward, that lay at the motivational heart of retainer relationships. Its most distinctive action, the assault at Gad's Hill, collapses in confusion and laughter explicitly resulting from internal division. Before long the Percy faction likewise dissolves into ineffectuality, and its prime representative, Hotspur—who has generally been seen as the fullest representation of the old feudal ideals in the canon—must stand alone and then fall to one who in various ways embodies more modern relationships to the world, including the relationships of service.

Indeed, and with a bemusing irony, it may be said that Hotspur falls because, idealist as he is, he has nonetheless violated the fundamental ideal of his type—loyalty to his feudal lord. This issue emerges anew early in *Henry V*, in the unmasking of Cambridge, Scrope, and Grey; in that play, Shakespeare balances the stumbling remnants of the Eastcheap band with a set of comic retainers—Gower, Macmorris, Jamy—who enact faithful and productive service, and especially Fluellen, who takes on Falstaff's responsibilities to amuse his patron and the audience in ways that sustain, not violate, his oath to defend his royal lord. That kind of loyalty—and its betrayal—remains, of course, an almost obsessive concern of the plays all the way to the end. It animates all the tragedies, in one form or another. It is also active in the romances (where it becomes deeply entangled with the idea of faithful disobedience we will investigate in chapter 6), and receives an emblematic expression in the tableau created in *The Tempest* when Ariel freezes Antonio and Sebastian with their swords raised to strike dead the sleeping patriarch, Alonso, echoing the patriarchicide of *Hamlet* and *Macbeth*.

In *Romeo and Juliet*, the Prince's efforts to bring the feud under control fail; it only ends when there is no one left to carry it on—when it has, in effect, killed itself. The retainer bands of the play are, in effect, leaderless. Old Montague is impotent from the outset; he arrives at the initial scene of conflict too late to participate (and even then is comically restrained by his wife, a Margaret in reverse); almost at once the Prince's decree recapitulates the two centuries of effort by the English civil authorities to bring retaining under control. Capulet's effective realm is the household, not the city, and even there his messenger admits the enemy into the camp (by in effect inviting Romeo and the others to the ball), his servants sneak prostitutes into the house under cover of the entertainment, his daughter evades his insistence that she marry Paris, his Nurse conspires with his daughter, and his nephew Tybalt rejects his efforts at peacemaking and so violates Capulet's oath to the Prince. Romeo and Juliet initially submit to Friar Laurence—within a concern for the alternative Christian understanding of community provided by the freedom/service paradox, a potentially benignant turn toward an order that honors voluntary, not enforced subordination. In such a community, an authentic patriarchy might flourish, in which the readiness of the physically, economically, and socially stronger to sacrifice themselves on behalf of the weaker would command a loving and thankful respect. Laurence, however, makes no effort to reeducate the Veronese, conducts no debate even within himself on where responsibility and authority ought to lie in this tangled affair. Instead, he merely temporizes— buys time by sending Romeo into exile with no one to support this not- yet-man, and launches Juliet into the romantic fantasy-plot of the potion, also by herself, to face ontological and metaphysical exile in the tomb. Romeo's return to Verona and the suicides of both lovers show up the hollowness of the friar's authority, and Laurence's behavior toward the end of the play—especially his precipitate flight from the crypt at the approach of the watch—is anything but masterful. We might perceive here a suggestion that the laity can sometimes enact a more complete *imitatio Christi* than the clergy.

Patriarchy has equally weak hams in *King Lear*. Lear himself, though he tries to keep "the name and all the additions to a king," finds his authority flouted and his servant stocked. Two-thirds of his retainers abandon him; those who remain are incapable of protecting him against his cormorant daughters. Gloucester's sons betray and escape him; when Edgar rejoins his father, it is he who exercises actual control, albeit from a nominally subservient position. Albany stands aside while Goneril assails her father's authority; she scorns him and turns instead to the youthful and more energetic Edmund. Cornwall is slain by his servant, for what may seem good cause, his callous and insulting attack on a man whose fatherly status is repeatedly invoked throughout the scene. Regan joins in by plucking white hairs from Gloucester's beard, then turns from her dead husband toward Edmund without an apparent backward glance. Yet, there remains the question whether the patriarchal authority that is so deeply and repeatedly offended in this play is not, for the most part, undeserved, is not a merely formal, even arbitrary insistence on submission on the grounds of an arbitrary, a merely chronological priority.

It is tempting to adduce a political ground for this: initially, the sequence of rulers following Henry VIII—that is, a child and two women—subsequently, the loosening of established patriarchal control in English political life in the mid-1590s at the moment when the old generation of Elizabeth's counselors and ministers was literally passing away—Leicester, Haddon, Walsingham, the grand patriarch Burghley, all within a few years of one another. Their deaths initiated a struggle for control (exacerbated by the uncertainties about the succession), focusing on the militarist Essex and the court intriguer Robert Cecil (a younger son), which culminated initially in Essex's pathetic rebellion, and, subsequently, in the frantic (and unpredictable) scramble for power at court that went on throughout the early years of the reign of James I. The implications of Essex's failure are important: it anticipates the effective end of the institution of retaining as a *political* force, and its effective replacement by a model of intra- and interinstitutional negoti-ation, that is, the monarch and Parliament. That end had not yet fully come: James brought with him from Scotland, where the older forms of service still had much vitality, a tendency to define service according to the retainer model, and the pattern carried on into the Civil Wars in various ways. But, its day was passing.

Still, in both history and drama, it appears to me that something other than the particular enactment of repressive patriarchy is at issue. Farrell's argument would attribute Tybalt's aggressiveness to the fact that, of all the young men, he is the only one we see fully dominated by a patriarch. But what then can we make of Mercutio? He, of all the young men, ought to be the most free from patriarchal domination—apparently already enjoying his own estate (no parent appears to mourn his death or demand justice), formally allied to the Prince rather than either of the families, free to be invited to the Capulet ball but to select affiliation with Romeo and Benvolio rather than Tybalt. Yet, he is just as irrationally aggressive as Tybalt.

A possible implication is that aggressive violence derives from some-thing more fundamental than particular patriarchal institutions or even from patriarchy in general; that is, from gender itself and its associated sexuality.[30] Such a proposition has, of course, been a commonplace of Shakespearean criticism for a couple of decades. The connection appears at the very beginning of *Romeo and Juliet*. In the prefatory sonnet,

"Where civil blood makes civil hands unclean" in line 4 is followed by "fatal loins" in line 5 and "star-crossed lovers" in line 6. The theme is immediately taken up by Samson and Gregory, whose images of aggression—"we'll draw" (1.1.3), "I strike quickly" (5)—almost at once become sexual: "thrust his maids to the wall" (16), "cut off their . . . maidenheads" (19–22), "My naked weapon is out" (30), that is, images of killing the enemy men and taking their women. This is an ancient characteristic of the activity of retainer bands—think of Achilles and his Myrmidons, spending their day off from the fighting at Troy on the raid that brings Briseis to the Grecian tents. How far it made part of the activity of early modern English war-parties is hard to know.[31] Shakespeare had represented such actions in *Titus Andronicus*; the theme is bizarrely mingled with resistance to patriarchy when Titus battles with his own sons over possession of Lavinia, and with clan vengeance when Lavinia's husband's life, as well as her tongue, her hands, and her chastity, pays for Titus's judgment on Alarbus. The activities are implied in Henry V's threat to the citizens of Harfleur to unleash his soldiers' lust on the citizens' daughters and wives (3.3), and are curiously displaced into comedy when Bassanio's conquest of Portia means similar sexual success for Gratiano. Likewise, we find in *Romeo and Juliet* a more or less socially acceptable displacement of the theme. When Mercutio, Romeo, Benvolio, and their friends and servants crash Capulet's party with masks instead of helmets and torches instead of spears or guns, they form up like an armed band: "Strike, drum," commands Benvolio as they "march about the stage" (1.4.114 and s.d.). They are, in effect, conducting a sexual raid, and Tybalt's cry to arms, though silenced by Capulet acting for the Prince, is validated by Romeo's theft of Juliet from their midst. In *Lear*, Edmund, seemingly triumphant on the field of battle, has Goneril and Regan striving to be his mate, and his own conqueror, Edgar, who as Mad Tom delineates himself as a former servant who has enjoyed his mistress's favors (3.4.78–79), later appears as the most effective fighter in the play, conquering the sworded Oswald with only a staff as a weapon, and defeating Edmund hand to hand.

Indeed, the language of these scenes reminds us that like soldiers on active service, Elizabethan retainers in the looser sense, and especially the servants in the larger households, led lives of sexual deprivation. Unlike the more modest establishments of the lesser gentry, yeomanry, and bourgeoisie, in which women constituted half or more of the typical household, the households of Tudor magnates consisted very largely of men, mostly under the age of 24.[32] And for various reasons, masters in all sorts of households sought to keep their servants' (and their sons') sexuality as well as other areas of their lives under strict control. We get a glimpse of this when Capulet's household servants hope to take advantage of the confusion caused by his party to smuggle some prostitutes into a house whose only visible female servant is the old Nurse: "Good thou, save me a piece of marchpane, and as thou loves me, let the porter let in Susan Grindstone and Nell" (1.5.7–8).

This material leads us toward the sexuality of the male-bonded group.[33] A striking characteristic of such groups is the degree to which the members are literally incorporated, express their membership physically, through the body, whether within the group, connecting its members with one another, or against other groups, marking them as alien. A defining instance occurs when Kent in disguise confirms his acceptance into Lear's retainer band by tripping up the outsider Oswald. Lear recognizes the act by choosing the new servant to carry the important message to Regan. In an important way, retainers extend the body of their master, allow him to do his deeds at a distance, or in several places at once, or with expanded force; and like the limbs of the body, they are dispensable in ways in which he, its head or heart, is not, as when the Danvers and Long servants were perhaps hanged while their masters went free.[34] Consider also Thidias, Octavius's messenger to Cleopatra, who bears the whips and scorns of Antony's rage at his master, and is told that should Octavius wish revenge, he can visit it on Antony's former servant Hipparchus (*Ant.* 3.13.85–154). Among themselves, however, retainers constitute a self-sufficient society in which all the roles are taken by men. Shakespeare, whose own theatrical company was just such a group, must have been sensible of this. And that those roles were sometimes sexual we know from various contemporary and modern sources.[35]

Modern psychology and social anthropology have not yet very adequately dealt with the personal and social dynamics of the male-bonded group—or, indeed, with the issue of violence in the individual male. Yet, a satisfactory analysis would make a very useful addition to the consideration of the dynamics of service by clarifying the question of whether ubiquitous types of human behavior are also fundamental—whether they represent some innate and, hence, finally inescapable element of human nature, or are only locally determined expressions of energies that might in changed circumstances be channeled into other, more socially productive behavior. (We look at the issue of altruism and self-interest in these terms later, in chapters 7 and 9.) The question with regard to the violence of the retainer band is whether tightly organized groups of young men will ineluctably seek opportunities to act out the violence that is in them, and hence inevitably provide destructive energy for the Tybalts and Edmunds, the Richards and Worcesters, the Macbeths and Iagos, to direct into war or murder or domestic abuse. This is also a question as to whether modern social science can throw useful light on early modern social life and writing.

Lionel Tiger's *Men in Groups* (1974), which traces the phenomenon of male violence back to the survival needs of primitive tribal hunters and hence argues that by now it expresses a genetic basis, gave the enterprise a bad name by rationalizing traditional macho behavior by means of bad science. Its kinder, gentler nineties counterpart, *Demonic Males*, has not been much more warmly received. Its argument that male violence has a genetic rather than (or even as well as) a cultural basis draws fire from the cultural constructionists who dominate contemporary social science; its sturdily impolitic conviction that genetic inheritance disposes women to seek mates who display the physical and psychological capacity for violence, to "want" even abusive partners (243), infuriates feminists; its attempts to trace the genetic lines are termed completely untenable by distinguished geneticists like Jonathan Marks. Its efforts to show how "evolutionary feminism" might continue to "tame the demon" do, however, accord with some of the elements in the ethos of service, in placing group survival over individual success as an ultimate criterion for evaluating behavior (241–51). They also chime pretty well with Dorothy Hammond and Alta Jablow's counterargument to Tiger—an approach based on literature rather than anthropological or sociological observation. Though they concentrate on dyads, Hammond and Jablow treat groups as well, and find that in all instances "the narratives of male friendship seem to be political propaganda for abrogating familial ties in favor of male solidarity. In them friendship was idealized, war glorified, and the warrior the ideal man." They recognized the force of intertextuality—the tendency of canonical texts like the *Iliad* or *Gilgamesh* to nourish across time and even across cultures a particular model of social relationships, in which Achilleus and Patroklos, not Hektor and Andromache, supply the pattern to be followed. But their research suggests that the model has arisen independently in many societies. They vigorously deny that the myth commonly involves overtly homoerotic components; subsequent writers would use the term *homosocial* instead. Their argument would thus imply that the behavior of the rival bands in *Romeo and Juliet*, and of individuals or pairs like Romeo, Tybalt, Romeo and Mercutio together, is at the very least highly predictable. Hammond and Jablow are useful in a consideration of *Romeo and Juliet*, moreover, because they emphasize the powerful if irrational antidote to death that marauding seems to supply: in the excitement of the battle, or the rape, time stands still, death is at once courted and flouted, the pleasures of paternity enjoyed as its tedious responsibilities are escaped. (Their emphasis on the lust for immortality connects their argument with Farrell's treatment of patriarchy.) The whole action of the play, indeed, can be usefully viewed as a struggle between the two modes of the play to win the battle for time: in the play's comic phase, to accelerate time—Romeo rushing toward Rosaline, toward Juliet; he and Juliet rushing toward each other; and Capulet and Paris rushing her toward comedy's normal conclusion, marriage—and in its tragic phase, Tybalt, Mercutio, Romeo, Juliet, and especially Friar Laurence desperately trying to stop time. The opening sonnet comments on it—the "two hours' traffic" (Lars Engle's marketplace negotiation, if you will) moving inexorably from comic beginning to tragic close. Within the play, temporal notations mark each stage— "an hour before the golden sun," "this morning early," and so on. Time's work, of course, is death; the play's radical shift in the treatment of time occurs at the point when time has, indeed, shaken its dreadful dart, and dragged Mercutio and Tybalt into its dark abysm. As Shakespeare repeatedly reminds us in the sonnets, the antidote to time is love. But, in this play, love is inevitably associated with personified Death, who, in two of the most memorable passages of the work, becomes Juliet's most urgent and successful suitor (4.4.62–66, 5.3.90–105).[36]

Walter J. Ong's analysis is more satisfying in the present context because it is both rooted in psychology and articulated through history. Ong argues that "adversativeness" is a necessary condition of our self-knowledge, quoting C. S. Peirce: "A thing without oppositions *ipso facto* does not exist" (17). He traces "deliberate cultivation of the adversative" in premodern Western life from the Greeks onward.[37] The issue is especially urgent for males, because, having started out in the female world of the nursery, they need contestation to establish not only their mental but also their sexual identity. Agonistic activity, therefore, has been ubiquitous in both the physical and the intellectual education of young men. The process, however, leaves the man essentially isolated; first, the female group from which he initially broke out and then the males around him with whom he customarily struggles for supremacy are defined as Other. Hence, "Male bonding groups are associations of loners. The male values a companion whom he can stand up against and who can stand up to him: each receives assurance from the other's decently adversative stance, for it reminds him of his own needs and resources" (80).[38] In terms of the present argument, the men serve one another's needs by resisting them. The agonistic relationship can be essentially verbal and symbolic; thus, Gregory and Samson express their bond by competing with one another in aggressiveness, each vaunting his own prowess and putting the other down. "I strike quickly, being moved." "But thou are not quickly moved to strike" (1.1.4–5), even as they turn out to be comically reluctant actually to draw and strike until Tybalt arrives to authorize it. In *Two Gentlemen of Verona*, when Valentine encounters the outlaws, it is hard not to be amused by the increasingly self-conscious understatement with which they top each other's boasted defiance of authority; Valentine apparently wins the contest, and gets to be captain of the band, because his accomplishments include physical beauty and a mastery of languages as well as murder (4.1). In an odd way, although the world has not room enough for both, Hal and Hotspur are friends—even closer than friends, siblings: "some night-tripping fairy had exchanged / In cradle-clothes our children where they lay" (1.1.86–87). Likewise, Antony and Octavius, later Caesar. But the contest need not lie between social equals: when Lucentio and Tranio change places or Petruchio quarrels with Grumio, it is implied that Petruchio needs a resistant servant, or Lucentio a competitive one, to complete their magisterial identities. Indeed, Bruce Smith has argued that in sixteenth- and seventeenth-century European society, homosocial male bonds were more commonly formed between superiors and inferiors—man and boy or master and servant—than between equals (216).

In both *Romeo and Juliet* and *Lear*, these elements, like the theme of patriarchal resistance, having been initiated by servants, are largely displaced into the language and actions of the play's retainers in the narrow, genteel sense, the aristocratic young men affiliated with the two families. In the early play, it is the group of young Montague men with Romeo as its heart and the brilliant, sexually obsessed Mercutio as its moving spirit, expended, alas, in a waste of shame. The agonistic relationships are figured in Benvolio's struggle to uncover the secret of Romeo's disturbance, then more fully in the wit-combats between Romeo and Mercutio, and finally, of course, in the duels: it is surely significant that Mercutio punningly insists on Romeo's freedom from Tybalt's magisterial control:

Tybalt.   Here comes my man.
Mercutio.   But I'll be hanged, sir, if he wear your livery. (3.1.51–52)

But the apparently warm association involves an underlying isolation—like the central figure in that powerful premodern expression of the discourse of retaining, *The Wanderer*. The first thing Benvolio reports to the Montagues about their son, Romeo, is that he wanders solitary through the Veronese night. Later, though briefly joined with his friends as they concoct the plan to crash the Capulet party, Romeo separates himself from them when he espies Juliet, escapes them again to enter the Capulet gardens, leaves them for good at his banishment. He is alone in Mantua when he gets word of Juliet's apparent death, sends his servant away while he alone buys the poison and enters the tomb, kills Paris to maintain his solitude, and dies, he thinks, alone beside his beloved's corpse. The male group that might have sustained and saved him, instead tries to drive the wedge of their gynophobic sarcasm between him and his *femme fatale*, and insists on their conventionally agonistic relationship to the Capulets rather than truly hearing and understanding his desperate attempt to avoid a fight. The group seems too merely accidental and adventitious to function as a real community—even to defend themselves against their enemy Tybalt. At the play's end, not one single member of it remains alive on stage, and their counterparts among the Capulets are equally futile. The implication that some alternative social structure, with an ideal of mutual and communal service rather than of violent competition at its center, would have generated some more desirable outcome, is hard to resist.

The pattern reappears in *Richard II*.[39] The play begins in conflict between a young man and his elder (like those in *Romeo and Juliet* and the Long–Danvers feud, carrying on a quarrel initiated in the past, in the struggle among Richard's uncles for power during his minority), and develops in terms of youthful resistance to patriarchal control—Richard against Gaunt, Aumerle against York. Once Richard and Bolingbroke have declared their struggle, the actual management of the conflict is largely displaced onto their retainers, in the full, formal, historical sense—Bushy, Bagot, and Green on Richard's side, the Percies on Bolingbroke's. Male–male relationships are privileged over relationships with women, and abstract concepts of honor over love. Richard and Anne (so completely divorced that the text gives the two only one brief scene together) are forced apart; the Duke of York vehemently opposes his wife's attempt to gain a pardon for their son. The play ends when a retainer, seeking preferment, carries out at a distance a murderous wish of his master that is not even a command, and that his master wishes had remained unsaid (or so he claims). Bolingbroke's brief comment on this act, and Exton's reply, form themselves around metonymies of the body:

> King. Exton, I thank thee not, for thou hast wrought
>   A deed of slander with thy fatal hand
>   Upon my head and all this famous land.
> Exton. From your own mouth, my lord, did I this deed. (5.6.34–37)

Indeed, a play that begins by placing great emphasis on tongues and teeth and words, and on the gloves that are synecdochic of action, but not on the action itself, ends by using the word *hand*, invoked as the primary agent of the male will, with striking frequency, 15 times in the last 500 lines.[40]

In *King Lear*, male bonds of both egalitarian and hierarchical service are made, frayed, broken, made again, and finally broken not to be reset. The play opens with men reaffirming their male solidarity in agonistic terms. The opening speech sees life as a contest: "I thought the king had more affected the Duke of Albany than Cornwall." Both dukes initially cede authority to their wives, but by the middle of the play they are competing with those wives, Cornwall in reckless cruelty, Albany in thoughtful responsibility; when the wives are disabled, the *agon* resumes between Albany and Cornwall's avatar Edmund. Gloucester, by contrast, is the kid brother, the hanger-on, genial, accommodating, needfully sensitive to political nuance, but also, and by the same token, conscious of the smiler with the knife, as his recital to Edmund indicates, and hence racked by agonistic anxieties: "Love cools, friendship falls off, brothers divide; in cities, mutinies; in countries, discord; in palaces, treason; and the bond cracked 'twixt son and father" (*TLr.* 1.3.98–100). Back in the first scene, politics gives way to sexual conquest, expressed as sport (1.1.20), and then to Gloucester's attempt to establish a bond between his bastard son and the powerful Earl of Kent. Lear's intent in dividing the kingdom is to prevent anticipated strife; he calls France and Burgundy "rivals," and France states his claim in contemptuous, competitive terms—"fair France" versus "wat'rish Burgundy." Lear initiates a contest among his daughters with chunks of England as the prizes. According to the terms of Ong's analysis, Cordelia's refusal to play this game is profoundly feminine, the willingness of Goneril and Regan symptomatic of their unnatural desire for power and dominance. And Lear's preference for the daughters who take the typically masculine line by competing for the prize fits into the scheme.

So does the role of the retainers. For all her own drive toward rule, to direct her own retainers, we have no reason to doubt Goneril's reiterated statements about the unruliness of Lear's. This may reflect a Tigerish disposition toward violence. Or, it may have more local causes. While Lear was king and master of his own household, much of the retainers' energy would have gone into the usual servants' tasks—carrying messages, escorting members of the family when they traveled, keeping accounts, serving meals, and so on. Now they are as idle as their master, and predictably their masculine aggression spills out toward the alien household around them, though all the text supplies for it to work upon is Oswald, seemingly no match for any one of them alone to say nothing of the full hundred.[41] Ong does not apply his analysis specifically to groups of retainers, but it seems to me that the aggressive behavior of the typical retainer band solidifies if it does not establish the group's bond: when overt resistance to Goneril's servants does not work and Lear instead begins to respond to his daughter's efforts to diminish his authority with petitions rather than assertions, his followers melt away.

In the second plot, Edmund competes against his brother, his father, his nominal ally Albany, and the army of France. When he is not striving directly, he provokes quarrels—between Gloucester and Edgar, Gloucester and Cornwall, Goneril and Regan. His readiness to wound even himself in his pursuit of power (by cutting his arm to help persuade Gloucester of Edgar's perfidy) identifies him as an exceptionally aggressive character. Indeed, I suggest that Shakespearean Machiavels, from Aaron the Moor onward—all loners *par excellence*—are men in whom the normal need for agonistic self-definition rules ungoverned by the alternatives, men for whom the struggle in and of itself, regardless of its outcome, is everything, and who are therefore obliged to keep upping the stakes as each particular aggressive action achieves its end. Thus, Macbeth—or at least Shakespeare through him—so contrives things that at the end of his play, he is, to all intents and purposes, single-handedly battling the joint armies of England and Scotland (a circumstance brilliantly realized in Roman Polanski's filmed version of the play). Eventually, of course, such men overreach and fall. This appears even in Edgar, carrying on his masquerade as poor Tom with more enthusiasm than the circumstances really require, and plotting as effectively against father and brother as Edmund has, if from different motives and to different ends.

The struggle between Antony and Caesar, each defining himself in resistance to the other, obviously satisfies Ong's terms. But as *Antony and Cleopatra* will be very fully considered in chapter 8, I shall make the last stop on the agonistic line at *Coriolanus*. No play except *Othello* makes the male bond as fully central to its action, although obviously it differs from *Othello* (as from the second plot of *Lear*) in that the agonistic struggle is between men who are, formally as well as naturally, enemies, as though Othello were, indeed, a Turk. It fits and does not fit this book because the one scene in the play that pays much attention to servants (4.5) involves them only verbally and peripherally in the *agon*. But it does set them up in comic retainer fashion, like Samson and Gregory, rather mindlessly parroting their master Aufidius's presumed prejudices (against low persons), scornfully if warily contemptuous of Coriolanus when he first appears, enthusiastic about "the rarest man in the world" when Aufidius welcomes him as comrade. So enthusiastic, indeed, that they suddenly begin to trade sly devaluations of their boss: "Here's he that was wont to thwack our general" (4.6.177–78). One can readily imagine them, had the events turned out otherwise, looking at service in economic rather than moral terms, abandoning Aufidius for Coriolanus at an early opportunity, and thus acting out a pattern we have observed before in the organization of early modern English service (and markedly anticipated in *Antony and Cleopatra*). Yet, from the phenomenological and structural perspectives, it is worth observing that this single scene in which servants have a large part stands at the point where the agonists, who to this point have been battling off the stage, now confront one another in the text—indeed, stands astride this point, the servants' dialogue being split between the beginning and end of the scene, with the masters' confrontation in the middle.

At issue here are questions of liminality, for the link between *bonds* and *boundaries* is more than phonetic: in *King Lear*, the sequence of *bounty*, *bound*, and *bond* (1.1.52, 63, 93) can be understood to summarize some of the fundamental issues of the piece, in particular the contrast between relationships based on money and land and those based on domestic reciprocity.[42] These are played out most fully in the relationships among fathers and children, but inscribed also in the emphasis on matters of service, and help to account for the importance of that shrinking band of retainers in the first three acts. (The first responsibility of the feudal retainer group was to defend the manor's borders against encroachment, and the old English retainer traditions seem to have endured longest in the national border country both north and west.[43]) In *Romeo and Juliet*, the quarrelsome retainers want to know how far they can go: "Let us take the law of *our side*. Let them begin. . . . Is the law of *our side* if I say 'Aye'?" (1.1.37–45; emphasis added). Joseph A. Porter has explored this theme with special attention to Mercutio.[44] Mercutio, Porter argues, like the classical divinity from whom he takes his name, is a liminal figure:

> Boundaries—that of the ancient feud, those of gender and generation, those between night and day and life and death—crisscross Mercutio's play, and much of its action transpires at such Mercurially liminal times and sites as dawn, the city walls, the garden and balcony, the interurban road, and the entrance to the tomb. Above all others Mercutio before his death manifests this liminality in his behavior. . . . Mercutio's social structures are themselves textbook examples of the liminal as expounded by Van Gennep, Turner, and others. As with that stage in rites of passage

and initiations when the initiates have left behind old social affiliations, and perhaps names, without yet having assumed new ones, so that they live together for a time outside the ordinary dwelling area, *in radical equality and strong bondedness*, so with the trio of Benvolio, Romeo, and Mercutio. (118–19; emphasis added)

The construction of a liminal band is hardly unique to Mercutio; Porter's analysis accomodates the behavior, not only of the three young men in *Romeo and Juliet*, but also of the Danvers gang, who attack the Longs at a roadside inn rather than in their home, flee to the stables and outbuildings of Southampton's estate, and are ultimately punished by exile.[45] And of Lear's retainers, alienated from productive social duties by their master's retirement from active kingship, forced to live on the sufferance of the daughters, constrained by the prudential hegemony of the domestic tyrant (all the more demeaning because articulated through the female, not just Goneril but her possibly effeminate agent Oswald), provoked into essentially futile adolescent resistance (summarized in Kent's skirmish against Oswald and Cornwall), and driven finally (in the form of the paradigmatic group of Lear, Kent, the Fool, and Mad Tom) to the wild margins of the realm. There they try with grotesque desperation to come to terms with patriarchy.

For we encounter here yet another paradox, which is that the liminal male group, many of whose energies are spent trying to escape from the center, from centralized patriarchal authority and the central hearth of the household and its crucially central presiding figure, the mother, is yet always drawn as toward a vortex by the centrist forms from which it is trying to escape. The individual patriarch tries to deny time and causality by embracing it in the procreation of children and the imposition on others of death. The liminal male group also seeks to escape, as speeches about and by the outlaws in *As You Like It* beautifully suggest:

> They say many *young* gentlemen flock to him every day, and fleet the time carelessly, as they did in the golden world. (1.1.101–03; emphasis added)

>   But whate'er you are,
>   That in this desert inaccessible,
>   Under the shade of melancholy boughs,
>   Lose and neglect the creeping hours of time. . . . (2.7.108–11)

In *Romeo and Juliet*, we see the young men's disposition to turn night into day and vice versa, while Lear proposes to "go to supper in the morning" (*TLr.* 3.6.38). But the procedures of the marginal male group, in contrast to full-formed patriarchy, are predicated on the avoidance of closure, of marriage and death; such a group lives best through merely gestural behavior—sports, games, the gents in *Love's Labour's Lost* as ascetics or Muscovites, Falstaff and Hal playing at being highwaymen or the king, the trapping of Parolles, the teasing of Achilles, the mock trial of the pelican daughters.

In such games, alternatives to patriarchal hierarchy can sometimes be explored, that is, the discursive marketplace, which in their violent moments the male group avoids, it also enters, on behalf of an observing audience bound in its quotidian actualities to prudential observance of some dominant ideology or other. Falstaff and his rag-tag retinue can play with the leveling possibilities of a Robin Hood world where men in buckram despoil the rich to feed the no-longer-rich, secure in the assurance that the Prince insulates them from normal causality. Lear can be moved to a recognition of injustice: "Take physic, pomp." For Shakespeare's most sensitive and malleable characters, the experience of the liminal group seems to prepare them to continue to experiment even when they have left the group behind. Thus Romeo and Juliet investigate the possibilities of a new domesticity in which the linear imperatives of patriarchal hierarchy give way to negotiation, mutuality. Edgar, caring for his sad, blind father, is as much mother as son. Lear and Cordelia, reunited, "will sing like birds in a cage," and take turns observing with dispassionate interest the pathetically foolish anxieties of those still trapped in the old patriarchal mode.

In the Shakespearean world, however, such social and moral initiatives are fragile. If Ong is right and the agonistic male is at his core a loner, male groups are basically unstable.[46] When something irreversible intrudes—when Mercutio's sportive flyting modulates into a real fight or the power-lust of Cornwall and Edmund escalates into the assault on Gloucester, the ideal collapses; into its place, the centrist discourse of patriarchy tends to intrude. *Romeo and Juliet* relapses into phallocentric violence; toward the end of *Lear*, not even Albany or Cordelia suggests that the quarrel be resolved by negotiation rather than pitched battle. Not a single one of Lear's original retainers remains to defend Cordelia or support him in his grief when he enters carrying her body; the last of them, the Fool, has vanished silently somewhere in that wild liminal place, while Kent and Edgar—they may or may not have abandoned the King, but certainly neither of them dies defending him nor shares his captivity—resume patriarchal behaviors and attitudes when they resume their titles and arms.

We are reminded that psychology must interact with history just as the individual must interact with society. Both individual males and the groups they form construct myths by which they seek to authorize their desires, articulate their needs, and preserve their histories. When these myths encounter the realities of quotidian living, dissonance always ensues. The more complex the enveloping social environment, the more extensive and various the dissonance will be. The mythology of aggressive English patriarchy, articulated through the retainer group, remained viable, even inviolable, while populations were relatively sparse, travel difficult, the difference between familiar and strange a matter of a few miles. As the population grew, commerce increased, and exchanges of all kinds proliferated, the mediation of masculine assertiveness through violence was challenged and then restrained, so that groups but also the individual agents comprising them were obliged to work their ways through extensive discursive negotiations.

In both *Romeo and Juliet* and *King Lear*, then, we find a patriarchal society beginning to investigate new, counterpatriarchal institutions. Yet the old patriarchal myths—including the myths of male friendship—retain sufficient vitality to explode into violence that destroys themselves but destroys the new initiatives, too. In significant ways, the process by which the English establishment sought to break down the institution of retaining, and the violence that attended it, was part of that great slow process by which the ancient forms of merely assertive dominance—the forms of the retainer band, with their swords and bucklers, their clubs, bills, and partisans—gradually gave way to forms in which negotiation and authentic mutuality was at least a possible alternative. This process occurred in concert with another, in which patriarchal domination over marriage gradually gave way to partner-initiated courtship and mutual agreement—eventually, to a weakening of patriarchal dominance within marriages. An aspect of this development was the gradual replacement of the extended patriarchal household, like that of the Capulets, of Gloucester, of old Lear, where kinfolk and servants were incorporated into even relatively modest establishments, by the nuclear family. One consequence was that where before at his marriage a young man might only transfer from one male-bonded group (his father's kinsmen, friends, retainers, and servants) to another (his own similar associates), now the kind of male group represented by Romeo, Mercutio, and Benvolio dissolves at the door of the church: "Wedding bells are breaking up that old gang of mine." At the end of *The Taming of the Shrew*, the former chums, Petruchio and Lucentio, are at odds. Love and prospective marriage divide Proteus from Valentine, and will scatter the young men of *Love's Labour's Lost*.

The most revealing disruptions occur in *Much Ado About Nothing*. The group of Don Pedro, Benedick, and Claudio constitutes a traditional retainer group, which a senior male, Don Pedro, has initially put together for military purposes. Their campaign successfully completed, they return for R and R to Messina, where they attract the local men— Leonato and Antonio—as temporary additions, for the sportive enterprises of masked balls (like the one in *Romeo and Juliet*) and the baiting of the horned bull, Benedick, with the apparently untamable heifer, Beatrice. (Note that none of these men is married.) Don Pedro, like a good lord, offers the gift of Hero, the heiress he has just won, to his faithful young retainer, Claudio—a classical instance of patriarchal match-making. Against the background of the alternative modes of courtship going on between Beatrice and Benedick, however, independent agents as wary as porcupines, the old-fashioned forms lead toward the dissolution of the male group. The formal instance is the "death" of Hero, homologous in its effects on the male group with the deaths of Tybalt and Mercutio, that is, the intrusion into their improvisational gaming of an act with seemingly irreversible consequences. This draws Benedick, now affiliated with a realigned group, into an agonistic stance. The focal moment occurs when he challenges Claudio to fight, in language that at least tries to put mere gesture away: "Fare you well, boy, you know my mind. I will leave you now to your gossip-like humour. You break jests as braggarts"—play-warriors in a couple of senses of the term—"do their blades which, God be thanked, hurt not" (5.1.176–78).[47]

At the same time, a retainer group of the newer kind is likewise at work. Borachio and Conrade, the associates of Don Pedro's bastard brother Don John, are "followers" of their master in the sense that Falstaff and the others "follow" Hal—bound to him not by traditional relationship but by immediate and particular economic advantage. Borachio, indeed, carries out customary servile tasks; he is "entertained for a perfumer" at the moment when he overhears Claudio reveal to Don Pedro his love for Hero (1.3.46), immediately brings the information to his master, and closes the scene in a line that locates both him and Conrade in the servant's role (and invokes the stoppage of time), "We'll wait upon your lordship" (59). Like the retainer band of the Danvers, this group conducts a raid on the enemy group; unlike the Danvers, but in a parody of traditional marauder tactics, they direct the assault at the enemy's womenfolk. For this exploit, Borachio is rewarded in cash. And in the comic exploration of male-group relationships, this group's efforts, initially successful, are ultimately frustrated by an even more parodic version of the retainer band, the watch, with the faux-genteel Dogberry as its leader, and furnished with bills for certain— "have a care that your bills be not stolen" (3.3.38)—and probably with clubs and partisans as well.

I believe that we can take these groups as comic representations of serious contemporary social forms—the traditional retainer band, bound by custom, military need, amusement, and mutual respect, and the early modern band, bound by cash. That the groups concur with and are both connected and disrupted by a corresponding pair of modes of amatory courtship suggests that the two movements represent domestic and public expressions of the same underlying process. At the end of the sixteenth century, the process was far from complete. Mediation by cash and negotiation disauthenticates the resolution of conflict by violence: it is to the point that Benedick and Claudio never come to blows. In Shakespeare, generally, violence arising from individual, personal conflict can only be approved upon the battlefield, and even there, as in the duel between Hal and Hotspur, the necessity occasions regret—which may even help explain Hal's odd refusal to claim in public the honor of killing his great adversary at the end of *1 Henry IV*. For all these pacific initiatives, however, the old modes, with their absolutist commitment to the resolution of conflict by violence rather than accommodation, had so much life—which means, of course, so much death—left in them that in events such as the confrontation between Charles Danvers and Henry Long they rose up to destroy the alternative modes in both the personal and the social spheres. But changes were underway. By testifying so effectively to the power of both the receding and the emerging discourses—and to the psychological as well as the social forces that shaped them—the plays in which Shakespeare inscribes these developments become landmarks along that road.

CHAPTER 6

FIDELIS SERVUS . . .: GOOD SERVICE AND THE OBLIGATIONS OF OBEDIENCE

During the Danvers–Long episode, Roger Fynch, one of Southampton's servants, found himself in a moral dilemma.[1] His master, to whom in general he owed unquestioning obedience, had entrusted him with a message that would help the fugitive murderers escape the law. His conscience called on him to reveal their whereabouts to the authorities so that the murderers could be brought to justice. Fynch, like Lancelot Gobbo trying to decide whether to leave Shylock, temporized, by taking the trip as slowly as possible, stopping for refreshments, carrying out the order but in a way that could have subverted its intention had not the officers of justice been even slower than he. His ambivalence takes us into the very center of the ethical and practical issues involved in the matter of Good Service—in particular, conflicts between the commandments of men and those of God or the moral code. This theme has been at the center of earlier critical attention to service in the early modern drama, especially with regard to *King Lear*, and especially in the work of Richard Strier. I propose to deepen those earlier analyses by taking fuller account than they do of the religious elements in early modern thought and life, however, and by looking closely at some plays and characters that have not been much regarded. And also by offering glimpses of ways in which servant relationships might reflect or refract important social relationships of other kinds, familial, economic, even political.

Dozens of early modern English texts—treatises, sermons, plays, letters and diaries, homilies distributed to every English parish church and sets of household rules—take up the matter of good and bad service (and its corollary, good and bad mastery) as an issue central not only to the lives of particular people in particular households but also of the entire common weal. The issue is expressed in a set of formulae that pass essentially unchanged from text to text. Not surprisingly, the concepts of service can be investigated with reference to both early modern and twentieth-century psychology. They reappear in the drama and fictional narrative of the time. But the theory, although it occasionally nods toward the clash of competing goods that appears in the case of Roger Fynch, is simplistic. In fiction as in life, the service relationship as enacted exhibits far less coherence and uniformity than the theory; and no set of texts presents more abundant and various images of both good and bad service than the plays of Shakespeare. Concern with the question itself, however, of what constitutes good or bad service—with the *ethical* dimensions of service, as it were—receives particular attention in *King John*, *King Lear*, *Othello*, *Timon of Athens*, and *Cymbeline*, and it is those plays that chapters 6 and 7 will especially engage.

In all of the contemporary treatments, the decisive factor was the submission of the servant to the master. We glimpsed this at the beginning; it is the fundamental element in the concept of willing service. Such submission, as sixteenth- and seventeenth-century authorities agreed (the dissenters were a few radical Protestants of the leveling kind), derived from social and economic actualities and from a long and unbroken if not unchanging set of social practices. It also arose, however, from perceived moral and even theological truth, for it had the authority of classical literature, history, and philosophy; of the law; of the church; and of Holy Scripture itself behind it (Baynes 1–11). Clerics across the theological range from fervent Calvinist to fervent Laudian took the same line. "Every Master, as hee is a Master, hath his Authority from God," wrote the Puritan Edward Elton in 1615, citing Romans 13:1; to resist the master's authority is to revolt against God Himself (577).[2] John Fit-John (1577), a secular writer of apparently centrist allegiance, identifies service to God as the model for all kinds of service (H3v).[3] On a more secular plane, masters ruled in their houses as monarchs did in their countries (Brathwaite 4–6; Elias 42; Filmer 63). And closer to home, as it were, masters ruled their servants as fathers ruled their children. So pervasive is this patriarchal view that although a good many women—most notably, Queen Elizabeth—ran their own establishments, not one of the contemporary works read for this study gives specific attention to female heads of household. How could it be otherwise when the tradition descended from the very beginning of things? For as Sir Robert Filmer, a defender of royal privilege, states in his treatise, *Patriarchia* (ca. 1635–42), patriarchal authority arose with Adam, and flows to us through Judah, Abraham, Esau; the 72 nations produced by the curse of Babel "were distinct families, which had Fathers for rulers over them" (58; Gen. 10:5). And the position established in the Old Testament by the examples of the patriarchs and the

precept of the fifth commandment was confirmed by many passages
in the New Testament, especially Ephesians 6 and Colossians 4 (Gouge
79–80).

But if the master was a father, the servant was not quite even a child.
As Henry Smith, the most popular Elizabethan preacher, explained,
"I may say of servants, that God hath made them a little lower than
children . . . as one would say, inferiour children, or sonnes in lawe"
(59). Even over their children, fathers' power was all but absolute: "To
fathers within their private Families Nature hath given a supreme
power," says Richard Hooker—notoriously henpecked, according to
legend, but then, we are discussing theory, not practice (1. 24; 1.10.4).
Their control over their servants, therefore, extended to every area of
life. William Gouge specifies speech, gesture, carriage, dress, diet, exercise,
religious belief and practice, companions and places of resort, sexual
behavior including marriage, as well as all the details of the servants'
work (*Exposition* 82–86). John Fit-John's citizen-spokesman summarizes
it very clearly as he explains to a country boy going to London to seek
his fortune as an apprentice: "you your selfe and all that you can do, is
your maysters" (D3v).

Patriarchal ethics, of course, assigned to masters responsibility com-
mensurate with their privileges. The benchmark passages in Ephesians
and Colossians spend nearly as much time on the masters' obligations as
on the servants', and generate corresponding proportions in the commentaries. Henry Smith privileges spiritual responsibilities, for "a master in
his family hath all the offices of Christ: for hee must rule, and teach, and
pray; rule like a king, and teach like a Prophet, and pray like a Priest"
(56). But as Christ fed the multitude and encouraged his disciples to rest
when they were tired, so the master must look to the bodies as well as
the souls of those committed to his charge (Henry Smith 52; see also
Cleaver and Dod A5v). Daniel Touteville reminded his readers that
Aristotle long ago not only prescribed servants' need of work and
correction, but also food and shelter; we now add wages, he says,
because under the new dispensation, our servants are no longer slaves—
an interesting recognition of commodification (423). John Fit-John
likewise calls on masters to govern their servants "Godly, & justly," and
to "exercise them not only in servil & manual works: but also in deeds
of godlynes, & vertue, and to forsee that no kind of sin be used of his
servants in his house"; yet they are also to be given their due "meate,
drinke, lodging, linnen, wollen, apparell, their occupation" (E4v).
Nicholas Byfield lists six particular Don'ts: (1) not to require "inconve-
nient things," (2) not to assign work beyond the servants' strength,

(3) not to turn them away when sick, (4) not to restrain them from going to church by giving them tasks that would interfere, (5) not to hold back on food or wages (unless as punishment for actual transgressions), and (6) not to discharge them without means to live after years of faithful service (158).[4]

In exchange, servants had one primary obligation: to obey.[5] The injunction applied to all servants, "though they were Nobles serving in Princes Court" (Byfield 128). J. M. claims that he would do reverence to "the meanest Carman that whistlest after his Horse" if fortune called him to take wages from such base hands (A2r). So essential is obedience, says William Gouge, that although dishonor in a servant is tolerable, disobedience is not (82). And the allowable penalties for disobedience were severe—beating, withholding of food, incarceration, summary discharge into a society in which masterless servants were regarded as criminals.[6]

Given the ubiquity of these views, it is striking when we begin to analyze good service in Shakespeare to discover how often it involves disobedience rather than obedience, as Horst Weinstock and especially Richard Strier have noted;[7] indeed, the effort to resolve this apparent contradiction will generate much of the following argument. Shakespeare begins, to be sure, by modeling the orthodox relationship: the Dromios trudge faithfully around Ephesus, safeguard their masters' money, reputations, and persons, undertake tasks whose purpose they cannot understand and carry them out responsibly and energetically, endure without revolt beatings they have not deserved (though not without a reasonable amount of *sotto voce* grousing).[8] In the later plays, however, mere obedience is never sufficient to win approval, and—with the conspicuous exception of the so-called tool villains, such as Clarence's murderers in *Richard III*—wherever Shakespeare directs more than local attention to a servant (I set aside here the dozens of places scattered across the canon where somebody or other is given a routine task and carries it out without comment), it is generally one who acts without or against orders, or who, like Ariel, takes some general order— "bring the rabble . . . here to this place" (*Tem.* 4.1.37–38) and executes it imaginatively:

> So I charmed their ears
> That calf-like they my lowing followed, through
> Toothed briars, sharp furzes, pricking gorse, and thorns,
> Which entered their frail shins. At last I left them
> I'th' filthy-mantled pool beyond your cell,
> There dancing up to th' chins, that the foul lake
> O'er-stunk their feet. (178–84)

We have already encountered some important instances of faithful disobedience, virtuous infidelity. One is the servant in *Lear* considered earlier.[9] Another is Antony's servant Eros, who kills himself rather than his master at his master's command. There is a striking instance in *2 Henry VI*, when the apprentice Peter Thump accuses his master Horner of treason, is granted the right to a trial by combat that all the onlookers expect to turn out as comically as the duel between Viola and Sir Andrew in *Twelfth Night*, and then, to the shock and astonishment of spectators on the street and in the theater, kills his master, who confesses his guilt before he dies (1.3.181–227, 2.3.47–106).

More extensively developed are Hubert, in *King John*, Camillo and Paulina in *Winter's Tale*, and Pisanio in *Cymbeline*.[10] Hubert is Shakespeare's first extended representation of the virtuously disobedient servant. He is also the most complex, in ways that reflect the complexity of his origins, in history and perhaps in the play's dramatic sources.[11] Indeed, not until *Othello* will the playwright investigate so richly the various interactions that one servant and one master may enter on.[12] The exploration is more or less extensive according to the solution to a textual problem: whether or not we accept Dover Wilson's suggestion, itself based on a couple of Folio speech headings, that the character named Hubert is also the character introduced by the Folio as a Citizen of Angers.[13] As spokesman for the town, this citizen announces its allegiance to England but refuses entrance to either John and his army or the French power fighting on behalf of John's young nephew Arthur, until the uncertainty about which of them is the legitimate ruler of England is settled. When the ensuing battle between the two armies is indecisive, a citizen now identified in the Folio speech prefixes as Hubert continues to refuse them entrance. And when they threaten to join forces and reduce the town before returning to their own conflict, this spokesman offers a diplomatic alternative to bloodshed, the marriage of John's niece Blanche to the Dauphin Louis (which much offends John's bastard cousin Falconbridge and gives rise to his famous speech about commodity). Two scenes later, after the intervention of the Papal Legate Pandulph has broken off the deal and restarted the war, John recruits a man called Hubert (not necessarily the same figure—but Shakespeare does not normally give two significant characters in the same play the same name) to be his close associate, commanded by the King by name to take charge of the captured Arthur: "Hubert, keep this boy" (3.2.5).[14] Toward the end of that scene, John hints that the boy's death would be welcome to him. Later, he sends other servants with orders that Arthur should be blinded. Hubert initially proposes to carry them out, but is persuaded by the youngster's appeals for mercy, and relents—giving out, however, that the boy is dead. When Arthur dies trying to escape from his captivity by leaping from the battlements, Hubert is blamed for it by a group of nobles but more or less exonerated by that less equivocally faithful servitor, Falconbridge.[15]

No one called Hubert appears in either Holinshed or *Troublesome Reigne* until the episode of Arthur's captivity. Holinshed identifies Arthur's keeper as Hubert de Burgh, who became one of the principal men in the kingdom during the last year of John's reign and most of the reign of Henry III. *Troublesome Reigne* repeatedly calls him Hubert de Burgh. The first folio uses the baptismal name only, and little in *King John*'s presentation of Hubert suggests a feudal magnate, a fact that may help explain why both Dover Wilson (ed. xlvii) and Braunmuller (ed. 277n.) doubt that de Burgh is intended. Indeed, after Arthur's death, when Hubert is willing to prove his innocence with his sword against the Earl of Salisbury, Lord Bigot is offended by what he perceives as a breach of social order: "Out, dunghill!" (The epithet anticipates the fate of the nameless servant in *King Lear* who defends Gloucester against Cornwall.) "Dar'st thou brave a nobleman?" (4.3.87). Yet the Hubert of *King John* has traits in common with Humphrey of Gloucester in *2 Henry VI* and Lord Hastings in *Richard III*, undoubted magnates who are also, by and large, faithful servants, suggesting that these characters are conceived primarily as royal servants, only secondarily as men of great command.

The textual problem is important because it affects our estimation of the character. If Hubert is also the citizen, his proposal would have rescued John from the uncertainties of war with France and extended if not insured his reign, albeit at the cost of most of the English territory in France. The proposed outcome could supply grounds for the effusive gratitude with which John greets Hubert as the latter is being appointed the captured Arthur's jailer—especially if, as Michael Manheim and others have suggested, Hubert had been a covert partisan of John prior to the two armies' arrival in front of Angers (Curren-Aquino 130).

> Come hither, Hubert. O my gentle Hubert,
> We owe thee much. Within this wall of flesh
> There is a soul counts thee her creditor,
> And with advantage means to pay thy love;
> And, my good friend, thy voluntary oath
> Lives in this bosom, dearly cherishèd.
> Give me thy hand. I had a thing to say,
> But I will fit it with some better tune.
> By heaven, Hubert, I am almost ashamed
> To say what good respect I have of thee. (3.3.19–28)

Moreover, if Hubert's allegiance to John predates the attack on Angers, his pretense of neutrality in the speeches from the walls makes him a hypocrite, a practiced intriguer, someone well able to interpret the evasion and innuendo with which John insinuates the murder of his young rival.

King John.	Good Hubert, Hubert, Hubert, throw thine eye
	On yon young boy. I'll tell thee what, my friend,
	He is a very serpent in my way,
	And wheresoe'er this foot of mine doth tread,
	He lies before me. Dost thou understand me?
	Thou art his keeper.
Hubert.	And I'll keep him so
	That he shall not offend your majesty.
King John.	Death.
Hubert.	My lord.
King John.	A grave.
Hubert.	He shall not live. (3.3.59–66)[16]

However we choose to resolve the textual question, we observe the speeches and actions of a man who has willingly put himself into the service of another, greatly his superior in rank and power, who negotiates nothing, accepts John's assertions with submissive assertions of his own, and who here at the outset imposes no moral or legal limits on the kinds of service he is ready to perform—even, he says, at the cost of his own life (56–57). The relationship appears to straddle the essentially personal and oral basis of the feudal vow of allegiance, and the contractual, literal grounds of emergent late Tudor capitalism. John refers early in the exchange to a "voluntary oath," which has however made John Hubert's "creditor," whose soul "with advantage means to pay thy love" (21–23).[17] Hubert bases his initial readiness to blind Arthur on this oath—"I have sworn to do it" (4.1.58).[18]

The exchange puts Hubert, thus far, on the boundary between two classes of servants obedient to intrinsically wicked, even blasphemous orders or suggestions, the two groups together making up the class of so-called "tool villains." The first comprises inferior characters explicitly suborned by their superiors to murder even royalty itself (Humphrey of Gloucester's assassins in *2 Henry VI*, Clarence's killers and Tyrell and his goons in *Richard III*, the murderers loosed on Banquo, Fleance, and the Macduff family in *Macbeth*, the Captain sent by Edmund to kill Cordelia and Lear, Thaliart the would-be poisoner of Pericles), together with the "executioners" sent by John with the warrant authorizing the blinding of Arthur.[19] The second is the class of men who carry out murders desired but not expressly commanded by their lords (Exton in *Richard II*). John himself so places Hubert:

> I faintly broke with thee of Arthur's death;
> And thou, to be endearéd to a king,
> Made it no conscience to destroy a prince. (4.2.228–30)

Some of these characters are apparently bound to their masters by feudal oaths or expectations, others by short-term, essentially contractual agreements. With them we might also associate Borachio and Conrade in *Much Ado About Nothing*, Charles the Wrestler in *As You Like It*, Oswald in *Lear*—characters less obviously malignant than these but who are still content to resign responsibility for morally dubious actions to the masters whose favor they thereby hope to win or keep.[20] These men (and Shakespeare was interested enough in the type to have used such characters over and over), might well plead that however dire the deed, moral responsibility for it lay with the master: the servants were only following orders, only carrying out the primary injunction of the service relationship, obedience.[21]

In the Shakespearean moral economy, however, just as in the orthodox economy of service expressed in contemporary sermons and treatises, the fact of service does not absolve the servant of moral responsibility, and as John puts it in the speech just quoted, does not "Ma[k]e it no conscience to destroy a prince." Most contemporary authorities, if a little reluctant to counsel disobedience, agreed that because the law of God supersedes the laws of nature and of men, servants were not only allowed to but were indeed obliged to disobey when ordered to do evil.[22] Strier cites Tyndale: wicked princes are not to be resisted, but "if they command to do evil, we must then disobey." The first Edwardian homily on Good Order and Obedience is more comprehensive: "we may not obey kings, magistrates, or any other, though they be our own fathers, if they would command us to do any thing contrary to God's commandments" (Strier "Faithful" 107).[23] Fosset expatiates: "All obedience must bee subordinate unto the devine obedience due unto God. If thy Master bid thee doe evill, hurt thy neighbours cattell, or steale his goods; if hee command thee, or give thee example to cogge and lie, to steale or use any fraud or deceipt in buying, or selling, to sell that which is evill for good, to exact more then a thing is worth, to doe any thing which you would not be content should be done to you . . ." (35).[24] As biblical precedents for such authorized disobedience, William Gouge names Joseph declining Potiphar's wife, the midwives who disobeyed the

Pharaoh's order to kill all male children and so saved Moses, and the servants of Saul who refused to murder the priests (1 Sam. 22:17; Gouge 91); Cleaver and Dod add the refusal of Shadrach, Meshach, and Abednego to worship a false god (Dan. 3:18–22), and the first Christians' defiance of the authorities' prohibition against preaching their new faith (Acts 4:19, 5:21). In the words of L. A. Beaurline, "the notion of absolute obedience is not a sure guide through a play like *King John*" (ed., 47); he is thinking in political terms, but the proposition holds true for domestic issues as well, and it holds true for more plays than *King John*.[25]

But *King John* pays particular attention to it. Hubert is, to be sure, obedient to such commands (e.g., "keep this boy") as are relatively unexceptionable; and he remains outwardly obedient even after he has spared Arthur's eyes, by having John's henchmen publish abroad the false report that Arthur has died.[26] Yet obedience is only one considera-tion. The complexity of the moral situation in *King John* is thrown into relief by the fact that in *Troublesome Reigne*, Hubert does strongly emphasize the obligations of retainer obedience: "I would the King had made choyce of some other executioner: onely this is my comfort, that a King commaunds, whose precepts neglected or omitted, threatneth torture for the default," and again,

> My Lord, a subject dwelling in the land
> Is tyed to execute the Kings commaund. (Bullough 1315–18, 1389–90)[27]

In *King John*, however—and in Shakespearean plays generally, to a quite remarkable extent—the issue of obedience is, if anything, suppressed. Hubert does not read the warrant aloud, merely shows it to Arthur (33, 37). He makes one oblique reference to his vow of fealty—"Yet I am sworn . . ." (123)—*after* he has decided not to obey the order. Otherwise the text is silent. The contrast with *Troublesome Reigne* is very sharp. And it continues on into the scene where John, having repented his order, taxes Hubert for the boy's death. At the corresponding point in *Troublesome Reigne*, Hubert again appeals to obedience:

> According to your Highnes strickt commaund
> Yong *Arthurs* eyes are blinded and extinct. (Bullough 1661–62)

King John is again oblique. The interview begins with two long, inter-esting speeches from Hubert, which report astral wonders (five moons), connected with talk by "Old men and beldams in the streets" of young

Arthur's death (4.3.183–86). References to an auditor's "rolling eyes" and to a smith "whilst his iron did on the anvil cool" recall the threatened blinding (193–95). John makes the first of several attempts to transfer the responsibility to his servant: "I had a mighty cause / To wish him dead, but thou hadst none to kill him" (206–07). In reply, Hubert invokes but does not directly refer to the King's command: "No had [sic], my lord? Why, did you not provoke me?" (208). The king's response would actually refer more appropriately to their conversation immediately after Arthur's capture than to the unaccomplished blinding, because that conversation involved innuendoes concerning Arthur's death (though the word *winking* is another reminder of the order to blind), and so parallels Henry IV's response to the news of Richard II's death:[28]

> It is the curse of kings to be attended
> By slaves that take their humours for a warrant
> To break within the bloody house of life,
> And on the winking of authority
> To understand a law, to know the meaning
> Of dangerous majesty, when perchance it frowns
> More upon humour than advised respect. (*Jn.* 4.2.209–15)

Thus, John, not Hubert, first mentions the warrant; and Hubert, when he picks it up, does so only by metonymy: "Here is your hand and seal for what I did" (216).[29]

John reacts with 33 impassioned lines, beginning with anticipation of "damnation" and ending with the desperate state of his kingdom and his own self, weakened by rebellious nobles, threatened with conquest by French invaders, all seemingly brought on by the reports of Arthur's death:

> Nay, in the body of this fleshly land,
> This kingdom, this confine of blood and breath,
> Hostility and civil tumult reigns
> Between my conscience and my cousin's death. (246–49)

And again he tries to shift responsibility for this grievous state of affairs to the servant. The terms of this discourse require particular attention. In its first movement, John posits an innate aptness for evil that takes a physical, visible form, the mark of Cain (explicitly invoked):[30]

> How oft the sight of means to do ill deeds
> Make deeds ill done! Hadst not thou been by,

> A fellow by the hand of nature marked,
> Quoted, and signed to do a deed of shame,
> This murder had not come into my mind.
> But taking note of thy abhorred aspect,
> Finding thee fit for bloody villainy,
> Apt, liable to be employed in danger,
> I faintly broke with thee of Arthur's death;
> And thou, to be endearèd to a king,
> Made it no conscience to destroy a prince. (220–30)

Further suppressing the issue of obedience, this speech shifts the basis of the relationship from vertical hierarchy toward reciprocity—"to be endearèd to a king"—words that recall the emphasis on friendship and love of his earlier hints about Arthur's death. Hubert's remonstrance subtly restores hierarchy: "My lord." John overrides him before he can go further, continuing to ignore hierarchy by discovering an intuitive sympathy between the two men that removes the need for explicit speech. His language carries forward the emphasis on outward and visible signs even as it introduces the very theme of this chapter, the good servant's responsibility to resist a master's wicked impulses:

> Hadst thou but shook thy head or made a pause
> When I spake darkly what I purposèd,
> Or turned an eye of doubt upon my face,
> As bid me tell my tale in express words,
> Deep shame had struck me dumb, made me break off,
> And those thy fears might have wrought fears in me.
> But thou didst understand me by my signs,
> And didst in signs again parley with sin;
> Yea, without stop, didst let thy heart consent,
> And consequently thy rude hand to act
> The deed which both our tongues held vile to name. (232–42)

This recollection accords well enough with the progress of the interview in which Hubert took service (although even a conscientious servant might be pardoned for deciding not to cross a master he does not yet know in the first five minutes of his employment). And as we have seen, early modern orthodoxy called on servants to resist evil orders from their masters: it is on just such grounds that Hubert accepts Arthur's argument for disobeying John in *Troublesome Reigne*:

> My King commaunds, that warrant sets me free:
> But God commaunds, and he commaundeth Kings.

That great Commaunder counterchecks my charge,
He stayes my hand, he maketh soft my heart. (Bullough 1435–38)

Such an argument retains obedience as the central element in service: Hubert's obligation to obey John yields to his obligation to obey God, who "commaunds" three times in the speech to John's one, and the playwright underlines the theme with alliteration, chiasmus, and other rhetorical exclamation points.[31]

What is fascinating about Shakespeare's treatment of these matters is that Hubert declines to use this argument. When we return to the scene with Arthur, we discover that the armature of their relationship is emotional, not legal, philosophical, theological, or economic—in the terms of the various discourses, domestic rather than feudal or commodified.[32] The first half of the preceding scene has emphasized natural affection, in Constance's extended lament for the loss of her son—a lament from which the political ambitions she expresses earlier in the play are conspicuously absent (3.4.16–105). In the second half, however, dominated by the Machiavellian Pandolf, Commodity returns in force: the Cardinal insists that in order to retain his throne, John will be obliged to murder Arthur, which means that John will perforce insist on murderous obedience from his agents, including Hubert. But natural affection, which Arthur and Hubert call "love"—the word occurs with surprising frequency—rather than the formal mutuality of master and servant, prince and subject, binds the jailer and the captive each to each, and exerts an imperative that mere obedience cannot resist. The social matrix is, indeed, invoked; the first exchange recognizes the existing hierarchical disparity between them, and the greater disparity yet lying potential in Arthur's strong claim to the crown:

Arthur. Good morrow, Hubert.
Hubert.   Good morrow, little Prince.
Arthur. As little prince, having so great a title
          To be more prince, as may be. (4.1.9–11)

But this exchange has been immediately prefaced by a different kind of language: "Young lad, come forth, I have to say to you." In Hubert's mouth Arthur is never "My lord" (a title owed to him not only by his royal blood and rank as Duke of Brittany, but also by the fact that John has said that "Hubert will be your man, attend on you / With all true duty" [3.3.72–73]), but "young lad," "little Prince," "young Arthur" (33), "Young boy" (40), "boy" (88, 104, 123). Indeed, Arthur himself at least rhetorically disowns his claims to mastery:

> By my christendom,
> So I were out of prison, and kept sheep,
> I should be as merry as the day is long. . . . (16–18)

Instead, he suggests another possibility: "I would to God / I were your son, so you would love me, Hubert" (23–24). Even more—he professes to serve Hubert as much as Hubert serves him, and in explicit recognition of their official disparity:

> When your head did but ache,
> I knit my handkerchief about your brows,
> The best I had—a princess wrought it me,
> And I did never ask it you again—
> And with my hand at midnight held your head,
>   . . .
> Many a poor man's son would have lain still,
> And ne'er have spoke a loving word to you,
> But you at your sick service had a prince. (41–52)

He goes on to concede the possibility of disingenuousness: "Nay, you may think my love was crafty love, / And call it cunning" (53–54). Hubert refuses to take this up, but also refuses to relent. So where his earlier speeches offered equality of experience if not of rank or age, Arthur begins to concede *his* submission to his servant:

> Nay, hear me, Hubert! Drive these men away,
> And I will sit as quiet as a lamb;
> I will not stir, nor wince, nor speak a word,
> Nor look upon the iron angerly.
> Thrust but these men away, and I'll forgive you,
> Whatever torment you do put me to. (78–83)

This inversion of their nominal relationship does not entirely turn the trick, for a few lines later Hubert is still threatening the boy with blindness. But it does move him to dismiss the King's executioners (84), potentially awkward witnesses of his upcoming disobedience. Arthur presses his sensed advantage by submitting even more radically:

> Hubert, the utterance of a brace of tongues
> Must needs want pleading for a pair of eyes.
> Let me not hold my tongue, let me not, Hubert;

> Or, Hubert, if you will, cut out my tongue,
> So I may keep my eyes. O, spare mine eyes,
> Though to no use but still to look on you! (97–102)

The iteration of Hubert's name recalls the earlier speech in which John asked the favor that is the negative pole of this one. Like that speech, this one is dense with rhetorical artifice, especially wordplay on Hubert's preceding speech, "Go to, hold your tongue!" (96). Whereas John's artifice tends to debase him, however—why lavish the arts of persuasion on a servant sworn to unquestioning obedience, in a situation where the artificer seems to have the upper hand?—Arthur's, under these desperate circumstances, helps rescue him from an appearance of mere helpless vulnerability, by implying that the young prince still has his wits about him, and by throwing the onus on the man.

So challenged, Hubert it is who appears vulnerable to the power he has feared from the beginning of the scene:

> If I talk to him, with his innocent prate
> He will awake my mercy, which lies dead. . . . (25–26)

Mercy will, he says, in a striking if conventionally sexist image, make "resolution drop / Out at mine eyes in tender womanish tears" (35–36)—an image that points toward some of the implications of gender that we will look at more closely in chapter 8. In any case, the image is one of many in the play that represent conversion, transmutation, exchange, and that help express the oscillations and inversions, the turnabouts and betrayals that constitute the dramatic stuff from which the play as a whole is made.[33] A particularly salient instance follows shortly; after Hubert relents, Arthur exclaims, "O, now you look like Hubert. All this while / You were disguised" (125–26). The speech contrasts intriguingly with John's later remarks about Hubert's savage nature and savage appearance: Arthur sees Hubert's true nature, and hence his aspect, as gentle.

That images of transaction and exchange should occur in connection with service relationships should provoke only recognition, not surprise. For such relationships, more than almost any other kind of personal relationship, are essentially transactional—tasks performed by the servants, sustenance provided by the masters. Many of those transactions, moreover, are carried on at close quarters, involve physical proximity, even physical contact, in ways that continue the theme of inversion, conversion, substitution; recall our earlier observation that servants are in a sense the physical extensions of their masters, detachable self-propelled hands, mouths, eyes. Early modern servants dressed and undressed their masters, carried their chamber pots, washed their dirty linen and dirty clothes, found and cooked and served their food, nursed them when they were ill—nursed them, indeed, in the first, literal sense of the term, when they were young, as *Romeo and Juliet* reminds us. There is a homology between weeping and lactation; it means that the "womanish" tears Hubert's pity threatens to make him shed for Arthur will nourish that child, convert Hubert from keeper to nurse just as (so we hear a few lines later) Arthur has been converted into Hubert's nurse—and just as Hubert apparently becomes John's nurse during the King's fatal illness (5.6), as though with the boy's death, by another homology, the uncle has become the child. In short, servants were to masters as parents are to children, yet masters were also in many practical and sometimes even emotional ways—John's reiterated sense of *dependence* on Hubert is striking—as children to parents.

These remarks forcibly remind us that in Ephesians and Galatians, injunctions to children fall between those to wives and those to servants; all three sets are grouped in the general class of subordinates, all three are thus linked. If there is a natural affiliation between women and servants, so is there between servants and children. In both relationships, the figure more powerful in either law or nature is nevertheless in important ways the dependent. A salient feature of Shakespeare's treatment of the character of Hubert is his diminution of Hubert de Burgh, "the Great Justiciar" as he is called in *DNB*, the man who in history would go on to become one of the most powerful men in England during the reign of John's son Henry, into a servant, a man of no apparent independent authority. Yet, his subordinate role gives him enormous responsibility: as both the plot of the play and many of its particular speeches assert, he has the life of a prince quite literally in his hands, in the form of red-hot irons. When the prince's rhetoric works on his conscience to the point where he recognizes his moral duty, he does all he can to protect the boy, not only sparing his eyes and life, but also using the dismissal of the executioners and the false report of Arthur's death to buy time until he can investigate the true nature of John's command (a further explanation for Hubert's delay in the scene with John in stating that the boy still lives). Thus, a chilling irony invests the subsequent image of this unfaithfully faithful servant bearing his little lord's dead body in his arms as a father might bear a tired child to his bed (4.3.140–60). But this irony is doubled when the care Hubert has shown for the spiritual as well as the material well-being of his master is mocked by that master's inability to ally the "fever" that rages in him, fired by a troubled conscience, his mother's death, his own vacillations, fear of the French and the papacy, and the disloyalty of all his noble English supporters except the faithful Falconbridge, a fire to which the monk's poison only adds the final log. The irony is further marked when the Bastard gives a valediction that strikingly anticipates Kent's farewell to his master in *Lear*:

> Art thou gone so? I do but stay behind
> To do the office for thee of revenge,
> And then my soul shall wait on thee to heaven,
> As it on earth hath been thy servant still. (5.7.70–73)

As are Adam and Pisanio and Timon's Flavius in their turns, Hubert is oddly absent from this closing scene. We can, however, suppose him waiting respectfully on the fringes of the scene for the coming recognition of his new master, Henry III, while Falconbridge's speech marks this play, like *King Lear*, as a tragedy of good service frustrated by bad mastery.

If the issue of obedience in master–servant relationships is first fully opened in the relatively early *King John*, it also draws explicit and extensive attention in the plays Shakespeare wrote for the King's Men toward the end of his career—*Antony and Cleopatra, Timon of Athens, Pericles, The Winter's Tale, The Tempest, Henry VIII*—but especially *Cymbeline*. In *Antony*, it gets an intriguing twist, when a servant, Menas, suggests to a master, Pompey, a dishonorable assault on Pompey's enemies and guests, Antony and Caesar. The honorable Pompey must reject the suggestion, though he wishes that like Henry IV, his servant had merely interpreted his implicit desire without asking for direct orders. An expression more like Hubert's occurs when Eros, whom Antony has made his body servant on his oath "that when the exigent should come . . . Thou then wouldst kill me," rejects the command and kills himself instead (4.15.62–94). Some of the acts of faithful disobedience are set off against corresponding acts of obedient villainy. In *Pericles*, in a scene structurally reminiscent of the scene between Hubert and Arthur, the tool villain Leonine has been ordered by his mistress Dionyza to murder young Marina, only because the latter's daily beauty makes Dionyza's daughter ugly. Like Arthur, Marina reasons, flatters, and appeals to his better judgment. Unlike Hubert, Leonine does not relent, though he is saved from committing the crime by the provident arrival of some marauding pirates (15[4.1].101–51).[34] In the following scenes, Marina, now the brothel slave of Boult and the bawd, not only refuses their orders that she prostitute herself, but also converts their customers, especially Lysimachus.

In *The Winter's Tale*, Camillo's virtuous rejection of Leontes's order to kill Polixenes is contrasted with Antigonus's obedience in abandoning the infant Perdita on the beach. Camillo, of course, lives to be rewarded; Antigonus becomes bear fodder. There are salient similarities between Hubert and Camillo. Both appear to accept their masters' original order, Camillo in terms that economically summarize the issues:

> I am [Polixenes's] cupbearer—

that is, even an important Bohemian aristocrat will perform domestic services for a king, standing at his elbow during banquets to keep his wineglass full—

> If from me he have wholesome beverage,
> Account me not your servant.

And he goes on to ground his analysis first in the servant's primary obligation, and then in Iagoan self-interest:

> What case stand I in? I must be the poisoner
> Of good Polixenes, and my ground to do't
> Is the obedience to a master. . . . To do this deed,
> Promotion follows.

The emphasis on Polixenes's goodness is worth noting; Cleaver and Dod, among other contemporary authorities, urge servants to seek service with virtuous masters, who will deserve their fidelity (Aa 7v).[35] Camillo goes on to adduce a motive that Hubert has not used, though familiar to us from references in *Hamlet* and *Macbeth*, the sanctity of monarchs, which gives him a chance to indicate that moral choice, not self-interest, will be his own guide:

> If I could find example
> Of thousands that had struck anointed kings
> And flourished after, I'd not do it. (1.2.346–60)

He then transfers his allegiance from Leontes to Polixenes, as Hubert transferred his from John to Arthur—the comparison becomes all the closer when Polixenes tells Camillo that

> I will respect thee as a father if
> Thou bear'st my life off hence. (461–62)

As Strier has argued, Paulina, wife of the unfortunately obedient Antigonus and future wife of Camillo, is also a faithfully disobedient servant ("Faithful" 122). At her first entrance, she announces her "best obedience to the Queen" as the ground on which she can be trusted to take good care of the newborn Perdita (2.2.39). She continues to serve her mistress, but obliquely, by concealing and guarding her until her restoration at the end of the play. Like Hubert, she brings her master, the king, false report of her charge's death. Like Hubert, she thereby assumes a responsibility not only for her master's physical well-being, but also for his spiritual health (the point is amplified by a name that recalls that towering spiritual counselor, St. Paul). Her delay in telling him that Hermione lives allows her to administer a rigorous penitential discipline. It may appear that this enforced contrition is unduly protracted—16 years to Hubert's quarter-of-an-hour. T. G. Bishop has some eloquent pages, however, on how Shakespeare derives from St. Paul a vision grounded in "a substrate of images and associations in which incarnation is the principal trope for all kinds of unification . . . including that which creates new community" (87). The community of this play cannot consist only of a reformed Leontes, his wife, and the woman who has served as their de facto priest. The principal victim of Leontes's injustice was the child Mamillius; reincarnating him is not literally possible, even in romance, but the figurative possibility is found in the union of Perdita and Florizel—which must await their sexual and social maturity. And reincorporation of the secondary victims, Camillo, Paulina herself, and Polixenes, must depend on that delay. Yet, for the audience, after all, the delay is not that great: the 16 years are nominal, the actual delay about an hour.

In *Cymbeline*, faithful disobedience is brought to focus in the character of Pisanio. That Pisanio has drawn no more critical attention than he has indicates partly the dark corner to which servants have been banished by previous critics and directors, partly the marginal status of the play within the corpus of Shakespeare's work.[36] Yet, he is the most fully developed of any of Shakespeare's purely domestic servant characters in the later plays, and his importance to the plot of *Cymbeline* is absolutely crucial. (Imagine what happens to the play if, like his theatrical near-contemporary Bosola, he carries out his orders and murders Imogen.)[37] By contrast, Hubert's impact on the plot of King John is slight—he disobeys the king to save the boy, but the boy dies all the same. *Cymbeline* thus places the issue of obedience at its center. Pisanio's servant status, his characteristic servility, and his fidelity, are all stressed in the language of his first appearance:

Queen.	Here is your servant. (1.1.160)
Imogen.	Why came you from your master?
Pisanio.	On his command. (169–70)
Queen.	This hath been
	Your faithful servant. I dare lay mine honour
	He will remain so. (174–76)

Later the Queen complains of his faithfulness to Posthumus: "He's factor for his master" (1.5.28); "A sly and constant knave, not to be shaked" (75–76). And Pisanio himself confirms it: "But when to my good lord I prove untrue, / I'll choke myself" (86–87).

This emphasis on fidelity and obedience makes Pisanio's readiness to disobey Posthumus's orders to kill Imogen all the more striking. Yet he reaches his decision much more rapidly than Hubert. And, it is worth noting, he reaches it in language that explicitly invokes obedience, fidelity, and hierarchy, but also grounds the decision immediately in the concept that good service is moral service:

> *Disloyal?* No.
> She's punished for her truth; and undergoes,
> More goddess-like than wife-like, such assaults
> As would take in some virtue. O my master,
> *Thy mind to hers is now as low as were*
> *Thy fortunes.* How? That I should murder her,
> Upon the love and truth and *vows which I*
> *Have made to thy command?* I her? Her blood?
> *If it be so to do good service, never*
> *Let me be counted serviceable.* (3.2.6–15; emphasis added)

The quibble in "good service" is particularly noteworthy. Similar terms provide the basis for the subsequent scene in which Pisanio reveals his dilemma to Imogen, first in Posthumus's letter, which we now hear verbatim: ". . . if thou fear to strike and to make me certain it is done, thou art the pander to her dishonour and equally to me disloyal"

(3.4.28–30); then in Imogen's reiterated reactions to it:

> Come, fellow, be thou honest,
> Do thou thy master's bidding. When thou seest him,
> A little witness my obedience. (63–65)

> Why, I must die,
> And if I do not by thy hand, thou art
> No servant of thy master's. (73–75)

> Where's thy knife?
> Thou art too slow to do thy master's bidding
> When I desire it too. (96–98)

Her challenges are framed in speech full of words such as *false* (five times), *betray* (twice), *traitors, obedient, disobedience.* (Her disguise-name will be Fidele.)

Pisanio, in turn, calls his master's commandment "bad employment" (109), and proposes to carry out as much of his task as he can by sending false news of Imogen's death and "Some bloody sign of it, for 'tis commanded / I should do so" (125–26)—the act recalls Hubert's false report to John and Paulina's to Leontes. He then assumes the role of the wily servant, revealing his plan that Imogen should lie low, disguised as a man, until the misunderstanding can be sorted out, carrying out his part of the deception by pretending to shift his loyalty from Posthumus to Cloten, and then sending Cloten on what he thinks is a wild-goose chase, and concealing Imogen's whereabouts from Cymbeline even under the threat of torture, and even as he asks the king to "Hold me your loyal servant" (4.3.9–16).[38] Eventually, his master commends his behavior, albeit at a distance and indirectly, explicitly invoking the concept of virtuous service:

> O Pisanio,
> Every good servant does not all commands,
> No bond but to do just ones. (5.1.5–7)

Three more things remain to be noticed. The first arises from the scene in which Cloten attempts to recruit Pisanio to his service, in language that specifically rejects the "bond but to do just ones" in language that recalls Camillo's in the same bind:

> Sirrah, if thou wouldst not be a villain, but do me true service, undergo those employments wherein I should have cause to use thee with a serious industry—that is, what villainy soe'er I bid thee do, to perform it

directly and truly—I would think thee an honest man. Thou shouldst neither want my means for thy relief nor my voice for thy preferment. (3.5.108–14)

Pisanio's comment on this suggests that he continues to serve Posthumus not out of mere duty, but because Posthumus is virtuous himself:

> Thou bidd'st me to my loss, for true to thee
> Were to prove false, which I will never be
> *To him that is most true.* (3.5.150–53; emphasis added)

The suggestion that virtuous service is the necessary reciprocal of virtuous mastery departs from the orthodox view of service; all the commentators wrote in the expectation that many servants would serve bad masters, and exhorted them to endure maltreatment in this world in order to earn glory in the next, citing one of the benchmark statements about service in Colossians (or its counterpart in Ephesians): "Servants, be obedient vnto them that are *your* masters . . . Knowing that of the Lord ye shal receiue the rewarde of the inheritance" (3.22–24). The notion of moral reciprocity is made explicit in the command to masters that follows in the two epistles: "Ye masters: do vnto your servants, that which is iuste, and equal, knowing that you also have a master in heauen" (Col. 4:1; Eph. 6:9). Good mastery is desirable, even practical; as Thomas Fosset put it, citing the solicitous centurion of Luke 7, since servants tend to reflect the behavior of their masters, "nothing maketh good servants so much as the goodnesse of the Masters" (Fosset 42; see also Topsell 101). Masters ought to know this directly, without the exhortation of preachers, because they themselves are also servants, of their own secular lords, of the monarch, of God (Byfield 158; Rollock 367).[39] After all, the angels serve God joyfully, and Christ Himself took on the form of a servant, and became obedient even unto death (Babington 116; Fosset 2–5; Homilies 90).

None of these texts, however, constructs master–servant reciprocity as a *necessary* condition of the secular world. They are all constrained by the traditional view of the servant's state as divinely ordained. Yet such a notion could be logically derived from the Biblical texts by someone arguing from within the emerging worldview that was beginning to see social status as an accident of birth or circumstance rather than a providential assignment (the familiar articulation of the emerging position is Edmund's, [*TLr.* 1.2.1–22]): if the servant's place is not ordained by God's particular will but only a whim of Fortune, his obligation to serve is equally adventitious, a matter of human law or custom rather than divine ordinance, equally binding but also equally not binding on both servant and master. Alternatively, on socioeconomic rather than onto-logical or theological grounds, reciprocity could be a corollary of the emerging ideology of service as a marketplace arrangement rather than a familial one: like other business arrangements, service binds both parties, and if either reneges on the deal, the other can call it off. In either the theological or the socioeconomic mode, reciprocity is a version of those transactional relationships that we came upon at the end of our treatment of *King John*.

Shakespeare develops the idea of necessary reciprocity no further with regard to Pisanio. But it does appear in other elements of the play. The simplest involves Belarius. He served Cymbeline well, he says; when the king forsook his magisterial obligation by basing a judgment on lying words rather than truthful deeds, Belarius forsook his retainer's oath of obedience, and reciprocated Cymbeline's injustice by stealing the princes. A much more complex and subtle treatment appears in Posthumus's reflections on his attempted revenge, which are larded with references to service, obedience, submission, bondage, as though his failure to live up to the spirit of his obligations to both Imogen and Pisanio can only be compensated by his reciprocal assumption of their subordinated roles: he will become a bondservant, even lower on the scale than Pisanio, he will be penetrated and eventually killed like Imogen.

> O Pisanio,
> Every good servant does not all commands,
> No bond but to do just ones. (5.1.5–7)
>
> [Gods, d]o your blest will,
> And make me blest to obey. (5.1.16–17)
>
> Most welcome, bondage, for thou art a way
> To liberty . . .
> My conscience, thou art fettered,
> More than my shanks and wrists. . . .
> . . . Must I repent
> I cannot do it better than in gyves
> Desired more than constrained. . . . (5.5.97–109)

The last speech is especially interesting because more than any we have seen so far, it inscribes the paradoxes of willing service and freedom from which this study was launched. Within the economy of freely chosen service initiated in the New Testament and articulated by the theologians, material bondage when "Desired," not "constrained," entrains supernatural rewards. Something like that does, in fact, happen to Posthumus; having made a slave of himself on behalf of Imogen, he dreams of freedom, not only from shackles but also from anxieties, and wakes to find it true (5.5.217–43). In the pre-Christian world of the play, the references are to Jupiter and fairies, not to Christian texts. The dynamics, however, are the same.

But we are getting a little ahead of ourselves. The second general observation to be drawn from this play is that the association of good service and right moral judgment is such a commonplace that Pisanio is never thanked by any of his superiors for bringing them unlooked for happiness by his disobedient initiative: when he has completed his expository tasks in the long, overcrowded final scene, he returns to the servant's customary marginal silence, and neither speaks nor is spoken of in the last 200 lines of the play—no Paulina for him, as is granted to Camillo for doing a similar deed, any more than the Dromii are explicitly freed for their faithful service. There is a powerful implication that good service is an end in itself. Michael Neill suggests a further, psychological understanding of this apparent contradiction. "True service . . . because of its function in a system of mutual obligation, implies self-respect, a solid conviction of one's own worth" (86); he might but does not go on to suggest that from that perspective social value can be assigned irrespective of overt recognition and reward.

The third point is that disobedience of specific orders and its global analog, violation of obligations of obedience and service, appear, indeed, in many other actions of the play. Imogen has violated her daughterly obligation to Cymbeline by marrying Posthumus against her father's will. Posthumus repudiates his wedding vows by plotting Imogen's murder and disobeys his order of banishment by returning to England from Italy. Cymbeline himself denies Rome's demand for tribute. Belarius has broken his oath to his liege by kidnapping the boys. The Doctor disobeys the Queen when she commands him to give her poisons.[40] Imogen leaves Lucius for her husband. Posthumus's readiness to believe Iachimo's lies implicitly contradicts his vow to honor his wife. Cymbeline's foolish insensitivity to the real worth of Posthumus, Belarius, the Queen, and Cloten besmirches his responsibility as king and father. The Queen's intrigues contravene her marriage vows; her attempts to murder Pisanio and especially her stepdaughter Imogen betray the inherent responsibilities of her role as mistress and mother. Cloten's intent to rape Imogen contradicts all the laws of chivalry. Iachimo flagrantly breaks the rules of both friendship and hospitality. This play also represents much romantic rupture of those class barriers of which the master–servant set may be regarded as prototypical—Posthumus's marriage to Imogen, Imogen's becoming Lucius's servant, Guiderius's killing of Cloten, the turning of the military tide by the supposed rustics. And there is, of course, the inversion of gender, apparent in Imogen's disguise, implicit in the Queen's manipulation of her husband. The play thus images a world discreetly in rebellion against all the traditional codes of hierarchy and hegemony. Like *King John*, it works to construct a society formed by transactional mutuality. Unlike *King John*, however, the outcomes of transactions in *Cymbeline* are not necessarily constrained by an essentially retributive logic, in which crime or error or folly entrains punishment.

For because the play assigns awards and punishments according to the motives of the actors rather than the customary legal or political assessment of their works, it gives primacy to ethical, not social values. (Is this a definition of romance?) With respect to service, this means that social hierarchy has been supplanted by moral hierarchy not only in the metaphysical realm of St. Paul's Epistles but also in the practical realm, however distant, mythic, provisional, of Cymbeline's England. These choices are never as easy in life as they are made in the romances, of course, which even more than most comedies allow at least some of their characters to have their cake. Such choices pressed with great force on all early moderns in England and elsewhere. Strong enough with respect to household masters, they fell with special urgency on those called by their religious convictions, whether they looked toward Rome or toward Geneva, to challenge the highest earthly master of them all, the one whom every citizen was legally obliged to serve, the monarch. Foxe's *Actes and Monuments of the English Martyrs* (1563, 1583) is a catalog of actions that from the Reformist perspective were the most admirable illustrations of virtuous disobedience; adherents of the Old Religion saw the work of the Jesuit missionaries and others in the same light.[41] Shakespeare and his company were forbidden by law from explicitly exploring the question of doctrinal versus national loyalties. But the constant presence of the dilemma in the early modern world, especially because it affected people of both Catholic and Protestant sympathies, may help account for the recurrence of the theme in the plays, in non-theological terms, from one end of the canon to the other. At any rate, as we shall now see, *King John*, *King Lear*, and *Cymbeline* are not the only plays, nor are these the only forms, in which Shakespeare investigates the relative force of ethical and social imperatives. And good servants like Hubert and Pisanio are by no means normative.

CHAPTER 7

. . . *PERPETUUS ASINUS*: BAD SERVICE AND THE PRIMACY OF THE WILL

That masters want obedient servants goes almost without saying. That images of disobedience distress masters, while images of obedience please them, is a necessary corollary. Mark Thornton Burnett and Thomas Moisan and others have amply demonstrated how early modern English drama repeatedly exploits magisterial anxieties by raising and then allaying them. *The Alchemist* is perhaps the definitive instance: for almost all of a long play, a servant, Jeremy Face, exploits his absent master's resources for his own economic and sexual ends, apparently without fear of retribution; he degrades the house by inviting a rogue and a prostitute to live there with him, and by using it as the base for an assortment of fraudulent enterprises. His behavior exhibits all the traditional servant vices except indolence. Jonson's comedy suits recent critics' materialist insistence on money and power. But that insistence largely confines the inquiry to social and political issues. I hope to show, however, that the issue of good and bad service had and still has spiritual and psychological dimensions that materialist analysis so represses as to blot and distort our understanding, if not of Jonson, then of Shakespeare, and perhaps of ourselves.

This is partly because materialist assumptions, like other critical assumptions, are inherently reductive and simplistic. The social, economic, and legal forces that establish the general conditions of service are the resultants of a myriad of individual decisions and the motivations behind them—although, of course, those forces are also affecting if not determining the decisions.[1] But the particular motives that lead individual masters to seek servants and individual servants to accept service with them can vary widely. In different situations, moreover, similar motives may well produce different attitudes and relationships. In particular, it may well matter a good deal whether the servant views her or his state as externally imposed, the work of providence, fortune, chance, law (or even the kind of impersonal social force just invoked), or as something freely and willingly chosen. John D. Cox has shown how the Augustinian recognition of the power of humility, *potentia humilitatis*, passed into Shakespearean dramaturgy through the demotic traditions of medieval drama. His argument supplements the analysis of the paradox of service and freedom traced in this book. The two analyses together supply a theological and theatrical basis for volitional primacy, that activity of the mind that conscientiously regards environmental conditions, such as social status or emotional disposition, as effects of choice, not chance, elected by an effort of will, not imposed by circumstance. There is a historical basis, too, because the will occupied such an important place in the dominant psychological theory of early modern England. These issues bear strongly on the way in which particular masters and servants work through concepts of service, good and bad. In the Shakespearean context, they become useful in understanding the plays in which service is an important element. They also lead to awareness of some ways in which an investigation of service helps interpret other situations in which the formal hierarchy, asserting or implying a top-down flow of power, may mask other sources and distributions of actual power, and of the satisfactions involved in its exercise, that are more complex.[2] Those complexities appear with special force in *King Lear*, where they gather around the figure of Edgar. But at the outset, we will concentrate especially on *Othello*, and in particular some features of the character of Iago and his relationship with the Moor.

As Michael Neill has suggested, Iago may be usefully regarded as Shakespeare's most extensively developed servant, and *Othello* as his most strenuous exploration of the servant–master relationship.[3] I invert the customary hierarchical order to emphasize the fact that as this terrible play unfolds, the master's dependence on and vulnerability to the servant come progressively further into view. Not the simple physical dependence of the homeless Lear, nor even his psychological dependence on his "additions"—in Othello's world, the "quality, / Pride, pomp, and circumstance of glorious war" (3.3.358–59). All masters are dependent on all servants in this way.[4] But the dependence is deepened under stress, and in Othello, we survey the almost childlike needs of a man accustomed to command and obedience, who loses his confidence in his own powers when the elements in his world that he thought he had under control suddenly develop minds, and especially wills, of their own, which are expressed not in the overt forms of conflict of which he is, indeed, a master, but in the forms of servitude.

We touched briefly on Iago as a perverse version of the wily servant type in chapter 4. Mark Thornton Burnett starts his book on early modern service with the proposition that "Iago's function hardly conforms to the role of the domestic servant" (1).[5] But in fact Iago conforms quite precisely to such a role, in something like the literal sense of that term: that is, he acts and talks like a servant through most of the play, though he appears not to think that way. We noted earlier that ten times Othello issues a direct order to his "honest" subordinate, and that nine times Iago carries out the order. The nature of those commands is significant, for most of them are domestic rather than military.[6] (A way to express the difference between Iago's position and his hopes, about which he complains so bitterly to Roderigo, is to call it reassignment as aide-de-camp rather than executive officer.) The first two orders clearly establish the essentially domestic nature of Iago's new duties: he is told off to escort Desdemona to Cyprus, and when Othello arrives there, he asks Iago to look after the baggage. The next two arise from the quarrel between Cassio and Montano, and apparently belong to the military sphere. Yet, the first of these involves a standard servant's task—to supply information on activity during the master's absence; and the second is the military equivalent of locking up the house for the night.

Thereafter everything is concerned with the emotional and sexual relationships among Othello, Desdemona, and Cassio, from Iago's initial innuendos to the assault on Cassio. Four of the commands demand additional information; the final two call for action, the murder of Cassio (a form of the servant violence we investigated in chapter 5) and the purchase of poison with which Othello can kill his wife. Only the last of these does Iago not try to carry out, in some way satisfactory to Othello: at that point, discreetly but unmistakably, the real inversion of their roles takes explicit form, for this time Iago's reply is in the imperative:

> *Othello.* Get me some poison, Iago, this night. I'll not expostulate with her, lest her body and beauty unprovide my mind again:—this night, Iago.
>
> *Iago.* Do it not with poison. Strangle, her in her bed, even the bed she hath contaminated. (4.1.194–98)[7]

It seems worth observing that when on one further occasion Othello seeks information from Iago, he will not or cannot demand it directly, but asks Cassio or perhaps Ludovico to seek it for him:

> Will you, I pray, demand that demi-devil
> Why he hath thus ensnared my soul and body? (5.2.307–08)

But Iago will serve and obey no more:

> Demand me nothing. What you know, you know.
> From this time forth I never will speak word. (309–10)

Hence the last words about service in this play come from Othello himself, recalling the days of his own faithful observation of the commands and needs of Venice as the ground for his last request, that he be remembered fairly—"I have done the state some *service*," and so on (5.2.348; emphasis added), just before carrying out his last act as executioner (which, as we have seen in the section on *King John,* can also mean "servant") of that professed alien and murderer, himself.

Through all of this Iago presents himself as serving Othello's needs: the ostensible relation is made explicit at the climax of the play, in the traditional terms of servitude, a diabolical parody of ceremonial indenture:

> Witness you ever-burning lights above,
> You elements that clip us round about,
> Witness that here Iago doth give up
> The execution [Q1 *excellency*] of his wit, hands, heart
> To wrong'd Othello's service. Let him command,
> And to obey shall be in me remorse,
> What bloody business ever. (3.3.466–72)[8]

The vow, of course, places Iago in the company of the murderers of Humphrey of Gloucester in *2 Henry VI,* Sir Piers of Exton, who kills Richard II on behalf of Henry IV, James Tyrrell, who arranges the murder of the princes in the tower for Richard III, the murderers in *Macbeth,* and the Captain sent by Edmund to kill Lear and Cordelia. In all those cases, however, the murderous servants are marginal characters who show up only just in time to satisfy their masters' already existing needs.[9] Iago, by contrast, is present from the beginning, onstage for much of the play, and, like a kind of upside-down Dr. Frankenstein, creates the dreadful master he apparently needs to serve, transforming the genial, generous Moor of the first two acts of the play into a deluded monster. Obviously, in the process, he contravenes the good servant's obligation to restrain, not encourage, his master's unacceptable impulses. Yet, it is only the spirit, not the letter, of the good servant's ethos that he violates, for until he has made sure of Othello's vulnerability, he conforms to all the stipulated requirements: he is available when wanted, deferential of speech and action (in the root sense as well as the familiar one, in that he apparently defers his own concerns in order to deal with his master's), and above all, as we have seen, obedient, in ways that emphasize by contrast the importance Shakespeare elsewhere places on judicious disobedience as a hallmark of truly good service.[10]

Iago's disaffection is known to the audience or reader from the very beginning of the play, from the very same speeches that establish service as a major theme. The passage is familiar but deserves to be quoted in full.

> *Iago.* Why, there's no remedy. 'Tis the curse of service,
> Preferment goes by letter and affection,
> And not by old gradation, where each second
> Stood heir to th'first. Now, sir, be judge yourself,
> Whether I in any just term am affined
> To love the Moor. . . .
>
> I follow him to serve my turn upon him.
> We cannot all be masters, nor all masters
> Cannot be truly followed. You shall mark
> Many a duteous and knee-crooking knave
> That, doting on his own obsequious bondage,
> Wears out his time much like his master's ass,
> For naught but provender, and when he's old, cashiered.
> Whip me such honest knaves. Others there are,
> Who, trimm'd in forms and visages of duty,
> Keep yet their hearts attending on themselves,
> And, throwing but shows of service on their lords,
> Do well thrive by 'em, and when they have lined their coats,
> Do themselves homage. These fellows have some soul;
> And such a one do I profess myself—for, sir,
> It is as sure as you are Roderigo,
> Were I the Moor, I would not be Iago.
> In following him, I follow but myself.
> Heaven is my judge, not I for love and duty,
> But seeming so for my peculiar end. (1.1.39–60)[11]

The episode invokes several *topoi* of service. It presumably had the effect in the Jacobean theater of provoking the deepest anxieties about their servants of all the masters in the house. Iago's remarks at the outset, comparing a decadent present to a good old past, recall J. M.'s *A Health to the Serving Men of England* (1598) and other *ubi sunt* treatments of service. The long second speech centers on the proverb that supplies the titles for this and the previous chapter: *Fidelis servus perpetuus asinus* (the faithful servant is always an ass)—not a proverb quoted with approbation by orthodox writers on servants, of course, but one that presumably ran current among servants themselves.[12] In this context, Iago somewhat amplifies the suggestion we caught from Pisanio that only good masters deserve good service: Iago implies that by ignoring "the old gradation," Othello has forfeited any ethical claim on Iago's real fidelity.[13] (By contrast, Cassio, perhaps as one expression of the "daily beauty" in his life that makes Iago "ugly" [5.1.19–20], remains almost desperately faithful even when he has been, like the old ass, "cashiered.") The final lines focus the issues. Iago's service, as he has already said, is only superficial, "forms and visages of duty," "seeming for my peculiar end"; he truly serves not his master but himself.

For materialist critics, this is the crucial statement (and it should be observed that Shakespeare certainly gives it the rhetorical emphasis of placing it at the end of the speech). Michael Neill summarizes the argument. The transition to a cash-based model of service around the turn of the seventeenth century, accompanied by a drop in the demand for servants that created a buyer's market, made for "progressively demystified relationships," so that "most household service was coming to seem like a form of wage slavery, more and more difficult to reconcile—whatever Kent would have us think—with honor or gentility" (33). In particular, he uses one of the few Tudor documents on service produced from within a life of service, Thomas Whythorne's autobiography, to argue that the service role, which obliges the dependent to mask his real resentments under a show of gratitude in order to keep his job, gives service a "histrionic" quality that leads to the kind of "eye-service" so often deplored by St. Paul and other commentators. This understanding of service may be peculiarly evident to us because it arises from what seems "a recognizably modern sensibility" (44).

Neill's primary exhibits are *The Duchess of Malfi*, where Antonio and Bosola mirror Cassio and Iago (32) in a play that expresses "a deep and persuasive skepticism about the very nature of service" (33), *Arden of Feversham*, with a focus on the "velvet dandy" Mosby (34), *The Changeling*, where De Flores rages against Beatrice's attempt to buy his service with cash (36–38), and *A New Way to Pay Old Debts*, where despite the apparent moralizing outcome, the real dramatic energy inheres in Overreach and his rapacious servants, not in the virtuous Lovell and the Alworth household (75–84).[14] But he introduces the problem with a close look at Iago, contrasted in many ways with Kent as the model for the older, idealized attitudes to service. No one, Neill says, better illustrates "the paradoxes of . . . strategic duplicity" (2). Nor is his malignity a result of any "diabolically unmotivated Machiavellianism"; instead, it is driven by his conviction of the essentially materialistic basis of service relationships (32). Thus, toward the climax of his speech, he honors those eye-servers, "trimm'd in forms and visages of duty" (50), whose duplicity so beguiles their masters that they can

> thrive by 'em, and when they have lined their coats,
> Do themselves homage. These fellows have some soul;
> And such a one do I profess myself. (53–54)

Iago, however, for all his theatrical appeal, is not, I believe, Shakespeare's last or deepest word on the subject, nor should the prominence of doubt about the validity of service ideals in other early modern plays distort our understanding of these.[15] Neill himself concedes that Shakespeare takes "a fundamentally conservative attitude" toward the ongoing early modern transition to a "capitalistic cash-nexus society" (74). And in its complexities, the Shakespearean canon as a whole blurs, I believe, the "sharp historical divide" Neill perceives between the "society of orders" exemplified by Kent and that of "competitive individuals" exemplified by Iago (45).[16] Even in *Othello*, the metaphysical dimensions of service remain active. Iago himself invokes them, if only in an effort to reject them. In particular, the cunning ensign denies not only duty, the motive that in the orthodox view should drive all servants per se, irrespective of the personal qualities of their masters, but also love, the motive that will ideally develop between servants and masters as they share the elements of their lives. With his characteristic audacity, Iago introduces his *Non serviam* (the Devil's motto) with an appeal to "Heaven"—"Heaven is my judge" (1.1.59)—that cannot, in this context, be merely casual: given the biblical identification of service as the distinctly Christian mode of being, the statement is positively blasphemous, and helps set up Othello's line, "I look down towards his feet" (usually construed to mean that he is looking for Satan's cloven feet) near the end of the play (5.2.292).[17]

The parodic elements in Iago's pretense at servitude thus reach much further than the language, as he mocks not only the social but also the metaphysical understanding of service as constituting at once the lowest and the highest mode of human life.[18] "Servants," says St. Paul, "be obedient unto them that are *your* masters, according to the flesh, with feare and trembling in singlenesse of heart as vnto Christ, Not with service to the eye as men pleasers"—Iago's "forms and visages of duty"—"but as the servants of Christ, doing the will of God from the heart, With good will, serving the Lord, and not men. . . . And yee masters doe the same things vnto them, putting away threatning: & know that even your master also is in heaven, neither is there respect of person with him"

(Eph. 6:5–9). The final phrase reminds readers that all persons serve some higher person, even the monarch, and that servitude is thus "an existential condition" (Hunt "Slavery" 45). This servitude is not to be confused with the social conditions—invoked in the Biblical passage—that marked some servants of God as masters of men because it is itself only one of many expressions of something even more fundamental, of that inescapable human servitude that arises from our corporality, our bodies' subjection to gravity, time, decay, and death.[19] After the Fall, Adam's doom was the servant's remorseless toil, Eve's not only the labor of giving birth but also that particular servitude which is the mother's to her endlessly demanding child. None of the metaphors of incarnation is more forceful and more frequent than that of servitude—the bondage of sin and death, the strong toils of mortality. God's chosen community, the Jews, enacted it in their own servitudes, in Egypt, in Babylon. Milton argues strikingly in *Paradise Lost*, that it is the incarnation, not the crucifixion, that constitutes Christ's definitive sacrifice of Himself on behalf of Man.

Paul has earlier indicated, however, that in all hierarchical relationships, those with the world at large, including the powers that be, those within the church, and those within the family, between husband and wife, parents and children, Christ's example makes the right response to existential servitude not to resist it, but joyfully, urgently, freely to accept it. "Giving thanks alwayes for all things vnto God . . . Submitting your selves one to another in the feare of God" (Eph. 5:20–21). As we saw earlier, the recurrent use of acts and images of servitude throughout the New Testament make of service the distinctively Christian role. For embracing servitude, "doing the will of God from the heart, With good will serving the Lord, and not men" (Eph. 6:6–7) is, of course, the *imitatio Christi*; all acts of service echo the primal Christian sacrifice, and the terms of the sentence supply an important gloss on Hubert's disobedience of the will of John in favor of what he perceives as the will of God. In that scene, Arthur assures his captor that he will submit, "quiet as a lamb," a type of Christ (*Jn.* 4.1.79); the iron that was to have been used to burn out his eyes (at this point a metonymy for Hubert himself) has grown cold: "The breath of heaven hath blown his spirit out / And strewed repentant ashes on his head" (109–10).[20]

Note the biblical text's stress on *will*. According to orthodox early modern psychology, the will is the faculty that turns mental activity into physical activity. In this model, information from the senses is assembled by the imagination into images, which are stored in the memory. The images stimulate the passions, which produce psychological motions, of desire or fear. The will translates them into action; the actor moves toward an object if the motive is desire, away from it if the motive is fear. Ideally, the whole procedure is under the control of the reason, which evaluates the images with respect to concepts such as truth and virtue, and directs the will sometimes to accept, sometimes to reject or convert, the motions of the passions. Often, however, the passions, stimulated by false imaginings, overpower or bypass the reason and govern the will directly; the actions that result are theologically or morally or socially destructive. The model pretty effectively accounts for the workings of *Othello*; Iago's irrational imaginings, communicated to Othello, overpower the Moor's reason; he goes on to will the deaths of Cassio and Desdemona, and, when he has slain the latter with his own hands, of himself. Iago himself grows increasingly addicted to his need for dominance, until he overreaches himself and is brought down. He thus exemplifies the Augustinian view of these things, in which the infected will becomes a raging tyrant, the psychological counterpart of the medieval drama's Herod, tearing cats, vaunting his repudiation of orthodox morality. In this connection, John Cox quotes *The City of God* (trans. Henry Bettenson), 1.1: "The city of the world"—the world of the arch-materialist Iago and his newly materialistic victim Othello—"aims at domination—but is itself dominated by that very lust of domination" (Cox *Dramaturgy* 12). But the particular lust of *Othello* is sexual lust, articulated, of course, in those images, of bestial couplings—Iago's "an old black ram is tupping your white ewe," Othello's of toads knotting and engendering in a cistern, and so on—*service* in the animal husbandry sense. And the climactic moment, in which the two men kneel to one another and Iago swears his undying service, recalls the climactic image of the marriage service and so brings together the social and sexual connotations of *service* in a spectacularly concentrated way.[21]

The relevance of all this to other relationships of service becomes clear in Thomas Wright's *Passions of the Mind in General* (1601), which supplies one of the best and liveliest accounts of faculty psychology just as the doctrine is about to be made obsolete by the work of Bacon, Hobbes, and Locke. Repeatedly, Wright uses the imagery of service to express the interactions of the model: "the spirits and humours wait upon the Passions as their Lords and Masters" (91); "for passions and sense are like two naughty servants who ofttimes bear their love one to nother [*sic*] than they are obedient to their Master" (95); most people give over their passions to their appetites in youth, and continue in maturity, so that "it were without doubt a great disorder to see the Lord attend so basely upon his serveaunts" (95–96); after many citations from

Scripture and the Fathers, "the Passions are not only not wholly to be extinguished . . . but sometimes to be moved and stirred up for the service of virtue" (101); and so on.

Will and service are thus powerfully connected in theory. They are also connected in practice. At bottom, at center, the essence of the service relationship is primacy of will. I say *primacy*. I could say *dominance*; at a first, second, or even third glance, it may appear to be a question of dominance—another word, after all, for mastery. One person, the master, imposes his or her will on another person, the servant. Hew wood. Draw water. In the old way of servitude, slavery, the imposition of one will on another began, at least, with force, the military defeat and capture of one person by another. Until very recently (and still in very many places and situations), such dominance was sustained by force or the threat of force. The Antipholi (and especially Antipholus of Ephesus—to whose citizens Paul addressed his letter), mark their control of the Dromii by binding and beating them; when an Antipholus in turn is bound and beaten, it is a mark of his loss of mastery. Yet, the fact or even the threat of force is not a necessary element in mastery: we acknowledge sheer urgency and persistence of will—of volition. The infant's will to cry is stronger than the mother's will to ignore the cries; she rouses, unwillingly, at 3 AM, to take the baby to her breast. Every fresher in Intro to Psych learns about passive-aggressive personalities, which by their will to resist, if not to act, gain the ends they seek against the less persistent wills of apparently superior others. In a contest of physical force, Othello would, we suppose, overcome Iago—against Cassio, Iago enlists the aid of Roderigo, strikes, himself, only from the rear, and even then fails to kill his man. In the flower of his self-confidence, Othello masters whole troops of armed men—"Keep up your bright swords" (1.2.60), "He dies upon his motion" (2.3.167). His confidence once undermined, however, Othello yields control to Iago. "Strangle her in her bed," the ensign says, in the imperative, and the general does so (4.2.202).[22]

Obviously, by making the Moor kill Desdemona, Iago, nominally the servant, has imposed his will on Othello, nominally the master. He has achieved this, however, not by *domination*, nor by force, nor by assertion (until this last—and first—command), not even obviously by persuasion, but by preemption, *primacy*, by arriving before his master at points along the transit from love to hatred where Othello is willing (in this context, the word is not merely a grammatical convention, but retains its substantive lexical sense) to go. Thus, Iago is *willing* to suspect Cassio and Desdemona of infidelity before Othello does, to imagine them making the beast with two backs before Othello can, to understand the implications of this for Othello's confidence in his own powers before Othello will. And this capture of initiative, of what I call *volitional primacy*, has occurred at the beginning of the play (as far as the audience or reader is concerned), at the moment when Iago tells Roderigo that he serves Othello not because God's providence has placed him in that role, or because the vagaries of fortune have brought him there, but because he chooses to:

> Roderigo. I would not follow him then.
> Iago. O sir, content you.
> I follow him to serve my turn upon him. (1.1.40–42)

The apparently innocuous preposition in the last phrase neatly marks the inversion of nominal status—the servant is now on top—as it suggests the image of a murderer preparing to strike his victim in the back. And it generates a shivery echo in the next line, "We cannot all be masters," where the apparently innocuous pronoun cloaks the implication that Iago, at least, can be a master, and eventually *will*—"serve my turn" entrains "serve *his* turn." We can imagine a history for Iago in which service to Othello was for all practical purposes forced upon him. But Shakespeare does not give us that history. Instead (and this is the crucial point, the point that establishes *primacy*), Shakespeare has Iago make his general service of Othello an act of his own will, the *first* significant action of the relationship. Othello, Cassio, the Venetian Senate, may suppose that the initiative was Othello's. Iago tells us otherwise. Othello's choice of Cassio as lieutenant and Iago as ensign was only the *occasion* of Iago's act; until he willed it (and let it be remembered here that commodified early modern service gave servants legal if not always practical freedom in the choice of masters), the relationship did not exist, was only a possibility. It follows, then, that each individual servile act, whether something as relatively base as to collect the baggage or something as relatively elevated as to ambush his former superior officer, Cassio, will equally be in obedience to Iago's own will, will be given both temporal and causal primacy by his initiation, Othello's commands again merely providing the occasion. We remember that from the beginning, Iago has insisted on being what he chooses to be, not what others choose for him, in words that are the dark negating mirror of the primal Will itself: "I am not what I am" (1.1.65).

Iago's primacy is not confined to Othello, of course. He manages Roderigo, apparently his economic if not social superior, by anticipating his desires and needs—it is easy to imagine some scene prior to the opening of the play in which Roderigo casually mentions the attractions of Desdemona and is egged on by Iago to suppose he might have her, as Sir Toby Belch, a kind of first draft of Iago, eggs on Sir Andrew. Iago then uses Roderigo to manage Brabantio. By pretending sympathy with Cassio and Desdemona, that is, by taking the emotional initiative, speaking first, imposing his will by making them think it is theirs, he gets Cassio to compromise himself by appealing to Desdemona, and Desdemona to compromise herself by taking Cassio's side.

I call this kind of feeling, thinking, and acting *volitional primacy* because it arises in an act of the will, in which the agent elects to regard the crucial circumstances of his or her situation as results of her or his own choice, not something imposed by accident or by the choices of others, and because that willed choice begins the sequence of significant actions.[23] A useful analog is furnished by games like chess, in which one of the important elements is what analysts call *the tempo*. At the beginning of the game, the player with the white pieces moves first, and the player with the black pieces is obliged to play in response to White's move. The moves of the responder are always more limited than those of the initiator, always to some extent forced. As long as White maintains the initiative, the tempo—the volitional and temporal primacy—he enjoys an advantage; the game will unfold along the lines he imagines, and, all other things being equal, White should always win. Should white make an ineffectual move, however, the tempo shifts to Black. The advantage is now on her side; in effect, from that point, from her first freely chosen move, it becomes a new game, in which, as long as she continues to make effectual moves and so keep White in the responsive position, she should always win. Life is more complicated than chess, to be sure. But it is not irrelevant to note how commonly we use the language of games to talk about life. Indeed, an important element of volitional primacy is that, in effect, the agent is making or perhaps revising the rules of the social game. Othello is playing in accordance with the chivalric rules, which stipulate that men speak only the truth, that women are chaste, and that servants are faithful. Iago, after he has seized a place in the game by willing to be a servant, then seizes the tempo when Othello makes the ineffectual move of bringing Desdemona to Cyprus—putting his queen in jeopardy, as it were—and uses the opportunity to change the rules. The outcome of the game we know.

Shakespeare's other Machiavels adopt this ploy. It appears early in the canon in *Titus Andronicus,* when Aaron the Moor, perhaps a slave but certainly a kind of chamberlain, exploits the lust and cruelty of his mistress Tamora (mistress in both the early modern and contemporary

senses of the term) and her sons to gratify his own lust and cruelty, then withdraws his service from them to save his child's life. Shakespeare develops the episode in ways that further our understanding of the place that the will holds in these affairs.[24]

Aaron has fled with his son, Tamora's bastard child, when the infant's black skin makes it clear that her husband, Saturninus, cannot be the father. Aaron is captured while trying to bestow the boy on a Gothic foster-parent. He is completely in the power of his captor, Lucius. His demeanor, however, is anything but servile; he apparently scorns to plead for his own life, caring only about the life of the child, and does not beg for that, but rather offers Lucius a deal, in language full of imperatives: "Touch not the child"; "Lucius, save the child"; "Swear that he shall [live]" (5.1.49–70). The effect is to make what follows Aaron's willed act. And the act that he particularly wills is to realize a traditional anxiety of masters by revealing all the dreadful household secrets, including especially the rape of Titus's daughter Lavinia by Tamora's sons.

At a higher social level, Richard, Duke of Gloucester, and Edmund, another Gloucester's bastard son, purport to serve their brothers and Edmund's father while actually advancing their own "particular ends." Both these characters speak in a register of almost servile humility when the situation requires them to gain trust or allay suspicion, then shift to registers of control or contempt when alone or in command. The pattern is especially clear in *King Lear*. The accident of his birth, making him not only the second son but also illegitimate as well, would, according to custom, force Edmund to accept service to some friend or neighbor of his father as the only legitimate way to make his living, and in the opening scene of the play, we see Gloucester introducing the young man to Kent as though to bring such a relationship to pass. Early on, Edmund seems to accept the role that circumstance has imposed on him: of his first 15 speeches to other characters (1 to Kent, 14 to his father), all but two contain honorifics—"my lord," "sir," "your lordship," as well as many other devices of rhetoric that imply hesitancy and deference. The mode is continued in his conversation with his legitimate (and elder) brother Edgar—"bethink yourself," "at my entreaty," "I pray you," culminating with "I do *serve* you in this business" (*TLr.* 1.2.138–55; emphasis added). The three soliloquies that are framed by these deferential speeches, however, have a radically different tone of cocksure arrogance. They make it clear that while Edmund, like Iago, may sometimes choose to act the servant, he has willed to replace the rules of custom with new, more "natural" rules more favorable to his own interests. Edmund returns to the dependent's mode when meeting

Regan and Cornwall—"madam," "my lord," again ending with *serve*: "I shall serve you, sir, / Truly, however else" (2.1.115–16); Cornwall's untimely death at the hand of a servant attempting to give true service by resisting his master's wicked orders presumably relieves Edmund of this obligation, at least, to hypocrisy. By the end of the play, he is master himself, courting the royal Goneril and Regan, standing on equal footing with Albany in the management of the war, and like King John, Richard Crookback, and Macbeth, recruiting a servant, the Captain, to carry out his murderous will. In his final speeches, the dominant register is the imperative—"Quickly send," "Nay, send in time," "Take my sword," "Give it to the captain" (5.3.218–24). Indeed, he has only been prevented from imposing his will on all of England by the intervention of Edgar, whose own willed assumption of the servant's role has qualified him phenomenologically to oppose his brother: why he should win out in the combat is a question to which we will return in a moment.[25]

So far, there appears to be much overlap between volitional primacy and the historically situated development that Stephen Greenblatt memorably named "Renaissance self-fashioning":

> . . . it is linked to manners or demeanor, particularly that of the elite; it may suggest hypocrisy or deception, an adherence to mere outward ceremony; it suggests representation of one's nature or intentions in speech or actions. And with representation we return to literature, or rather we may grasp that self-fashioning derives its interest precisely from the fact that it functions without regard for a sharp distinction between literature and social life. (3)

Self-fashioning is developed from the confrontation with "an alien," like Othello (9). And though it is peculiarly well-exemplified by Iago (229), it is a decisive element in over-reaching nondramatic and dramatic characters from Marlowe's Tamburlaine, Faustus, and Barabas, through Richard III to Edmund—characters, that is, driven by a kind of desperate self-interest, whose genesis categorically contradicts "the theorists of empathy" (236). In anatomizing self-fashioning, then, Greenblatt places himself with Burnett and Neill and the other materialists.

I will argue, however, that the pairing of Edmund and Edgar tells us that volitional primacy as a more fully conceived self-fashioning is not the exclusive domain of self-interested Machiavels. As Greenblatt discerns it, self-fashioning is a function of struggle. But all struggles are not alike, and the attitudes and assumptions of the participants affect the process and the outcome. In particular, I want to follow Richard Strier in charging Greenblatt with the failure to distinguish between self-fashioning as

an intrinsic feature of a kind of character: "selfhood *as* role-playing"; and self-fashioning as a response to particular situations: "role-playing *as an option*" (*Resistant* 71–72). We can develop this by arranging some Shakespearean characters along a range according to the degree in which their assumption of a subordinated status seems to express the element of choice, of will—unpacking Strier's affirmation of the validity of *intention*, so that, to adapt his phrase, volitional primacy's name "is not only Iago" (*Resistant* 79).

We can start with Malvolio. He exemplifies the materialist insistence on servants' *ressentiment* because his discontent, indeed, is not with his particular mistress, Olivia, nor with his particular work, which he carries out with a kind of sour enthusiasm, but with his servant's status per se. Rather than embracing his dependent inferiority, he seeks to rise. Rather than seizing the initiative, however, he only dreams. And his particular gestures, when they come, are merely reactive; instead of studying the needs (and weaknesses) of his superior and serving them (to either good or bad ends), as do Iago, Falconbridge, Edmund, he is so ignorant of Olivia's real desires that he can blindly follow the suggestions of the forged letter. They lead him, asslike, into yellow stockings, cross-garters (a kind of nether bridle), inane smiling, ludicrous presumptions of sexual and social desirability, and eventually the physical bondage of the madman's cell. In effect he declines to make a self for himself, but allows others to make it for him. And thus Malvolio misses both elements of volitional primacy—he neither wills his servitude nor assigns it a moral or ontological or temporal priority, and just as Shakespeare generally rewards servants who grasp those elements virtuously, he generally frustrates those who, like Malvolio, fail to grasp them, or who, like Rosencrantz and Guildenstern, Seyton in *Macbeth*, and Oswald do so for bad ends.[26]

By contrast, Grumio, who might well have started out as "gaffer russet-coat's second son," asserts himself. His struggle does take the form of a kind of self-fashioning because he does establish and then take account of his resident alien, Petruchio. On the face of it, his willfully literal interpretation of his master's order to knock at Hortensio's door makes no sense (*Shr.* 1.2.5–46); one effect of the episode is to establish Petruchio as irascible, but even a master as genial as Lucentio might well be irritated not only by Grumio's initial misprision but also by his blockish resistance to merely verbal correction.[27] With regard to *will,* however, the exchange has the effect of capturing the tempo for Grumio. Petruchio, as master, always has the white pieces, and moves first, with a demeaning phrase: "Here, sirrah, knock I say" (5). Grumio replies, not with obedience, but with questions, which not only put Petruchio in a rhetorically responsive position but also threaten to overturn the entire hierarchy, for if Grumio can strike even Petruchio, he must logically be Petruchio's master. Petruchio is miffed, and strives to regain the initiative by using an even more demeaning term—followed, however, by an even stronger invitation to revolt: "Villain, I say, knock me here soundly." Grumio's reply forecasts Iago, who also begins his subversion of Othello in the interrogative: "Why, what am I, sir . . .?" (9). Within a few lines Petruchio has regained the tempo, but only by shifting the discourse from speech to physical force, compelling Grumio into a suppliant position by twisting his ear. Grumio retreats to language that concedes his servant's status—"Help, masters, help!" (18). But he refuses to submit altogether; his master is mad (18); if not that, then his behavior gives Grumio grounds for breaking their contract: "If this be not lawful cause for me to leave his service . . ." (28). And the apparent standoff between the two is only resolved by Hortensio's intervention (42–44). Moreover, if the Folio stage directions are complete, Grumio never does carry out this particular command, in either Petruchio's interpretation of its meaning or his own. Yet, Petruchio keeps him, and he stays with Petruchio. Grumio is Petruchio's servant; under the legal and social codes of late Tudor England, he must have a place of some kind, and no other is offered him. We must also recognize, here as in most human situations, the powerful force of sheer inertia. In many real ways he has no choice: circumstances have made him dependent on an irascible master. But the "knock me" exchange shows him insisting, at the cost of a sore ear, that he retains a will of his own—which he can also express by treating the lower servants as Petruchio treats him, and by acting as his master's confederate in the taming of Katherine, his social superior. And only in this first appearance does he articulate discontent, as though, having demanded a kind of recognition, he finds the rest of his service satisfying enough. Unlike the Machiavels, in other words, he does not continue to struggle until either there is nothing left to struggle with, or he is defeated and destroyed.

We can find similar modes of resistance in Katherine's responses to the first moves in Petruchio's game of wooing a few pages later:

> *Petruchio.* Myself am moved to woo thee for my wife.
> *Katherine.* Moved? In good time. Let him that moved you hither
> Re-move you hence. I knew you at the first
> You were a movable. (2.1.192–94)

The parallel is strengthened by the fact that Katherine converts Grumio's verbal threat to strike his master into action (215 s.d.). A few lines earlier, she has succeeded in wresting the rhetorical tempo from him; through the first exchanges he introduces most of the images on which the wordplay works, but from "tongue" onward (213), Katherine takes the lead, until as he did with Grumio, Petruchio shifts from verbal to physical restraint, if we read his "you scape not so" and her "Let me go" as implying that he has grabbed her and perhaps put her in position to be spanked, as Richard Burton does Elizabeth Taylor in the Zeffirelli film. The stychomythia of this passage imitates the form of many New Comic exchanges between masters and servants; so does the switch to physical dominance. Both these features join the recurrent resistance of the tone in signaling another instance of that natural affiliation between servants and women that is discussed more fully in chapter 8. Again, however, the relationship begins but does not end in the assertion of physical supremacy. And again, although she maintains the struggle far longer than Grumio, she eventually moves beyond it. In short, the kind of self-fashioning I call volitional primacy can be personally and socially productive.

In these plays, the interactions of masters and servants develop the *topoi* of classical comedy, including abusive masters and long-suffering slaves who nevertheless retain their self-respect by taking verbal or actual initiatives. It seems appropriate here to observe that none of these figures enjoys any significant material reward for either their service or their initiative. Indeed, there is a pattern in the plays implying that material self-interest is not, finally, enough to account for faithful service. One who is rewarded is the misanthropic Timon's "singly honest man," his steward Flavius (*Tim.* 4.3.524), whose faithful service continues past Timon's fall, and whom Timon honors not only verbally, but with the gift of some of the gold he has found in the forest.[28] Service is a major concern of *Timon of Athens*; not even *King Lear* and *Antony and Cleopatra* (all seemingly written during the same period of Shakespeare's career) have so many servants as characters—seven with names, at least seven others distinctly identified by function or master (including a page and a fool), and other, supernumerary figures.[29] On the whole, the servants come out of this grim work better than their masters; as a group they are humanized, in the idealizing sense, so that none of Timon's servants betrays or abandons his master, even those other servants who serve Timon's hypocritical friends are conscious of their masters' immorality, and while none goes so far as to refuse to obey orders, none seems to share freely in the depravity.[30] And two neighboring scenes (4.2 and the latter part of 4.3) dramatize the fellowship that continues to bind Timon's servitors even after the collapse of the household. At the heart of this group is Flavius.[31] Like Adam in *As You Like It*, he seems to have prospered along with Timon; he retains money of his own to divide with his less fortunate fellows (4.2.27). The fact ought to free him to become the kind of dark rising star we see in Iago or Edmund. But his free choice is to continue to act in all ways as a servant. His demeanor is uniformly deferential and reserved. In a long aside early in the play, he laments his inability to get Timon to recognize the financial disaster awaiting him, and in the process separates himself from servants who take advantage of their masters when their masters are in trouble:

> Well, would I were gently put out of office
> Before I were forced out.
> Happier is he that has no friend to feed
> Than such that do e'en enemies exceed. (1.2.196–99)

His respect and affection for his master are such that he would rather be fired by Timon himself (though he has given no cause) than forced out by creditors after the collapse of the household into bankruptcy. In the event, however, that collapse, though it may force him out of Timon's house, does not force him out of Timon's service; he chooses to retain his subservient status, seeks his raving master in the wood, pledges continuing service, offers (like Adam) to give his master his savings. Timon is amazed, calling to mind how many servants "arrive at second masters / Upon their first lord's neck" (4.3.506–07).[32] Flavius explains his motives:

> That which I show, heaven knows, is merely love,
> Duty and zeal to your unmatchéd mind,
> Care of your food and living; and, believe it,
> My most honoured lord,
> For any benefit that points to me,
> Either in hope or present, I'd exchange
> For this one wish: that you had power and wealth
> To requite me by making rich yourself. (4.3.507–14)

"Merely love" is, indeed, quite precisely what is missing from the list of motives in Greenblatt, Neill, and the other materialists—the quality that is also absent from Iago and Edmund and other bad servants, present in Adam and Hubert and Edgar.[33] As usual, Burnett is exemplary. In a survey of the sixteenth- and seventeenth-century treatises on service, he concedes that "some lasting ties developed," but nevertheless chooses to emphasize those arguing that servants "were, by nature, dissatisfied and restless" ("Treatises" 58). All of Burnett's evidence is anecdotal, however, and a glance at any daily paper will support the truism that unhappy households are far more likely than happy ones to attract outside attention, legal or homiletic. We can say that Shakespeare repeatedly offers an alternative vision. Nothing in the speeches or actions of Flavius himself or anybody else suggests that his statement is insincere. It earns Timon's commendation of Flavius as the only honest man he knows, and a reward of gold (4.3.515–17).

The customary materialist judgment on such statements by servants and other subordinates, expressing love and respect for their social and economic superiors, is to invoke Engels, Nietzsche, and the concept of false consciousness. As initially formulated by Engels, this argument treats what Greenblatt calls "the unproblematic accord affirmed by the theorists of empathy" (*Self-Fashioning* 236) as a social construction developed and sustained by the dominant to maintain their privilege, and imposed on subordinates by complex and subtle campaigns of indoctrination and constraint. Nietzsche's ingenious twist—which can, indeed, be turned against the idea of volitional primacy—concentrates on what he views as the essentially hypocritical preemption of the ideal, especially by Jews and their successors, Christians, to deny true aristocrats the freedoms their superior gifts of body and mind ought to authorize. In either case, professions of love by inferiors for superiors are ultimately hollow.

There is no space here for full consideration of this complex issue, still being actively debated not only by philosophers and social scientists, but now also by evolutionary psychologists. The issue has practical as well as intellectual significance in our time because of the way it ties into political activity. If the consciousness of empathy and service is false, its falsity needs to be revealed so that those victimized by it can struggle to gain the rights denied to them by systematic exploitation and injustice. According to this way of thinking, we postmoderns need to read early modern texts in ways that recognize the workings of false consciousness, even or maybe especially in the writers we particularly admire, as a way to recognize similar features of our own culture. Such an approach accounts for the materialist emphasis on *ressentiment* and ambiguity.

And it cannot be denied that ambiguity there is. Flavius's fidelity is not enough to rescue Timon from misanthropy; he drives even this good man away:

> If thou hat'st curses,
> Stay not. Fly whilst thou art blest and free.
> Ne'er see thou man, and let me ne'er see thee. (526–28)

Flavius, in fact, stays, to act as Timon's door-keeper, faithful to the end. But he is, like Hubert, Pisanio, Lear's Fool, and other faithful servitors, marginalized at the end. The particularly striking case is Adam, in *As You Like It.* He joins the class of those who demonstrate faithful disobedience by transferring his allegiance from his legal master, Oliver, to the victim of Oliver's unjust and unfraternal malice, Orlando. He bases his decision on general family loyalty (invoking the young men's father, Sir Rowland), but especially on the contrast in virtue between the two brothers, as though, like Flavius and much more explicitly than Pisanio, he believes that virtuous service should be the complement of virtuous mastery. His service is remarkable: under no compulsion but his own goodwill, he offers his penniless young master his substantial life savings of 500 crowns (£125, well beyond the £40 of means required by the Statute of Artificers and ample to support him in "settled low content" when he grows too infirm to serve), and readily abandons the house that has been his home for 63 of his 80 years to risk the uncertainties of the road. Orlando interprets this as the kind of utterly ungrudging familial service celebrated with retrospective nostalgia by J. M.'s *A Health to the Serving Men of England*:

> O good old man, how well in thee appears
> The constant service of the antique world,
> When service sweat for duty, not for meed! (2.3.57–59)

Adam himself makes the act a work of conscience, in language similar to Flavius's:

> But fortune cannot recompense me better
> Than to die well, and not my master's debtor. (76–77)

Within two scenes he collapses from hunger and weariness as the two of them wander in the forest; Orlando carries the old man offstage on his back, in a gesture often interpreted as an allusion to Aeneas carrying his father out of burning Troy. When succor is found, Orlando declines to take it until he has looked to his "fawn" (2.7.128). The language sets up a useful contrast, as idealistic as the rest of this episode, "second childishness" in a very different key from the cynical Jaques's grim dismissal of old age, which immediately precedes Orlando's reentry still bearing the old man, and contrasted, too, with Jaques's earlier description of the abandonment of a wounded stag by the rest of the herd, image for the contemptuous indifference of "fat and greasy citizens" to the sufferings of the "poor and broken bankrupt" (2.1.47–57), which it echoes in the word "fawn."

The ambiguity in the representation of all this virtue arises partly from the fact that it is implicitly ironized by what follows, for the episode has already been distanced and deprived of sentimentality by Amiens's song about the winter wind, "not so unkind / As man's ingratitude," not so biting "As benefits forgot" (2.7.175–86). We might interpret this as a recollection of the selfish ingratitude of Oliver. But the text makes no such connection; at this stage, Oliver is still apparently enjoying the favor of the usurping Duke Frederick. And the sequel is even more disturbing. For at this point Adam simply disappears, not to reappear (at least in the text, although in production he often continues to swell a scene or two). Burnett, in his dour way, follows some recent directors in stating that Adam "declines and presumably dies, which suggests that the virtues of the antique world are unsustainable" (*Masters* 85). From an idealizing perspective, he has, indeed, thematically died—willingly embraced a life of faithful service, capped by his remarkably generous and self-denying final acts, been rewarded by the equally self-denying gratitude of his master, and passed on to well-earned rest. I find neither textual, generic, nor psychological warrant for literal death, however, anymore than we need to suppose that old Corin, who likewise makes no appearance in the final scene, dies when he has carried out his thematic obligations. The characters simply disappear.

There are ways outside the bleak vision of the materialists to account for it. One is generic. In comedy, Orlando and most of the others are young, and have youthful business to occupy them, in which the aged have no part. In their world—Touchstone's world, if you will—even those old servants who are not actually cashiered may retire into the greenroom (how aptly named!), not to return until the curtain call.[34] Alternatively, and perhaps more probably, the old servant's thematic role has been taken over by his master, for the new Adam, Orlando, with the old Adam as his model, serves Adam as Adam has served him (recall Arthur serving Hubert), ministering to him like a nurse to a child. More fully yet, we see that in Orlando, the concept of service has come to extend to all the elements in his life. He begins in a position of largely self-regarding solitude, friendless, impoverished, and without apparent purpose:

> . . . if I be foiled, there is but one shamed that was never gracious; if kill'd, but one dead that is willing to be so. I shall do my friends no wrong, for I have none to lament me; the world no injury, for in it I have nothing. Only in the world I fill up a place which may be better supplied when I have made it empty. (1.2.155–60)

By the play's end he arrives at the center of a network of servitudes. He serves the banished Duke, as a member of the latter's retinue: "I must attend the Duke at dinner" (4.1.154). He is *cavaliere servante* to Rosalind, as lover, suitor, and future husband, and Silvius, invited by Rosalind to define love, says, among some other things, but in terms numerous enough to constitute the dominant strain, "It is to be all made of *faith* and *service* . . . All adoration, *duty*, and *observance*, / All *humbleness* . . . all *obedience*" (5.2.79–88; emphasis added). Despite the wrongs done him by his brother Oliver, Orlando freely chooses to serve the latter at the risk of his own life, saving him from the lion and the snake, leading him to the same succor Orlando has found among the servants of the banished Duke. And even more than Adam, he freely chooses to do these things.

As You Like It is a comedy, of course. Like other comedies, this one becomes a kind of secular enactment of the metaphysical vision of the Bible, where willing attention to the needs of others in this life (Acts 1–4) is freely rewarded in the next (Act 5, and the predictable sequel). But in comedies, service, like romantic love and other valuable things, comes pretty easy, by grace, indeed, more than by works, and not by real suffering. Orlando's only sacrifice, apart from the scar on his arm, is a brief delay in the enjoyment of his love, a delay filled with the intellectual and emotional pleasures of his instruction by Ganymede and the agreeable *fête champêtre* life of the bandits. Touchstone's service costs him a few days in Arden and the arm-filling stresses of the love of Audrey. The stakes are higher in the histories and tragedies, where the consequences of both good and bad service are irrevocable. Bushy, Bagot, and Green enroll themselves in the list of bad servants by their unwillingness to resist the destructive commands of their master, Richard II. So does Buckingham, whose resistance to Richard III is fueled not by any revulsion at his master's villainy but by Richard's failure to come across with the promised reward. The point is that these servants, like Oswald, choose to be merely obedient, or merely disobedient. A much more interesting and complex case is Falstaff. Like Tranio and Iago, he demonstrates a good deal of volitional primacy; he argues at length that Hal should disregard morality and law in order to sustain his entertaining servants, is insolent to the Lord Chief Justice, twists the commissions in the army his master has obtained for him into instruments for his self-enrichment. We explore later the idea that characters in whom volitional primacy is strong treat life as playwrights do: they write their own scripts, as it were, in which their own understanding of the world determines the courses they take. The sheer effrontery of such figures testifies to the power of their will. Like Iago, however, Falstaff's uncontrollable self-regard finally brings him low—at the point in the tetralogy when the magnitude of Hal's own obligations as king means that he must have reliable servants about him.

The stakes are higher still in *King Lear*. Service costs Kent his comfortable status at the top of the social pile, a night in the stocks, another night on the heath, the anguish of watching his master through his madness, and of standing helplessly by at his death and the death of Cordelia.[35] Service costs the nameless defender of Gloucester's poor eyes his life. Service may even cost Oswald his life, if we suppose that he sees it genuinely in his mistress's interest to complete Cornwall and Regan's intention and slay the blind fugitive. Edgar suggests as much in his epitaph:

> . . . a serviceable villain,
> As duteous to the vices of thy mistress
> As badness would desire. (*HLr.* 20.239–41; *TLr.* 4.5.243–45)

The two episodes are made verbally as well as structurally homologous, indeed, by Oswald's contemptuous rhetoric toward this second nameless defender—"slave," "villain," "dunghill"—and by the reminiscence in all three words of the earlier servant's fate (*HLr.* 20.232–34; *TLr.* 4.5.235–38). And a circle is neatly closed, for it was the first episode and its aftermath that brought Edgar and Gloucester together in their radically reconfigured relationship.

It is no accident that at this moment Edgar begins to reassume his rightful position, and suggest two further antidotes to materialist nihilism. Neill notes briefly that Edgar belongs in the list of Shakespearean servants, but does not analyze how deeply this personage is implicated in the issues and ideologies of service, in ways that throw brilliant light not only on good service versus bad, but also on the crucial matter of free choice and hence of volitional primacy.

The role of Mad Tom has perhaps been thrust upon Edgar by desperation. But the first character he creates for himself (and the fact that he appears in a series of different service identities is in itself significant), of the prototypical bad servant, seems his own free selection, from among any number of plausible alternatives. This gib's vices recur in dozens of early modern invectives on service: pride, vanity, worldliness, lust, fornication, false swearing, drunkenness, gambling, rumor-mongering, violence, indebtedness:[36]

> A servingman, proud in heart and mind, that curled my hair, wore gloves in my cap, served the lust of my mistress' heart, and did the act of darkness

with her; swore as many oaths as I spake words, and broke them in the sweet face of heaven; one that slept in the contriving of lust, and waked to do it. Wine loved I deeply, dice dearly, and in woman out-paramoured the Turk. False of heart, light of ear, bloody of hand; hog in sloth, fox in stealth, wolf in greediness, dog in madness, lion in prey. Let not the creaking of shoes nor the rustling of silks betray thy poor heart to women. Keep thy foot out of brothel, thy hand out of placket, thy pen from lender's book, and defy the foul fiend. (*HLr.* 11.72–83; *TLr.* 3.4.77–88)[37]

Many of these are the vices of Edmund, especially lust, several times reiterated, and at this point let it be observed that Mad Tom's fictional history could well have been the history of Edmund—may already be the history of Edmund prior to the play. We have earlier noted that as a penniless bastard, his only livelihood beyond the generosity of his father would have been found in the service of some other man; in the opening scene Gloucester introduces him to Kent as a possible master, and at that stage Edmund is still willing to go along: "My *services* to your lordship. . . . I shall study de*serving*" (1.1.26–28; emphasis added). Had he taken such service, his manifest proclivities would have made a transit such as Edgar describes predictable: the falling off, from three suits and six shirts and horses to ride, to whippings and stockings and grilled rat for dinner (3.4.119–24).

But these vices are not, indeed, the vices of Edgar. Nor is his service bad. In fact, in a striking way, Edgar's history of service defines good service, and not only in that the things he does are the things good servants do, "became his guide, led him, begged for him"—including the faithful disobedience of leading his father/master to the supposed brink of the cliff to save him not only from death but also from despair and damnation (*TLr.* 5.3.181–82). His time with his blind father also outlines the traditional pattern of retainer service (appropriate to the setting and themes of this play): first relatively menial assistance and faithful following (in a conspicuously rural accent), then military service (against Oswald), and finally a kind of tacit battlefield advancement from rustic man-at-arms to manorial dignity, with corresponding change in manner of speech. I said earlier that I would comment on the fact that Edgar defeats Edmund hand to hand. How has he deserved this? The answer is obvious enough, of course—he has been a faithful rather than a faithless son, and a faithful supporter of the old King. He is also reclaiming his own legitimate inheritance. Yet, it is on Albany's account, not his own, that he frames his challenges: "thou art a traitor . . . / Conspirant 'gainst this high illustrious prince" (*TLr.* 5.3.123–25). In other words, it is as the faithful supporter of his feudal lord that Edgar comes forward. His victory thus vindicates him not only as son, and as subject, but also and importantly as servant. Good service in *Lear* is certainly in some sense ironized: Edgar's efforts cannot reverse the effects of his brother's false service, enabled by the false service of Goneril, Regan, and Cornwall, and so restore Gloucester, Cordelia, and Lear to life and honor and dignity. Yet, the play can be read as setting some kind of seal, however partial and transitory and flawed, on the ideals of service: without them Albany, Edgar, and Kent, too, would have been brought down, the self-fashioning Machiavel set in their place, and the moral tragedy made complete.[38]

Two further kinds of argument validate our recognition of this. The first, just invoked, is heuristic. Recognizing the corrosive consequences of bad service does not preclude Shakespeare's endorsing its antidote; leaving the theater, we are as free to remember Kent and Edgar as Edmund and Oswald. Linda Woodbridge has argued persuasively that in *King Lear*, the sustaining integrity of home and of country is radically broken down; the center cannot hold, and by the end of the play almost everybody in it has become a helpless vagrant (208–09). In the absence of explicit familial or institutional agency, however, the only effective resistance to this process within the play is offered by those who serve. The second is practical. With the Marxian analysis of a hypocritical altruism available to us, we can and should be wary of voices and postures that invite us to cast aside our legitimate goods to serve some undeserving exploiter. Early modern servants, however, did not have that analysis to guide them. They were obliged to make lives for themselves in the world they lived in. Volitional primacy, richly consonant with contemporary psychological and ontological theory, offered a mode of life that allowed servants and other permanent or temporary marginals to lead lives emotionally if not materially satisfying. And I think that true for moderns, too. My reasonable assessment of my culture tells me that it is not going to change in fundamental ways overnight. While I am waiting and hoping that my support of trade unions, my protests at the state house, my letters to Congress, will eventually help bring about radical social changes, in the meantime, I have to get through today, and tomorrow, and the tomorrow after that. Feeling that I choose to do my work and treat my boss in ways that potentially nourish us both makes more sense than a progressively more bitter and alienating *ressentiment*.

This analysis connects the theme of service, in the narrow, vocational sense, to larger issues. Shakespeare repeatedly promotes the notion of volitional primacy: characters who exhibit it fare better, for shorter or longer periods, than those who act according to custom, habit, compunction, or fear, whether they are virtuous figures like Orlando or villains like Iago. Edmund exhibits it in large measure. Edgar also has it, however: from the depths of his servility he *wills* to save his life, ease his father, defeat his brother, by means that differ from the means of his brother only in the motives and ends. So does Cordelia, whose initial resistance to her father's foolish game connects her with those disobediently faithful servants we met in the last chapter, and who certainly sacrifices her comfortable position as the wife of the King of France to try to serve her father back in England. Like Edgar's, her behavior differs from her sisters' more in motive than in form—they, too, disobey and step out of their formally subservient positions, but in order to gain power over their father, not to serve him. Those differences arise, I believe, from a related concept, the concept of *willing servitude*, of the willing suppression of a character's own apparent best interest in favor of another's, which we have already encountered at several points. On close inspection, this proclivity seems to be connected with matters of economy, matters of affiliation, and matters of gender, which we will now investigate, with particular reference to *Antony and Cleopatra*.

Chapter 8

"A Place in the Story"

Gender, Commodity, Alienation, and Service

We have previously noted some places where issues of service and issues of gender seem to intersect—in the fact that St. Paul's injunctions to servants follow shortly on his injunctions to wives, in the fact that increasing numbers of women begin to appear on rosters of servants in early modern English households, in particular relationships such as that between Grumio and Katherine or Lancelot Gobbo and Jessica. And we can further correlate the two sets of relationships by remarking that in almost all the normative paradigms of social relationship in early modern England, both servants and women occupy formally subordinate positions. Moreover, we can note that in this period, English women and English servants began to gain more freedom than they had generally enjoyed before to choose—not the formally subordinate roles they would occupy, which continued to be ineluctably set by the society as a whole, but the particular conditions of their subordination, the particular husband or master they would serve. Historically, these developments are synchronous with the shift, also previously noted, from service mediated by the direct exchange of goods and services, in which servants exchange their labor for food, clothing, and shelter, to service mediated by money, by cash wages—a shift that entailed additional freedom of choice, such that servants who in earlier times would have committed themselves to serve at least through the lifetime of a particular master, now signed on only for a quarter or a year or the stipulated years of an indenture. Some early modern writers on service related this development to a breakdown in the old ideals, which they saw as meaning that servants felt themselves increasingly alienated from their masters and the conditions of their lives. But at least some servants—including women—themselves appreciated the additional freedoms.[1] Implicitly, these included a larger measure of choice in the structure of the household, with correspondingly complex redefinition of roles that had earlier been traditionally determined by the data of gender and class. Indeed, study of the early modern discourses of service leads to a heightened awareness that the Shakespearean understanding of the household, beginning with the nuclear couple and opening out to include all those who live and work under their roof, sees the domestic unit, including both husbands and wives, masters and servants, as something whose characteristics and relationships ought ideally to be invented, as a playwright invents the characters and relationships of a play, rather than simply imitated from a socially stipulated template.[2]

Gender, service, and the family are closely linked in those most crucial biblical texts from Ephesians and Colossians that provide the basis for the early modern ethos of service, for the injunctions to servants in those texts are closely preceded by the injunctions to wives. Both injunctions specify nurture by the superior and obedience by the inferior as the raw material of familial mutuality, and they have the effect of putting women and servants at the same level, in the same group. That is, these injunctions, so strongly endorsed by virtually all early modern writers on service, imply a natural affinity between women (even those who are also masters) and servants, and suggest that the roles of servants and women overlap. Shakespeare gives us fewer representations of service relationships between women than between men (and surprisingly few between male masters and female servants). When he does represent women serving women, however, mutuality and familiarity are the norm—the alienation that characterizes male servants like Grumio or Iago does not appear. No Shakespearean female master beats or upbraids or otherwise puts her woman servant in her place as Antipholus does Dromio, Cornwall his nameless follower, or Cleopatra the unfortunate messenger who brings the news of Antony's marriage to Octavia. No Shakespearean female servant expresses resentment toward her mistress as Grumio does toward Petruchio; no Shakespearean female servant is insolent toward her superiors as Oswald is to Lear. The exchanges among the Princess of France, Juliet, Hero and Beatrice, Desdemona, and Cleopatra and their female attendants are almost uniformly cheerful, good-natured, mutually supportive—models of ideal mastery, ideal service. And they are strikingly marked by an element of sheer fun that appears only sporadically in male–male relationships.

The most fully developed instances occur in plays that are deeply concerned with economic exchange, *Merchant of Venice* and *Antony and Cleopatra*. Nerissa, the most extensive of all the waiting-gentlewoman roles in the canon, supports Portia in her anxiety over the caskets, her passion for Bassanio, her legal imposture. Portia treats Nerissa with respect, encourages her marriage to Gratiano, urges her to assert herself against her new husband just as she is challenging Bassanio. The text per se indicates that they readily extend their sustaining mutuality to the stranger Jessica.[3] In these relationships there may be a certain amount of amiable mockery, even of conspiracy, as when Hero and Ursula and Margaret gang up on Beatrice. An actor performing Nerissa might well invest with a glint of amusement her reminder to Portia of the latter's earlier meeting with Bassanio (1.2.94–99). But these moments are without malice. When betrayals occur—the Nurse urging Juliet to give up Romeo for Paris, Margaret supplying the ground for Claudio's rejection of Hero, Emilia stealing Desdemona's handkerchief—it is always at the behest of some man.[4] To these points we can add the remarkable fidelity of those female characters who leave their privileged situations to take positions as servants—Julia in *Two Gentlemen of Verona*, Viola, Imogen. Arguably, then, Shakespeare strongly suggests that women know, somehow, how service ought to work. Whether that knowledge is innate or learned is not easy to discern. When Shakespeare discusses service directly, it is always in conjunction with male servants: the female characters take it all for granted. In other words, they exhibit the contentment with their roles that is a concomitant of the exercise of volitional primacy.

The model of female mutuality is set in explicit contrast with male analogs in *Antony and Cleopatra*. Initially, the entourage of Egypt's beguiling queen is mixed with and in the process set over against the retainers of Marcus Antonius. We might characterize the difference between the two establishments thus: one based on Roman custom, independent of the particular personality of the master, tending, indeed, to form the character of the master, or at least the way that character expresses itself within this context, and the other based on the particular personality of the mistress, responsive, adaptable, even changeable. In that view, Antony's household is typical, Cleopatra's idiosyncratic. Antony and his men seem to be responding to the pressure of anterior and exterior expectations and habits; Cleopatra and her women seem to be choosing their own ways of doing things.[5] Both of these focus their attention and energy primarily in the present moment, whether through inertia or self-indulgence. Antony's, as we saw earlier, represents a relatively pure form of the traditional retainer household, deeply masculine, rooted in military activities. It has an economic component—the servants expect to share in the booty as they have shared in the danger—but this is treated as an expression of an essentially man-to-man relationship rather than as an end in itself. In Cleopatra's, material resources, to the extent (not great) that they are regarded at all, are regarded only in terms of use—neither the Queen nor her servants show any interest in acqui-sition per se.[6] A third model—whose lineaments we can discern in the household of Caesar—is much more purely based on economic rather than personal relationships and organized for the systematic pursuit of long-term economic and political goals. In the world of the play—and perhaps that of the playwright—this one emerges dominant over the other two, destroys them, indeed. But the play asks us to consider what has been lost when they are undone.

Shakespeare's treatment of Caesar's Imperial Roman model of house-hold order is marked by radically diminished *personal* relationships between master and servants. This group pretty fully exhibits the under-standing of service that Barnett and Neill and others identify as increas-ingly prevalent in earlier Stuart society. No overt emotional component inhabits the interactions between Caesar and any of his subordinates. They share no histories, express no feelings for one another, make no sacrifices, spend no time together that is not devoted to business. All stands on a purely practical footing. This development seems to me to anticipate the historical process wherein the early modern bourgeois household, of master (and/or mistress), journeymen, apprentices, and other servants, all living and working under the same roof, grew not only increasingly more complicated but also increasingly less familial (an alternative use of the new domestic freedoms noted above). The master moved into a private dining room, then into a separate house, then the workers moved away from the workshop into their own separate houses, so that eventually the business was carried on in a building consecrated only to that work, by people who had few if any dealings outside the workplace, and the modern company or corporation appeared. A similar process occurred in government, as the extended royal or baronial household evolved toward the modern bureaucracy. The contrast is wound up with other economic and social developments: as the respon-sibility for the defense of life and property passed from individuals to government, as the complexity of social order increased, as the sources of wealth multiplied and its distribution widened, both the emphases and the organization of individual households became more various. This was a process of *commodification*. In this analysis, Lear's household and Cleopatra's are old-fashioned (and perhaps Antony's, though we never see him "at home" in Rome), Goneril's is more up-to-date—more fully commodified—and Caesar's more so yet. And the structure of

King Lear implies that when Lear admits the values of commodity into his domestic relations by explicitly linking allegiance and economic reward, then alienation of child from parent, servant from master, begins to occur.

I say "explicitly" recognizing that in the long-standing retainer model, masters were expected to reward faithful servants with drinking cups or earldoms. But the expectations were tacit, not, as it were, contractual.

Antony's household ("camp" might be a better term), is a predominantly male military grouping. Caesar's is likewise masculine, though predominantly diplomatic or bureaucratic rather than military, and notably less stable than Antony's: people come and go. Cleopatra's is a less homogeneous group than the others, especially in terms of sexuality and gender; it seems significant that the play devotes a whole scene to this group (1.2) right at the outset. It comprises two women, the ladies-in-waiting Charmian and Iras; an unmanned man, the eunuch Mardian; an apparently manly man, Alexas (to judge from the way the women tease him—see especially 1.2.52–72—though the remarks may be addressed ironically to someone who is in fact anything but a stud); plus two more ordinary servant types, Diomedes and the treasurer, Seleucus, whose sexuality never becomes an issue.[7] As the play unfolds, Antony and Enobarbus are also in, though never fully of, the establishment—we have already noticed Enobarbus's assumption of household tasks, and J. Robert Baker has suggested that we read "fool" in Philo's opening description of the relationship so as to relate Antony to domestic fools like Feste and Touchstone (109). (We can introduce another paradigm by observing that the mixture is reminiscent of the households of Elizabeth or Anne of Denmark: an inner circle of ladies-in-waiting who greeted their mistress when she awoke, attended her throughout the day, and put her to bed at night; a choice group of mostly young and sexually attractive gentlemen on duty in the anteroom, available to defend against unwanted intruders, fetch wine, carry messages, or merely supply company and amusement to the queen and her familiars; and the other members of the household working at their assigned tasks in the rest of the house.[8]) A further way to look at it is in terms of larger if vaguer issues of political theory and style: courts, Lear's and Cleopatra's and sometimes Antony's, where royal rule is based on metaphysical constructions of monarchy, versus courts, Cornwall's and Caesar's and sometimes Antony's, where rule is based on practical actions and accomplishments; courts, Lear's and Cleopatra's, devoted to recognition and satisfaction of immediate interests and desires, versus courts, Caesar's and Edmund's-in-the-making, committed to longer-term goals, and so on. Historically, we can read contrasts between the old nobility, such as the Howards and Stanleys, whose power, like Kent's, Gloucester's, and Enobarbus's, derived from long-standing retainer loyalties, and *arrivistes* like Robert Carr, men without traditional legitimacy, advancing, as Edmund or Proculeius advances, primarily by charm, cunning, and force of will.

Cleopatra's waiting women repay particular scrutiny.[9] As Kent, the Fool, and Edgar as Mad Tom echo or amplify Lear's truculence, impetuosity, and irrationality, so Iras and Charmian resonate with their own versions of Cleopatra's wayward brilliance. Significantly, their official task is to supervise the queen's personal appearance. But they look after manners as well as mantles. They are witty, vigorous, independent; one of their important functions is to call ironic attention to the queen's more outlandish inconsistencies. Thus, Charmian tells Cleopatra that she thinks too much of Antony, and when the queen threatens her with "bloody teeth" for daring to "paragon" Antony with Julius Caesar, responds wryly, "By your most gracious pardon, / I sing but after you"; the queen's reply suggests that she accepts the rejoinder as reasonable, and so does not violate our earlier proposition about the fundamentally cordial relations figured in female households (1.4.65–74). When the test comes, however, they make their mistress's causes and attitudes their own. After Cleopatra's love for Antony has been confirmed, then strained by her flight at Actium, they offer ungrudging support to both members of the couple. (The contrast with Enobarbus is inescapable.) They themselves confine their aggressive behavior to words, and those tending rather to inclusion than exclusion; when Cleopatra assaults the messenger who brings word of Antony's marriage to Octavia, Charmian intercedes on his behalf (2.5.75–81), and their deaths, like hers, are strikingly gentle.

In all this, but especially in those deaths, Cleopatra's gentlewomen develop and sustain a sense of community in marked contrast with the intensely masculine retainer bands of *Romeo* and *Lear*.[10] I cited earlier Walter Ong's insistence on the single state of men; even when ostensibly gathered in groups, he says, they are loners. Tybalt dies with no friends or relations at hand, Mercutio in a state of vehement alienation— "A plague on both your houses!" Romeo sends Balthazar away before encountering an equally solitary Paris, and is so eager for a unique death that he misses his chance to be reunited with his beloved. Hotspur and Hal are effectively alone on stage (Falstaff is there, of course, but declines to participate), separated from their kinsmen and allies; at their ends,

Richard II, Richard III, Macbeth, Othello, and Timon are practically and psychologically alienated from their former supporters and their current adversaries. In supposed or actual defeat, Cassius and Brutus have friends in attendance—whose service at this point is to kill, not preserve them. At the end of *King Lear*, most of the old king's followers have fled. The Fool has vanished; Gloucester attempted suicide, and has found a world in which he is morally as well as physically blind intolerable; Edgar is too bound up in his own affairs any longer to worry about the king; and in the first Quarto, even the faithful Kent has absented himself, "tranced" by contemplation of the "piteous tale" he has just told (*HLr.* 24.204–17), during the crucial moments when his presence might have saved Lear and Cordelia. Lear himself dies with friends around him, but so cut off from them that he rails on them as murderers and traitors, greets the restored Kent with courteous indifference, and is, as Albany perceives, quite in a world of his own: "He knows not what he says, and vain is it / That we present us to him" (*TLr.* 5.3.267–68).

The male retainers of *Antony and Cleopatra* are equally unreliable, so that male alienation and solitude remains part of the tragic picture.[11] Alexas, Cleopatra's manly man, betrays her:

> Alexas did revolt, and went to Jewry on
> Affairs of Antony; there did dissuade
> Great Herod to incline himself to Caesar
> And leave his master, Antony. For this pains,
> Caesar hath hanged him. (4.6.11–15)[12]

Decretas not only abandons his dying master for Caesar, but also steals the very image of the shared military endeavors that have bound them through all those campaigns:

> Thy death and fortunes bid thy followers fly.
> This sword but shown to Caesar with these tidings
> Shall enter me with him. (4.15.110–12)

(In fairness, it should be noted that he continues to honor his master's name when he comes to Caesar, and offers to die if the new master does not welcome him.[13]) Enobarbus, Antony's Kent, who has stood firmly beside his master through all the predictable vicissitudes of war and Roman politics, is unable to find or make a place for himself in the exotic, unstable Egyptian court; he achieves, of course, an inverted apotheosis of infidelity and solitary repentance when he leaves Antony for Caesar and then apparently wills himself to die alone in a ditch, an epitome of the masterless man:

> O Antony,
> Nobler than my revolt is infamous,
> Forgive me in thine own particular,
> But let the world rank me in register
> A master-leaver and a fugitive. (4.10.17–21)

Such betrayals may seem to substantiate the materialist emphasis on the ambiguities and incompletions of service. To observe that they occur is not necessarily to deny the validity of the ideal, however, only to recognize the practical difficulties of realizing it. Note that in most of these cases, the commodification that we will consider later has intruded, in the form of Caesar's powerful if not otherwise attractive counterclaim: the bad apple has been introduced into the barrel.

The issue is not merely one of fidelity and infidelity. Enobarbus's status is ambiguous; like Iago in relation to Othello, he appears sometimes as Antony's personal servant, sometimes as a military comrade. In a puzzling passage, Leeds Barroll tries to distinguish his relationship with Antony from Proculeius's with Caesar: "Body- and table-servants, guards, and soldiers of undetermined rank such as Enobarbus have 'masters,' but Proculeius is obviously no table-servant" (123). But neither is Enobarbus, nor is anybody's "rank" all that clearly specified anywhere in the play. The historical figure was a man of considerable wealth and consequence, initially a follower of Brutus, under whom he commanded a fleet opposing the triumvirs, and after going over to the side of Antony highly enough regarded in Rome to become consul. In the play he is admitted to the high councils of Antony and Caesar, though rebuked for plain speaking (2.2.108–19), accepted as a friend by Agrippa and Maecenas, and otherwise accorded substantial importance and dignity. Yet we first see him supervising the service of wine and being asked to carry messages (both typical domestic servant's tasks), and his brusqueness and seeming indifference to his master's anger recall Grumio in The Taming of the Shrew (1.2.11–12, 75). In short, he exemplifies something Barroll seems to lose sight of here—the extremely wide social range of the concept of service in early modern England, which means that man or woman might be both master and servant at the same time.

And it seems clear that the issue of service—of what that might mean—is central to Shakespeare's development of the character and the play. This appears most fully in the changes he makes from his source, Plutarch. First, like the members of Cleopatra's entourage, Enobarbus's role is greatly expanded. Plutarch gives only an initial brief reference early in the account of the campaign against the Pythians, in which the subordinate is appointed to ease the general's shame by telling the army to retreat, and the five-line passage quoted below. In the play, his is the fourth largest part. To some extent, this allows him to articulate a Roman (and Plutarchan) view of Antony's conduct and especially of his obsessive love for Cleopatra. But the question of service is also much expanded from the suggestions in the source. In Plutarch, Domitius, as he is mostly called in North's translation, seems moved as much by illness and incapacity as by disgust to leave Antony for Caesar.[14] And the episode serves primarily to amplify the emphasis on Antony's generosity that is a strong line in Plutarch's account. "For, he being sicke of an agewe when he went and tooke a litle boate to goe to Caesars campe, Antonius was very sory for it, but yet he sent after him all his caryage, trayne, and men: and the same Domitius, as though he gave him to understand that he repented his open treason, he died immediatly after" (North 6.65).

Shakespeare retains the event of Enorbarbus's departure, Antony's gift, and the former subordinate's death. But, strikingly, he moves these events, from the period prior to Actium when Antony and Caesar are building up their forces, to the aftermath of the naval disaster. Thus, he places the betrayal as the climax of a swelling indignation at what Enorbarbus sees as the debilitation of Antony's Roman manhood by his epicene passion for his Egyptian whore, running from his ironic comments in Alexandria, through his extended descriptions to the other Roman soldiers at Pompey's parley, to his comments on Antony's flight from Actium. The play drops altogether the suggestion of prior illness, however, so that Enobarbus's death becomes his final expression of devotion to the master he served; note that he uses the language of service and not of military comradeship, in specific terms—"master-leaver" and "fugitive"—that invoke the moral and legal requirement of all to serve set forth in the Statute of Artificers. There is an instructive contrast with Antony's body-servant, Eros, who according to Plutarch had long before sworn to kill his master "when he did command him" (ch. 76; North 7.175–76), but refuses to obey Antony's order when the time comes. His response, however, to kill himself instead, is interpreted by Antony as an expression of fidelity whose effect is to reverse their roles: "Thou teachest me, Eros. . . . Thy master dies thy scholar" (4.15.96–102).[15] (The episode contrasts strongly, of course, with the ending of *Julius Caesar*, where both Pindarus and Strato kill Cassius and Brutus at their masters' request; the latter is rewarded by being taken into Caesar's service.[16])

The fact is, however, that these men, unlike Cleopatra's women, do not serve their master to the end.[17] Iras, indeed, dies a few moments before Cleopatra—maybe because she takes poison from Cleopatra's own lips during a farewell kiss (5.2.286–88).[18] But she remains in close and loving attendance on her dying mistress. Charmian watches Cleopatra die, then does her one last loving service, closing her eyes and making her presentable yet once more before she applies the asp to her own breast:

> Downy windows, close,
> And golden Phoebus never be beheld
> Of eyes again so royal. Your crown's awry.
> I'll mnd it and then play. (5.2.306–09)

Suicide, as viewed in terms of faculty psychology with its strong emphasis on the will, and as evaluated within the Stoic values of classical Roman thought, seems to belong in the realm of volitional primacy. Such Shakespearean suicides as those of Cassius, Brutus, even Antony, are grim, but still assert in a fully conscious way that what might appear to be one's inescapable fate is in fact freely chosen and embraced. Cleopatra's, however, and those of Iras and Charmian as well (and to a lesser extent those of Romeo and Juliet), have long struck readers as transcendent, even joyous. The quality is brought to clear focus by Charmian's final wonderful verb, *play*, which has been given to her by Cleopatra 75 lines earlier (228), and which makes the viper one last toy to end a reign, a world, consecrated to pleasures mutually created and enjoyed.[19] And its *discordia concors* with the Roman emphasis on individual work and accomplishment brings forward important questions.

At issue is the very essence and expression of service, and in particular, the question of the place where it is grounded. All of the several forms of service, different as they are, can be seen to have their roots in any of three different bases or values. These *modes* of service are distinct from the ideologies or practices of service outlined earlier; each of the ideologies may be worked out in terms of all three modes. The possibilities, as we have seen them developing, are these:

(1) The relationship of *ordination*, an essentially metaphysical union laid down by superior powers—fate, Nature, God—that have decreed such unions to be the lot of all, some in the master's, some in the servant's shoes, but all called to one or the other role and fixed there until called again, each role defined primarily in terms of its

responsibilities to the other, which are to be carried out at whatever necessary cost to the self. Because such relationships express the underlying order of the universe—whether Platonic, Stoic, Germanic, or Christian—they are inherently idealized.

(2) The relationship of *familiarity*, an essentially social reciprocity in which master and servant recognize each other as fixtures in their respective lives, related for as long as circumstances encourage it by habit, custom, activity, shared experience, the kinds of things that also link spouses, parents and children, siblings. Such relationships are understood to be sometimes good, sometimes bad, according to fortune or circumstance.

(3) The relationship of *commodity*, an essentially economic exchange of goods and services: over a given period, the master supplies the servant with the necessities of life and perhaps a cash wage, and in return, the servant does the things the master asks him or her to do. These relationships, too, will be subject to vicissitude, but imply an element of choice absent from the other three.[20]

Most master–servant relationships, in life or in fiction, will involve some mixture of the modes. A man like the Adam of *As You Like It* ordinarily went to work for someone like Sir Rowland de Boys at the instigation of his own family and friends as a way to provide a living for himself—that is on economic grounds, grounds of commodity. Over the years his life became so bound up with the de Boys family that to live another way became almost unthinkable. But Adam's decision to leave the official head of the household, Oliver, and to sacrifice his apparent self-interest for that of Orlando, because he perceives the latter as his true master, implies that he has imbibed and incorporated an essentially metaphysical ideal of service, a divine Statute of Artificers, affecting masters just as much as servants, that supersedes anything enacted at Westminster or the county assizes.[21] As in this case, however, the particular relationships represented in the plays are generally dominated by one or another of these modes.

The retainer relationships in *Romeo and Juliet* are of the familial kind, as the division into Montagues and Capulets demands, while that between the Nurse and her three masters mixes modes two and three: if her assistance in the marriage to Romeo expresses her surrogate-mother's love of Juliet, her apostasy when she moves into Paris's camp is predicated on fear of losing her job. In *King Lear*, Oswald seems driven by commodity, Gloucester and the Fool by familiarity, Kent and the nameless slayer of Cornwall by ordination; Kent's final words assert an affiliation that transcends life itself: "I have a journey, sir, shortly to go: / My master [Lear's spirit? God?] calls me; I must not say no" (*TLr.* 5.3.296–97). Edgar's period of service comprises the whole range; he affiliates himself with Lear for protection from pursuit and the storm, serves his father out of filial duty as well as love, and offers his life as a sacrifice on behalf of himself, his father, his king, and his gods (*TLr.* 5.3.125–26).

Commodification is a marked feature of *Richard III* and the second historical tetralogy. In distinction from the traditional retainer relationships that organize most of the affiliations in the three parts of *Henry VI*, Richard casts off Hastings (the very pattern of the feudal retainer) and replaces him with Buckingham, whose service is insured by some very particular commodities, "the earldom of Hereford, and all the movables / Whereof the King my brother was possessed" (3.1.192–93). Richard interprets Buckingham's reluctance to condone the murder of the princes as breach of contract; when Richard fails to come across with the promised compensation, Buckingham feels free to leave his service (4.2.122–25), if not to escape his wrath. Indeed, in this play, commodity has so strong a grip that it seems to interfere with normal female solidarity; the four dowagers, each identifying her interest with a particular man or men, rising and falling with that man's rise and fall, can grieve and rail together but never find enough true common cause to offer one another more than occasional compassionate mutuality. Bushy, Bagot, Green, and the other caterpillars benefit materially from their allegiance to Richard II, and the Percies initially go to Bolingbroke's aid because Richard's raising these obscure men to political eminence and so breaking established lines of allegiance seems to threaten all the traditional feudal values (*R2* 2.1.225–302). Richard's treatment of Bolingbroke—a cousin, but also officially a servant, one who has sworn to sustain and protect Richard in taking the coronation oath—is only the final unbearable straw on a pile of commodifications:

Ross.	The Earl of Wiltshire hath the realm in farm.
Willoughby.	The King's grown bankrupt like a broken man. . . .
Ross.	He hath not money for these Irish wars,
	His burdenous taxations notwithstanding,
	But by the robbing of the banished Duke. (257–62)

In *1 Henry IV*, the Percies apparently fall under the spell themselves, however, revolting at least in part because Henry claims their captives and hence their ransom after the battle with the Scots. Prince Hal gives rather than takes, progressively distancing himself from the acquisitive parasite Falstaff, and dismayed by the readiness of his erstwhile friends and retainers Cambridge, Scrope, and Grey to betray him for "a few light crowns" (*H5* 2.2.86).[22]

In *Antony and Cleopatra*, most of the male relationships (between equals as well as between masters and servants, to be sure) are commodified.[23] Plutarch's life of Antony is full of references to servants who disobey their master's commands or betray their confidence to acquire a possession or save their necks.[24] The old historian's emphasis (perhaps unconscious, for the *Parallel Lives* contain no explicit concern with service as an abstract idea) may account for Shakespeare's intensive investigations of the theme in *Antony and Cleopatra*.

An episode near the end of the play provides some suggestive materials (5.2.134–86). Caesar has conquered; Antony is dead. The victor is consolidating his gains. Seleucus, the Egyptian treasurer, who has apparently served Cleopatra from childhood—"one that I have bred" (167)—and who ought therefore to serve her in the familial mode, reveals to Caesar Cleopatra's financial deviousness in concealing half her wealth, perhaps because he is compulsively honest but more likely because he wishes to ingratiate himself with the conqueror.[25] The emperor-to-be respects the prudence of both Cleopatra's cunning and Seleucus's candor: "I approve / Your wisdom in the deed" (146). But his concession fails to stem her wrath at "mine own servant" (158), which runs on for 25 lines.[26] The terms of her harangue are instructive. Some of them put the steward in his place—*slave, villain, dog*: terms commonly used in these plays by superiors to unsatisfactory inferiors, or between nominal equals to imply differences in merit, as when Henry Long called Sir Charles Danvers "puppy." She questions his manhood: "Wert thou a man / Thou wouldst have mercy on me" (170–71); this might convey the suggestion that Seleucus, like Mardian, is a eunuch,[27] but seems more likely to bear the construction, common throughout Shakespeare's work, of cowardice.

Even more to our purpose are two other statements. Toward the beginning of the episode, Cleopatra indicates that in what we might call the Roman context, all values are commodified:

> See, Caesar! O behold
> How pomp is followed! Mine will now be yours,
> And should we shift estates, yours would be mine. (146–49)

Almost at once, however, she goes on to denigrate commodification by railing on Seleucus's act as the behavior of a mere wage earner: "O slave, of no more trust / Than one that's hired!" (150–51);[28] the image will be amplified later in the scene when Cleopatra invokes the vulgar many in Rome who would be witness to her humiliation should she allow Caesar to lead her in triumph through the streets of the city:

> Mechanic slaves
> With greasy aprons, rules, and hammers shall
> Uplift us to the view. In their thick breaths,
> Rank of gross diet, shall we be enclouded
> And forced to drink their vapour. (205–09)[29]

A few lines further on, she characterizes the concealed treasure as "lady trifles," "immoment toys"; at best, as "nobler token[s]" with which to honor Livia and Octavia (162–65). These remarks, to be sure, are scarcely disingenuous; Cleopatra is at pains throughout the interview to present herself as a poor helpless female, an enterprise that culminates in her wonderfully hypocritical valediction (a line that notably links womanhood and servanthood), "My master and my lord!" (187), no doubt because her defeat has left her in the situation that conquered women have endured throughout the history she knows. But I do not agree with Linda Charnes that she remains fundamentally acquisitive (7); pretty consistently throughout the play, she has denied material wealth any *intrinsic* worth, independent of the comforts and securities it can provide. In the opening scenes, the talk is of relationships, not things; she values even the body only as a means to express something metaphysical, in language that suggests that physical perfection is not a gift of fortune but something willed:

> Eternity was in our lips and eyes,
> Bliss in our brows' bent; none of our parts so poor
> But was a race of heaven. (1.3.35–37)

Her most concrete images, though conventionally Roman, are also intensely ironic, as she sends Antony back scornfully to the despised Fulvia:

> Upon your sword
> Sit laurel victory, and smooth success
> Be strewed before your feet. (1.3.100–02)

Her first appearance to Antony in her barge on the Cydnus is a breathtakingly costly piece of stage business; but we know that she takes just as much pleasure in laying her state aside to go with him dressed as a commoner through the streets of the city. She understands others' interest in money, and initially proposes to reward Antony's messenger with gold and pearls. When his news of the marriage to Octavia enflames her to strike him and drag him up and down, her repentance for what she understands to be unjust is to reward him with the "merchandise"—presumably, more rich gifts—he has brought with him; its value for her has been canceled by her distress at his message.[30] The "jewel" of her world, for which she would "throw [her] sceptre at the injurious gods," is a man, not an emerald (4.16.78–80). In treating with Proculeius, she asks nothing for herself, only for her son (5.2.19); her person she values only at "many babes and beggars" (5.2.47). To the end, land and possessions are signs only of spiritual greatness. Antony, she says, was all-giving, as she applies a cosmic elevation to a term—*livery*—normally specialized to domestic service:

> In his livery
> Walked crowns and crownets. Realms and islands were
> As plates dropped from his pocket—

that is, the mere casual overflow of his generosity (5.2.89–91). Hence it is quite in keeping that she should end her response to Seleucus's revelation in words that concern a reciprocity of actions, not of things:

> Be it known that we, the greatest, are misthought
> For things that others do; and when we fall
> We answer others' merit in our name,
> Are therefore to be pitied. (5.2.171–74)

The conqueror replies that neither does he deal primarily in material possessions:

> Caesar's no merchant, to make prize with you
> Of things that merchants sold. (179–80)

But Dolabella, coming in a few lines later, reveals this as mere policy, not an expression of the victor's own basic values. Not, however, to our surprise; for from the outset Octavius Caesar has tended to commodify not only the negotiations between victor and vanquished but also indeed all kinds of relationships. Thus, he commodifies service quite explicitly, in words (especially *waste*) that imply a general tight-fistedness:

> Within our files there are
> Of those that served Marc Antony but of late
> Enough to fetch him in. See it done,

And feast the army. We have store to do't,
And they have earned the waste. Poor Antony! (4.1.12–16)

Caesar, we are told, "gets money where / He loses hearts" (2.1.13–14),
and taxes Antony for failing to send him money and soldiers as he had
sworn to do (2.293–94).

The attitude is not personal, however; it belongs rather to Rome. We
see it extensively in Antony himself, in his Roman moods. In the opening
scenes, in Egypt, he denies commodification of that on which he sets
most value: "There's beggary in the love that can be reckoned" (1.1.15);
when Cleopatra is by him, "Kingdoms are clay," and the "nobleness of
life / Is to do thus"—a pronominal adverb without an antecedent,
suggesting some essentially metaphysical activity (1.1.38–39).[31] In a
universe so conceived, to "wander through the streets and note the qualities of people" is as good an activity as to vanquish the Parthians
(55–56). He will return to this mode toward the end, when to fight
Caesar is only a game—

> What, girl, though grey
> Do something mingle with our younger brown, yet ha' we
> A brain that nourishes our nerves, and can
> Get goal for goal of youth. (4.9.19–22)—

and when he asks those who serve him still to kill him for love, not gain:
"Let him that loves me strike me dead" (4.15.108).

Fulvia's summons, however, when it calls him back to Rome, calls him
back to Roman attitudes. Re-Romaned, Antony sends Cleopatra not a
kiss but a pearl, in earnest of kingdoms to follow. Cleopatra is more interested in the words that accompany it, and will respond, she says, with
unceasing letters. When Antony marries Octavia, it is as if she were the
common stock that cements his joint enterprise with Caesar (see especially
3.2.27–31); he certainly does not do it for the woman in and of herself.
Antony expresses his resentment of Caesar in terms of commodity:

> When perforce he could not
> But *pay* me terms of honour, cold and sickly
> He vented them, most narrow measure *lent* me.
> (3.4.6–8; emphasis added)

He grounds his rupture of the detente with Caesar on the latter's failure
to give him his share of Sicily after Pompey's defeat, some ships lent and
not returned, and Caesar's detention of the deposed Lepidus's revenues

(3.6.24–29). After the disaster at Actium, he rewards those who have stayed with him with a ship full of gold. He perceives Caesar's power in terms of "coin" as well as of ships and soldiers (3.13.21). When he goes out to fight one last time, he talks of an "occupation" in which he is a "workman," though with a gleam of his other, ordinal self: "to business that we love we rise betimes" (4.4.17–20). He proposes to reward Eros "Once for thy sprightly comfort, / And tenfold for thy good valour" (4.8.11–13). The second betrayal by Cleopatra's forces he interprets in commercial terms:

> Triple-turned whore! 'Tis thou
> has sold me to this novice. . . .
> . . . The Witch shall die.
> To this young Roman boy she hath sold me, and I fall
> Under this plot. (4.13.13–49)

When Mardian brings feigned news of Cleopatra's death, Antony contemplates killing him, relents, but offers no reward (messengers commonly received "vails" or tips for their service): "That thou depart'st hence safe / Doth pay thy labour richly" (4.15.36–37). His final request of Eros is posed as a commodifying *quid pro quo*—something contractual, like the increasingly dominant forms of Jacobean service, rather than something intrinsic to the service relationship:

> When I did make thee free, swor'st thou not then
> To do this when I bade thee? Do it at once,
> Or thy precedent services are all
> But accidents unpurposed. (4.15.81–84)

These matters find their most concentrated and salient locus in the three scenes comprising Enobarbus's betrayal of his master Antony. At his first appearance, considering the freedom with which he later speaks, Enobarbus seems oddly subdued by the jocund frivolities of Cleopatra's court. When he returns to the stage, in Antony's company, away from Alexandria, he recovers his voice, his spirits, and his Roman contempt for Asiatic irresponsibility. Almost immediately, he begins to commodify: "Under a compelling occasion let women die. It were pity to cast them away for nothing, though between them and a great cause they should be esteemed nothing" (1.1.125–27). Through the remainder of the scene, his prose commentary on Antony's passionate verse tends mainly to disvalue the women, Fulvia as well as Cleopatra.

His next striking speech occurs in the midst of the negotiations between Antony and Caesar, expressing skepticism about an agreement between two men whose only real common interest will vanish with the defeat of a common enemy: "Or if you *borrow* one another's love in an instant, you may, when you hear no more words of Pompey, return it again" (2.2.108–10; emphasis added), and although he is rebuked by Antony, and becomes for the remainder of the parlay "your considerate stone," he has spoken a truth recognized in Agrippa's subsequent suggestion that Antony marry Octavia. When he speaks again, it is to recount to Agrippa the wonders of the Egyptian encounter—"The barge she sat in," and so on, with heavy emphasis on the material richness of the scene, culminating in a deliciously bathetic commercial image:

> Our courteous Antony,
> Whom ne'er the word "No" woman heard speak,
> Being barbered ten times o'er, goes to the feast,
> And for his ordinary pays his heart
> For what his eyes eat only. (2.2.228–32)

He tells Pompey of praising him "When you have well deserved ten times as much / As I have said you did" (2.6.78–80), and claims a few lines later that he will praise any man who will praise him—tit for tat (90).

Much of the rest of his discourse is in this blunt, debunking, com-modified vein. Yet, like many cynicisms, his is only an idealism disgusted by stupidity and triviality. We see the other side when he discusses mil-itary strategy, trying to persuade Antony that attacking Caesar at sea is folly, with arguments grounded in practical observations, but also in his real admiration for his lord, in their shared experiences, in the military version of the familial bond (3.7). Antony has "absolute soldiership," "renowned knowledge" (42, 45). After his hero's shameful flight from Actium, Enobarbus can find no refuge in irony:

> Mine eyes did sicken at the sight, and could not
> Endure a further view. (3.10.16–17)

Yet this retainer resolves, against the claims of his own practical reason, to "follow / The wounded chance of Antony" (3.10.34–35), and for a time, though continually irritated by Antony's follies, holds fast, in terms that place loyal service in the face of adversity as the most honorable possible behavior:

> The loyalty well held to fools does make
> Our faith mere folly; yet he that can endure
> To follow with allegiance a fallen lord

> Does conquer him that did his master conquer,
> And earns a place in the story. (3.13.41–44)[32]

To the extent permitted by the materialist disposition of the underlying philosophy, the grounds are ideal, even metaphysical, and at no point in the play is the evaluation of things by life, not cash, more absolute.[33]

In short, we find in Enobarbus, as in his master, a somewhat awkward mixture of attitudes, of idealism and pragmatism, commodity and faith. By the light of practical reason, Antony's continuing belief in something like "absolute soldiership" before overwhelming odds seems brainless posturing: "A diminution in our captain's brain / Restores his heart" (3.13.200–01), and Enobarbus resolves to leave him. His next speeches are pure commodification, as though Antony's refusal to think in those terms has pushed Enobarbus to balance him by thinking in no other:

Antony.   He will not fight with me, Domitius.
Enobarbus.   No.
Mark Antony. Why should he not?
Enobarbus.   He thinks, being twenty times of better fortune,
                He is twenty men to one.

Yet again, however, he chooses service over survival:

Antony.   To-morrow, soldier,
                By sea and land I'll fight: or I will live,
                Or bathe my dying honour in the blood
                Shall make it live again. Woo't thou fight well?
Enobarbus.   I'll strike, and cry "Take all." (4.2.1–8)

Invoking the values of the *comitatus*, Antony chooses to fight, not negotiate, will either live or die, will value the enterprise in terms of life alone, as idealized under the absolute rubric of honor. In the remainder of the scene, Antony addresses his servants, thanking them for their service, calling them good fellows, identifying himself as "a master / Married to your good service," whose concern for their good interests leads him in effect to invite them to leave: "Tend me tonight two hours. I ask no more" (30–32). (The word *married* powerfully highlights the familiarity of this; yet in this context it is invoking not domestic household but the hall or camp of the traditional retainer band—*family* defined as the group sharing a hearth—to say nothing of Christ and the disciples at Gethsemane.) His apparently unqualified generosity reduces even the grizzled Enobarbus to tears—"I, an ass, am onion-eyed. For shame, / Transform us not to women" (35–36). But in the morning Enobarbus has defected to Caesar, during the bridging scene in which the soldiers report with wonder the music beneath the stage that signals the defection of the god Hercules. In a phenomenological sense, moreover, he *has* been turned into a woman; Cleopatra it is, not some hardened veteran, who arms Antony for the final battle.

The effect is to stand commodification on its head. While Enobarbus has claimed that he would "take all" (4.2.8), he has, in fact taken nothing, has left empty-handed.[34] Still the well of Antony's generosity continues to flow; he sends his old follower's treasure after him, together with "gentle adieus and greetings," wishing "he never find more cause / To change a master" (4.5.15–16). But cause Enobarbus does find; the practical Caesar hangs Alexas, gives Canidius and others "entertainment but no honorable trust," and plants "those that have revolted in the van" (4.6.8–17); the decision may imply that Caesar places a principled value on fidelity for its own sake and a corresponding disgust with faithlessness, but it also suggests a purely practical desire to test new servants' loyalty the quickest way. In either case, the contrast undoes Enobarbus. Commodity, he sees, can reward evil as well as good:

> O Antony,
> Thou mine of bounty, how wouldst thou have paid
> My better service, when my turpitude
> Thou dost so crown with gold! (4.6.31–34)

He now sees himself as "the villain of the earth." The recognition leaves him alienated and alone. His final speeches, addressed to the moon (changeable, of course, and associated throughout the play with Cleopatra), are free of commodification; he returns instead to the Stoic concern for reputation: "O Antony, / Nobler than my revolt is infamous" (4.10.17–18), and dies, with his master's name on his lips, "a master-leaver and a fugitive" (21). In the absence of any obvious external agency, the act seems an inverted triumph of volitional primacy.

Enobarbus's flip-flop from commodification to idealization anticipates his master's. As I noted earlier, when the next day's defeat, at sea like the one at Actium, brings on despair, Antony commodifies his anger at Cleopatra, and at Mardian bringing the news of her supposed death. Mardian's account, however, very closely echoes the death of Enobarbus:

> What thou wouldst do
> Is done unto thy hand. The last she spake
> Was "Antony! most noble Antony!"

> Then in the midst a tearing groan did break
> The name of Antony. It was divided
> Between her heart and lips. She render'd life,
> Thy name so buried in her. (4.15.27–34)[35]

Thereafter, Antony, too, abandons commodity for familial and sacrificial love. It is on the latter ground that he appeals to the palace guard to finish the suicide he has botched ("Let him that loves me strike me dead" [4.15.107]); he offers those whom he asks to carry him to the monument only his thanks (138); his last speeches to Cleopatra mingle the themes of love, honor, and a judicious awareness of Fortune's vagaries that nevertheless bespeaks independence from Fortune's service. His example seems to inspire Cleopatra. She belittles Caesar as "Fortune's knave, / A minister of her will" (5.2.3–4), uses a feigned interest in commodification to divert Roman suspicions (recall the confession of Seleucus, discussed earlier), and brings about her death (and those of Iras and Charmian) on grounds of love and honor. Even Caesar seems drawn into this ambit; he assures Cleopatra that "Caesar's no merchant, to make prize with you / Of things that merchants sold" (5.2.179–80), and although Cleopatra doubts his sincerity ("He words me, girls" [187]), the rhetoric of commodification is much less insistent in his speeches toward the end of the play than it is earlier.

In its place is a remarkable mixture of the familial and ordinal that enacts if it does not formally invoke the Pauline linkage of gender and service, with its implication that faithful marriage, parenthood, and service have both practical and metaphysical rewards. Cleopatra tells Charmian to do her chores (5.2.227), talk of "the worm" is in terms of feeding and eating, "a woman is a dish for the gods" (269); Antony becomes "Husband," the asp is a baby at Cleopatra's breast, and Charmian's last observation is that the crown is crooked on her dead mistress' brow.[36] At the same time, the clown brings ultimate liberty, Cleopatra is a marble statue, more constant than the moon, full of "immortal longings," "fire and air"; Antony's kiss is "heaven," the asp's bite "soft as air," the eyes of "golden Phoebus" forever robbed of their most majestic spectacle. The couple's weakness is noble, their fame great enough to deny the tomb, these high events only to be marked by "great solemnity."

Much recent criticism of *Antony and Cleopatra*, arising as it does from postmodern hostility to the metaphysical, has taken the debunker's stance toward Cleopatra's staging of the imperial couple's final scene, and the concept of mutual service that it enshrines.[37] Within the play, in the obvious ways, commodity rules—and not in *Antony and Cleopatra* alone. Antony, Cleopatra, Iras, and Charmian are dead. Caesar commands the field, the city, and the world. It is not he, however, whom most readers and playgoers remember. Historically, the apogee of the Roman imperium, honored by generations of Renaissance writers as the highest achievement of secular humanity, is just about to come. Yet, in the tragedy, if this day has come, it seems, by contrast with the fecund play of the lovers and their servants, thin, shallow, impoverished, and gray, sustained as it must be by revolted allies to whom mere survival was all. This is in part the case because Caesar is, throughout the play, essentially alone, without confidant, friend, lover, or spouse. His closest relationship is that with his sister. But using her as a commodity, seeking closure in contracts rather than human relationships, he leaves himself finally at the base of the monument, not the top, with his back to the audience, helplessly looking up. The lovers' assertion of volitional primacy, abetted and joined by their servants, has put all of them beyond even Caesar Augustus's power.

That assertion seems to me inflected by gender, in ways already suggested by what we have observed of the servants in this play. It would be pretty foolish to propose that women in the world at large are indifferent to commodity. It seems to me generally true of the women of Shakespeare's world, however, whether they are masters or servants. At wooing time, no Shakespearean woman prefers a rich suitor to a poor one; to the extent that commodification is upheld, it is by the men— Baptista, not Bianca, Page, not his daughter Anne, Brabantio, not Desdemona (if we can suppose that a lack of land and settled wealth makes part of Othello's inadequacies in the senator's view), Cymbeline, not Imogen. Mistress Quickly presents her bills to Falstaff, but continues to serve and cherish him when he does not pay. When ambition does appear, it has an almost metaphysical quality—power as an end in itself, not a means; not for Lady Macbeth, Goneril, or Regan Tamburlanian or even Malvolian fantasies of earthly crowns and rich jewels, but simply to "be great." Once committed, moreover, Shakespearean women are almost without exception faithful, as wives, as lovers, as servants, regardless of changes in circumstance. Shakespearean men may well, as we know, waver and change, forsaking parents, siblings, wives, lovers, and masters. But the women are almost always ready to take risks, leave home, put on a new and dangerous identity, to serve those to whom they have pledged themselves.

The model for their behavior seems to me to be the marriage vow. The formula in the Prayer Book of 1549, which includes a commitment to obey, reiterates the homology noted above between wives and servants—"to have and to holde from this day forwarde, for better, for woorse, for richer, for poorer, in sickenes, and in health, to love, cherishe, and to obey." In other words, choose, freely, to set the welfare of the family higher than that of the individual self. Our postmodern awareness of the imperative force of economic and social actualities has, of course, alerted us to the external constraints that enforce and reinforce apparently free choices. They appear in Capulet's explicit ultimatum to Juliet: marry my choice of husband or starve in the streets. They appear in Caesar's implicit ultimatum to Cleopatra: die in your way or die in mine. These women, however, transform acceptance of the practical fate imposed on them by their male opponents into an artistic, psychological, perhaps ethical triumph, by choosing to feel and so to express the event as liberating rather than confining. This is the essence of volitional primacy—the essence, as I will argue further in the next and final chapter, of Shakespearean service. That essence is not, as I trust I have already indicated, confined to women. But because the a priori subordination of women in early modern society gives women earlier, deeper, more comprehensive opportunities to exercise it, they tend to assert it sooner and more often. And *Antony and Cleopatra*, in the contrasts between feminine and masculine households and societies, in the contrasts between feminine and masculine ways of living and of dying, illustrates the point with exemplary fullness.

CHAPTER 9

"As Willing as Bondage E'er of Freedom"

The Vindication of Willing Service in *The Tempest*

The concept of volitional primacy provides a way to account for the verve and energy with which many Shakespearean persons carry on. It is not surprising, for the concept is fundamentally rhetorical: not so much the verb—*serviam*—as its intonation. It is also fundamentally theatrical. Lars Engle reminds us of the what-if procedures that generate theatrical plots. "What happens if the man who hates usury is obliged by circumstance to borrow money at interest? What if a black soldier marries a white lady?" (56). What if a subordinate acts (in a theatrical sense) as if his or her subordinated position was reached by conscious choice? In *The Taming of the Shrew*, Lucentio does exactly that—though only to selected audiences; in his whispered asides to Bianca, he retains his masterly identity. It is also true, however, and perhaps more deeply, that Petruchio in his sphere and Katherine in hers refuse to allow the customary patterns of society to determine their actions. Petruchio wills to reject the established interpretation of Katherine's character and the established ways of courtship in order to achieve his ends; along the way he makes a mockery of wedding customs and other social niceties. From the beginning of the play Katherine opposes her will to that of her father, her sister, and her suitors, including Petruchio; her turnabout into a vigorous endorsement of traditional gender hierarchy at the end of the play, however discomfiting to moderns, continues the pattern, allowing her to astonish the male onlookers and silence the other women. In *King John* a young man of "large composition" (1.1.88) actively seeks the social stigma of illegitimacy, and throws off his secure but confined identity as the legitimate heir of Sir Robert Falconbridge for landless but royal bastardy and the opportunity to risk his life to rise; he serves first his grandmother and then his uncle the king, though primarily in a military rather than a domestic or even a political way. Julia, Portia, Nerissa, Rosalind, Viola, and Imogen likewise abandon their socially acceptable selves, by dressing as men (it is relevant to the present study to note that all but Portia and Rosalind also take identities as domestic servants); their willingness to shatter the rigid canons of sexual identity brings them the freedom within which they can negotiate new and more productive relationships. Falstaff—and his young master Hal, as well— prowl the uncertain margins of society, where the readiness is all, and errors in judgment or just plain bad luck entail the same risks of imprisonment or death as the intrigues of the courtly center, but are at least sought in a spirit of improvisational play that contrasts radically with the deadly earnestness of the court. Hal goes on in *Henry V* to bring something of the same spirit to both war and wooing in France. In the same play, Fluellen, member of a geographically and socially marginal nation, by insisting that his leek stands for honor, not shame, triumphs over not just Pistol but the King; Pistol himself, like Parolles a play or two later, by confronting and embracing his fallen state, manages at least to recover his dignity (and the affection of the audience).[1]

As the fates of Falstaff and Pistol indicate, seizing the social initiative does not always bring the approbation of material rewards or long-term earthly happiness. Romeo and Juliet defy the customs, of familial feud and prudential marriage, that govern life in Verona; custom and circumstance ally with their own impulsiveness to bring them down.[2] Hotspur, willful as a two-year-old, animates the courtly world of *1 Henry IV* with his restless vitality. But his reductive commitment to an outmoded concept of honor and his imprudent trust in his unreliable and selfserving kinsmen leave him vulnerable to Hal's more comprehensive resourcefulness. Antony and Cleopatra, forced to choose between the ludic hedonism of Alexandria and the calculations of Rome, are also forced to choose between life and death. Aaron, Richard III, Iago, Edmund, and Iachimo enjoy success until Act 5 (and the pleasure they take in their Machiavellian freedom from ordinary moral constraints is manifest), but are all brought to judgment in the end. Even Edgar, though he has defeated his brother and helped to cleanse the realm, looks out at the close of *King Lear* over the bodies of Lear and Cordelia toward the place where he has watched his father die of a broken heart. In the moral economy of Shakespearean drama some measure of prudence remains a virtue, and improvidence, recklessness, gullibility rarely go unpunished, to say nothing of adultery, private vengeance, and murder. Yet characters as wicked as Richard and Edmund compel audiences' admiration, perhaps their affection, by their sheer vitality.

That vitality, even in tragic plays, is essentially comic. For it is the vitality of improvisation. The contrast between Richard or Edmund and Octavius Caesar illustrates what I mean. The latter, in both *Julius Caesar* and *Antony and Cleopatra*, certainly takes advantage of opponents' weaknesses and the opportunities presented by chance. Certainly he has a plan. Certainly he wills his own success. But he operates always within the parameters of political and military custom. He never seems, as the others do, to have flung himself, without hesitation, into the waters of experience, letting the current take him where it will in a way that makes its will his will, and gleefully disporting himself in whatever psychological or moral or economic eddies he finds. To return to the earlier theatrical metaphor, he never operates by creating a scenario, then placing someone he wishes to control in it in a role that the other character can play only one way. Indeed, when he tries to do that, by having Proculeius extend a duplicitous offer of clemency to Cleopatra, her own suspicions confirmed by Dolabella's lead her to frustrate his intention. The offer is too merely calculated: it lacks the element of surprise that is also the element of grace.

The index, it seems to me, is always language. Characters of the kind I am talking about, from Petruchio to Caliban, exploit linguistic resources more fully than their fellows; they shift freely from verse to prose, change register on a dime, make jokes and puns, swing from mood to mood, like a gibbon in a tree. There are some essentially moral limits here; Shakespeare gave Othello and Lear strains of a wild, terrible, ecstatic music that Iago and Edmund cannot produce. But the major exponents of volitional primacy in these plays are always all-round verbal athletes, who make lesser, more inhibited characters seem verbally limited. Hence Octavius, although his language is vigorous, polished, urbane, never delights us the way Antony, Enobarbus, and especially Cleopatra can; none of the memorable phrases of the play come from him.[3]

As I have said, there are limits, both moral and ontological. Improvisation, though it may postpone the closure of discovery or death (Tranio and Edmund), cannot avert it. Hamlet's desperate vitality, the epitome of Shakespearean improvisation in both language and actions, yields finally to a wise passiveness: "The readiness is all" (5.2.160). At the base of the concept of volitional primacy is recognition—or is it precognition?—of those things that cannot be changed. Remember that Iago does not initiate his service of Othello: he is by definition, from the outset, no better than an ensign, a subordinate to the general. But he takes control of his service by going out to meet it, as it were, by submerging himself, in Othello's presence, at least, in his servant's role. (The difference in his demeanor just before and just after Othello's arrival in Cyprus makes a fine instance of the rhetorical versatility discussed above, when he jests with Cassio, flirts with Desdemona, and generally plays the role of the ironic courtier to the hilt, then after Othello's entrance switches abruptly into deferential subordination.[4]) Having cast himself as the title character of a drama called Iago the Servant, he serves the play, in theatrical parlance, and thus comes to control it. That control is very extensive. In important ways he rewrites the other players' roles, recasting Othello from commander-in-chief to cuckold-in-chief, Desdemona from virginal bride to whore, Cassio from place-holder to place-beggar. When we last see Iago he is exposed, defeated, wounded, bound, facing the prospect of torture and certain death. Yet in these depths of submission and degradation, he retains some measure of volitional primacy: "Demand me nothing. . . . From this time forth, I never *will* speak word" (5.2.309–10; emphasis added). Having freely elected the appearance of servitude, he now freely gives it up. And his refusal to speak in some way despoils the "censure" Cassio will impose on him of any real satisfaction: for a man so fully and as it were merely verbal as Iago, the self-imposition of silence is a sentence of nonbeing as severe as any Cassio can lay on him.

Still, Iago is free only to a point. It is not just that he must, in fact, and presumably against his will, be hauled off to prison to be confined, tortured, and probably executed. It is that in ways that run much deeper than his service of Othello, he is the servant of his own infected imagination.[5] Iago's imagination is vivid. He readily converts the conjugal embrace into the coupling of animals—"the old black ram is tupping your white ewe . . . making the beast with two backs." He knows before asking how Brabantio will react to the news of his daughter's marriage to the Moor. It is easy for him to imagine that his own wife, to say nothing of Desdemona, is unfaithful, and Cassio an unprincipled seducer. Almost effortlessly, by a kind of ventriloquism, he appears to communicate his sordid vision of sexuality, as the coupling of toads in cisterns, to his master. But his imagination is defective. He can *perceive* virtue in Cassio ("He hath a daily beauty in his life") and in Othello ("a constant, loving, noble nature"). But evidently he cannot imagine a Cassio whose respect for his superior puts his superior's wife off limits, a Desdemona who herself refuses to imagine infidelity; he cannot construct an image of virtue that he can make real by becoming virtuous himself.[6] As Aristotle put it, "He is by nature a slave who . . . shares in reason to the extent of apprehending it without possessing it" (*Politics* 1254b, quoted in Hunt "Slavery" 45). As a result he can never fully realize the paradox of servitude as liberation, which must involve the spirit as well as the letter of the role.

As I have suggested earlier, that paradox is expressed in the Collect for Peace of the Anglican Prayer Book's service of Morning Prayer:

> O God, which art author of peace, and lover of concord, in knowledge of whom standeth our eternal life, whose service is perfect freedom: Defend us thy humble servants, in all assaults of our enemies; that we surely trusting in thy defense, may not fear the power of any adversaries; through the might of Jesu Christ our Lord.

Recall that Cranmer had taken this prayer from occasional use in the *Missa pro pace* in the Sacramentary of Gregory the Great, and placed it where it would be said or heard every day by every conscientious Anglican priest, heard almost every Sunday by every Anglican churchgoer, and said or heard almost every day by the masters and servants of pious Anglican households (Brightman 148; Legge 395). And in adapting the prayer, he made changes that strengthen the features of the prayer most germane to a consideration of service. The concept passed deeply enough into orthodox Anglican thought that the genial Thomas Fosset would thus describe how the servant should willingly and cheerfully answer the call to serve:

> . . . to obey, and to be in subjection, to have no will of his owne, nor power over him selfe, but wholly to resigne himselfe to the will of his Master . . . *Spontaneum & rationabile voluntatis propriae sacrificium*, a voluntarie and reasonable sacrificing of a mans owne will, voluntarily, freely, and without any constraints: and reasonably, that is, according to reason and religion, in the obedience, and feare of God. (1612, 22)

And while the emphasis of the paradox in these explicitly theological documents is spiritual, the practical extension of the love of God to the love of neighbor in the Golden Rule carries the paradox as enacted into the ordinary concerns of secular life.

Fosset's emphasis on *will* invokes my concept of volitional primacy; it both brings us back into the problematic areas of the subject, and points a way out of them.[7] Post-structuralist criticism of early modern texts has tended to *amplify* the discontent of dramatic figures cast in subordinated roles—women, Jews, the colonized—not to *ameliorate* it, as the concept of volitional primacy tends to do. Readers made skeptical by such criticism will surely have been saying to themselves, it must have been all very well for these preachers, eloquent as they were, to try to bring the erected wits of the servants listening to them (compelled to come and stand at the back of the church or chapel, no doubt, by their masters) to some understanding that their earthly servitude could be the prelude to some heavenly freedom. But their infected wills were surely grumbling the while, "Give me some food." And drink. And better wages. And a free shot at seducing the chambermaid or marrying the widow who kept the tavern on the green. The problem involves the masters, too. For all Chrysostom's eminence among the church fathers, and for all his obvious influence on Luther and even Calvin in this connection (Luther *Works* 29.660; Calvin 3.892, 4.102), he is not extensively or frequently cited by any of the Tudor and Stuart commentators I have read. The fact is that his vision of a truly egalitarian Christianity was too subversive of the status quo to be expressed by Establishment preachers to socially mixed audiences, even in explicitly idealistic contexts. We must also concede Shakespeare's characteristic hesitancy to utter unambiguous assertions about metaphysical matters.

For my purposes, therefore, it is crucial to note those statements and images that find in cheerful, willing obedience, the conscious and voluntary subordination of one's own immediate interests to those of another, not only the hope of future bliss but also the experience of present satisfaction. Before the Fall, Luther had said, carrying out God's will had given Adam joy; if attaining a similar joy in the postlapsarian world can only be accomplished through Christ, it is nonetheless still accessible (Althouse *Theology* 253). Hence Daniel Touteville's stress on Paul's requirement of single-minded servants, serving "*freely, from their heart* . . . when the heart not onely desires to doe it, but withall rejoyceth, and is much delighted in the doing of it" (349). It is not my intention to argue that Shakespeare endorsed in a creedal way any specifically Christian concept as the only way to freedom. The concept was active around him, his fellows, and his audience. There was much emphasis on servants in the narrow modern sense of the term, but all the commentators insist that the concept applied to people of every rank, and assumed greater force than it might have for us, given the fact that people of every rank sometimes, if not at all times, found or placed themselves in servant roles. The demotic theatrical tradition of the mystery cycles and many of their humanistic derivatives, the moralities, had set a high value on the *potentia humilatatis* (Cox *Dramaturgy* 26). Shakespeare and his fellows belonged to a social group whose legal subordination and marginality must have made these ideas appealing. And whatever Shakespeare's doctrinal views, I believe that the concept directs our attention to a moral if not a theological ideal that he enacts so repeatedly and effectively that it seems to me to become finally the cornerstone of his ethical vision.

The operative term is *enacts*. Shakespearean texts do not very often or very explicitly discuss these issues. Instead, they repeatedly ask their audiences to watch characters performing acts of freely elected service. These acts earn rewards, sometimes for the characters themselves (especially in the comedies and romances), in the form of social and economic gains in status, wealth, the emotional security of stable married love, but sometimes only heuristically, only for the audience (especially in the tragedies), in the form of feelings of satisfaction (perhaps in that word's etymological sense of completion). A conspectus of the possibilities appears in *The Tempest*, analysis of which constitutes a summary of our study of Shakespearean service.[8]

The Tempest offers about as many different images of service as *The Taming of the Shrew*.[9] The topic is introduced in the second line of the play, in the word *master*, and runs discreetly through all of that first scene, in assertions and reminders of proper hierarchy within the crew, within the aristocratic party, and between the two groups. Virtually all the characters except Alonso and perhaps Sebastian are at some point formally identified as masters and servants, in relationships that exploit all the early modern discourses of service defined and illustrated heretofore. There is the consistently rebellious slave Caliban, who also has affinities with the crabbed servant of New Comedy; two unreliable and finally mutinous household servants, Stefano and Trinculo (caricatures of contemporary servant types, it would seem); the grumbling but faithful servant Ariel (one of Shakespeare's most interesting developments of the wily servant); two gentlemen-in-waiting, Adrian and Francisco; old Gonzalo, the fruitful courtly hop who climbs and truly serves both Duke Prospero and King Alonso; Prince Ferdinand, who willingly embraces domestic service to the master Prospero in order to act out his erotic service to his mistress Miranda; and Miranda herself, who seeks to outdo Ferdinand in her readiness to serve. Antonio, though now Duke of Milan, is the vassal of Alonso, and nominally if not practically subordinate to Sebastian as well, while Sebastian must follow and obey his brother; these two, along with Gonzalo, Adrian, and Francisco, comprise Alonso's retinue.

These categories are not just invoked but are also developed. Caliban is the prototypical servant, hewer of wood and drawer of water. For the most part Stefano and Trinculo act as early modern domestic servants, of the kind hired for the term, but when they hook up with Caliban, and Stefano's access to spirituous liquors allows him to lord it over the other two, the three become a ridiculous parody of a retainer band, typically consecrated to marauding assaults on their neighbors.[10] Their behavior also recalls the not-quite-parodic image of the bad servant constructed by Edgar as Mad Tom. The aggressive Boatswain represents a group not much considered heretofore, subordinates engaged short term to carry out specialized duties; other instances would include barbers, blacksmiths, physicians, midwives, bailiffs (like the one sent by Mistress Quickly to arrest Falstaff)—people whose social status might well be inferior to that of their temporary employers but whose special skills or powers sometimes give them a brief preeminence. Ariel serves Prospero in various roles—as footman, executioner (as the term is used in *King John*), steward, chamberlain, master of revels, master of horse, counselor. Gonzalo is a definitive instance of the aristocratic servant (bearing many affinities with Polonius, and also with the Duke of York in Richard II, Lafeu in *All's Well*, and the Earl of Gloucester in *King Lear*), with Adrian and Francisco as his underlings.[11]

Service is a theme of the play from early in Act I.[12] Prospero explains to Miranda how his usurping brother Antonio used the machinations of service in the court to advance his ambitions (1.2.79–116). Shortly he summons the chief agent of his power, Ariel, by the name of "servant"; Ariel in turn calls him "great master," and goes on to use other terms that imply service—"thy best pleasure," "thy strong bidding" (190–94). Ariel recounts how he has carried out his master's instructions in separating the royal ship from the rest of the Neapolitan fleet, staging the apparent wreck, dividing the court party from the crew and the King's son from his fellows. He seems pleased with himself, and Prospero is pleased, too: "thy charge / Exactly is performed" (238–39). But when the mage goes on to request "more work," Ariel resents it:

> Is there more toil? Since thou dost give me pains,
> Let me remember thee what thou has promised
> Which is not yet performed.
> *Prospero.*   How now? moody?
> What is't thou canst demand?
> *Ariel.*   My liberty.
> *Prospero.* Before the time be out? No more!
> *Ariel.*   I prithee,
> Remember I have done thee worthy service,
> Told thee no lies, made thee no mistakings, served
> Without or grudge or grumblings. Thou did promise
> To bate me a full year. (243–51)

Despite the extraordinary situation, a magician talking to an elfin sprite about magical acts performed on a mysterious and exotic island, the passage represents an arrangement similar to that between Lancelot Gobbo and Shylock. Ariel has contracted to serve Prospero for a period that appears to be 13 years. Prospero has offered to remit one year in exchange for faithful service.[13] Ariel claims that he has carried out his part of the bargain, and longs for liberty. Prospero insists on getting every last hour's worth of work: commodification, at this stage of the play, is still in force. In the exchange that follows (supplying a good deal of exposition and revealing more fully some irascible aspects of Prospero's character only hinted at in the preceding dialogue with Miranda), it transpires that the basis of the agreement is not money or other material benefits, but the very thing for which Ariel now asks, his liberty. Prospero has released the spirit from 12 years of cruel confinement in a cloven pine, in exchange for a corresponding period of service plus a year. In his anger at Ariel's presumption (which recalls Petruchio's at Grumio and the Antipholi's at the Dromii), Prospero threatens his servant with further confinement (one of the standard punishments imposed by contemporary masters on servants who got out of line, extended among others to the uppity Malvolio). The threat is sufficient to restore Ariel to at least vocally willing subordination:

> Pardon, master.
> I will be correspondent to command,
> And do my spriting gently. (298–300)[14]

Prospero responds by setting an explicit term on the relationship— "after two days / I will discharge thee"—and then a specific task:

> Go make thyself like to a nymph o' the sea. . . .
> . . . Go; hence with diligence. (301–07)

This scene firmly establishes Prospero's hierarchic and hegemonic control of Ariel; it is followed by one that confirms his corresponding control over Caliban. There are significant differences. Ariel, as we have seen, is a kind of all-purpose upper servant, analogous to, though more powerful than, Gonzalo; he has substantial freedom of movement and of action. Caliban, as Prospero explicitly says in first mentioning him, and repeats several times thereafter, is a slave. He performs the prototypical tasks of the domestic: "He does make our fire, / Fetch in our wood, and serves in offices / That profit us." And he is indispensable: "We cannot miss him" (314–17). A second difference is in the means by which Prospero keeps him in line. The mage controls the spiritual Ariel by fear only, the fear of further confinement. The bestial Caliban demands stronger and more various controls.[15] The most important is physical pain (during the play mostly only threatened, but apparently in the past frequently applied)—not unlike the beatings suffered by the Dromii and Grumio, though more inventive:

> If thou neglect'st, or dost unwillingly
> What I command, I'll rack thee with old cramps,
> Fill all thy bones with aches, make thee roar,
> That beasts shall tremble at thy din. (371–74)

A second means of control is confinement. Caliban is already confined, as Miranda says:

> . . . therefore wast thou
> Deservedly confined into this rock,
> Who hadst deserved more than a prison. (363–65)

Evidently he can only leave this rocky cell at Prospero's command; while immured, he can do no mischief (although once released, he has enough freedom of movement to fall or climb into his association with Trinculo and Stefano). Caliban thus does, indeed, inhabit a state of bondage more radical than most actual English servants, and something akin to those slaves in the New World whose status has helped to actuate the great flood of postcolonial writing about this play.

An active question here is whether his status is merely a function of the system of Eurocentric patriarchal hegemony. Servant or slave, he embodies with comically nightmarish thoroughness most of the anxieties of early modern masters. In his dialogue with Prospero and Miranda, at his best he is insolent, truculent, sullen, foul-mouthed, physically unattractive (at least by European standards), malodorous. Few English masters would have tolerated for long—or would tolerate now—a servant who, like Caliban, resisted every order, did his work only under compulsion, and returned curse for curse. His attempted rape of Miranda exposes the vulnerability of gently born Tudor and Stuart children (boys as well as girls) to the servants who normally spent much more time with them than did their parents. He, not his drunken associates, initiates the murderous plot against Prospero; in the process, he reveals family secrets and proposes to take violent advantage of his knowledge of the way the household works. For all that, he apparently participates in the tide of forgiveness that washes over the play in the final act, for whereas an attempt by a servant on the life of a master was accounted an act of petty treason, punishable by death, he, like Tranio, is merely returned to his normal status and duties (Dolon, "Subordinate"). Beyond that, there is the recurrent metaphysical imagery within which Caliban sees first Prospero, then Trinculo and Stephano, then Prospero again, as gods. And while early modern people spoke sometimes of God as love, the emotion specified as appropriate was far more often fear. For all that, the centrality of Caliban in recent criticism of the play will require us to consider his status more fully later in the chapter.

To Ariel and Caliban, we may add the nameless attendant spirits who occupy in this play the roles given in other plays to obedient, nameless, household servants and retainers. Offstage, they help Ariel carry out tasks such as the movement of the ship to safe harbor, the conveying safe ashore of the Neapolitans and Antonio, and the hunting of Caliban and his confederates. Onstage, their duties are those of the domestic servants of wealthy households involved in the entertainment of guests. They bring in and take out again the tantalizing banquet, and supply music and dancing for the masque of the goddesses—a range of duties very similar to those carried out by the servants of the Danvers and Southampton, and by the members of the King's Men as Grooms of the Chamber of James I.

In and around his treatment of the domestics, Shakespeare organizes a complex though largely implicit exploration of the role of the courtly servant (the *hop* of Holles's metaphor of hop and pole), through the speeches and actions of the Neapolitan party—Adrian, Francisco, Gonzalo, Antonio, Sebastian, and Ferdinand—and of Miranda. Ferdinand and Miranda we deal with later. Sebastian, like Don John, Claudius, Edmund, and Antonio himself, perforce serves as younger brother in a system based on primogeniture; in practical terms he serves Antonio, too, for in their dealings the latter tends to take command (in a relationship like that of Iago and Roderigo), so that the Neapolitan not only accepts from the Milanese tutelage in the arts of murder and usurpation, but also tends to follow his lead in scorning the true and loyal service of Gonzalo and the others. Antonio, the last in the line of Machiavels that runs from Aaron through Iago and Edmund, is ruler (albeit by usurpation) in his own land, the duchy of Milan. He is formally a vassal of Alonso, and offers the latter some faint, and mainly verbal, shows of servility. He sees himself, however, as having left service behind him: "My brother's servants / Were then my fellows; now they are my men" (2.1.269–70). He has earned his promotion, of course, by the Machiavel's self-centered version of volitional primacy. As Prospero himself notes, he used the mechanisms of courtly service to organize his *coup d'état*:

> Being once perfected how to grant suits,
> How to deny them, who 't'advance and who
> To trash for over-topping, new created
> The creatures that were mine, I say—or changed 'em
> Or else new-formed 'em; having both the key
> Of officer and office, set all the hearts i'th'state
> To what tune pleased his ear. . . . (1.2.79–85)

(The speech implies a court organized much like Octavius Caesar's.) Antonio finally achieved his ends by putting Milan itself into a servile position as a vassal state—"confederates . . . wi'th' King of Naples / To . . . do him homage, . . . and bend the dukedom . . . To most ignoble stooping" (111–16). Having found servants susceptible to his management during his own *coup*, he expects all of those now on the island but Gonzalo to acquiesce in the one he plans for Sebastian: "They'll take suggestion as a cat laps milk" (2.1.284), with the clear implication (normative not only to Machiavels but to most postmodern criticism) that overt self-interest drives all men. His goal in offering to murder Alonso and in suborning Sebastian to murder Gonzalo is to rid himself of the last vestiges of his own servitude, as Sebastian recognizes:

> One stroke
> Shall free thee from the tribute which thou payest,
> And I the King shall love thee. (288–90)

Of all the persons in the play, only these two fail at some point to assert in apparently sincere terms that they accept their servile state. I return to this issue later.

Adrian and Francisco join the legion of largely indistinguishable functionaries (neither is identified by name in the spoken text, and the roles are sometimes combined in performance) who swell scenes in the anterooms and throne rooms of the plays; they supply information, run routine errands, second the views of their masters. Since they are never tested, there is no way to know whether Antonio is correct in viewing them as moral ciphers who will go wherever they are led, or only as cynical, but as far as it goes, their service is exemplary. Antonio and Sebastian, betting on whether Adrian or Gonzalo will pontificate first on the castaways' situation, do imply that Adrian is a Gonzalo-in-training, who takes his cues about appropriate courtly speech and attitude from his elder (2.1.24–37). Francisco's major speech encourages Alonso to believe that his son Ferdinand has survived the wreck (113–22).[16] This is not mere sycophancy, especially to an audience that knows he speaks the truth, for the servant's call was to support the master emotionally as well as physically; and Shakespeare places Francisco's demeanor in sharp contrast with that of Sebastian and Antonio when Sebastian follows with words designed to cast the king back down: "Sir, you may thank yourself for this great loss" (123).

Gonzalo, as close as this play comes to an ideal servant like Kent, comments on the contrast: "You rub the sore / When you should bring the plaster" (137–38). He is much more fully developed—the fullest Shakespearean portrait of a senior court official after Polonius, and much more gently figured, his detractors being men we are generally invited to condemn. In his first appearance, during the storm of 1.1, he worries about the king ("Good, yet remember whom thou hast aboard" [17]), keeps his head, and closes the scene with a wry jest that keeps it in comic perspective. Prospero remembers him with great respect and affection for his charity—unlooked for from a foedary of the enemy, Naples—in supplying Prospero and Miranda with food, water, clothing, and especially magical books, in the aftermath of the *coup d'état*. Once on shore he comforts the grieving king, like Francisco; as chamberlain he also takes stock of the situation ("Here is everything advantageous to life"), notices significant facts ("Our garments . . . hold notwithstanding their freshness"), and attempts to settle and cheer the anxious party with the philosophical speculations for which he is now best known—"Had I plantation of this isle, my lord" and so on (2.1.1–9, 53–54, 63–65, 147–68).

In this disquisition, a man who moves so comfortably within the hierarchy of the court nevertheless counsels equality—"use of service, none" (151)—and hence goes farther than even Edmund or Iago in proposing to alter the customary hierarchies of early modern Europe; they wish only to make places for themselves higher up the ladder, not to lay the ladder on the ground. The structure of the speech implies that the institution of service is ultimately counterproductive, for this leveling talk precedes talk of the spontaneous abundance that renders service superfluous. The manifest impracticality of his vision (about which, of course, the incessant wisecracking of Sebastian and Antonio leaves no doubt) makes it difficult to know how we should interpret this potentially subversive view. Much will depend on whether the actor generally commands respect as well as affection from the audience, or whether he allows the character to amuse the spectators in the way the courtly mockers are amused. Either way, the subversive idea is assigned a merely speculative or fanciful status, temporally associated with the sleep that Ariel then brings upon Gonzalo, Adrian, Francisco, and Alonso (who is apparently so distracted by grief for Ferdinand that he has not heard a word) and so marginalized. And it is implicitly subverted by the fact that within every new relationship of the play—right from the outset, in the Boatswain's insistence that the fact of the storm and of the mariners' expertise in dealing with it means that the aristocrats must yield up their customary dominance—some contest for primacy goes on, just as within all those relationships carried over from before the play begins, primacy has already been established. The only exception is the relationship between Ferdinand and Miranda, in which the contest is about who shall serve, not who shall dominate. Like a good retainer, when roused from his magic sleep, Gonzalo leaps to the defense of the king ("Let's draw our weapons"), encourages him to believe his son lives still, and is evidently told off by the king to lead the search (2.1.318–22). This he undertakes until exhaustion drags him down (his fatigue recalls that of Adam in *As You Like It*). The scene of the mystic banquet follows, in which he correctly discerns the underlying gentleness and goodwill of the spirits.

The dominant elements in the character of Gonzalo are thus charity and optimism. Such a stance can be seen as an existential version of volitional primacy, making (in a literal, agential sense of the idiom) the best of things. It does not quite define him, however: he has moments when he sees, clearly enough, the dark side. In particular, although his last thought is for his wicked companions' welfare, not their punishment, he has not misunderstood the moral realities of the usurpation of Prospero's throne:

> All three of them are desperate: their great guilt,
> Like poison given to work a great time after,
> Now 'gins to bite the spirits. I do beseech you,
> That are of suppler joints, follow them swiftly,
> And hinder them from what this ecstasy
> May now provoke them to. (3.3.104–09)

I believe that his recognition of their guilt and his concern for the state of their minds and souls arises from similar concerns for himself. At his next (and last) appearance, in the final scene, he stands amazed with the others as Prospero reveals himself. Given his largely optimistic interpretation of the island heretofore, his response to Prospero's revelation is strikingly *not* optimistic:

> All torment, trouble, wonder, and amazement
> Inhabits here. Some heavenly power guide us
> Out of this fearful country! (5.1.106–08)

The reaction seems particularly odd because Prospero has welcomed the good old man in terms of marked respect—"Holy Gonzalo, honourable man . . . O good Gonzalo" (62–68); he is Prospero's "true preserver," and his good acts are "graces" (69–70). Yet Gonzalo now seems to speak from dismay, even remorse. Observe, after all, that his efforts on Prospero's behalf did not extend to actual disobedience of his orders.[17] He did not, for example, procure a sound boat rather than "a rotten carcass of a butt" (1.2.146); he certainly did not go so far as to attempt to ally himself fully with the legitimate duke rather than the usurper, perhaps by joining him in the boat. Like his counterpart in *The Winter's Tale*, Antigonus, who carries the infant Perdita off to "some remote and desert place" and exposes her there to the "protection / And favour of the climate" (3.1.176–79), his fidelity to his master makes him at least partly complicit in a potentially deadly act. Unlike Antigonus (and the sailors of his ship), he does not suffer a terrible death from the savage nature of the place. But he recognizes that savagery as an element of the island, and he does stand, apparently anxious and silent. The moment carries forward the vivid image reported by Ariel of Gonzalo mourning with the other aristocrats in the aftermath of the failed coup against Alonso: "His tears run down his beard like winter's drops / From eaves of reeds" (5.1.16–17). It seems to me that part of his reaction here may involve recollection of his complicity in a similar assault on Prospero. Thus his normal good cheer has given way to remorse. His next speech is an equivocal reply to yet another of Prospero's offers of honor:

> *Prospero.*   First, noble friend,
> Let me embrace thine age, whose honour cannot
> Be measured or confined.
>   *He embraces Gonzalo.*
> *Gonazalo.*   Whether this be
> Or be not, I'll not swear. (5.1.122–24)

The speech is no doubt normally interpreted as expressing his uncertainty as to the material reality of Prospero and his astonishing effects. Yet it can equally well sustain a more immediate and local application, to the truth of the assessment of his moral quality that Prospero has just uttered.

A similar equivocation adheres to his next speech, 80 lines further on, which follows the discovery of Ferdinand and Miranda: "I have inly wept, / Or should have spoke ere this" (203–04)—tears of joy, no doubt, for the recovery of the Prince and the union of two fair youngsters, but perhaps tears also of mingled sorrow and joy for his recognition of his own inadequacy and for his share in the general forgiveness, as the remainder of the speech also suggests:

> Look down, you gods,
> And on this couple drop a blessèd crown,
> For it is you that have chalked forth the way
> Which brought us hither. (205–08)

Hither, that is, not only to the geographical but to the moral and emotional places where they find themselves, which he summarizes handsomely at the end of his next speech: a place where Claribel found a husband, Ferdinand a wife, Prospero his dukedom, and, finally and climactically, "all of us ourselves, / When no man was his own" (215–16).

In the aftermath of a direct confrontation with the moral obligations of status (of both servants and masters), the integrity thus recovered is not merely moral and psychological but also theological: Gonzalo witnesses, albeit discreetly, to an infusion of grace—that pouring out of the oil of divinity for which good service—subtly invoked in the final clause—is a preparation but not a guarantee.[18] It lets Gonzalo recover his habitual role as the enthusiastic optimist, bearer of good news and cracker of jokes. His final speech in the play's last scene, like his final speech in its first (which it explicitly recalls), turns off solemnity but also invokes divinity:

> O look, sir, look, sir, here is more of us!
> I prophesied if a gallows were on land
> This fellow could not drown. (*To the Boatswain*) Now, blasphemy,
> Thou swear'st *grace* o'erboard: not an oath on shore?
> Hast thou no mouth by land? What is the news?
>   (219–23; emphasis added)

The transition is social as well as tonal, from the courtly servants to the domestic, down the hierarchy; for the debriefing of the Boatswain leads on to the reappearance of Stefano, Trinculo, and Caliban. As I suggested earlier, these three have turned themselves into an uproarious parody of the retainer band, with Stefano as gift-giver (the gift being the wine he dispenses in his *al fresco* mead-hall). During their first scene together Caliban moves from being his worshipper ("I do adore thee") to being his subject ("I'll swear myself thy subject"); the contrast with his enslavement to Prospero is sharp enough to register as "freedom" (2.2.132, 144, 177). In the second scene, the mood grows more martial: Caliban serves Stefano rather than Trinculo because the latter is "not valiant," and from offering to find berries and sticks and to bear wood for them rather than for the mage, he advances to the murderous plot against Prospero—a comic refraction, of course, of the plot of Antonio and Sebastian against Alonso. Revealingly, as Caliban begins to think in the same way as the scheming aristocrats, his speeches shift from prose to blank verse, and his language to the language of courtly service:

> I thank my noble lord. Wilt thou be pleased
> To hearken once again to the suit I made to thee? (3.2.36–37)[19]

For all his temerity in transferring his allegiance from Prospero to Stefano and proposing the assault, Caliban cannot bring himself so far as to assume the full lead role—Macbeth's role—in the plot: ". . . *thou* mayst knock a nail into his head," he says (59; emphasis added)—in contrast with Antonio, who fears not to break through the divinity that hedges kings.[20] Yet it is he who sustains the plot despite the vacillations of the castaways, encouraging his nominal leader by assuring him of the infidelity of the other servants (echoing Antonio's assessment of the Neapolitan courtiers)—"they all do hate him / As rootedly as I" (89–90)[21]—and upping the estimate of the booty by including Miranda. At the end of the scene it is he who leads the group off, following Ariel's distracting music, with Stefano behind and Trinculo bringing up the rear. When the three reappear after their detour through the "filthy-mantled pool," he is still in the lead, and issuing instructions: "Pray you, tread softly" (4.1.194). His fellow marauders have lost some confidence in him—"Do you hear, monster, if I should take a displeasure against you, look you" (201–02)—and he is obliged to return to the language of servitude: "Good you my lord, give me thy favour still" (203). But the Neapolitans shortly reveal their unworthiness to be even followers when the "fripperies" Ariel has hung near the cave mouth distract them from their fell purpose, and all of Caliban's exhortations cannot prevent his troops from looting before they have secured the town.[22] In the end, they force him all the way back into his slave's role, as beast of burden

> *Stefano.*   . . . Go to, carry this.
> *Trinculo.*   And this.
> *Stefano.*   Ay, and this. (249–51)

before all three are driven off in terrified disarray by Ariel's spirits in the form of dogs. The episode is almost certainly designed to remind viewers of the welcome commonly offered vagabonds (sometimes discharged servants) hoping to steal laundry from the clotheslines or shrubbery of rural English homes: so low have these pitiful descendants of the Viking raiders sunk.

We meet them next after the step down the social hierarchy initiated by Gonzalo as noted above. Stefano evidently sees them as still a united band, offering each other mutual support against a hostile world:

> *Stefano.* Every man shift for all the rest, and let no man take care for himself; for all is but fortune. (5.1.259–60)[23]

Many editors (among them Kermode, Orgel, Ribner, and Righter) gloss this as a piece of drunken confusion: the butler's intention is to say in effect, "Every man for himself," but it comes out backward. If I am right in discerning in this group the tattered remnants of the retainer tradition, however, the commitment to solidarity, however badly enacted under pressure, will remain in effect as a public ideal. The remark does indicate his resistance to informing nurture—as Aldous Huxley somewhere says, experience teaches only the teachable—for it was his shifting for himself in the matter of gaudy duds that broke their discipline on their first approach to the cave. Caliban appropriately ignores the appeal. He has been driven by "dry convulsions," shortened sinews, and "agéd cramps" (4.1.255–56) back into fearful respect for Prospero. When the mage orders him to take the other two into the cell and do their servants' work by readying it to entertain the visitors ("trim it handsomely"—though perhaps with a more general metaphoric sense, something like "behave yourself according to your station"), he obeys with seeming alacrity (no more grumbling), recognizes his folly in preferring Stefano to Prospero, and resolves to change his ways, once more in terms that invoke the theological context of good service:

> Ay, that I will; and I'll be wise hereafter,
> And seek for grace. What a thrice-double ass
> Was I to take this drunkard for a god,
> And worship this dull fool! (5.1.298–301)

He has apparently been set in charge, and confirmed in a kind of superiority for which his de facto leadership of the retainer raid has prepared him.[24]

The resolution of this part of the plot has angered postmodern commentators offended by an obedience apparently extorted by force, and by a pardon conditional on Caliban's accepting traditional patriarchal hegemony; in some recent productions the Caliban, confirming that he has an indomitably independent nature on which Prospero's hierarchizing nurture will never stick, has given the speech only the most grudging utterance.[25] Within the guidelines of late twentieth-century leftist thought, the refusal to celebrate Prospero's restoration to power is unimpeachable. It does, to be sure, put the critic outside the reestablished circle, like Antonio and Sebastian (though on the opposite side), in a Darwinian (more properly, Spencerian) world where every relationship at every moment must be contested. From inside or outside, however, the critic can ask some questions. Has Prospero *learned* anything from these instances of faithful and faithless service, and the range in between (besides the political usefulness of perpetual suspicion)? Does he exhibit any deeper and more generative understanding of the master's proper behavior here in the close of the play?

I tend to disagree with Greenblatt (*Negotiations* 146), and others who see Prospero's attempt to reform Caliban as "having comprehensively failed" (Gillies 150) and Shakespeare as inscribing here a somewhat reactionary image of indigenous New Worlders as "naturally inferior," which runs counter to his "career-long tendency" to offset "profound ethnic difference" by "dignity of character" (150, 151).[26] The issue turns on two points. The first is whether Caliban does, indeed, represent the New World, or whether, as Meredith Skura has argued, the New World references that gather around him are essentially similitudes that make only part of the construction of an essentially unique figure. The second is whether or not Caliban's "I'll be wise hereafter / And seek for grace" is to be taken at its face value. If so, the failure was not comprehensive, only temporary; second time's a charm—the speech then is not simply incantatory, like the ephemeral images of tempests and banquets, only a kind of radically enhanced lyric, whose effects fade with the final chord, but something grounded in discipline and experience. Generically, the process enacts that fundamental pattern of comedy in which rigid causation, such that foolish or inappropriate acts necessarily entail irreversible suffering, is suspended—for instance, Tranio not getting his nose slit despite Vincentio's threat. Socially, the process depends on the superiority of experience to precept and of love to fear as pedagogical devices: the Caliban who declined to respond to Prospero's exhortations or to his cramps and pinches is persuaded by his time with Stephano and Trinculo that the willing service of a worthy master can elevate rather than demean the servant.[27] Psychologically, the process may rest, as Skura proposes, on changes in Prospero himself. Having initially projected "his own repressed fantasies of omnipotence and lust" onto Caliban, his subsequent rejection of the darkness in himself opens the way toward a state from which acts of reconciliation can freely flow (310–11).[28]

Some critics treat all the actions that occur on the island as somehow directly responsive to Prospero's will, so that he controls Alonso and Ferdinand and Miranda as he wishes to control Caliban; thus Greenblatt: "To compel others to be 'all knit up / In their distractions,' to cause a paralyzing anxiety, is the dream of power, a dream perfected over bitter years of exile" (*Negotiations* 143). In this view, all the other characters except perhaps Ariel become actors in Prospero's script. Nothing in the text explicitly supports this view, however; it seems to me that Prospero behaves much more like a director using improvisational techniques to rehearse a play than like a writer. His power does bring the Neapolitan party to the island, and he does apparently arrange to draw Ferdinand, the one important member of it he does not already know, away from the others and under Prospero's survey and that of his daughter. Thereafter his actions mainly respond to initiatives that arise unprovoked by him from within the others according to their natures—love from Ferdinand and Miranda, murder and usurpation from Antonio and Sebastian and Caliban, service from Gonzalo. In other words, Prospero needs initiation into the understanding of the power of volitional primacy and willing service as much as anyone in the play or in the audience: I would describe *The Tempest* as a theatrical *Basilicon doron*, a heuristic that completes the education of a prince.

We can develop this proposition further through a literal interpretation of a clause in Caliban's last speech: "I'll be wise hereafter, / And seek for grace": that is, not only that he will think before he acts and act so as to be in a position to get rewards (he did that, in effect, in his service of Stephano), but that wisdom itself consists in so leading one's life as to be ready to receive the unsought, unearned, unconditional dispensation of divine or cosmic bounty. Prospero himself has been blessed by an almost miraculous opportunity to recover his lost dukedom and discomfit his erstwhile enemies.[29] In taking advantage of it, he has apparently come close to forfeiting the moral superiority that validates his actions. But provoked by Ariel, or at least confirmed by Ariel in a decision already made by himself, he has resolved to side with reason, not passion, and to take a vengeance that is only mental and moral, not physical and political, a tacit request (not even a demand) for penitence (5.1.25–30). (A decision that his treatment of Caliban at the end of the act carries out quite literally.)

The context of Prospero's resolution is complex. Most immediately, it comprises a powerful provocation to revenge, already present at the beginning of the play, now refreshed by the frustrated assault of the drunken servants, which adds the insult of violated hierarchy to the injury of projected murder—an injury in its way more grave than the original injury of Antonio and Alonso, since it aims at his life, not just his power. It will not do, of course, to take this too seriously, since the threat is comic.[30] It does, however, recall the actual injury of the usurpation, and the threatened assault on Alonso. The larger context (which will draw us back toward the issue of service) is set forth in the masque of the goddesses, promising the unconditional abundance of the good gifts of the earth to Ferdinand and Miranda. These two, in the terms of the present argument, are the play's fullest image of grace in action, in all the senses of that term. Most particularly, it is important to observe that their love is a gift, unsought by them and, if sought by Prospero, not something whose action he could guarantee: they both utter their commitment at first sight, without any prompting from him, though the utterance is more striking in the prince, since he has had earlier opportunities to love, now believes he carries the political responsibilities of the kingdom of Naples, and yet offers to wed her on the spot.

Love thus is grace; it does not come because it has been earned by some patient apprenticeship, even by some daring action such as Romeo's invasion of the Capulet household, or in satisfaction of some established set of criteria—good family, good dowry, good education, modesty, chastity, and so on, none of which Miranda has yet confirmed.[31] Once granted, however, love verifies itself in acts of mutual service.[32] Ferdinand, indeed, serves more fully and responsively than anyone in the play, even Gonzalo. Prospero strips him of his sword and his royal identity, and by assigning him Caliban's badges and diet, assigns him status as a mere slave:

> Come;
> I'll manacle thy neck and feet together:
> Sea-water shalt thou drink; thy food shall be
> The fresh-brook mussels, wither'd roots, and husks
> Wherein the acorn cradled. (1.2.464–68)[33]

After some initial resistance, Ferdinand embraces his servitude: the loss of father, friends, and freedom is nothing,

> Might I but through my prison once a day
> Behold this maid: all corners else o' the earth

>   Let liberty make use of; space enough
>   Have I in such a prison. (494–97)[34]

Prospero imposes the servitude to test the boy's love. Stephen Greenblatt's argument that Prospero's actions toward the others are designed to arouse "a salutary anxiety" deserves attention (*Negotiations* 144). So does his suggestion that "evacuating . . . the majestic vision" of the nuptial masque, with its "majestic vision of plenitude" is meant to make Ferdinand " 'cheerful'—secure in the consciousness that life is a dream" (145). A more satisfactory reading, however, proposes that for all its fantastic qualities, the island serves primarily to force those who inhabit there (including Prospero himself) to confront and accept their existential situations for what they are. Alonso as ruler needs to recognize that the short-term advantages of usurpation and merely dynastic marriage may be offset by longer range consequences. Antonio and Sebastian and the drunken servants need to accept, maybe to choose, their subordinate status. Ferdinand and Miranda, young and dizzy with love, need to recognize that Adam's curse fell on kings as well as gardeners. Life is precisely *not* a dream. The good things of this world sometimes come unsought, but must usually be gained and must always be sustained by labor—by service. Such recognition is the necessary precondition for the assertion of volitional primacy and true service. It may be peculiarly important that it come to people like Ferdinand, partly because the conditions of their lives tend to insulate them from quotidian realities, partly because their own dreams of power can bring misery to so many others. Both of these conditions appear in the history of Prospero himself; *his* recognition is a necessary precondition for *his* effective service of those under his control, on the island and, subsequently, back in Milan.[35]

In Ferdinand's case the service to which he is called is, at least initially, to Miranda; for her sake he is ready to sacrifice all that has previously mattered to him:

>   Hear my soul speak.
>   The very instant that I saw you did
>   My heart fly to your service; there resides
>   To make me slave to it. And for your sake
>   Am I this patient log-man. (3.1.63–67)

This is the most striking exercise of volitional primacy in the play, a man who thinks himself a king going out to meet a servitude—"fly to your service"—more complete than anyone's but Caliban's, sharing Caliban's task, giving up (metaphorically, at least) his very humanity, passing from prince to billet of wood.[36] Miranda proves her worthiness by joining him in work, posture, and terminology, expressing the central value of volitional primacy by noting that "I should do it / With much more ease, for my good will is to it, / And yours it is against" (29–31). Ferdinand, however, has said as much himself: "the mistress which I serve quickens what's dead, / And makes my labours pleasures" (6–7)—remember my earlier emphasis on the core of joy at the center of freely elected service. Indeed, if we take him literally, service is life ("quickens what's dead") itself. All this comes to a focus in their exchange at the end of the scene, after they have assured themselves of their mutual, freely elected affection:

> *Miranda.* . . . I am your wife, if you will marry me;
> You may deny me; but I'll be your servant,
> Whether you will or no.
> *Ferdinand.* My mistress, dearest;
> And I thus humble ever.
> *Miranda.* My husband, then?
> *Ferdinand.* Ay, with a heart as willing
> As bondage e'er of freedom: here's my hand.
> *Miranda.* And mine, with my heart in't. . . . (83–91)

Indeed, she seizes primacy away by preempting his proposal of marriage, and by insisting that she serves independent of his will. But this is not a contest. Ferdinand, too, speaks of bondage freely chosen. The editors are virtually unanimous in glossing *willing* as *desirous*, so that lines 90–91 can be paraphrased "With a heart as desirous of it as bondage is of freedom" (Kermode ed. 156n.). Holding the tradition of the Cranmerian paradox in view, however, I would propose an alternative, perhaps superior reading: "with a heart as willing as true bondage is ever willing true freedom." In any case, if she is first with the words, he is first with the essential gesture, the taking of hands that is the visual expression of betrothal.

This willing exchange of servitudes infuses joy into much of the remainder of the play. It is immediately followed, to be sure, by twin parodies of right service acted out by two pairs of human characters who imitate the two elemental social levels of early modern service, Stephano and Trinculo at the lower, Sebastian and Antonio at the higher end of the scale. (Note the ways in which they illustrate the agonistic masculine nature described by Ong and discussed in chapter 5.) These are characters in whom essentially selfish attitudes seem deeply enough imbued that even Ariel's mystical interventions cannot produce a real change of heart, characters whose nature repels nurture of any kind—more precisely, from whom the good nature that produces good service has been by bad nature or nurture somehow driven off:

> Flesh and blood,
> You, brother mine, that entertained ambition,
> Expelled remorse and nature, whom, with Sebastian—
> Whose inward pinches [like Caliban's outward ones]
>   therefore are most strong—
> Would here have killed your king. I do forgive you,
> Unnatural though thou art. . . . (5.1.74–79)[37]

In this connection, it is worth noting that when confronted with his villainy, Antonio retreats into silence. He makes no response to Prospero's forgiveness, and his only speech in the remainder of the play is a trivial aside whose final word invokes the commodifying that has dominated his behavior from the beginning:

> . . . one of them
> Is a plain fish, and no doubt marketable. (5.1.268–69)

It is impossible to imagine him continuing to house with Prospero in a renewed Milan; I much prefer to see him as akin to Autolycus or Parolles, wheeling and scheming through some kind of marginal life, perhaps in the company of his accomplice, Sebastian. At any rate, from this time forth he never does speak word in the play and thus, like Iago, achieves an upside down triumph of volitional primacy.

By contrast, however, the scene in which the lovers exchange servitudes seems to inspire Prospero (more accurately, to offer the audience a Prospero reflecting what it might have learned from the scene), for when we next see him with Ariel the testy, snippy dialogue in which Ariel earlier asked for freedom and Prospero put his servant off has given way to mutual expressions of love: "Do you love me, master? No?" "Dearly, my delicate Ariel" (4.1.48–49). Their next exchange deepens this sense of harmony; when Prospero calls, Ariel responds, "Thy thoughts I cleave to" (the verb recalls the cloven pine in which the mage has earlier threatened to confine his sulky sprite; it also echoes the Biblical injunction to husbands and wives). Ariel then reports, with obvious delight, the punishment he has so far dished out to the drunkards by leading them into the pond (scum in the scum), and goes on at Prospero's request to coax them with the fripperies to reveal both their plot and their ineptitude and then to set the spiritual dogs on them.

But Ariel's pleasure in the discomfiture of low-class scoundrels gives way to a more melting mood. The next exchange swings on a prime instance of the kind of moral support (in a more than usually literal sense of that phrase) that early modern orthodoxy asked of good servants, as Ariel (now anything but amused), describes the misery of the tormented aristocrats, in terms that call for mercy:

> Your charm so strongly works 'em,
> That if you now beheld them, your affections
> Would become tender.
> *Prospero.*   Dost thou think so, spirit?
> *Ariel.*   Mine would, sir, were I human. (5.1.17–20)

We cannot say that Ariel's intervention determines Prospero's choice of "the rarer action, virtue over vengeance": much in the previous scenes has tended that way. It certainly confirms the choice, however, by helping Prospero link "reason" and "feeling" (26, 21)—so often dichotomized. At this point, Prospero can be said to have served Alonso, at least, and perhaps Caliban (if not Antonio and Sebastian) in one of the senses in which Luther's priests were to serve their flocks, by bringing the wicked to penitence. At this point, he can only commend their spirits to a higher mercy[38]—as he commends his own, calling attention to his own penitence by invoking the tradition of *memento mori* ("every third thought shall be my grave") and asking the audience to intercede for him:

> And my ending is despair,
> Unless I be relieved by prayer,
> Which pierces so, that it assaults
> Mercy itself, and frees all faults.
> As you from crimes would pardoned be,
> Let your indulgence set me free. (Epi. 15–20)

In the context of that memorable phrase in the Collect for Peace, identifying *service* and *freedom*, this last word of the play cannot but be powerfully significant. It has rung like a bell in this work—11 occurrences, more than any other play except the much longer *Othello* (also much occupied with service, as we have seen)—plus seven occurrences of *freedom* (far more than any other play), one of *freely*, and one of *frees*. Six of these occur in the last scene and epilogue.[39] To these we may add three uses of *liberty* (one in the final scene), and repeated instances of such words as *confine, release, untie.* There are onstage representations of bondage such as that of the aristocrats frozen in their guilt by Ariel's power, and reports of things like Ariel's imprisonment in the tree,

Caliban's immurement between his episodes of labor, Ferdinand in manacles, and the confinement of the crew in the hold of the ship.[40] To these we may add recurrent metaphors on similar lines, such as that with which Prospero comments on the dazed state of his former enemies:

> The charm dissolves apace,
> And as the morning steals upon the night,
> Melting the darkness, so their rising senses
> Begin to chase the ignorant fumes that mantle
> Their clearer reason. (5.1.64–68)

The epilogue is especially rich: *confined*, *release*, *frees*, and *free* in 20 tetrameter lines (this is the traditional rhetorical order of climax). There are multiple freedoms in view. The Neapolitans have been freed from the toils of Prospero's spells and (some of them, at least) the guilt of their earlier wrongdoing. Alonso, burdened with grief at the loss of a son occasioned by an earlier marriage we must suppose to have a merely commodified basis, rather than the relation of love between Ferdinand and Miranda, is released from the tormenting shackles of remorse (the sentiment Antonio explicitly cannot feel) and anxiety—the stage direction at his entrance calls for him to make "a frantic gesture" (5.1.58). He is now free to enjoy a properly mutual relationship with Prospero and Milan, the spectacle of his son and his miraculous wife, and the prospect of grandchildren. His courtiers, especially Gonzalo, can return to the life they know and seem to like. Ferdinand has earned his way out of the servitude imposed on him by Prospero and into the bonds of marriage, which, nonetheless, freely elected as they are, promise sexual freedom and freedom from solitude at the very least. Miranda, joining him in those bonds, will escape her isolation as the only person of her age and sex, and gain a productive place in a brave new world—she seems to have had no proper function in the old one. It is significant that the decisive image of them in this scene is of their playing chess— a game in which only the tempo—and the quality of play—can unbalance perfect equality. It is further significant that the game gives Miranda, at least, a further opportunity to subordinate her interests to those of her beloved: having charged him with cheating, she goes on by an act of her will to convert that cheating into "fair play" (5.1.174–77).[41] Caliban has at least temporarily escaped the shackles of drunkenness and folly; it seems probable (though it is never made explicit) that when Prospero departs he will remain as king of the isle, such as that monarchy might be, given the absence of any being like himself to rule over or with.[42]

Ariel, by or to whom many of the uses of *free* and *freedom* have been addressed, as the being most galled by constraints, will explicitly, of course, be released from his servitude to Prospero and his fear of the cloven pine. Prospero himself will be liberated from the island and his anger. His antepenultimate utterance of the play proper—the last, significantly, completes the freeing of Ariel—recognizes the continuing bondage of sin and death, and hence of the human nature of which they are the inescapable consequences. But his renunciation of book and staff, and hence of the *super*natural solicitings they symbolize, bespeaks a willing acceptance of his merely human state that in terms of the great paradox must lead to freedom in service.[43]

Prospero goes on, then, to invoke, in his final actions as de facto ruler of the island and in a prelude to his resumed identity as Duke of Milan, that form of grace, of unconditional generosity, that is forgiveness. This is the essential realization of the spirit of comedy—Dante calls it divine. It seems to me related at its base with willing service, in that both spring from the subordination of the self-interest of the servant or the forgiver to that of the served or the forgiven. In a way, willing service *is* forgiveness: the servant forgives the master for enjoying (in either sense of the term) the benefits that accrue from the merely circumstantial inequality of their status. Both ideals carry an implicit burden, to be sure: they invite the beneficiary to respond in kind, to enter into a reciprocal mutuality of the kind modeled by Miranda and Ferdinand.[44] But such reciprocity will govern the attitudes and actions of the inhabitants of an ideal community—a community like the utopias of Gonzalo or Thomas More. And the context of Prospero's statements of forgiveness is the imminent return of all these temporary co-sojourners to their own original communities, of Milan, Naples, and the island, where, having undergone the heuristic of the island, they can henceforth lead better lives.

The language of the previous paragraphs—indeed, the previous chapters—presents the persons of the play as real people. They are not, of course; they are mere dramatic images, strings of words sometimes physically reinforced by the inflections and gestures of actors. From the theatrically heuristic point of view, these images are presented for the delight and use of spectators and readers. And the heuristic structure of the play centers, I am arguing, on ideas of service that would have been powerfully present in the minds and lives of the audience at the Globe in 1611, and that are less obviously but not perhaps less powerfully relevant to ours. In this structure, a series of speeches and acts of servants who are refractory (the Boatswain and Caliban), grudging (Ariel), ineffectual (Gonzalo), or even deeply and treacherously subversive

(Antonio and Sebastian, the drunken conspirators), set the stage for a potent instance of willing and generous service, right service, by Miranda and Ferdinand, which is then followed by further invocations of not only right service but also of the kind of service that arises from right mastery, in the actions of Ariel, Caliban, Alonso, and Prospero himself.[45] And by representations of that mode of service we call forgiveness—the service specifically requested by Prospero, now in his character as a mere performer, merely one of those immaterial and fugitive spirits so memorably invoked in his earlier speech to Ferdinand after the breaking of the vision of the nuptial masque.[46] The speech reminds us that in the discursive marketplace of a play, the logic of events is not so much truly causal as phenomenal, although some images, such as that of Prospero observing right service and Caliban seeing up-close the differences in masters, can be seen to have causal force within the fable of the play. And it is by means of such a phenomenal logic that the play has urged the value of service.

I am not arguing here that *The Tempest* is itself, to borrow a descriptor from Stephen Greenblatt, a land of Cockaigne. The end of the play, in consonance with its beginning and middle, has patches of deep shadow. There seems little likelihood that Stephano and Trinculo, should they chance to come by a barrel of sack while free of their masters' immediate control for an hour or two, would not get rebelliously drunk, and perhaps fantasize once more an inversion of the commonwealth that would bring them atop the hierarchy. Apparently unrepentant, Sebastian remains to threaten Alonso and Ferdinand, Antonio to trouble the dreams of Prospero and Miranda. The lovers, like all of Shakespeare's married personages and like us, will ineluctably face the hazards of childbearing, parenthood, illness, old age. Prospero himself plans to direct one-third of the life that remains to him to contemplation of his impending death. The questions the play has raised about the validity of the established order, patriarchal, radically hierarchical, commodified, Eurocentric, which postmodern criticism has quite rightly examined in detail, will have as much claim on the memories of the audience as the spectacle of the two lovers at play in their secure alcove. Stephen Orgel finds that "Shakespeare, in the development of his comedy, increasingly finds the promised restorations and marriages of comic conclusions inadequate to reconcile the conflicts that comedy has generated. This is not to say that Shakespearian comedy does not end happily, but that its happy ending does not exhaust the energies of the drama" (ed. *Tempest* 55; see also Pierce). Still, it is that spectacle, not the recalcitrance of the younger brothers or the echoes of colonialism, that occupies the center of Act 5. And it is Prospero, not Caliban or Antonio or even Ferdinand, who gets the last word, with its emphasis on freedom and service, freedom *in* service.

We end by noting that, as he stepped out of character, the actor of this role began his own return and that of his fellows from their mastery over the playhouse and its occupants to their condition as servants of James I, the King's Men, one of them preparing to exchange the crown of Naples for a workaday jacket with a servant's badge. And the audience, too, was about to be loosed, by their applause, from the spatial confinement of the playhouse, the perceptual, emotional and intellectual enthrallment of the play, and perhaps, in the long run, from one or another of the inhibitions on their ability to see truth and follow it. Because nobody except the actors is obliged to attend a play, that confinement, that esthetic and emotional and ethical servitude, was, and is still, freely chosen, perhaps repeatedly chosen, on grounds that, I believe, spring from such a recognition of our situational inadequacies as is the necessary prelude to initiatives of volitional primacy, of willing service, and of the existential joys inherent in both.

NOTES

1 The Paradox of Service and Freedom

1. Booty 60.
2. In the oldest surviving manuscript of the so-called Gelasian sacramentary, the opening phrase drops *caritatis* (H. A. Wilson 272). The first occurrence of the *servire/regnare* formula I can find is as follows: *jugum enim ejus obedientiae merito est suave, cui servire est regnare.* This is from a sermon on Matt. 6, formerly attributed to Augustine but now ascribed to other fifth-century authors, Pseudo-Maximus of Turin or perhaps Eusebius of Emesa (no. lxiv in *P.L.* 39, 1866). See Dekkers 140. My thanks to James J. O'Donnell for this reference.
3. This is the version in the English edition of 1545, explicitly authorized by "the King and the Clergy . . . none other to be used throughout his dominions." But the prayer appears in this place without significant differences in all of the hundreds of surviving books of hours in both Latin and English.
4. The prayer it replaced continued and continues to be heard; it was transferred to the corresponding spot in the service of Evening Prayer.
5. On this point, see Lindberg 686.
6. Most former monks continued in various forms of religious employment, but some needed to find secular employment. Nuns returned to their families; though officially forbidden to marry, a few seem to have done so. Lay servants received good severance pay and most seem to have found places in secular households (Dickens 172–74).
7. The Bible is quoted throughout from Lloyd Berry's edition of the Geneva translation.
8. The point is echoed in 2 Cor. 12:9: "And [the Lord] sayde unto me, My grace is sufficient for thee: for my strength is made perfect in weakness."
9. A comment by George Downame (1609) suggests the possibility that the Christian paradox is developed from a pagan one: he proposes to "refute the paradox of the Stoicks, who held that the wise men of the world were only free, when they also, being not freed by Christ, were and are no better than seruants" (17).
10. The passage also echoes 1 Pet. 2:20: "For what praise is it, if when ye be buffeted for your fautes, you take it paciently? but and if when ye do wel, ye suffer *wrong* and take it paciently, this is acceptable to God."
11. "Haec est vera, haec perfecta, haec sola religio, per quam Deo reconciliari pertinet ab animae, de qua quaerimus, magnitudinem, qua se libertate dignam

facit: nam ille ab omnibus liberat, *cui servire* omnibus utilissimum est, et in cujus servitio placere perfecta et sola libertas est" (*Opera* 1.732; emphasis added). According to Martin R. Dudley, the crucial phrase in the Collect, "whose service is perfect freedom," comes from a prayer by St. Augustine, but he does not specify the precise source (120). If it exists, I have been unable to identify it. The closest I have been able to come is a marginal note in a work by a seventeenth-century clergyman, John Denison, giving the pre-Cranmer form of the paradox, and referring it to "Augustine, *de temp. ser.* 182": "*iugum eius [ejus obedientiae] merito est suaue, cui seruire est regnare.*" See earlier, n. 2.

12. "*Ipso vero qui vobis preest non se existemet potestate dominante sed caritate serviente felicem*": "Let not him who is set over you consider himself fortunate in power, as governing, but in charity, as serving" (Clark 18).

13. The Latin is *sciatque sibi oportere prodesse magis quam praeesse,* suggesting that the *servire/regnare* formula from the Latin collect has influenced the translator but not the original compiler of the order.

14. He cites as primary scriptural authorities for the right understanding of service Gal. 2:4 and 5:13, and 1 Cor. 6:12, 7:21–23, 9:19–22 (25.473–74).

15. There are conspicuous exceptions, notably the parable of the disobedient tenants (Matt. 21:33–41; Mark 12:1–9; Luke 20:9–16—one of the few parables that appears in all three synoptic gospels). In the Hebrew Bible, the touchstone is Ahithophel, whom Luther identifies as the definitive wicked servant (*Comm. Psalm* 101, *Works* 13.179).

16. The reference is actually to Matt. 20:26–27, with parallels in the other synoptics.

17. This commentary and the one on Titus cited below were actually sets of lectures that Luther delivered at the University of Wittenberg, and have survived as notes taken by his friend George Rörer; they were not published until much later (1 Tim. in 1797; Titus not until 1902). Thus, they are not texts we can point to as potential sources or direct influences on the theology and sociology of Cranmer and other English writers. Nevertheless, they do display Luther's thinking, and the ideas are likely to have been disseminated by his students and friends.

18. A similar tone appears in a prayer "Of Servants" included in the miscellaneous intercessions of the Church of England Primer (1553), and obviously intended to be used by servants in their own daily devotions: "O Lorde Jesu Christ, we are commaunded by thy blessed apostles, that we shoulde honoure and obey oure bodily maisters in feare and trembling, not only if they be good and courteous, but also thoughe they be frowarde, & serue them: not unto the eye as menne pleasers, but with singleness of heart, not churlishly aunswerynge them agayne, nor pykynge, stealynge or conveyinge away anye parte of their goods, uniustly, but shewing al good faithfulnes vnto our maisters, as thoughe we serued God and not men: Graunte me grace I most humblye beseech thee, so to serue my maister & my superiours, that there maye be founde no fault in me, but that I, behauing myselfe upryghtlye, iustlye, faythfullye, and truelye in my vocation, may doe worshyppe to the doctrine of thee my God and saviour in all thyngs" (Qvv–Qvir). Phrases

from this, such as "picking and stealing," recur constantly in early modern sermons and treatises. There was ground for such anxiety; one authority cites PRO LS13/280 as evidence that a significant cause of the financial problems of James was the incessant pilfering of the royal servants (Akrigg *Pageant* 89).

19. I find it highly interesting that the passage goes on to talk about the images of service in Plautus and Terence—a development that moves us toward the application of these considerations to Shakespeare. "If you read the comedies [as most adolescent scholars in early modern Europe did], you will see what the poets think about slaves—good-for-nothing fellows doing things in such a way that they neglect their duties to their masters." The remark is not altogether fair to New Comic servants, especially the wily ones who go to a good deal of trouble to advance their masters' interests. But the point is to establish a rhetorical contrast with the dutiful if sadly rare servant who follows his orders to the letter: "if he does that, he is saved" (29.60).

20. There is perhaps a distant echo of these ideas in Étienne de la Boétie's *De la servitude volontaire* (ca. 1550). He seems to have had Protestant sympathies, but his focus on formal political relationships—specifically, monarchy—rather than those that are either religious or personal leads him to well-known statements about the radical undesirability of any kind of servitude.

21. According to Packer and Duffield (349, 354), Cranmer's library included two editions of Chrysostom's works, plus an edition of his commentaries on the Bible, including Galatians, Ephesians, and Colossians (Basle 1536). In the early 1540s, when Cranmer first began work on the reformed liturgy, there was a striking spate of English editions of Chrysostom's homilies, in Greek, Latin, and English.

22. Strier observes that the servant who resists wrongful orders—a concept that we explore in detail in chapter 5—acts out the ideals of the radical Protestant theologians ("Faithful Servants" 119).

23. Strier observes that the question of "limits of obedience" was constantly debated: "both the humanist and the Reformation traditions were ambiguous and self-contradictory" ("Faithful Servants" 104), and notes a development in the period from "a concern with the maintenance of order to a concern with corrupt and corruption-inducing authority" (111). The development anticipates the tendency of postmodern treatments of service to emphasize the repressive and coercive arguments over the liberal.

24. Ridley calls Cranmer "almost a Lutheran by conviction" (259); Hall says his "theological sympathies were clearly Lutheran" (27).

25. Henry, at least, insisted on this kind of subservience; even so assertive a person as Wolsey claimed on his deathbed that "I have often kneeled before him, the space sometimes of three hours, to dissuade him from his will and appetite: but I could never dissuade him therefrom" (Hutchinson 20). But there were also many occasions when Cranmer "stood against Henry, in defense of what he thought to be religious truth, a perilous matter" (Hall 27).

26. This echoes the passage from Augustine's *De quantitatae animis* quoted earlier in n. 12.

27. Burnett surveys this literature from a very different perspective, choosing to emphasize elements of anxiety and *ressentiment* ("Treatises"). Kronenfeld finds a strongly marked strain of "Christian egalitarianism or 'spiritual equality' " in early modern nonconformists (126–69); she is less ready than I to find the concept within the Establishment, or to extend it to quotidian as well as to spiritual activity (139). But she argues that there was a core of common values that was the basic substratum of all the competing early modern ideologies (246), particularly important for assessing probable audience response to particular dramatic moments and theatrical gestures.

28. Denison's marginal note cites the Augustinian sermon cited earlier in n. 2.

29. My thanks to Debora Shuger for this reference. Baynes's and Herbert's are the only unmistakable echoes of Cranmer's formula I have found.

30. The city acting companies had been forced by the Statute of Artificers and various London ordinances to seek formal affiliation as servants of protecting magnates; hence the Admiral's Men, the Lord Chamberlain's Men, etc.; we will see more of this in chapter 2 (Gurr 29–30).

31. The view places me at odds with materialists such as Sommerville: "The equality of Jew and Greek, slave and free, male and female was strictly confined to the spiritual sphere . . . it had no necessary implications for social and political relations" (50–51); she is writing about women, but the position holds true for other subordinates as well.

32. A comparable view appears in Horst Weinstock's study of "Loyal Service," though without the historical materials presented here. He distinguishes the moral and psychological grounds visible in Shakespeare from those in "Kyd, Green, Marlowe, Jonson, Webster, or other Elizabethan or Jacobean dramatists" (470).

2   The Hop and the Pole: The Limits of Materialism

1. I have already named Burnett. Neill's more ideologically complex study will get detailed treatment later. Other critics cited in this book whose work I would place in this class are Barker and Hulme, Belsey, Breight, Charnes, Dolan, Greenblatt, Hunt, Moisan, Newman, Prager, Sheen, Skura, Sommerville, and Willis.

2. Hoffman begins his treatment of Gramsci by observing that "classical Marxism, in emphasizing the coercive nature of politics, has been correspondingly weak in analyzing the problem of consent" (1).

3. The importance of the episode has been widely recognized in *Lear* criticism; see especially Barish and Waingrow, Delaney, Kronenfeld, Mahood 167–69, and Strier. The argument looks simplistic at this distance, and ignores the actual complexities of early modern English society, some of which are discussed below. Unless otherwise indicated, citations of Shakespeare's works refer to *The Norton Shakespeare*, which uses the text of the Oxford *Complete Works*, ed. Wells and Taylor. References to *Lear* distinguish between the quarto *History of King Lear* (1608, abbreviated *HLr.*)

and the folio *Tragedy of King Lear* (1623, abbreviated *TLr.*); Wells and Taylor number the scenes of *HLr.* consecutively through the play, but use traditional act-scene numbers for *TLr.* Where the texts are identical or similar, reference is to *TLr.*, as likely to be more useful to readers who do not have the Norton or Oxford ready to hand.

4. Mahood discerns a similar, though less striking, pattern in *JC*: immediately after the assassination, the first figure to appear is Antony's servant, probably only a boy, whose bold and eloquent message from Antony stops the conspirators from carrying out their plan to proclaim liberty to the people right away, and so initiates their fall (122).

5. Representative instances are Phyllis Rackin's book on Shakespeare's histories, which describes itself as looking "to discover the traces of the daily experience of ordinary people" so as to recover "the voices erased by the repressions of the dominant discourse" (xi), but actually gives little space to either service relationships as such or to most of the characters in those plays who occupy service roles, and Howard, who proposes to focus on "non-elite social groups: servants, rogues and vagabonds," etc. (12), but whose index has no entry for "servant" or "service," and whose text nowhere treats servants as a group.

6. Griffiths proposes that service was "the typical experience of plebian youth" since common people "spent the greater part of their youth in some form of service" (353–54).

7. Sharpe's book actually largely ignores service. The treatment of servants in English social historiography was largely anecdotal until Peter Laslett's *The World We Have Lost* inaugurated both a new attention to previously marginal groups and a new methodology. See also Beier, Dolan, and Kussmaul. There is a good survey of the resources in Frye and Robertson.

8. The earliest extensive treatment I have found was Barnes's Brandeis dissertation of 1982—not, to my knowledge, published anywhere in part or whole. Its limited accessibility, and the fact that it was written from a thoroughly modernist point of view (it begins with extensive citation from Tillyard's *Elizabethan World Picture* and ends by treating Ulysses's speech on degree as normative for the canon and the period) have muffled its potential influence. Barnes's analysis does, to be sure, reflect the idealizing and hegemonic treatment of service that informs nearly all the early modern treatises and sermons that take up the topic. Berry's *Shakespeare and Social Class* does not give servants extended or concentrated attention, though there are many passing references.

9. See especially Dolan, Moisan, and Strier.

10. The phrase is Enobarbus's: "The loyalty well held to fools does make / Our faith mere folly; yet he that can endure / To follow with allegiance a fallen lord / Does conquer him that did his master conquer, / And earns a place in the story" (*Ant.* 3.13.41–44).

11. The list of plays in which servants do not have significant places is short: *Cor., 1H6, 2H6, Tro., Wiv.,* and *Tro.* drops out of the list if we consider Thersites as Achilles' parasite or jester.

12. A representative approach is that of Thomas Moisan, who traces "a concept of service infusing devotion and terror, in which the servant's duty is to divert 'knocks' from the master or absorb them from him," citing Foucault's analysis of early modern service as "a constant, total, massive, nonanalytical, unlimited relation of domination, established in the form of the individual will of the master, his 'caprice' " (279). Very few of the orders issued by Shakespearean masters to their servants, however, seem to me "capricious"; most are sensible and practical, and most of the rest arise from logical if not necessarily laudable motives. Mahood does call attention to one place (*H8* 4.2.100–08) where a master (Katherine of Aragon) and an upper servant (Griffith) join to put an underservant in his place by undeservedly rebuking him for lack of ceremony. The act may seem merely capricous; but the episode may also reflect Holinshed's report that, after her deposition, Suffolk tried to hire as servants for Katherine only those sworn to deny her the courtesy due to her royal birth (53).

13. Neill, addressing the question whether anxiety about unruly servants around the turn of the sixteenth century was warranted by an actual rise in resistance to authority, rightly notes that "it may be more important to understand what people *thought* was happening to their world than to gauge the accuracy of those beliefs, since what people believe to be true is typically what determines the way they act" (3–4). The statement is as applicable to postmodern scholars, however, as it is to Elizabethan householders.

14. Mac Cullough demonstrates that the traditional English form of "unfreedom," villeinage or serfdom (never as confining as Greek or Roman slavery), remained more common through the mid-sixteenth century than many earlier historians have supposed. Even so, this status had almost wholly disappeared by 1600 ("Bondmen" 99).

15. The fluidity of the situation is indicated by the fact that none of the early modern sources cited by Wrightson in his analysis of social class in the period identifies servants as a distinct social group ("Estates"). Modern readers are often surprised to learn that in the late sixteenth century, many apprentices (perhaps 30% of the total) were gently born—the proportion is far higher than the 2–5% of gentlefolk in society at large (Wrightson *English Society* 28). An intriguing instance of the blurred frontier appears in Middleton's *Trick to Catch the Old One*, when the Host (very likely a former servant, since servants leaving service for independent life often used their savings to set up an inn), in order to advance the interest of his customer Witgood and hence his own, leaves his position as master of his own house to become, temporarily, a servant. The move suggests that the servant position had its advantages—easier to influence various household decisions from inside the household group than from outside, and incomparably better for acquiring information.

16. Margaret Gay Davies notes that this act imposed conditions of service that were uniform all over the country (2), a fact that might seem to make generalization for the Elizabethan and Jacobean periods easier than for earlier Tudor England—were it not for the other economic and social forces that were, in fact, working to make the situation more, not less, complex.

17. Burnett finds in the mobility of English servants in this period grounds for the anxiety with which servants in general were regarded (*Masters* 58–59; see also Woodbridge). Even though the stipulated period might not be up, servants were free to leave at the death of their masters—not always welcomed, since it had the effect of turning them loose on a sometimes-hostile world. Indeed, although it was common for masters to leave their servants bequests to tide them over until they could find other situations, and even to urge their heirs to keep them on, or their executors to help them find positions, it was by no means universal practice, and a good many were left high and dry—perhaps to join that body of disaffiliated servants, ready to beg, steal, or riot, so feared by contemporary writers. Neill notes that the contracts of servants, like those of modern athletes, could be sold or willed to other masters (23).

18. When some of the companies began to acquire property, the Act for the Punishment of Vagabonds specifically ordered actors to "belong" to a "Baron of this Realm or . . . any other Personage of Greater Degree"; in 1598, the authority to license such a relationship was further narrowed to great peers (Gurr 27). This development presumably represents recognition of the power of the playhouse to shape people's attitudes.

19. John Fit-John, in *A Diamond Most Precious* (1577), a treatise especially addressed to "the Maysters, and Wardens, of the companies of the cittie of London," uses "servant" and "apprentice" indifferently. The kinds of service normally carried out in England under short-term verbal agreements were often supplied in the New World under indenture; see Kussmaul and Abbot Smith. A character in Jonson's *The Case is Altered* suggests the possibility that some servants were men of other professions making a little extra money by hiring on for short periods—an evening or perhaps a weekend; Juniper, who is identified as a cobbler, is hired by his friend Onions, groom of the hall to Count Ferneze, to act as a waiter at the latter's feasts.

20. During the time when he was a servant, says Ben Jonson's Subtle, his confederate Face, at that time a "good, / Honest, plain, livery-three-pound-thrum," had by a combination of vails and the selling of (stolen) household goods been able to save up no more than 20 marks (*Alchemist* 1.1.51–56)—well short of the statutory requirement for independence. In *Eastward Ho* (1605), it is said that at court even the trencher-bearers and the groom of the close-stool must be feed (2.2.72–77). The Old Woman in *H8* who brings the news of the birth of Elizabeth is furious because her tip is only 100 marks—sufficient, she says, for "an ordinary groom" (more than the £40 needed to get him out of service, if he wished), but presumably not for a lady-in-waiting like her (5.1.173–74). The King is evidently disappointed because the baby is not the male heir he longs for.

21. Shylock's assessment of Lancelot's proclivities seems to be borne out by the sequel: he gets "the Moor" pregnant, is insolently familiar with his boss's guests, and quibbles with their orders in very much the same way as Grumio quibbles with Petruchio, though with less belligerent results (*Mer.* 3.5).

22. Idealized, nostalgic treatments of traditional household service were produced by John Fit-John, J. M. (probably Gervase Markham), and an anonymous writer who may have been Walter Darrell.

23. The most positive expression of master/servant commonalty in the period is doubtless Deloney's *The Gentle Craft* (1597?) and Dekker's play from it, *The Shoemakers' Holiday* (1600), which give narrative and dramatic expression to the images of bourgeois service earlier advanced by John Fit-John—apprentices and journeymen working away with a will for a master who in return shares his prosperity with them. Most recent social and literary historians are disposed, of course, to see this as arrant idealizing.

24. Mahood stresses the familial quality of Lear's household (162).

25. For discussion of this development, see McClung, especially 18–45; he notes that the process of separation must have begun at least as early as the late fourteenth century, because it is one of the complaints of *Piers the Plowman* (McClung 29).

26. Griffiths argues that the master–servant relationship is intrinsically ambiguous and "on occasion inherently unstable" (298).

27. The recognition renders untenable Amussen's statement that the relationship between servants and masters, unlike that between wives and husbands, was "straightforward"—respect and obedience from servants and care, protection, and guidance from masters (41).

28. Douglas Bruster argues that *servus* figures in Shakespearean comedy, unlike those in its Roman sources, "are important not for their wit or intelligence but instead for their geographic and class mobility" (125)—in other words, for the degree to which they stretch the boundaries of customary roles and relationships. He seems to have characters such as Tranio in mind—even though Tranio's mobility is in crucial ways enabled by his wit and intelligence.

29. As Robert Miola puts it, "Shakespeare's moralized and romanticized New Comedy retains the deep structures of its origins, particularly the traditional opposition between masters and servants" (162); the remark can be extended to tragedy and history as well.

30. Veyne states that in late Republican and Imperial Rome, subjugation and the frontier were only a secondary source of the slaves on whose labor the Roman economy was almost totally dependent; most slaves were the children of other slaves, were bought from slave traders, or were former free persons sold into slavery for debt (51).

31. Paul Baynes, in his extensive commentary on Ephesians, is very conscious of these historical developments, which affect considerations of freedom in service; he makes a nice distinction between "mercenary servants" and "bondsmen." The same passage, by the way, includes one of the rare early modern English references to Africans purchased as slaves, "whose bodies are perpetually put under the power of the master, as blackamores are with us" (365).

32. That question was forcibly raised not long before Shakespeare began to write by Montaigne's friend Étienne de LaBoétie (*Discours de la servitude volontaire*, ca. 1550), but his early modern life in a society full of servants apparently so muffled his awareness of the domestic aspects of his concern that he focuses only on the matter of monarchs and subjects, and never brings it down to the domestic level.

33. Quoted by Peck, "For a King not to be bountiful" (43); it comes from MS HMC, *Portland* 9:6. Peck states that the sentiment was "copied from Lord Burghley," but gives no particulars.

34. The image corresponds with that expressed in Heal's study of early modern English aristocratic households, where "service can still be seen as the basis of personal connection and political influence" (167).

35. The pamphlet is discussed by Ann Rosalind Jones.

36. Latent in the image, to be sure, is the use of poles as weapons, a signification that recalls that in archaic societies, masters often achieved their status by military prowess, and even in early modern society had both responsibilities and privileges in the use of physical force.

37. The image might be thought less appropriate for relationships like those between master crafter and apprentice, for the master shoemaker or goldsmith by himself could and often did make shoes and spoons himself. In his specific relationship with the apprentice, however, the master is pole-like: even in preindustrial society, beyond an initial investment in tools and furniture and some ongoing overhead, all the productivity in that relationship that is above and beyond the master's own productivity is generated by the servant.

38. Griffiths insists that apprentices, treated *en bloc* by Burnett, did not constitute a socially homogenous group, as more and more gentlefolk began to arrange for their children to be indentured rather than sending them to become part of the household of some relative or neighbor (168–69).

39. Burnett makes very effective use of these materials, particularly as they appear in the city comedies; see especially. *Masters* ch. 2, "Crafts and Trades."

40. Actually, Sidney plays in rewarding ways with master—servant relationships in *Arcadia*—Mucedorus is enabled to woo Pamela by his disguise as a shepherd apprenticed to Dametus, and some of the best comedy in the book arises from the jealousy of Mopsa. And there is a prototype for the Adam of *AYL* in Lodge's *Rosalynde*. On the possible relations between *The Faerie Queene* and *Arcadia*, the Peasants' Revolt, and the affirmation by violence of early modern hegemony, see Greenblatt, *Learning*.

41. Neill cites Laslett: the issue is not one of *class* but of *status* within a "one-class society" (41). He goes on, however, still following Laslett, to discuss the "fiercely contested border" between the common people and the gentry (56–57).

42. Note that *functionally* the two men are level, here: both are carrying messages to Cornwall and Regan.

43. On this issue, see Dowd.

44. Similar views are argued by Kronenfeld; see her summary, 230–31.

45. A number of other scholars have noted the special importance of *Shr.* to studies of service in Shakespeare; see especially Mahood 46–48, Miola passim, and Moisan.

3 "Surprising Confrontations": Discourses of Service in *The Taming of the Shrew*

1. An earlier version of this chapter used the term "ideology," in the complex sense developed by Raymond Williams, to cover both the systematically

articulated intellectual systems of institutional spokespersons and the loose and often internally contradictory practical philosophies of ordinary people (*Keywords* 127–30). In contemporary historical scholarship, the terms "ideology" and "discourse" slide in and out of one another to the point where no systematic distinction can be made. But some rough and ready division between thinking and speaking may be supposed.

2. We might remember here the explicitly stated assumption of many Shakespearean characters, male and female, that women are inconstant and weak—and the many actions of Shakespearean female characters that belie the assumption.

3. Engle's argument parallels that of Weimann, who finds that theatrical interaction between *homo sapiens* (intellectually and socially orthodox) and *homo ludens* (intellectually and socially vsenturesome) produces "dynamic modulations . . . a dazzling play of difference in identity" (*Author's* 106–07).

4. In English society of around 1590 sailmakers were, I suppose, craftsmen, and could presumably be masters rather than servants themselves, with apprentices and journeymen as servants in their own households. But Vincentio seems very much to want to put Tranio in his place, here—a low one. According to the maritime historian Markus Redeker, sailmaking was a relatively "disreputable" occupation—no livery company or other institutional structure to protect and elevate its practitioners (private communication).

5. According to its Q1 title page, *The Taming of a Shrew*, the alternative version of the play, was performed by "the Right honorable the Earle of Pembrook his servants."

6. We are reminded of this relationship early in the play, when the traveling actors who will eventually perform the main plot arrive and are announced as "players / That offer *service* to your lordship" (Ind. 1.75–76); the same term is used of the Players in *Hamlet* (2.2.319). The extent of the services that actors actually performed for their noble patrons is not clear. T. W. Baldwin has documented the process, from at least 1572 onward, by which players became nominal members of aristocratic and then royal households, with the right to wear their lords' livery and enjoy the benefits of their protection (including, for companies serving monarchs, some protection against arrest); thus, the familiar designations of Admiral's Men, Chamberlain's Men, King's Men. A royal patent of James I established Shakespeare and eight named associates as "these our servants" (Schoenbaum 195–96). Baldwin believes they took no regular pay but were paid piecemeal for performances (*Organization* 6–10). James Burbage, appealing to Leicester for patronage in 1572, calls himself and his fellows "your houshold servants and daylie wayters," as though they were regularly to be seen serving in Leicester's hall (Gurr 29), and it is not unlikely that on special occasions actors did perform this task—it is certainly the case that householders routinely engaged additional servants to help look after guests at important entertainments. Shakespeare and others were granted four and one-half yards of red cloth apiece with which to costume themselves for the

king's ceremonial entry to the city in March 1604, and two of the eight, Augustine Phillips and John Heminges, "and some of their followers," are identified as "grooms of the chamber" paid for "waytinge and attendyinge on his Majs person & by commaundemente uppon the Spanishe Embassador at Somersette House the space of xviii dayes viz from the ixth day of Auguste 1604 untill the xxviith day of the same" (Schoenbaum plates 156–59). Gurr insists, however, that the professional companies of actors were "independent commercial organizations, not doing what pleasure-bent lord or royalty commanded, but going where and doing what brought most money and best audiences" (28). As Neill puts it, they belonged "more to the fluid world of urban commerce than to the ostensibly unchanging domain of feudal retainers." Still, their real dependency is indicated by the many companies that were forced to disband when their noble patrons died or withdrew their patronage (Gurr 19). Kernan calls some of the plays "openly serviceable," and Shakespeare himself "a helpful royal servant," but goes on to observe that this only puts the plays, especially the later ones, among "the master oeuvres of European patronage art," along with the Sistine Chapel, many great paintings by Titian and Velazquez, and much of the finest music of Mozart (xx–xxiii).

7. As David Kathman has shown, the surviving records indicate that the boys were apprenticed by means of the usual kinds of indentures, and that many though not all went on to become journeymen. Since there was no actor's guild, however, their masters in the legal sense were members of other companies—John Heminges and many of his own apprentices were freemen of the Grocers, Robert Armin and John Lowin of the Goldsmiths, and so on. Similar procedures governed the status of the members of the boys' companies, though they were typically bound for 3 years, not 7, and since some of them went on to become adult actors, it is possible that at the end of their initial indenture, when their voices were beginning to change, they moved over to the adult companies. Not much is known about the actual lives of the boy actors, but once indentured, the boys seem to have been at least as fully in the master's control as other apprentices.

8. Note the distinctly English character of this episode; Sly identifies himself as "old Sly's son of Burton-Heath," and cites "the fat alewife of Wincot" as a character reference; these are Cotswold villages south of Stratford.

9. I prefer the familiar Folio spelling of this name to the Oxford's and Norton's *Petruccio*.

10. The editor of the facsimile edition of this work, A. V. Judges, asserts that in the early sixteenth century, about one-quarter of the servants in great households were of gentle birth and education (vi–vii). Its author may have been Gervase Markham, author of books on housewifery, archery, country sports, farming, and soldiering—a range of interests that spans the broad scope of domestic and courtly service. Markham seems to have been gently born himself.

11. Gabriner remarks suggestively that the Induction depicts a "natural hierarchy" outdoors, in pursuits where ability counts more than family or wealth, and an "inverted" or "repressive" hierarchy indoors (209). Because the

discourse of household service overwhelmingly dominates early modern treatments of service, it also dominated such treatment of service as appeared in romantic and modernist scholarship and criticism, before postmodern materialism shifted attention to the rise of wage-ordered service. The fullest early modern treatments are by Cleaver and Dod (at least 7 ed. 1598–1624), whose subtitle indicates the biblical origins of the discourse, and Gouge, *Domesticall Duties* (3 ed. 1622–34). Neill gives a fine brief survey of this literature (77–78), and Amussen's book constitutes a summary of it, though much fuller on husband–wife and parent–child than on master–servant relations.

12. See Erickson 52–59. She says that only 10% of indentured women were apprenticed to the male-dominated trades. There was no Worshipful Company of Housewives, of course; indenture was, finally, a private contract between one individual and another, and in fact there were many occupations for men as well as women not controlled by guilds; it was mainly those centered in London and in which it was possible to grow rich whose leading members were eager to control access.

13. The speech contains several elements—"win my love," "honourable action," "observ'd in noble ladies"—seeming to recognize that the gently born page will at some point stand on the same social level as the lord.

14. Masters always in some sense stood *in loco parentis* to their servants, but that status was even more marked vis-à-vis youngsters—pages and maids-in-waiting, apprentices. A salient instance of the blurred boundaries between categories is Bertram, in *AWW*; after his father's death the King becomes both his guardian—his acting parent—and his liege-lord.

15. The Arden editor glosses *goodman* as merely "husband," but *OED* offers an early and more general sense of the term as meaning "the master or male head of a household" (2).

16. The development was not a simple one. Large trains were always a sign of wealth and power, for Anglo-Saxon chieftains and for Elizabethan magnates. But political and economic forces worked throughout the early modern period to reduce the average size of aristocratic English households, by half to two-thirds (Beier 23; Neill 28); we will encounter some consequences of this fact later. Alvin Kernan sees the adoption of theatrical companies by great lords as an easy and relatively cheap way for them to increase the size of their retinues—on demand for grand occasions, but not a drain on the household budget from day to day. James's centralizing these relationships in the hands of the royal family diminished the public relations power of some of his courtiers while giving himself "a powerful propaganda medium" (9–10).

17. In this play, Shakespeare explores these relationships in one of those Italianate households that mingle bourgeois and aristocratic characteristics—city dwellers who own both land and ships (see the discussion among Baptista, Gremio, and Tranio, 2.1.338–75). But they reappear in Oberon's relationship with Puck, Lear's with the Fool, and Prospero's with Ariel, among other more purely aristocratic master–servant pairings, and in a rural context between Justice Shallow and his steward Davy (*2H4*).

18. There are, indeed, many archival materials—household manuals and rosters, account books, letters, legal and other civic records. From all these, it is possible to piece together a composite image of the *structure* of households that may be reasonably accurate; Burnett calls on them, and on the social historians who have worked with them. The fullest single source is perhaps the diaries of Anne Clifford Herbert, Countess of Pembroke, which report on household activities over several decades; these were written in the seventeenth century, but she seems to me to have an Elizabethan rather than a Jacobean sensibility, and certainly ran her household on conservative lines. Friedman's account of life at Wollaton, which draws on a variety of archival materials, gives a very informative window on master–servant relations in one aristocratic household. In any case, virtually all of these documents take a magisterial point of view: very little survives to authenticate the feelings of subordinates.

19. Examples are J. M.'s *Health*, and Whythorne's manuscript autobiography. Whythorne's text is especially revealing; his struggles to maintain his psychological as well as his economic independence as he moves from one dependent situation to another, over and over again, are particularly evident in the poems interspersed among the narrative segments of the book.

20. In *Twelfth Night*, Shakespeare will offer a fascinating image of the struggle between an upper servant, Malvolio, ruling the household as his lady's agent, and a set of other dependents, the parasitic Sir Toby, the waiting-gentlewoman Maria, the upper servant of no stipulated duties, Fabian, and the bird of passage, Feste. As Olivia's uncle, Toby is probably Malvolio's social superior, though because many stewards were gently born—younger sons and what not—it could be that, had Shakespeare chosen to give this one a history, it would include the gentle birth and education his language implies. But Toby, like Malvolio, is economically subservient to Olivia and hence dependent on the goodwill of her servants: if Malvolio refuses to unlock the cupboard, no more cakes and ale unless the mistress can be persuaded to overrule. Maria's status is ambiguous, but no one perceives in her marriage to Toby the kind of social disparity remarked in Armado's passion for Jaquenetta in *LLL*. See also Middleton and Rowley's *Chaste Maid in Cheapside*, in which Davy Dahannet, Sir Walter Whorehound's "poor kinsman and attendant," reveals family secrets and otherwise violates his servant's obligations as he tries to frustrate Whorehound's plans to marry and thus remain Whorehound's heir. Another kind of struggle occurs between Lear's retainers and those of Albany and Goneril (see Mahood 160–62).

21. Maurice Hunt has argued that although formal slavery of the kind practiced in classical Greece and Rome was not accepted by English law, de facto enslavement can be discerned in early modern English social practice, and in the treatment of the servants in the early comedies of Shakespeare, including *Shr*. The argument seems to me to depend on a somewhat quibbling use of the term. Elizabethan servants may have been moved to take service by economic necessity and statutory obligation, but they were not chattels; they could choose to work for one master rather than another, and

for a fixed period, not for life, and while the law gave masters much power over the lives of their servants, there were remedies in law if not always in fact for abuses of that power. In any case, the historical materials he cites have a tendency (perhaps illustrated in the present study, to be sure), to turn anecdotes (in this case, of abuse by masters) into general conditions.

22. The anxiety finds a much more serious expression in *Macbeth:* "There's not a one of them" (his possible enemies) "but in his house / I keep a servant fee'd" (3.4.130–31). The second version of Rowland Lockey's portrait of Sir Thomas More and his descendants (London, V & A, ca. 1598) shows a male servant partly concealed by an arras, in shadow, behind the seated members of the family, who seem unaware of him. The meaning of the figure is uncertain; but to a modern eye it looks vaguely sinister. Servants are rarely figured in surviving Elizabethan and Jacobean pictures (though Thomas Whythorne had his own portrait painted on a set of virginals (12)); a defining image is Robert Peake's picture of Henry, Prince of Wales, and Sir John Harington, hunting (Metropolitan Museum of Art, N.Y., 1603)— the prince stands before his horse, which is held by a groom, but the horse's neck conceals all of the groom's face except one eyebrow and part of one ear.

23. Heal sees the fashion of classical education for the sons of the aristocracy as one of the elements in the decline of retaining (164–66).

24. Among others, see Jameson 201; Robbins 68–77, 146, 175; Neill 28ff.; and Burnett and Moisan, passim. Barnes argues that the "moral lapses" in early modern drama are repeatedly connected with "breakdowns of the order of service" (4); he does not address the moral dimensions of *Shrew*, however.

25. In law, violence by servant against master was regarded as petty treason, punishable by death (Dolan "Subordinates('s)").

26. I do not accept Stephen Marx's proposal that in *Shrew* we can find "glorification of violence" (59).

27. The Shakespearean locus that has particularly stimulated comments of this kind is the ending of *The Tempest*, where interest in the discourses of colonialism seconds interest in political and gender issues. See the useful survey in Dolan, "Subordinate('s) Plot." I return to these matters in chapter 9.

28. The editorial and critical discussion of the fact that the frame story is never brought to closure in the Folio text of *Shrew* is a mare's nest (it takes up 38 pages in Brian Morris's Arden ed.) that I will not try here to comb out. But one important strand compels attention. In the parallel play, *The Taming of a Shrew* (1594), an induction very similar to the one in The *Shrew* is carried through by four subsequent interludes and an epilogue, in which the dead-drunk Sly is carried sleeping back to the place where the lord and his men took him up. He awakes, marvels at what he takes to have been a dream, and resolves to apply Petruchio's teachings about the taming of shrews to his own wife. This speech supplies much firmer ideological closure to the play than does the Folio text; an implication is that if The *Shrew*'s intention (in the speech-act sense) is to interrogate various forms of social hierarchy rather than to affirm conventional patriarchy, then the play's relatively open ending is appropriate.

29. The same sequence supplies the structure for Cleaver and Dod's manual.

30. We can read this line as requesting sisterly equality, within a proto-feminist discourse in which Katherine, by abusing Bianca, denies her own true nature by adopting the actions and attitudes of their common male oppressors. Bianca makes no other gestures toward solidarity, however, and seems to me otherwise quite content to advance her own interests within the patriarchal framework until her marriage secures her a customary base from which to resist it.

31. Within the household model, women were to be responsible for the punishment of women servants, men of men (Cleaver and Dod D1r).

32. Some of Bianca's audacity is present in the source, for Polynesta, her counterpart in Ariosto and Gascoigne, is there forward enough to have gotten unremorsefully pregnant. That kind of defiance is, almost by definition, indirect and secretive.

33. Burnett (*Masters* 168–71) and Lamb argue persuasively that even though the actual incidence of sexual relations between mistresses and servants, and of mistresses stooping to marry a servant as Bianca appears to do here, was probably low (the evidence is skimpy and merely anecdotal), such relationships were very threatening to early modern patriarchy, and hence likely to provoke fictive representation all out of proportion to their practical significance. Lamb makes good use of material from Whythorne's autobiography and the diaries of Anne Clifford.

34. I base this reading on the fact that Feste appears in both Orsino's and Olivia's houses, and tells us that he dwells in neither but lives next to the church (3.1.5–7)

35. A reading of the play along these lines informs the version directed by Jonathan Miller for the BBC Time-Life series, with John Cleese as a gentle, thoughtful Petruchio.

4   "Monsieur, We Are Not Lettered": Classical Influences and the Early Modern Marketplace

1. For an informed if still rather speculative account of Shakespeare's early exposure to drama on page and stage, see Greenblatt, *Will*, ch. 1.

2. Shakespeare's other earliest work was presumably on the first historical tetralogy. There is, of course, no classical dramatic prototype for these plays (although in its way *R3* is almost as Senecan as *TAn*); but Roman historiography, especially that of Livy, another standard grammar school text, helps account for the relatively simple structure, emphasis on big public moments and especially on highly rhetorical speechifying, and other characteristic features of *H6*. See L. B. Campbell, Velz passim.

3. On Shakespeare's possible experience as a schoolteacher, see especially Honigmann.

4. The starting point for any consideration of the New Comic heritage of Elizabethan and Jacobean comedy is Baldwin, *Small Latine*; also, his *Five-Act Structure* remains the fullest exploration of Shakespeare's response to the tradition. Indeed, the dozens of books and articles summarized in Velz

mostly either repeat that Shakespeare was influenced by Plautus and Terence and sometimes suggest one or another particular play likely to have served as a source, or refer the reader to Baldwin. (Velz's own comments, in his introduction and elsewhere, are lively and sensible.) But Baldwin and his immediate followers insisted that only direct verbal echo supplied acceptable evidence of influence. Thus, Riehle insists on the extensive direct textual influence of the Roman writers, especially Plautus, and especially on *Err.*, and generally downplays the significance of theatrical inspiration, either domestic or imported. Miola works from the rhetorical concept of *contaminatio*, the *combination* of sources, to produce a much more rich and flexible understanding in which the influence of New Comedy on Shakespeare and his contemporaries was communicated not only directly but also indirectly, through Italian and other Continental plays, both read and seen, and the works of other English writers and performers. My own views of these matters were early shaped by Doran's treatment of them, and especially by her sensitivity to the effect of classical devices on audiences as well as on readers.

5. Notice that *deserve* is etymologically close to *service*.

6. Neill's characterization of the gulling of Malvolio as "vicious" seems to me exaggerated (41).

7. There is as yet no clear consensus on the date of *Err.*, with informed arguments setting it anywhere from 1589 to 1594. Since it shares features including the treatment of servants with the other early plays, however, I do not think it crucial to determine whether it preceded or followed *Shrew* or *Two Gentlemen*.

8. The name seems to have been suggested by *Dromo*, used of more than one slave character in Terence; Riehle suggests that Shakespeare added the *i* to give "a lively rhythm" (179).

9. Miola cites Bernard Knox on the "many scenes in which the comedy slave surpasses the master in qualities which are traditionally those of the free man—in intelligence, courage, self-sacrifice" (163); Riehle proposes that Plautine slaves "often become intellectually superior to their masters" through their skill at devising intrigues or through their wit (48). Douglas Bruster argues rather tendentiously that Shakespeare's servants are not, by and large, the *loci* for the figuration of the artist's own economically dependent but artistically dominant status that they are in Plautus and Terence, and attributes this fact to Shakespeare's "deference to political authority" (130). My own analysis challenges Bruster in both general and particular ways.

10. The passages are as follows: *Tro.* 2.1; *AWW* 2.2.42–47; *WT* 4.3.82.

11. *TLr.* 1.4.72–75, 97, 147.

12. This is a good place to invoke Michael Neill's perceptive comments on the importance in the discourse of the period of verbal status-markers such as the *thou–you* distinctions in this speech (6–7, 64).

13. A fully deconstructive reading might see in the name of this hostelry an image of the master–servant relationship, yoking the controlling mind and hand and the controlled strength and speed in the one composite body.

14. There is an odd kind of anticipation of this in Marlowe's *Dr. Faustus*. Faustus engages Mephistopheles as his servant for an unusually long period, 24 years, by means of an unusually demanding indenture, signed in blood and offering as the servant's "wage" the master's soul. Mephistopheles is certainly wily, and he does some of the things wily servants do, like insuring Faustus's physical comfort and helping him get the girl (Helen of Troy, or at least her image). But of course he is really working against Faustus's best interests, not for them.

15. Reliable information about sexual relationships among masters and their servants, like many other features of early modern social life, is impossible to find. The fullest single source is probably Simon Forman's diary; the extracts of it reproduced by Rowse indicate not only that Forman himself had sex with many of his female servants, but also that he either knew or supposed that many of the bourgeois women who were his patients and mistresses had sex with their own male servants. Nor does he suggest that he found such relationships at all exceptional; indeed, his tone implies that in Salisbury and London, at least, people were hopping in and out of other people's beds all over the place. Forman's veracity, however, may be subject to doubt.

16. It is possible that the two roles were doubled in performance. In Plautus's *Mostellaria*, the play opens with a conversation between characters named Tranio and Grumio. In that play, Grumio, the rustic, remains faithful to his absent master, Theuropides, while the wily Tranio lives high on Theuropides' hog with Theuropides' son, Philololaches, whose attempt to marry the girl he loves, Tranio tries to assist. Plautus's Tranio also serves as a source for Face in Jonson's *Alchemist*.

17. J. M. views this issue from the perspective of traditional retaining, when servants were "the Dukes sonne preferred Page to the Prince, the Earles second sonne attendant upon the Duke, the Knightes second sonne the Earles Servaunt, and the Gentlemans sonne the Esquieres Servingman" (B3r). A bare ten years later, the scene had changed so much that an alternative perspective appears in Middleton, whose Lucre commends his rustic servant George: "There's more true honesty in such a country serving-man than in a hundred of our new cloak companions: I may well call them companions, for since blue coats have been turned into cloaks, we can scarcely know the man from the master" (2.1). As the old feudal bonds relaxed, and the variety of paths by which a man could make his way in the world increased, it is possible that the number of gently born men and women who went into service decreased, according to J. M.'s editor, A. V. Judges (J. M. 1931, vi–vii). Joan Thirsk, however, has argued that the extension of the principal of primogeniture to an ever-larger number of estates during the sixteenth century actually forced more young people, especially men, to seek positions as servants or apprentices, at the very time when decreases in the size of households were reducing the number of available places (366–67). It is nonetheless likely that in country households most of the servants would have been the children of husbandmen or yeomen, not gentlemen.

18. The gesture was also commonly used to control unruly livestock and schoolboys.

19. *OED* does not honor the invention by including *rebuse* in its list of English words.

20. The Statute of Artificers gave servants the right to leave abusive masters before their term was up, with the permission of the magistrates. Griffiths records a number of instances with regard to apprentices. Editors gloss the odd expression "two-and-thirty" as a reference to a card game implying that Petruchio's action was excessive.

21. In Plautus's *Poenulus*, the lovesick Agorastocles announces himself willing to have his servant Milphio tie him up and beat him; but Milphio declines, on grounds that once released, Agorastocles would give the beating back with interest (1.1.20–28).

22. Brian Morris has commented on the oddity of making Tranio's father a sail-maker in Bergamo, a small city in the foothills of the Alps north of Milan, not far from lakes Como and Iseo but not a major seaport (ed. 283n.).

23. Miola assigns primacy to Tranio, as *architectus doli*, noting that his is the second largest role in the play, after Petruchio (66–67). He also calls attention to the subtler, more ambiguous, and more complex version of the exchange that occurs in *AWW* when Helena advances from *bourgeoise* to *chatelaine* by way of effective royal service; she "reprises the role of the clever slave" (132). The exchange of places between master and man occurs, under very different circumstances, in Plautus's *Captivi*—not one of the plays regarded by Baldwin and others as likely to have been read by Shakespeare, but perhaps a source for Ariosto's *I Suppositi* and thus for Shakespeare's immediate source, Gascoigne's *Supposes*, and accepted as an important influence on this and other plays by Miola. In Gascoigne's play, the event is not staged, only recounted second hand by Polynesta, the counterpart of Bianca. Gascoigne follows Ariosto in this.

24. Another instance of the juxtaposition, vis-à-vis obedience, of children and wives, as in Ephesians and Colossians.

25. We may note here the parallel with Jonson's *Alchemist*. There, the wily servant Face, who has taken advantage of his master's long absence to plot and scheme not for the latter but for himself, by turning over his ill-gotten gains to his master on the latter's unannounced return escapes the punishment he has deserved and is restored to his place.

26. A few speeches later, when the new husbands are testing their wives' obedience, it is Biondello, not Tranio, who is sent by Lucentio and Hortensio to carry their summons.

27. Riehle cites Erich Segal in assuring us that although the plays of Plautus "tend to mock the ruling system of values, they by no means overturn it" (6). Early modern servants also attended the London public theaters, at least the outdoor amphitheaters like the Globe, though in what numbers it is hard to know; the several authories—Harbage, Cook, Gurr—dispute the issue, though the most recent of them argues that in this period, as later, the audiences seem to have been mostly from the propertied classes (Gurr 214–17).

28. In general, the language of the two Romans, especially Plautus, was much more highly artificial than the language Shakespeare produced for those scenes most largely involving servants. Charles and Michelle Martindale state that Shakespeare quite fails to represent the verbal brilliance of his Roman sources in *Err.* and *Shr.* otherwise, they completely ignore his debts to his Roman comic models (29). But they are generally insensitive to dramatic issues. Velz proposes, however, that the metrical peculiarities in *Err.* may result from "Sh's attempt to imitate Plautus' metrical legerdemain" (82).

29. Miola calls him the "antitype" of the wily servant (92); he belongs rather with the blockheads.

30. In both eras, the threadbare independence of the parasite marks the figure as someone distinguished from his patron by economic rather than truly social distinctions. Feste's possession of a house "beside the church" (*TN* 3.1.2–6) would explain his free movement between the households of Orsino and Olivia: as owner of freehold property he would be exempt from the obligation to be somebody's servant.

31. The Nurse's griping could also owe something to another character in *Amphitruo*, Sosia, Amphitryon's man—an additional argument (in addition to the similarity of the frame story to that of *Err.*) for the suggestion that the play as we have it is a reworking of an older play. And her maddeningly dilatory way of releasing her hold on important information is very like that of Staphyla in *Aulularia*. Some suggestions for the Nurse may have come from New Comedy via Ariosto and Gascoigne; *Supposes* begins with a scene in which Balia, the nurse, and Polynesta, the Bianca-figure, discuss the nurse's assiduous contributions to the secret affair between Polynesta and the supposed servant Dulippo.

32. Information about the sexual trades in Shakespearean London is scanty and unreliable, but it makes sense to suppose that something like a master–journey(wo)man–apprentice system was at work, so that people who had served as whores or doorkeepers could eventually become brothelkeepers. Mistress Quickly apparently masks her brothel as a legitimate tailoring business, where she and Pistol "lodge and board a dozen or fourteen gentlewomen that live honestly by the prick of their needles" (*H5* 2.1.29–30)—an oblique reflection on the nominal membership of actors in liveried companies?

33. The subsequent appearance of the type—tripled, this time—in *Per.* has much less energy, the Pander, Bawd, and Boult (two of the three not personalized as far as a name) serving mainly as foils for the goodness of Marina.

34. Neill observes in non-Shakespearean drama after the turn of the century, a renewed interest in characters of this type because "they speak to the very anxieties about domestic enmities that I have traced" (44). Shakespeare thus here as in other things seems to anticipate his contemporaries. DiGangi has interesting things to say about this type as representing the new negotiational relationships entrained by the shift from retaining to wages as the normative basis for service, though he concentrates on Volpone's Mosca.

35. The speech produces a mild crux, for in the scene of the meeting between Shylock and Bassanio (1.3), no such discussion occurs; as often happens in Shakespearean texts, discussion of an issue by one set of characters can be attributed by the audience, without awareness of the transfer, to another relevant set. Thus, having heard Lancelot discussing the matter with his father, we are prepared to suppose that Shylock has similarly spoken to Bassanio. Later, we learn from Shylock that he finds Lancelot an unprofitable division of which he wishes to divest himself: "Drones hive not with me"—with the additional motive that the glutton will help Bassanio "waste / His borrowed purse" (2.5.44–49).

36. Miola analyzes the way Maria mirrors Malvolio, succeeding to improve her social position where he failed, and treats Viola as a version of the wily servant (44–45).

37. The ahistoricism of Trevor Nunn's film of this play, and his willingness to sacrifice narrative logic to feeling and mood, appears when he shows us Toby and Maria not only marrying but also loading their luggage into a carriage and driving away.

38. An interesting non-Shakespearean analog is Trapdoor, in Middleton and Dekker's *Roaring Girl*. He himself is a "roaring boy," a down-at-heels soldier who is moved by a combination of love and need to seek service with Moll, the Roaring Girl; like Falstaff, when tested by the person he serves in disguise, he fails the test, but escapes punishment by claiming to have recognized her all along (3.1).

39. We get no histories for either Parolles or Thersites. It is possible to infer from Justice Shallow's elegiac memories of his time with Falstaff at the Inns of Court in *2H4* that Falstaff, too, had been a young heir, who subsequently squandered, not improved, his inheritance.

40. The moment echoes Pistol's resolution to turn bawd, thief, and liar, of course (*H5* 5.1.75–80); he calls more on circumstance than Parolles ("Old do I wax," etc.), and does not receive a subsequent validation analogous to Lafeu's of Parolles.

41. Kent's splendid barrage of insults (*TLr.* 2.2.13–21) is designed to attack Oswald's pride by denying that there is any social distance between them, although Oswald's place in Goneril's ducal household appears to be one that would normally be occupied by a man of gentle birth and substantial education.

42. Iago will be treated more fully in chapter 7. His social status is uncertain. As a professional soldier, he occupies a world on the edge of Venetian society. Brabantio seems not to know him, but Ludovico does; they greet one another familiarly and speak as man to man, without honorifics (*Oth.* 4.1.213–16, 261–74). His wife Emilia attends Desdemona in the office of waiting gentlewoman, on a par with Nerissa in *Mer.* and Margaret and Ursula in *Ado.*

43. For a treatment of the early modern aspects of Viola's service, see Dowd.

44. Miola quotes Iago in reference to Palaestrio and Gnatho, "the slave and parasite who serve their boastful masters only to serve their turn upon them" (in *Miles Gloriosus*), but does not explicitly include Iago in the *servus callidus* category (128–29).

45. Emilia herself seems to be pretty fully an example of the early modern waiting gentlewoman, with little or nothing of the classical *lena* about her,
except perhaps her readiness to accept the ways of a fallen world.

5 "Clubs, Bills, and Partisans": Retainer Violence and Male Bonding

1. Stanley's commitment to the ideal of retainer fealty is too strong, however,
to allow him to violate directly his own oath of service to Richard, which
presumably he has sworn at the latter's coronation, and on which he insists
when charged by Richard with treachery (4.4.422–28). He will plot against
the King by corresponding with Richmond; he will delay to call up his
forces and then withhold them from the decisive battle; but he will not lead
them out in direct opposition to his liege lord.
2. Information about this episode is assembled from several sources.
Contemporary documents include notes of a judicial commission
appointed to investigate the issue with special attention to the Danvers's
flight to France (Salisbury MS 5.84–89); a somewhat fuller account gathered, probably by Sir Walter Long's lawyer, probably for a legal hearing of
some kind, likewise focused on the escape (Lansdowne MSS 827.6 and
830.13.3); a statement by Lady Elizabeth Danvers, perhaps intended for
the Privy Council as part of her campaign to win pardons for her sons
(S.P. 12/209/78 and S.P. 12/251/123); and a discussion of the case by
Sir Edward Coke (3.246–50), which includes a copy of the coroner's report.
John Aubrey treats the event (41–42); his grandfather, Richard Danvers,
had been involved. Modern accounts, in addition to the biographies
of Charles and Henry Danvers in *DNB*, include the lives of the Earl of
Southampton by Charlotte Stopes, G. P. V. Akrigg, and A. L. Rowse; see
also Bradbrook, *Poet* (100–101), and Forse.
3. A. Wall places the episode in the context of an ongoing struggle for local
domination in Wiltshire among several prominent county families.
4. Shakespeare's treatment differs from that of his source, Arthur Brooke's
Romeus and Juliet, in a way that makes it closer to the Long murder; in
Brooke, Mercutio (Romeo's friendly rival for Juliet's attention at the ball)
does not appear in the conflict at all, so that the fight is only between
Romeo and Tybalt. The difference between Shakespeare and history, of
course, is that Romeo/Henry Danvers is trying to stop the quarrel by
peaceful means when Tybalt/Henry Long assails Mercutio/Charles
Danvers, and that Mercutio, unlike Charles Danvers, dies on the spot.
5. The proposal is weakened by the statement in *DNB* (entry for Henry
Danvers) that Sir John died on December 16, 1593, nine months prior to
the Long murder. Lady Danvers soon married Sir Edmund Carey, the
Queen's kinsman; Aubrey suggests that it was to gain court support for her
efforts to win pardons for her sons (42).
6. She was, Aubrey says, "an Italian, prodigious parts for a woman. I have
heard my father's mother say that she had Chaucer at her finger's ends.
A great polititian; great witt and spirit, but revengefull" (42).

7. At this point in his book, Akrigg is trying to account for the strong Italian flavor of Shakespeare's work in this period, and is seemingly indifferent to other aspects of the plays.

8. Forse's historicist approach calls on work on patronage and on popular theater to account for both the connections with Southampton and some particular features of the work. He argues that as Southampton's client, Shakespeare could repay some of his obligations by sympathetic reminders of his patron's needs and achievements; he sees a particular connection between the marriage plot of *Rom.* and Southampton's own troubled amatory history, involving Burghley/Capulet's attempt to force marriage (with Elizabeth de Vere/Paris) on Southampton/Juliet and Southampton's own courtship (as Romeo, now) of Elizabeth Vernon/Juliet.

9. Brooke's poem, first published in 1562, had been reprinted in 1587, which makes recent publication of the source text improbable as an immediate motive for writing the play—unless, as has sometimes been suggested, there had been an intermediate version.

10. This recalls Kent threatening and then assaulting Oswald for similarly essaying to impose the constraints of established authority on Lear's company.

11. Romeo's servant, Balthazar, is held for interrogation in the aftermath of the tragedy (5.3.181–82). Some of the servants involved in the Danvers affair said that they were troubled in their consciences about it all. Roger Fynch, for instance, porter of Calshot Castle, carrying a letter from his master Captain Parkinson to warn the Danvers to leave that place before letters bearing orders for their arrest could arrive, dawdled en route, stopping for a couple of beers at Chadd's tavern: "and all the way he went his heart was heavy and tormented, and he wept most part of the way to think he should be messenger to so evil a purpose as he was commanded, and he was very desirous that the said letters from Sir Thomas West might be at the Castle to apprehend them before he should come thither" (Salisbury MS 5.86–87).

12. I have not found any contemporary confirmation of this report. None of the scholars cited earlier mentions it; their lack of interest is not conspicuous only because until recently a lack of scholarly interest in mere servants was so normal.

13. Charles Edelman has proposed that the servants, who would not normally be carrying weapons, have swords and bucklers because Shakespeare is thinking of London servants, who on Sundays commonly made their way to Smithfields, to join servants from around the city in military exercises, no doubt regarded as sports. Popular literature of the period attests to the interest of servants and apprentices in military action. For example, Richard Johnson's *Nine Worthies of London* (1592) records the military achievements of various mercers and grocers; it was addressed "To Gentleman Readers, as well Prentices as others" (Heywood xxiii). It may have inspired Thomas Heywood's *The Four Prentices of London* (1615, probably written 1592–94), which makes its four young heroes proud to serve their city masters—but so much prouder yet of heroism in battle as to run off to join the Crusades at the first opportunity.

14. This is one of Shakespeare's conspicuous alterations of his source; in Brooke, the only fighting occurs in the middle, in connection with Romeo's killing of Tybalt; the retainer violence at the beginning and the fight between Romeo and Paris at the end are Shakespeare's inventions.

15. For the distinction, and much other material on retaining, see Dunham. The two most extensive Elizabethan treatments of service, J. M.'s *Health to the Gentlemanly Profession* and even more so the *Short Discourse of the Life of Serving Men*, probably by Walter Darell (1578), present the retainer model as the ideal pattern of service, to which both the equally traditional domestic and the emerging cash-nexus ideologies are inferior. Mervyn James uses a different terminology, "countenancing," to cover a variety of relationships among elite masters and their noncontractual servants.

16. James insists that Tudor and Stuart retaining does not articulate "a mere cash nexus" (52).

17. On the pervasive violence of early modern British culture, see James, 308ff.

18. "In London itself the fields about the City and even the main arterial roads were continual scenes of upper-class violence" (*Crisis* 230–31). Darell specifically excepts "quarrelling in the streets" from the list of behaviors appropriate for the ideal servant (A3v).

19. See A. Wall, who reports mutual accusations of riot by John Thynne (builder of Longleat) and James Marvin, with a band of servants at their backs (124), and Mildred Campbell, who reports "a good deal of the feud element" among the Tudor and Stuart yeomanry as well as the gentry (365). Alan Macfarlane, in his detailed study of crime in Westmoreland in the third quarter of the seventeenth century, found no evidence of "vendettas"; it is not clear whether the 50-year interval was significant (*Justice* 188).

20. On the rioting, see especially Manning. Retainers and servants were used to suppress rioters. In Huntington in 1607 an anti-enclosure mob of perhaps 1,000 was broken by a force that comprised "the retainers and servants [note the distinction] of the most prominent gentry" of the area, led by Sir Edward Montagu and Sir Anthony Mildmay; 50 of the rioters are said to have died in the affair (McMullan 43).

21. On this topic, see James, chapter 2.

22. The Proclamation against Retaining of 1572, which allowed only actual members of a lord's household to wear his livery in times of peace, had the unintended effect of encouraging actors to enroll as nominal members of a patron's household (Baldwin *Organization* 5), since one effect was to secure for actors some of the protections extended to other members of great households.

23. The development seems to encapsulate that traced by Stone, in which conflict between retainer bands gave way to duels involving several gentlemen on either side (though these were apparently much more common on the Continent than in England), and finally to the two-man fight with rapiers or guns. Southampton was apparently involved in both types during his protracted quarrel with Lord Grey of Wilton. In 1599, Grey challenged him and they may or may not have fought on the Continent in defiance of a Council order forbidding it. In January 1601, Grey and several followers attacked Southampton, accompanied by only his boy-servant, on their way

to visit Ralegh; the Earl held them off until help came—perhaps in the form of citizens bearing clubs, bills, and partisans—but the boy lost his hand (Akrigg "Shakespeare" 101–10).

24. Hall reports the profound anxiety in the city occasioned by this outburst: "so that the citezens of London fearyng that that [sic] should ensue upon the matter, wer faine to kepe daily and nightly, watches, as though their enemies were at hand, to besiege and destroye them: In so muche that all the shoppes within the cite of London wer shut in for feare of the favorers of these two great personages, for each parte had assembled no small nombre of people" (in *1H6*, ed. Cairncross, 136).

25. Q only; F cuts the phrase, leaving only "some company" four lines earlier. Is it possible that in the interval between 1605 and 1623, the significance of retaining has declined to the point where the term lacks force, or the royal distaste for the idea has affected the King's Men?

26. On the Montague side, Mercutio is following a similar line; his projection of his own characteristics, not only onto the bellicose Tybalt, but onto the pacific Benvolio, is even more blatant.

27. Kirby Farrell has noted the ambiguity of "The quarrel is between our masters, and us their men" (88; l.l.18–20).

28. McEachern proposes that Shakespeare's "portrayal of fathers refuses to authorize patriarchical power" (288); her argument largely focuses on *Ado* and *Lr.*

29. This is perhaps a postmodern way to restate Barnes's modernist discussion of failed service as a consequence of broken order.

30. In Bishop's words, "the ethos of male challenge and desire as ruled by a logic of repetitive violence from which there is no escape" (98). McEachern, resisting the notion of patriarchy as unitary and coherent, sees in it an intrinsic contradiction between the familial elements, which must incorporate feminine desires and needs, and the external male alliance. Violence would then express, among other things, unbearable tensions arising from unresolved contradictions (273).

31. Thomas Malory of Newbold Priory, possible author of *Morte Darthur*, compiled a criminal record in which, as a member of one armed band or another, he was said to have engaged in all the forms of retainer violence, from sheep-stealing to the attempted murder of a duke. He was accused (but not convicted) of raping Joan Smyth twice during raids on her husband's house and property, though his biographer argues that in the context the word *raptus* is more likely to mean that she was knocked around in the course of the robbery than that she was sexually violated (Hicks 52–53). No comprehensive historical study of rape in early modern England has, to my knowledge, yet been published.

32. If married rural or domestic servants appear at all in Elizabethan and Jacobean drama, they are extremely rare—I cannot think of a single Shakespearean instance.

33. Recent treatments of this issue as a theme of Shakespeare's work have tended to concentrate on men's relationships with women more than with each other; thus both Garner and Adelman ("Male Bonding") look at

male–male relationships as means for avoiding fully mutual heterosexual relationships. For early modern servants, however, such avoidance was not something that most young men were free to choose, given the overwhelmingly male nature of large households, both aristocratic and bourgeois, and the fact that servants could not marry without their masters' consent.

34. Norman Holland writes that "The son does for the father what the father does not or cannot do for himself, much as hawk, horse, and hound (all favorite Shakespearean images) act for their gentlemen masters in aggressive contexts. The pattern applies to king and subject, master and servant, officer and soldier, and many other such pairs of figures" (Holland et al. *Shakespeare's Personality* 8). A shocking and relevant instance appears in the 1638 trial of the Earl of Castlehaven, a probable homosexual who assisted in the rape of his wife by one of his "favourites" (a retainer, in other words), presumably giving the acting out of his own sexual ambivalence to this organ of his extended body (Bray 49).

35. How common is not now and probably will never be very clear. The pioneer study, Bray, finishes by assuming that homosexual activities at all social levels were quite common, and that although they were anathematized by all the powers that were they were also quietly institutionalized within households both domestic and academic—if true, a clear instance of the distinction drawn by cultural materialism between official and practical ideologies. But Bray documents surprisingly few actual instances, and must rely on the assertions of the satirists and pamphleteers to support his contention that homosexual practices were widespread. Bruce R. Smith makes similar assertions on the basis of similarly skimpy evidence. Smith's arguments, more complex and subtle than Bray's, are persuasive. But they are founded rather on what we know of human behavior generally than on the testimony of particular sixteenth- and seventeenth-century documents. Most of the large and growing body of scholarship on early modern sexuality now assumes that sexual attitudes and behavior of the period were so different from ours that our modern terminology obscures rather than clarifies the evidence, which is skimpy and ambiguous to begin with.

36. I hope it not specious to note here that killing time was one of the most urgent needs of domestic servants, forced—like actors, especially those in relatively subordinate roles—to wait, in both senses of the term, for the moment when their masters called on them. The terms *waiting gentlewoman/man* had much literal force. In fact, there is an interesting sense in which servants, as servants, only exist when they are actually performing service. While they are doing something else—waiting, or smuggling prostitutes and otherwise acting in their own rather than their masters' interest—they become something else. In any case, the sheer boredom of their quotidian lives was replaced in the violent moment by the loss of self-consciousness, which is time-consciousness, in "deindividuation," submersion in group identity (Wrangham and Peterson 198).

37. *Western* may be an important limiting condition, for some of Ong's propositions, especially the one concerning the necessary instability of the male

group, seem to be contradicted by things such as contemporary Japanese business practice. Coppélia Kahn observes that in the ideology of *virtus*, which she sees as central to the ethos of classical life and literature, a crucial element is *emulation*, "agonistic rivalry that isn't exclusively martial in form," and thus might express itself in party-crashing or exchanges of verbal insults (15).

38. The proposition seems particularly relevant to the young male groups in *LLL*, *Ado*, and *AWW*.

39. My thanks to T. G. Bishop for calling this to my attention.

40. Neill has a brilliant chapter on this word and its associated images.

41. In the anonymous *English Courtier* (1586), the Country Gentleman sees a large retinue as a sign of the master's social significance; the English Courtier looks at actual usefulness, and would discharge any servant not performing useful work (summarized in Neill 29–30). The disagreement seems obviously consonant with the dispute between Lear and Goneril.

42. Mahood contrasts the familial nature of Lear's retinue and "the hire-and-salary world" of Goneril and Regan, who "can conceive of service only as a way of meeting practical needs" (161).

43. Attention to boundaries appears in *Titus Andronicus, Julius Caesar, Hamlet,* and *Macbeth*, and distinguishes the tragedies of *Othello* and *Antony and Cleopatra*, which play themselves out on the frontier between east and west. In *1 Henry IV*, another prolonged adolescent, Hotspur, asserts his readiness to "cavil on the ninth part of a hair" (3.1.136) as he and Glendower carve up England.

44. Porter's central enterprise is to show that Mercutio expresses Shakespeare's highly complex tribute to his great predecessor and rival, Christopher Marlowe, and that Marlowe/Mercutio, not its source, Brooke, nor its titular hero, Romeo, truly presides over the play. The second part of the assertion, at least, seems to me untenable; as I have been arguing, Mercutio's behavior is ultimately anachronistic and futile, and in the *agon* of Romeo and Mercutio, the wit-combat of 2.3.32–87, Romeo more than holds his own, and gets the last word.

45. The analysis suggests an understanding of that peculiar episode, Essex's rebellion. Recall that Elizabeth stood in relationship to those closest to her *in loco parentis*, for they were, practically and often formally, members of her household, and that her customary method of discipline for transgressions against her rule was rustication—the courtly equivalent of "Go to your room!" Essex, thus banished to the fringes of the establishment, exhibits an essentially adolescent mode of behavior, gathering a band of (mostly younger) friends around him, constructing with them fantasies of domination and revenge (the latter focused on the *male* parental figures around the queen), finally acting them out in that pathetic, self-destructive gesture that might be construed as marking the symbolic, if not the practical, end of the retainer tradition.

46. Wrangham and Peterson cite an experiment in which pairs of friends split up and assigned to rival groups began to express commitment to group identity over individual friendship within a few days (194–95). The readiness with which modern male executives and athletes move from firm to

firm or team to team, regardless of the success they may have achieved as part of a particular group, supports the point.

47. Similar conflicts occur at similar moments in *Twelfth Night, Troilus and Cressida*, and *Cymbeline*.

6 *Fidelis Servus* . . . : Good Service and the Obligations of Obedience

1. See earlier chapter 5, n. 10.

2. Once, the argument goes, man was free. But all sin is disobedience of God (Chrysostom observes that no servants appear in the Bible until after the Flood); hence "service is a state of subjection, grounded partly in the curse of God for sin," and confirmed by the fifth commandment (Baynes 365; Chrysostom 303; Greaves 322). Even the new dispensation, as Calvin reminds us, promises only a spiritual, not a carnal freedom. And since it is God who has placed servants in their subordinate state, it is He whom they really serve (3.828). For that reason, the primary motive for obedient service, as stated in Ephesians 6:5 and enthusiastically echoed by all commentators, is the fear of God. The scoldings, beatings, confinements, deprivations, and summary discharges by which law and custom allowed masters to punish disobedient servants only gave corporal expression to a spiritual chastisement of far graver import.

3. The derivation of secular from divine authority grounds some important instances of disobedience, for instance, Hubert's in *King John*. A by-product of this idea was the insistent emphasis through all the authorities—mostly clergymen, to be sure—on masters' obligation to give their servants religious education and to require of them regular, daily religious observances (Brathwaite 4; Byfield 134; Cleaver and Dod B4r; Touteville 346).

4. See also Elton 1637, 598; Gouge *Exposition* 104–10. A model of patriarchal mastery is supplied by Touchstone the goldsmith in Jonson's *The Case is Altered*. To his virtuous, obedient apprentice Golding, he gives trust, responsibility, his daughter's hand in marriage, and a substantial jointure. To his rebellious apprentice Quicksilver, he gives only the freedom the young rake demands. The division is so paradigmatic, so much a dramatized pamphlet, that it declines to take on much theatrical life. However, it does handsomely illustrate the orthodox views of these matters.

5. The concordance reveals a high concentration of uses of *obey* and its derivatives in many of the plays in which servants are numerous and important: *H8* 13, *Shr.* 11, *Lr.* 11, *Ham.* 10, *Oth.* 10, *Cym.* 8, *Ant.* 7, *Err.* 6, *Tem.* 6, *Jn.* 4.

6. On corporal punishment of servants, see Fleming 20.

7. Strier summarizes the development of the idea of responsible disobedience through the sixteenth century, and then provides a detailed analysis of its workings in *King Lear* (*Resistant* 165–202). See also Kronenfeld, especially 123–69; she treats the issues in largely political rather than personal terms.

8. Analogs are pretty common in the plays of the period. Among the most striking: Brainwit, in *Every Man in His Humour*, whose efforts to serve

assorted masters lead him through a Protean series of disguises and pretenses; Shadow, in *Old Fortunatus*, who like the Dromios grumbles a lot as his old and young masters ride Fortune's bouncing ball; Babulo in *Patient Grissel*, whose fidelity to his young mistress Grissel mirrors at the servants' level hers to her foolish husband at that of the gentlefolk.

9. This moment has its equivocal features, since Cornwall's authority here is double—he is acting as regent on behalf of his wife Regan, as well as master. On the other hand, the legality of his order for the blinding of Gloucester, which must resonate with early Stuart notions of due process, seems dubious, since there has been no formal trial. Strier notes Shakespeare's stress on "the extrajudicial, purely private nature" of the act (*Resistant* 192). Nor is blinding (threatened by John against Arthur in order to disable him as a rival without necessarily killing him) a proper punishment for treason.

10. Strier mentions but does not explore Hubert's acts of service; he treats the other three at greater length. He argues that Kent's resistance to Lear's folly in preferring his older daughters' flattery to Cordelia's truth and his disobedience of Lear's order of banishment "most fully articulate" virtuous disobedience ("Faithful" 113). He seems to me, however, to take less full account of his master's spiritual well-being—equally the good servants' charge—than do Hubert and Camillo. By the same token, he dismisses Cordelia's initial resistance as a mere evasion (112), discounting by disregard her return from France and her deeply submissive solicitude for the king in his derangement.

11. The question of Shakespeare's relationship to his sources in *King John* is notoriously difficult. For a summary of these issues, see the introductions to their editions of the play by Beaurline, Braunmuller, and Honigmann. Quite apart from the contention over the nature of the Folio text (author's text? author's text corrected by playhouse annotator for publication and later theatrical use? playhouse text?) and its connections with *The Troublesome Raigne of King John* (1591, hereafter *TR*), authorities disagree about the extent and nature of the debts to the various chronicles, and especially the manuscript chronicle of Radulph Coggeshall. This last was evidently Holinshed's primary source for the story—highly ambiguous—of Hubert de Burgh's treatment of John's nephew and rival Arthur, and hence of the character of Hubert—although that character is more fully developed in *TR* than in any chronicle, and much more fully developed in *Jn.*— especially as regards his relationship with John—than in *TR*. Braunmuller notes that Holinshed "said too much about Arthur"—presents sometimes conflicting materials from his sources without choosing among them, and passes the confusion along to Shakespeare ("Historiography" 316). I will consider elements of these problems only as they affect the present argument—i.e., not attempting to participate in the debate per se, but only noting ways in which contrasts between chronicle and play or between *TR* and *Jn.* bring out aspects of the service relationship.

12. Critical emphasis on this play's political elements and on the dynamic outsider Falconbridge has meant that Hubert has attracted very little prior

attention. Neither Strier nor Weinstock analyzes his part in the action of the play. The fullest treatment is by Barish, "Oath-Breach."

13. The confusion arises from the fact that the Folio introduces the Citizen in a stage direction: "Enter a Citizen upon the walles" (2.1.201, presumably on the gallery at the back of the stage), and three succeeding speeches presenting the position of the people of Angers are headed "Cit." (267, 270, 281). Both King John and King Philip address "men" of Angers (203, 204 and thereafter) and whoever speaks for the city repeatedly uses *we* and *our*; evidently more than one person has come on. During a brief interval during which the kings lead their armies off to do battle, and in the absence of any stage direction calling for his exit, this character (or these) presumably remains in place. When the kings return, and without any stage direction marking another entrance on the walls, the speech prefixes for the spokesman for Angers (except for one, 368, obviously belonging to him, mistakenly given to the King of France) name him "Hubert." The suggestion that the Citizen and Hubert are the same person was made by J. Dover Wilson in his edition of the play(xl–xlvi, 121n.); it was accepted by Honigmann (New Arden), Evans (Riverside), Matchett (Signet), and Smallwood; it was rejected or queried by Beaurline (New Cambridge), Bevington, Braunmuller (Oxford), Wells and Taylor (*William Shakespeare: A Textual Companion*), Harrison, and Ribner.

14. There are a good many doublings. Of characters not father and son, the most intriguing is in *R3*, where Lord Hastings meets, names, and converses with Hastings the poursuivant (3.2.91–103), in what Antony Hammond can only explain as a moment of rather labored irony (ed. 338); we also find two Bardolphs in *2H4*, two Cinnas in *JC*, two Jaques in *AYL*. Within families, pairs of Antipholi and Dromii (*Err.* where the confusion is explicit and intentional), Stanleys (*R3*), Gobbos (*Mer.*), Siwards (*Mac.*), Hamlets and Fortinbras, plus various Henrys, Yorks, Gloucesters, Edwards, Richards, etc., in the histories. In all these cases, however, the two individuals are distinguished by family (Jaques de Boys versus Jaques the traveler), age, status ("my lord"), function (Cinna the conspirator versus Cinna the poet). Only in *Jn.* is no such distinction made: the fact seems to me to support the proposition that Hubert the citizen becomes Hubert the servant.

15. The political dimensions of these events are explored by Edwards. He treats the assault on Arthur as "the climactic scene of sacrilege which serves as the focus for the whole play"—but has virtually nothing to say about Hubert (118).

16. The beginning of the speech, with its three-fold repetition of Hubert's name, directs attention to the fact that Hubert is called by name strikingly often: 32 times during the 571 lines during which he is unquestionably on stage, including long periods when, as befits his servant's station, he is an unobtrusive onlooker. (I ignore the debatable scene, 2.1; he is not named in the dialogue of this scene, one reason for doubting the validity of the speech headings.) For comparison: Romeo is named 132 times, Hamlet 72, Iago (sometimes in a servant role) 60 but his master Othello only 24, Lear (as *Lear* rather than *King*) 15; of those characters comparable in extent and role, the two Dromios between them 36 times, Tranio 34, Lancelot

Gobbo 27, Pisanio 26, Grumio 23, Kent (in *Lr.*) 15, Enobarbus 14. Hubert is not unique; many servants are named more frequently than their masters because they are addressed by name, not only to attract their attention for an upcoming order but also because using someone's personal name implies intimacy, yet also superiority, especially when the someone is obliged to reply with an honorific, such as "My lord." The force of this act of naming is illustrated in another way by the 88 occurrences of the name of Katherine/Katherina/Kate, mostly addressed directly to her, and mostly by Petruchio, to 35 for Petruchio, mostly by people talking about him in his absence (Katherine never once uses his name). In *Jn.*, Hubert is named with particular frequency in the two scenes where his two masters are trying to persuade him to do something wrong—John, to kill Arthur; Arthur, to disobey John.

17. The force of oath-taking and oath-breaking in the play is analyzed by Barish.

18. The personal dimension is emphasized not only by John's repeated use of Hubert's name but also by the words *friend* and *love*. Hubert, however, never presumes to make similar gestures of intimacy toward John.

19. English antecedents for these characters can be found in the murderers and torturers of the mystery plays. Indeed, there is a clear homology between Herod, his retainers (the York cycle calls them "knights," *Herod* 150, 163, 212, etc.), and the innocent boys of Bethlehem, and John, his "executioners," and Arthur.

20. Mowbray, in *R2*, is a special case, since the event, the assault on the Duke of Gloucester, has taken place some time before the beginning of the play, and is represented as an extra-legal execution of a true traitor. So are Rosencrantz and Guildenstern in *Hamlet*, who may, but also may not, know the contents of the letter requesting death for Hamlet that they carry to England.

21. The epitome occurs, of course, not in Shakespeare but in Webster's Bosola. It may be that the prevalence of such characters refracts the anxiety provoked in late-sixteenth- and early-seventeenth-century English society (with some reason) by the large numbers of former soldiers, trained and hardened by fighting in the Low Countries and France, who found it difficult to return to civilian life, especially during a period of economic stress.

22. Weimann finds the fullest expression of this in William Perkins, *The Whole Treatise of the Cases of Conscience* (1606), a response to all the anti-Protestant actions of the government in the preceding decades (*Authority* 88–89). Perkins, however, only gives explicit political expression to a thought that had been gathering force from Luther onward.

23. Strier goes on to note that the Elizabethan version of the Homily on Obedience is far more authoritarian: "Conscientious nonobedience vanishes as either an option or an obligation" (107–08). The shift is part of the retreat from early Lutheran political liberalism discussed in chapter 1.

24. The doctrine imposed immense stress on English Catholics throughout the reigns of Edward and Elizabeth, and on Protestants under Mary.

25. In an interesting way, Shakespeare suppresses some potentially relevant political issues. Generally in *Jn.*, the question of service is wrapped up in the question of legitimacy, which engages all the important characters from the beginning to the end. But Hubert rather conspicuously does not use the uncertainties about John's claim to the throne to help ease the stress of his disobedience. Arthur's claim is such that Hubert could, in good enough conscience, give fealty to him rather than to John. Indeed, sparing Arthur is an act of practical allegiance. But only in subtextual terms; the issue does not explicitly appear in the language of this scene, or of those that follow it, in which Hubert reports his faithful disobedience to the King and defends himself against the enraged lords. He thus distinguishes himself from characters like Lord Stanley in *R3* and the revolted Percies in *1H4* whose disobedience is explicitly or implicitly based on a conviction that the ruler is not, in fact, a rightful one.

26. An intriguing question, but one that remains, as it were, buried in the text, not receiving any explicit notice at any point, is generated by the fact that the warrant for Arthur's torment is brought by men whom the Folio stage directions and speech headings term Executioners; the usage also occurs in *TR*. Braunmuller's gloss notes that Elizabethan usage did not confine this word to those who inflict injury or death, but used it for any person carrying out instructions; but all the other Shakespearean instances use the term in the limited modern sense. The question is why Hubert does not simply let them carry out the deed, as Brackenbury does when Richard's tool villains come for Clarence, but rather takes responsibility for it himself. Hubert calls them "dogged spies" (4.1.128), and uses them to spread the false rumor of Arthur's death. One of them, like his counterpart in *R3*, expresses deep discomfort: "I am best pleased to be from such a deed" (85)—but nothing suggests he would not carry out the order if given.

27. It is worth noting that in the first speech the act is explicitly motivated by fear of punishment—torture—rather than the abstract obligation of obedience.

28. Editorial consensus dates the composition of *Jn.* in the mid-1590s; some place it shortly before, some shortly after *R2*.

29. The corresponding speech in *TR* both emphasizes hierarchy and adds a reminder of the consequences of disobedience: "Why heres my Lord your Highnes hand & seale, / Charging on lives regard to doo the deede" (1714–15).

30. The emphasis on the *visual*, which obviously connects with the blinding of Arthur, is a general theme of the play, which explores the conventional interactions of appearance and reality in many striking ways; see Braunmuller ed. 43–48. The speech has led some producers of the play to make Hubert strikingly ugly or disfigured, but although Hubert admits that his form is "rude" (4.2.57–58), nobody else says anything uncomplimentary about Hubert's appearance, and John himself goes on to suggest that the deformity lay in imagination, not Hubert's lineaments: "for my rage was blind, / And foul imaginary eyes of blood / Presented thee more hideous than thou art" (4.3.265–67).

31. Barish perceives that Shakespeare "plainly does not believe" in vows that arise from abstract notions of "place" and "status," e.g., of servant to master. But he does not situate the issue theologically ("Oath-Breach" 13).

32. Burkhardt also notices the shift from the political toward the emotional, but regards Hubert as a master rather than a servant (123–33).

33. This is the sustaining theme of A. R. Braunmuller's treatment of the play (ed. "Historiography").

34. This episode falls within the part of *Pericles* accepted by Vickers and the many scholars he cites as Shakespeare's (ch. 5).

35. On good mastery in general, see James 54.

36. Strier recognizes Pisanio but does not go into much detail. So does Horst Weinstock, though his emphasis on the plays of the 1590s prevents even him from treating Pisanio at length. Erica Sheen has a long, complex, and finally not very persuasive argument that sees the play's nominal endorsement of orthodox understandings of service as undercut by subtle echoes (structural, not verbal) of Seneca's *Hercules furens*; in her analysis, Pisanio's loyal disobedience expresses Shakespeare's insistence on his freedom to rebuke his own master, James I. She does not treat Pisanio himself very fully.

37. I use the traditional "Imogen" in preference to the Oxford and Norton "Innogen."

38. For servants to lie on behalf of their masters appears to be acceptable to all; not even the most stringently moralizing commentators condemn such practices, either general or particular. A casual instance occurs elsewhere in this play, when Imogen has Pisanio arrange for her lady-in-waiting to pretend illness so that Imogen can leave the court in character of the maid (3.2.73–75). Mahood notes the maid Helen's vigorous defense of her mistress (45); she thus supplies a female version of Pisanio's good service.

39. Few carried this understanding as far as Daniel Touteville, the gentlest of the commentators, who told his readers, "If thou have a servant, therefore, treat him like a brother" (326). But the conception lay deep enough to inform the best and richest visions of the relationship, as we shall see in chapter 7.

40. Whether Shakespearean doctors are servants who might be hired for exceptionally brief periods, or independent practitioners as they are now, is a nice question. If the former, then this Doctor makes a clear counterpart to Pisanio.

41. Strier details the Protestant view of faithful disobedience in his treatment of the controversialists John Ponet, Christopher Goodman, John Knox, and George Buchanan (*Resistant* 108–10).

7 ... *Perpetuus Asinus*: Bad Service and the Primacy of the Will

1. On the complex personal and social matrices that generate theatrical images, see Grady 9–10, and Yachnin, *Stage-Wrights* 41–42.

2. The analysis is easier to carry out in looking at texts than at actual society, of course. Some sense of the difficulty in generalizing about early modern social relationships produced by the paucity of reliable data and the overlapping of ideological paradigms is outlined by Keith Wrightson. At the

turn of the seventeenth century, he says, we find "a persistent, unresolved tension between bonds of social identification and the conflicts of interests and ideals produced by intensified differentiation [of social identity]" ("Social Order" 201). Such tensions should produce precisely the ideological variations we find in Shakespeare's representations of social hierarchies.

3. Neill and I reached very similar conclusions about Iago by independent ways. But the uses to which we put our analysis are significantly different.

4. Miriam Slater speaks to the general vulnerability of masters to servants expressed in the Verney papers.

5. He goes on to categorize Iago's long speech on service as an "analogy." Neill does not go as far as I do in perceiving Iago's service as essentially domestic, but does reject Burnett's term, arguing, I think rightly, that military "place" is only another aspect of the central early modern system of dependence (27). Burnett has some lively pages on the manner in which "the male domestic servant can achieve power, not in acts of open revolt but through a gradual, persistent weakening of aristocratic defences" (*Masters* 109). His instance, however, is not Iago, whom he does not even name, but DeFlores in *The Changeling*.

6. The orders are as follows: (1) with Emilia, to escort Desdemona to Cyprus (1.3.293–96); (2) to look after Othello's baggage (2.1.204–06); (3) to report on the fight between Cassio and Montano (2.3.160–61); (4) to take charge of security in Cyprus after the brawl (2.3.239–40); (5) to give his thoughts on Cassio (3.3.136–38); (6) to report further on Cassio, and to set Emilia to spy on Desdemona (3.3.244–45); (7) to provide "the ocular proof" of Desdemona's infidelity (3.3.365–71); (8) to supply "reason she's disloyal" (3.3.414); (9) to kill Cassio (3.3.475–76); and (10) to obtain poison (4.1.194). Of these, only (3) and (4) are germane to the Venetian military expedition; all the others relate to Othello's personal effects and affairs. And all of them are variants—albeit increasingly perverse—of the routine tasks of domestic servants in early modern Europe.

7. Another instance of that repetition of servants' names we noticed earlier in connection with Hubert.

8. The passage involves two textual cruces, both germane to the matter of service. The first is the variance between the "excellency" of Q1 and the "execution" of Q2 and F (469). Bibliographical questions aside, either term suits the tenor of the speech, that Iago places himself, including all his most efficacious powers and qualities, at Othello's disposal, to do with as he will: the most comprehensive reading would include both words. But the use of *executioner* as a synonym for *servant* (in the stage directions of *KJ* 4.1, the Arthur-Hubert scene, e.g.) tends to support the Q2/F reading. The second is the apparent illogic of "to obey shall be in me remorse" (471, further complicated by the omission of *in me* in Q1). The line has occasioned much commentary, to which I will add this suggestion, that the line of reasoning according to which moral responsibility for servants' actions is transferred to the master when the servant is following direct orders (carried further in the next line, "What bloody business ever"), leads to this paraphrase: "Obedience will so dominate my thoughts and acts that it will completely take the place of remorse and other motions of my conscience

and so liberate my will as to allow me to carry out any order, commit any act, no matter how savage."

9. For informative treatment of these tool villains, see Mahood 49–52. She notes that in most of these plays one or more of the hired killers expresses remorse after the deed is done; Iago expresses none.

10. As he so often does, Shakespeare doubles the expression of the theme, in the speeches and actions of Emilia. When she pushes by the promptings of her conscience to "steal" the handkerchief at her husband's command (3.3.297), she does her mistress harm; only by directly disobeying both her husband Iago and her master Othello can she reveal their crimes and so recover her moral integrity, if at the cost of her life.

11. Given the emphasis in recent studies of the play on the differences between Q and F, it is worth noting that the speech is virtually identical in the two texts.

12. I came across it in a manuscript allegory of Fortuna, ca. 1585; the phrase is connected with two Iago-like figures standing next to Fortune's chariot. The first is "lyke a magnifico or some greate p[er]son: hys face fayre & commely for an old man: havynge a graye beard forkyd: But in the hynder parte of hys head, he muste have the face of a devyll. over hym this writynge. *Malitia vult illa quidem videri se esse prudentiam, sed abest ab ea distatque plurimùm* [Cicero, *De officiis* 3.71]. . . . Also one attendynge vpon this grave gentleman shall stand in a gowne lyke a servaunte . . . Barehead . . . havynge a penne in his eare & a scrowle in his hand: he shall poynte wyth his forefinger to this speeche placyd in somme meete roome. *Imperavi egomet mihi et servitutem servio* [stitched together from Terence, *Eunuchus* 252 and Plautus, *Miles gloriosus* 95]. But an Italyan smilynge standynge by hym shall poynte vnto hym wyth this speeche. *fidelis servus perpetuus Asinus*" (Brit. Lib. MS Sloane 1096 fol. 5r). The motto does not appear in either Tilley's *Dictionary of the Proverbs in England* or in *The Oxford Dictionary of English Proverbs* (3rd ed.), though both give *A good servant should have the back of an ass* (Tilley S33). Shakespeare connects servants and the word *ass* in *Wiv.* 2.2.300; *Err.* 3.1.14, 3.1.18, 3.1.47, 3.2.77; *TN* 2.3.149, 2.3.162, 2.3.163–64; *JC* 4.1.26. The most salient instance is a long aside by Dromio of Ephesus when his master has called him an ass: "I am an ass indeed. You may prove it by my long ears.—I have served him from the hour of my nativity to this instance, and have nothing of his hand for my service but blows . . . and I think when he hath lamed me I shall beg . . . from door to door" (4.4.27–35). In another relevant speech, Iago anticipates the inversion of servant–master roles when he observes that Othello "will as tenderly be led by the nose / As asses are" (1.3.383–84). Wyrick has extensively explored the iconographic background of Shakespeare's asses. Burnett has studied the development and dispersion of an emblem of "the trusty servant," a composite image incorporating an ass's ears (for patiently hearing the master's orders and especially reprimands), a hog's snout (for eating any diet, however poor), and a deer's feet (for dispatching his tasks swiftly); he quotes a verbal instance of the topos, in English, of 1543, and generally demonstrates that it was widely known ("Trusty").

13. The problems do not always involve clear black-and-white moral choices. Brainwit, in Jonson's *Every Man In*, is torn (in the traditional New Comic way) between serving his master and his master's son. The first he must obey; the second he must "insinuate with . . . for so must we that are blue waiters, and men of hope and service do, or perhaps we may wear motley at the year's end"—be dismissed, like any fool, should the old master die and his heir be indifferent or resentful—"and who wears motley, you know" (ed. Wilkes, 21.24–28).

14. Neill also includes the much later *Double Dealer* of Congreve (1693), noting that both Massinger and Congreve were the sons of men who had been stewards in great houses and thus learned up close the peculiar frustrations of knowing that most of the benefits of one's faithful labor are going to somebody else (41).

15. Burnett's book, which shares many of Neill's positions, pays strikingly little attention to Shakespeare—a couple of dozen references to only seven of the plays in a book of 200-plus pages.

16. A posture closer to mine is Kronenfeld, who in the end chooses to emphasize moral over political or economic issues, in comparing Kent and Oswald (237–44).

17. Iago's refusal to speak to his judges ("From this time forth I never will speak word") may also be construed as a blasphemous parody, of Christ's silence before Pilate.

18. What follows owes much to Maurice Hunt's treatment of slavery in early modern England, "Slavery, English Servitude, and *The Comedy of Errors*," to John D. Cox's analysis of the Augustinian treatment of power and vulnerability in medieval and Shakespearean drama, and to comments by Carol Chillington Rutter on an earlier draft of this book.

19. Barrington Moore, writing from within the modern libertarian understanding of the service role as inherently undesirable, locates the sources of asceticism in the suffering inevitably encountered in any life; if the suffering is accepted, the hostility aroused by it is directed "inward against the self instead of outward against its social causes" (55).

20. Greenblatt begins his discussion of Renaissance self-fashioning, to which we will return shortly, with a summary of Tyndale's treatment of the *imitatio* (2).

21. Some recent criticism, and a good many recent productions of the play, have investigated the possibility that Iago is attracted, homosocially if not homosexually, to Othello, and plots against Cassio and Desdemona as great rivals for his beloved's love. The idea enriches the motivational field but does not, I think, affect my argument.

22. Paul Yachnin offers the provocative suggestion that "men and women are loyal only to masters whose will is unconditionally free and sovereign in that it is undetermined by ideology, law, or morality" ("Politics" 352). I do not think that the statement holds universally true for all of Shakespeare's works—it will not account for the Dromios, for instance, and it is hard to reconcile with the instances of loyal disobedience we have just been considering. It is the case that the most conspicuous instances of servant loyalty are exhibited by servants whose masters have broken through ordinary

social constraints—Orlando, Lear, Posthumus, Timon. How the proposition might fit *Othello* is not clear. Othello has not obviously consulted any will but his own in promoting Cassio, marrying Desdemona, and governing Cyprus, and none of these actions is inherently antisocial. Iago's defection, then, seems to spring fully from himself.

23. My concept of volitional primacy seems to me consonant with the recurrent attention in the work of Robert Weimann to what he terms "self-authorizing expression" (*Authority* 3), of which he finds instances all over early modern culture, but especially in the theater, where juxtaposing and evaluating "the ideas and attitudes of both service and individualism, honor and property, sophistication and simplicity, cynicism and naivety" led to "a heightened sense of both the congruity and the incongruity between the *mimesis* of society and the expression, no longer the embodiment, of the self" (*Shakespeare* 251–52).

24. Vickers, citing many other scholars, gives authorship of the beginning of the play, and hence the first introduction of Aaron, to George Peele (ch. 3). The development I find most interesting occurs in Shakespeare's part, however.

25. For what it is worth, the other leaders who survive, Kent and Albany, have also gone through a servile phase: Kent as Lear's servant Caius, Albany as the marginalized if not absolutely suppressed husband of the domineering Goneril. Neill has a trenchant paragraph contrasting Kent and Iago as types of the ideal and the materialistic conceptions of service (25–26).

26. I have not previously discussed Seyton; he appears in the Folio text by name only toward the end, though in production the same actor often appears as one of the nameless servants who do customary servant work earlier in the play—bringing and taking messages, serving the banquet, carrying torches—and/or as one of the murderers who kill Banquo and the Macduff family. He apparently remains faithful to his master longer than anybody else, and is compliant, even obsequious, to the end, when he comes in to inform Macbeth of his lady's death. He will presumably suffer with the rest of the "cruel ministers / Of this dead butcher and his fiend-like queen" whose trial and punishment is implied in Malcolm's final speech (5.11.30–41).

27. Thomas Moisan gives this episode a Foucaultian reading, seeing it as just one of many expressions of service as a "constant, total, massive, nonanalytical, unlimited relation of domination, established in the form of the unlimited will of the master, his 'caprice' " (279). You could enact that reading in the theater by having Petruchio stand a yard from the door while he gives the order to Grumio clear on the other side of the stage. I must say, however, that few if any orders given by Shakespearean masters to their servants—including Petruchio's order here—strike me as overtly capricious; most are reasonable reactions to particular situations. Indeed, the scene will be funnier if Grumio is, indeed, close to the door and Petruchio at a distance.

28. Toward the end of an argument attempting to discuss general characteristics of the Shakespearean plays, I must tread a little gingerly here, in the no-man's-land between those editors who are sure that Shakespeare shared authorship of this play with Thomas Middleton (to whom the Oxford editors and Vickers assign some of the development of the character of

Flavius the Steward) and those who are equally sure that all is Shakespeare's work. Middleton gets the first introduction of Flavius, exposing Timon's bankruptcy (1.2). Shakespeare develops the character most fully as he reviews his unsuccessful efforts to arrest Timon's mad career even as he expresses his continuing support (2.1, 14 speeches, 77 lines), then a long speech in which he offers to share his own savings with the other servants (4.2.1–29), then a final scene in which he acts as Timon's doorkeeper and gives a short, bleak valediction (5.2). To Middleton are assigned moralizing comments on the hollowness of wealth (4.2.30–51), the important scene in which he meets Timon in the forest, offers him money, and is in turn offered some of the buried gold that Timon has found there (4.3.451–528), and two short transitional scenes (3.4, 3.5; Vickers 277). Despite the stylistic differences on which the allotments are based, and the assertion that the collaboration is too loose to produce real coherence (Vickers 480), Flavius is coherently conceived, recalling Pisanio in his realism and fidelity.

29. It is interesting that in a play where so many servants have names, so many other characters, as David Bevington notes, are identified only as types (ed. Bevington 1251).

30. It is thus in contrast with *Thomas of Reading* (ca. 1597–1600), in which a prosperous clothier drawn to emulate his betters by distributing lordly *largesse* goes broke. The servants to whom he has been prodigally generous desert him, although they return when he acknowledges his bourgeois condition again (Burnett *Masters* 68). The issue here seems to be not the ethics of service but something like its esthetics: when the clothier restores decorum, the servants return.

31. Flavius's virtuous stewardship is discussed by Burnett (*Masters* 163–64). He goes on to state that among early modern dramatic stewards, he is exceptional, though the focus of his argument, on Antonio in *Duchess of Malfi*, strikes me as strained.

32. An instance of the other kind appears in Jonson's *The Case is Altered* (ca. 1597). Jacques de Prie, former steward to the hero Chaumont, achieved independence from his servile state by stealing both his master's treasure and his two-year-old daughter. But fear of revealing his crime by spending too freely has made him a miser, unable to enjoy the fruits of his crime; before the play is over, his desperate efforts to protect his hoard have led to its discovery (and enjoyment) by the dim-witted Onion. Jonson took a general interest in the ethics of stewardship; both Mosca, in *Volpone*, and Face, in *The Alchemist*, exercise a good deal of private initiative in managing their patrons' resources, though to different ends, since Mosca, trying to garner all for himself, is discomfited, while Jeremy Face, working on behalf of his master (so, at least, he insists), is rewarded by not less than the verbal reversal of the dependence: "I will," says Lovewit, "be ruled by thee in anything, Jeremy" (ed. Wilkes, 5.5.143). He goes on to promise some material expression of his gratitude, too: "That master / That had received such happiness by a servant, . . . / Were very ungrateful if he would not be / A little indulgent to that servant's wit, / And help his fortune" (146–52). Yet it must be noted that he admits that the reward has placed "some small

strain / Of his own candour," and perhaps "outstripped / An old man's gravity" (152–55).

33. The lack may be related to that inability to deal adequately with the place of religion in early modern culture, and especially with that aspect of it that Greenblatt dismissively calls "glad tidings," which Strier sees as a major weakness in the work of Greenblatt and other new historicists (*Resistant* 73).

34. The Fool in Lear is altogether a more complicated instance; because the play is a tragedy, and a particularly distressing one, because there seems in him something febrile from the outset, by contrast with the "strong and lusty" Adam (2.3.48), and because the stresses to which he is subjected go well beyond mere fatigue and hunger, sending him off like an animal to find a private place to die makes sense. But again, no warrant in the text.

35. In Q, Edgar reports how the stress of recounting these events has brought Kent to literal collapse, so that "the strings of life / Began to crack" (*HLr.* 24.210–15), setting up the strong suggestion at the end of the play that Kent will soon follow his master into death.

36. Woodbridge cites Raman Selden on Edgar's "double consciousness here," in seeing poverty as a punishment for bad service, not a sign of bad mastery (214), and links his disguise with the "fraudulent poverty" depicted in the popular literature of roguery (221–23). She goes on to describe a more purely existential vision shared by Lear and Gloucester, and notes that it finds its focus in a more generally disturbed and disturbing Tom who "really has lost everything, and . . . really is homeless" (224). But she does not pick up on service.

37. The list of animal attributes makes this monster a savage parody of the composite beast who emblematizes trusty service, discussed earlier.

38. The fact is recognized though not developed by Kronenfeld (158) and reaffirmed in her conclusion, quoting Alan Shapiro: "Perhaps, indeed, 'a "hermeneutics of suspicion," in and of itself, despite its intellectual sophistication, is as crudely incomplete as a sympathetic imagination divorced from the disciplines of intellectual and historical inquiry' " (244).

8 "A Place in the Story": Gender, Commodity, Alienation, and Service

1. See, for instance, the view of service in the anonymous pamphlet *A Lettere from the Maids of London* (1567), threatening that if such freedoms as they had were withdrawn in accordance with the proposals of Edward Hake, no more country girls would want to take London service, and without them the society would collapse (Fehrenbach 37).

2. In an essay that has perhaps not received the attention it deserves, Lawrence Danson contrasts what he calls "the ego-self," crucially developed within the family, and the social self developed in response to the larger world. Danson assigns concern with the former to Shakespeare and the latter to Jonson, and goes on to discuss in detail Jonson's inability or refusal to represent normal family relationships. Jonson's emphasis on the social self may also account for the relatively skimpy attention he pays to service.

3. Some modern productions, notably that directed by Jonathan Miller with Laurence Olivier as Shylock and Joan Plowright as Portia, have contrived to suggest that Jessica's Jewishness puts her outside the group, and it is certainly true that Portia and Nerissa do not take her into their confidence. But Nerissa and Portia bid her welcome (3.2.236, 311), Portia acknowledges her as her deputy during the Venetian mission (3.4 38), and in Venice works to secure her financial comfort, and there is certainly no textual evidence of any tension between them.

4. This fact may be related to the striking absence from the Shakespeare plays of adulterous and otherwise faithless women, by contrast with the work of other early modern dramatists. The exceptions, Jane Shore in the first tetralogy, Tamora in *Tit.*, and Goneril in *Lr.*, are conspicuous by their lack of company. (I decline to put Gertrude in this list; though there are a good many critics who think she belongs there, I have not found their arguments compelling). By contrast, Shakespeare multiplies instances of faithful wives and lovers falsely accused of infidelity—Hero, Desdemona, Imogen—and puts their stories at the center of their plays.

5. A more familiar analysis, of course, relates these differences to those between Roman and Egyptian, Western and Eastern cultural expectations.

6. My reading challenges that of Linda Charnes, who sees both Cleopatra and Antony as unable to think "in *any* terms other than those of an acquisitive expansionism . . . the stakes of the conflict . . . are the ability to lay claim to authoritative space in which the things acquired can be *appropriated* (in senses both personal and political) as *property*" (7; emphasis in original). I am persuaded, however, that although both the lovers occasionally use the commodifying rhetoric of the Roman ethos, their most urgent desire is for freedom from the stultifying commodity of that ethos. I argue this more fully later.

7. All these personages appear in Plutarch's life of Marcus Antonius. Mardian, Iras, and Charmian are grouped in ch. 60, where Iras is identified as Cleopatra's hairdresser and Charmian as her lady-in-waiting; Octavius accused them of being "mainly responsible for the direction of affairs" (Plutarch 9.273–74), and it is interesting in the present context that although Cleopatra listens to her maids (it is Charmian's idea to send news of Cleopatra's death to the desperate Antony), they are not presented primarily as political advisors. In Plutarch, there seem to be two men named Alexas: Alexas the Syrian and Alexas of Laodicia; both are clearly followers of Antony, for the former accompanies Antony in his flight from Actium (ch. 66; Plutarch 9.289), while the latter was introduced by Timagenes to Antony in Rome, and "he had come to enjoy more influence with him than any other Greek" (ch. 72; Plutarch 9.303). But in Shakespeare's play, the character is associated with the group around Cleopatra at his first entrance and thereafter, and editors since Rowe have placed him among her attendants in their lists of *dramatis personae*. Mahood thinks him "a kind of Lord Chamberlain" and calls him "an out-and-out time-server" whose self-centered artificiality represents the worst in Cleopatra's way of life (182, 185). Diomedes is said to be Cleopatra's secretary (ch. 76; Plutarch 6.79–9.313). Seleucus was "one of her Stewards" (ch. 83; Plutarch 9.323).

8. Speculations about relationships between the fictive households in Shakespeare's Jacobean tragedies and the actual households of Elizabeth, James I, Anne of Denmark, and Henry Prince of Wales are tempting but obviously risky. H. Neville Davies makes a plausible case for seeing parallels between James and Octavius, and for Christian of Denmark, James's brother-in-law, as a prototype for Antony. He largely ignores Cleopatra, perhaps because while Anne, like Cleopatra, was a foreigner, whose Catholic leanings distressed the Protestant faction in both Court and Parliament, and, like Cleopatra, was often accused of frivolity and giddiness, she does not appear to have been particularly fascinating to anybody in 1606, when her brother paid his visit. Elizabeth A. Brown's article on the waiting women of Elizabeth and Cleopatra concentrates on the differences between the two sets. "The notable difference is the absence in the staged court of the complex kinship networks that are precisely what made Elizabeth's women most politically useful. As staged, Cleopatra's women have no family ties and no obligations to anyone apart from her [unlike the women in the histories, especially the first tetralogy], and this contrast to the elaborate network of Elizabeth's court exposes the extent of Cleopatra's political isolation" (136). But this is true of everybody in *Ant*. Antony is married twice, but the first union is totally ruptured before the play begins and the second is never more than a gesture. Neither Octavius nor Cleopatra has a spouse, as far as the text is concerned. Cleopatra almost wholly ignores her children, but so does Antony. Nor are there significant uncles or aunts or cousins, by contrast with the courtly situations in the two tetralogies. For all that the scope of their activities is geographically vast, the three courts (four, if we include the glimpses we get of Pompey's) are equally hermetic. Shakespeare is not here interested in the political ramifications of kinship.

9. On the whole, they have attracted little critical attention. J. Leeds Barroll, in his stimulating book-length study of the play, gives three whole pages to Antony's servant Eros but refers to Iras (once) and Charmian (twice) only as auditors of speeches by others. Janet Adelman's study of the play is no more attentive. Mahood devotes a chapter to the minor characters in *Ant*. that necessarily touches on servants and service at many points. Mahood's chronological approach means that she mentions the women several times, but does not treat either at length. There is, however, a valuable recent study of the women by Elizabeth A. Brown.

10. Observe that although men of her court are present when Cleopatra is first introduced (1.2), thereafter they appear only insignificantly (Alexis in 3.3) or as de facto representatives of the Roman court (Seleucus in 5.2). Shakespeare's play accords with the research of Shelley E. Taylor and others showing that under stress, women in almost all cultures tend to seek support from one another and nurture one another, whereas men, "lone warriors," tend to fight or fly (Goode).

11. Janet Adelman has noted the pattern of betrayal, which extends even to Octavius if we count Dolabella's warnings to Cleopatra (46–47). She observes that the unreliability of some of the servants only mirrors the sometime unreliability of their masters and mistress. Barroll notes moments in which

the actions and attitudes of servants mark stages in Antony's fall; he argues, for instance, that Antony's anger because no one instantly responds to his summons for help with the punishment of Thidias, and the fact that the folio stage direction registers the entrance of only a single servant (3.13.89–93), constitute "threats of disintegration" (105). Barroll wonders later whether a similar sluggishness afflicts Antony's personal guard in the aftermath of the botched suicide (118–19).

12. Because it is Enorbarbus who speaks, the character on whom the question of fidelity is centered, Shakespeare may at this point be recalling Alexas's original affiliation with Antony as presented in Plutarch.

13. On this ambiguity, see Mahood 199–200.

14. The name calls for some comment. Plutarch's text calls him Δομίτιο[ς] ∂ὲ 'Αηνρόβαρβο[ς] initially, Δομίτιοσ in the two subsequent references (9.230, 264, 280). North similarly uses Domitius Ænobarbus in the first reference, Domitius in the second (North 6.42, 65). The text of the play refers to him as Domitius twice, Enorbarbus 14 times, 6 of them before the first use of Domitius; Enobarbus (or any of several abbreviations) is the form in all the F speech headings and stage directions.

15. The language enriches North's original: "O noble Eros, I thanke thee for this, and it is valliantly done of thee, to shew me what I should doe to my self, which thou couldest not doe for me" (6.79).

16. Plutarch reports that Strato later did good service to Caesar until the battle of Actium; Pindarus, by contrast, "was never seen again," a fact that suggested that he might have "slaine his master without his commaundement" (ch. 53, 43; North 6.235, 226). Shakespeare's decision to ignore this possibility deserves note.

17. Elizabeth A. Brown explicitly contrasts the fidelity of the women with the infidelity of "their Roman [and male] counterparts" (138).

18. Plutarch says only that when Caesar's soldiers arrived they found Cleopatra and Iras dead, Charmian still alive but dead after one short speech (North 7.185). Mahood suggests that she wills herself to die, thus becoming a female counterpart to Enobarbus (203): in the absence of any explicit cause from the text, we are free to speculate.

19. Plutarch tells us that after Actium, Antony and Cleopatra changed the governing principle of their lives from "*Amimetobion* (as much to say, no life comparable) and did set up another, which they called *Synapothanumenon* (signifying the order and agreement of those that will die together)" (North 7.170). Shakespeare seems to see Cleopatra at the end combining the two principles.

20. This model improves on those proposed by Charnes and Neill by including the second, familial mode—the mode that actually governs millions of actual relationships; Charnes's dichotomy is between "love as a poetic construct or usable material for a fiction, and love as *realpolitik*" (9); Neill's between a "society of orders" and one of "competitive individuals" (45).

21. Adam uses the word *master* 5 times in the 15 lines of his first speech to Orlando (2.3.2–15). In the second speech, of 13 lines, mostly about Oliver, the word does not appear. At the beginning of the play, Adam advises

Orlando of the approach of "my master, your brother" (1.1.22). In his next speech, he affiliates himself with both: "Sweet masters, be patient" (53). Oliver seems to suspect the old servant of confederacy with his rebellious sibling, though it would be stretching things to interpret his line of dismissal—"Get you with him, you old dog" (69)—as meaning "leave my service" rather than "leave my presence." At their next encounter, the old man goes on to make it clear that he will follow Orlando on his own initiative, not because Oliver has driven him off: "Let me be your servant. . . . Let me go with you . . ." (2.3.47–54). We know that he has sufficient money to live on his own if he wishes.

22. I am perfectly aware of the large body of materialist criticism of these plays that sees Henry IV and Henry V as only more discreetly acquisitive than Richard III or Falstaff, and focusing for the most part on power rather than property. I have argued against that view elsewhere (Evett "Types" 153–58); as the sequel shows, I am persuaded that Shakespeare generally promotes relationships based on either the familial or the ordinal ethos over those based on money.

23. Mahood does not make this point as such, but notes that Roman *imperium* "is not a civilising mission but conquest for loot"; perhaps influenced by Plutarch, she sees Enobarbus's defection as evidence that the authority of Roman leaders is solely based on their ability to give material rewards (189,196). Carol Cook perceives a related quality, "the drive toward coherence and closure . . . the unwavering drive toward unification and control" (246–47).

24. The most conspicuous involves the soldier rewarded with armor of gold for his gallantry during Antony's brilliant, reckless skirmish outside Alexandria, which briefly postpones the Roman victory: "Cleopatra gave the man a golden breastplate and helmet as a reward for his valor. He accepted them and the very same night deserted to Octavius Caesar" (ch. 74; North 7.173). In *Ant.*, the gift goes to Scarus, who as far as we know is faithful to the end (4.9.26–29); the element of betrayal is transferred to Enobarbus, whose repentance and death occur in the following scene.

25. As Plutarch puts it, "But by chance there stood Seleucus by, one of her treasurers, who to seem a good servant came straight to Caesar to disprove Cleopatra—that she had not set in all, but had kept many things back of purpose" (ch. 83; North 7.182); Mahood notes the comment (201). A number of critics, including Godshalk and Levin, have sought to discern in the scene some kind of collusion between Seleucus and Cleopatra—the whole thing staged to persuade Caesar that Cleopatra wants to live and so make the suicide possible. But as Stirling long ago noted, if so, it must all lie in the playing, since there is no clear sign of it in the text (302). Perhaps for that reason, Yachnin suggests a similar motive without arguing for collusion ("Shakespeare's Politics" 351).

26. Seleucus first appears in Plutarch as the governor of Pelusium; when he surrenders it, Antony kills his wife and children, with Cleopatra's concurrence (ch. 74; Plutarch 9.307). The event would supply some motive, beyond either a constitutional inability to lie or a self-interested fear of offending Octavius, for his betrayal, but no trace of it remains in the play. Shakespeare

follows Plutarch closely in reporting the episode of the concealed wealth, but the long speeches expressing Cleopatra's rage mightily expand Plutarch's laconic narrative: "she flew upon him, and took him by the hair of his head, and boxed him well-favoredly" (ch. 83; North 7.182).

27. A possibility negated by the reference to the death of his wife and children cited in the previous note.

28. The line shows how far the literal meaning of the term *slave* had been occluded in early modern English speech.

29. The references to cloud and vapor have the force of representing the women as fallen goddesses.

30. Her behavior contrasts with Antony's; he abuses Octavius's messenger Thidias without remorse, and is willing to sacrifice his own former servant in exchange (3.13.45–154). The messenger, by the way, has more to do than most of his kind in Shakespeare's plays, and handsomely illustrates elements of the practical ideology of Elizabethan–Jacobean service. Having run his errand faithfully, and come close to suffering extremely for it, on his second appearance he is at pains to satisfy his mistress's desires, and while he can not deny that Antony and Octavia were married, he can represent her person in terms that give or allow an unfavorable impression—"low-voiced," "She creeps," "She was a widow. . . . And I do think she's thirty," with a round face, brown hair, and a forehead "As low as she could wish it" (3.3). His mistress rewards him with gold. For more on this character, and messengers generally, see Mahood.

31. Oddly, Cleopatra here seems briefly to assume the commodifying role: "I'll set a bourn how far to be beloved" (1.1.14). I would note, however, that *bourn* is a pun, carrying on the imagery of the forge of love (probably with an oblique reference to the myth of Venus, Mars, and Vulcan) so prominent in the first lines of the play—*glowed, bellows, fan, cool*—and when Antony responds "Then must thou needs find out new heaven, new earth," the language glances at the familiar Ptolemaic cosmology in which the most distant sphere is pure fire.

32. This decision qualifies if it does not challenge Yachnin's proposal that servants remain fully loyal only to masters who retain their own volitional integrity ("Politics" 352). But it is true that his commitment will not survive the further follies Antony commits after they have returned to Alexandria.

33. Classical stoicism was grounded in the materialistic belief that the soul dies with the body.

34. The fact seems to contradict Mahood's insistence on the purely economic basis of Roman military authority (196): it is the soldier and the servant, not the entrepreneur in him that is disgusted by what has happened.

35. Robert Miola has a thought-provoking page on what he calls "transformative fictions"—initial fictions that subsequently turn into truth, such as Petruchio's insistence during the wooing scene that Katherine is gentle and loving (76). Cleopatra's fiction takes this course.

36. Helms stresses the bathetic elements here: "Cleopatra's suicide . . . would reiterate the classical protocol for a death in which a hero dwindles into a wife" (560).

37. Charnes has already been noted. See also Belsey, Bushman, Hamer, Helms.

9 "As Willing as Bondage E'er of Freedom": The Vindication
    of Willing Service in *The Tempest*

1. I have long thought that nothing more summarizes Shakespeare's remarkable generosity of spirit than the observation that virtually no character in the plays ends degraded, driven from the stage in abject humiliation or completely broken in spirit. It is equally true of comic fools like Don Armado and Sir Andrew Aguecheek and of villains like Edmund and Iago. Malvolio and Shylock perhaps come closest. Shylock's "I am content," though often pronounced with the verbal and postural equivalent of crossed fingers, is nevertheless a total capitulation, recognizing his loss not only of his economic power but also of his ethnic and religious identity. Malvolio's final threat to "be revenged on the whole pack of you" is ludicrously hollow. Yet it is followed by Olivia's recognition that he has been put upon, and by Orsino's proposal that he be invited back into the circle. For the present purpose, it behooves me to note that Shylock and Malvolio make my case, in a way, because they eschew volitional primacy by refusing to embrace the facts of their situation. By the same token, those figures who are allowed a dignified exit have mostly recognized their folly or wickedness. Two who do not, indeed, Antonio and Sebastian in *Tem.*, we deal with later in this chapter.

2. A way to describe their fate—and to account for its pathos—is to say that they are obliged by circumstance to cram a whole lifetime of mutual service and sacrifice into a few hours.

3. In this connection, it is appropriate to note that Thomas Wright, like other early modern authorities, sets up his psychological model in *The Passions of the Mind* as prelude to an argument concerning the power language has to control the passions and so affect human behavior, with respect not only to secular interests but also to the most serious issues of theology, individual as well as corporate: the ultimate purpose of rhetoric, he concludes, is to save souls.

4. Cox observes that in early modern texts "stylistic ambiguity is invariably an ambiguity about social standing" (*Dramaturgy* 63). He notes elsewhere that false humility is a typical device of the predatory materialist (29).

5. I follow here a suggestion from Hunt ("Slavery"). Hunt applies the notion to the masters in *Err.*: "If the Dromios are slaves of their masters' passions, then the masters themselves must in one sense be considered slaves—slaves of their emotional selves" (45). In discussion of this proposition during the seminar on service at the 1993 meeting of the Shakespeare Association of America, Richard Strier objected to Hunt's shifting of the term from literal to figurative use. But the model supplied by early modern psychology suggests that to early modern thinkers, at least, the usage was not figurative but literal; while the will is under the control of forces—in this case, the imagination—over which the person exerts no rational control, the will and hence the person are in a state of servitude. Hunt's language is therefore appropriate when applied to early modern work such as *Err.* The idea gains historical support from Cox; in the Augustinian view of things that had

come to saturate European culture, identity is shaped by desire, and those whose desire is for power become slaves of their lust (*Shakespearean* 12–17). Cox does not say so, but the idea that identity is not just shaped but constructed by desire is central to the work of Lacan.

6. An interesting contrast is offered by Malcolm, in *Mac.*, whose imagination allows him to construct an elaborate (and apparently very persuasive) image of the corrupt and corrupting monarch as a test for Macduff.

7. My approach in what follows is not very fully theorized, in either psychological or sociological directions. A postmodernist psychological theorization on Lacanic lines might see in what I call volitional primacy a strategy of deferral by which desire—the thing, Lacan says, that gives life meaning—is perpetually frustrated and so sustained. A significant accommodation is possible, I think, with Marxian materialism (certainly some Marxists can be cited in support), using the concept of consent as developed by Marx and especially by Antonio Gramsci, who places will at the base of his argument. Roger Simon quotes Gramsci's prison notebooks (Q 751): "The collectivity must be understood as the product of a development of will and collective thought attained through concrete individual effort and not through a process of destiny extraneous to individual people" (118); Holub points out how the proletariat will "spontaneously . . . invent practices which, by meeting personal fantasies and desires, can simultaneously transcend the boundaries of domination" (55). Sociobiologists and evolutionary psychologists have used the widespread phenomenon of altruism in ways that connect the paradox with innate dispositions of the human organism. In *The New York Times* Natalie Angier reports a substantial scientific study demonstrating that cooperative behavior stimulates the same endorphin-producing regions of the brain as do chocolate and sex (July 23, 2002, D1, 8). But that argument is still too hotly contested within the physical and social sciences for me to use it with confidence here.

8. I have not tried here to respond fully to the immense history of *Tempest* criticism. Some particular scrutiny will fall on recent work, especially on postcolonialist lines. I owe a large general debt to the play's distinguished editors, especially Kermode and Orgel. Neither, however, pays particular attention to the theme of service, though Orgel anticipates the conclusion of my argument by observing how Prospero's epilogue shows him as both servant and master of the audience (ed. 56).

9. Neill has also recognized the centrality of the theme: in *Tem.*, service "comes to include virtually every character in the play" (21). He does not, however, recognize Miranda.

10. Within the colonialist treatment of the play, they can, as Skura argues, be usefully connected to the uncooperative and unproductive colonists discussed in the contemporary accounts of the Virginia colony by William Strachey, Robert Johnson, and others (302). For further discussion of these relationships, see especially Paul Brown, Gillies, and Takaki.

11. Mahood observes that Alonso's attendants comprise "the very smallest retinue that could accompany the King of Naples together with his brother and the tributary Duke of Milan," citing but rejecting David Bevington's

note that a couple of stage directions imply a larger group (205); it is hard to imagine any actual early modern European ruler traveling with so few. By Shakespearean standards, however, the company actually required by the text is not conspicuously smaller than that accorded other rulers, an obvious consequence of the size of the early modern acting company. It is also the case that there were evidently other ships in the "royal fleet," which could be carrying any number of additional servants (5.1.320).

12. Brower long ago noted evocation of "slavery and freedom" as part of the play's complex pattern of mainly metaphoric references (110–12).

13. Breight proposes that Ariel's account of this history is unreliable, because it supports Prospero's version of the wickedness of Sycorax and hence of Caliban and thus legitimizes Prospero's usurpation of the island (10). No alternative history is provided, however, nor does Breight explain why Ariel would be motivated to distort the truth.

14. "Gently" may have a social as well as an attitudinal meaning: like an upper servant of good family and breeding, not a coarse hind (like Caliban).

15. Paul Brown argues that in Caliban, the two main concerns of the early modern discourse of colonialism, "masterlessness" and "savagism," come together (208). Stephano and Trinculo more particularly invoke the anxieties aroused by the "masterless men" (210) who are also discussed by Beier and Woodbridge.

16. Mahood calls attention to the rhetorical efficacy of this speech (205).

17. Whether Gonzalo's instructions come from Alonso or Antonio is not clear. Antonio, having made his deal with Alonso, opened the gates of Milan to "a treacherous army," after which "the ministers for th'purpose" seized Prospero and Miranda and set them adrift (1.2.127–32). The fact that the "ministers" were inhibited from killing their captives because of the love of the people of Milan for their Duke may suggest that apart from Gonzalo they were themselves Milanese.

18. This element in the play is strongly emphasized by John D. Cox, in explicit resistance to materialist readings of the play ("Recovering").

19. I follow the Oxford Shakespeare (and many other editions) in lineating this speech as verse; my argument does not suffer much if it is taken only as prose more rhythmic, hence more orderly, than the surrounding speeches of the other two. In any case, the explicit statement of the core of the plot is certainly a pair of regular iambic pentameter lines:

> Yea, yea, my lord. I'll yield him thee asleep
> Where thou mayst knock a nail into his head. (58–59)

20. The proposed means of Prospero's death is odd. It derives, presumably, from Jael's killing of Sisera (*Judges* 4.21); the homology is appropriate for a slave deemed inferior to his master on account of his ethnicity as well as his individual subordination. It appears also in *R2*: Death "Comes at the last, and with a little pin / Bores through the castle wall, and farewell, king" (3.2.166–67).

21. If this were true, it would add substantially to the force of the materialist argument. But Ariel, for all his chafing, never says he hates his master, and none of the attendant spirits ever speaks *in propria persona*, so we have only Caliban's word for it—under the circumstances, not decisive.

22. I do not know if it has been noticed that the Neapolitan drunkards' detour affords a comic analog to Prospero's failure while duke: they turn aside from power itself to its signs, the "additions to a king," as Prospero was distracted by study for its own sake rather than as a means to good government.

23. The same ideology binds together that other rag-tag fellowship, Falstaff's band in *1H4, 2H4*, and *H5*, until death and the King's discipline finally dismantle the group, and reduce Pistol to a parodic yet pathetic counterpart to the Old English Wanderer.

24. Cox sees this speech as "the ultimate expression of anyone's humanity in *The Tempest*" ("Recovery" 47).

25. The most extreme version is Curtis Breight's. Stephen Greenblatt's much more sophisticated and subtle analysis is treated below. Barker and Hulme inaugurated the focus on the play's possible relationship with colonialism, and a corresponding emphasis (which has seemed to some a distortion) on Caliban; their opening has been widened by Paul Brown, Takaki, and many others.

26. Willis likewise discusses an "educable" Caliban, paired with an Antonio who is even more "savage" and "masterless" than he—a pairing that, she says, undermines a colonialist reading of the play (259–63).

27. Willis argues that Caliban is converted on his own (266).

28. Skura's argument has Freudian roots: it relates to the problems of moving from a world dominated by "large strong people with problems of their own" into a grown-up "social and linguistic community" (320). Greenblatt likewise sees changes in Prospero, but relates them mainly to a new awareness, which is also Shakespeare's, of the deeply ambivalent power of mimetic art to arouse and then allay anxiety (*Negotiations* 145–46, 156–57).

29. This is one way to understand the rather odd insistence by Sebastian that the marriage of Alonso's daughter Claribel to the King of Tunis, and the trip to Tunis to celebrate the wedding, occurred over the strong objections of the Neapolitan advisors and the girl herself:

> You were kneeled to and importuned otherwise
> By all of us, and the fair soul herself
> Weighed between loathness and obedience
> Which end o'th'beam should bow. (2.1.128–31)

Such circumstances make it all the more remarkable that the group should have come within reach of Prospero's power. According to Breight, the various moments in the play where Prospero or someone else sees miraculous agency are meant to invoke a corresponding, and even more specious, *topos* of the discourse of treason (12–14).

30. Breight argues that at this last entrance the conspirators are only comic in the hands of directors "complicit with hierarchical discourse," because

the description of their punishment unequivocally connects them with the unjustly tortured scapegoats of the various phony treasons devised by the cunning intriguers who served Elizabeth and James (23); if so, the connection was obvious enough to viewers of 1611 to alter the expectation of comic behavior developed by *all* the previous appearances of Trinculo and Stephano if not necessarily of Caliban. This seems to me a fine instance of the kind of stretched interpretation of peripheral words and phrases on which, Kernan argues, most of the materialist readings of the play depend (185). Greenblatt likewise relates the play to Jacobean trials for treason (*Negotiations* 136–46).

31. The contrast with the merely dynastic marriage of Alonso's daughter with the King of Tunis is instructive. Robbins observes that love is "that passion which, by putting characters temporarily in the power of underlings, allows brief but memorable foretastes of social equality" (185).

32. Neill notes the mutuality of service inscribed in the relationships of "the ideal couples" in one of his prime examples of plays articulating a demystified view of service, *New Way to Pay Old Debts* (89). The *iuventus* Sebastian, in Middleton and Dekker's *Roaring Girl*, speaks perhaps more wisely than he knows when he connects the ideas of love and service: "If a man have a free will, where should the use / More perfect shine than in his will to love? / All creatures have their liberty in that. / Though else kept under servile yoke and fear, / The very bond-slave has his freedom there" (2.2.1–5).

33. The language also recalls the parable of the Prodigal Son. According to Breight, Prospero's intention here is to break Ferdinand to his will and so insure his own dominance over a potentially more powerful son-in-law after the return to Europe (11–14).

34. To Neill, Ferdinand's service is only "a self-consciously extravagant mimesis of social subservience"—only, that is, a lover's gesture (24). But Prospero's power, in this context, is real enough, the logs are real enough, the aid of the girl real enough to give the speech more depth than that.

35. The proposition raises that possibility that the heuristic forces of the play are particularly aimed at Shakespeare's patron, James I, and the other great persons of the court; Greenblatt suggests as much (*Negotiations* 156–67). Barker and Hulme call the Milan–Naples struggle "a minor dynastic dispute within the Italian nobility" (203), but the replacement of Prospero by Antonio was not less radical than that of Edward VI by Mary, and while the play does not give explicit voice to the lives of the Milanese and Neapolitans, the traditional image of countries as ships, in conjunction with the images of disrupted governance presented in all the scenes of the play in which Antonio and the Neapolitans appear, invites an audience to consider what those lives might involve. Kastan joins Orgel (*Tempest* 30–31) and Greenblatt (*Negotiations* 129–46) in finding in the play refractions of important dynastic concerns of the Jacobean court, with special reference to the marriage of Princess Elizabeth to Frederick V, the Elector Palatine; he also sees the construction of Prospero as affected by the history of Rudolph of Bohemia, a notable polymath with a deep interest in the occult who had been deposed as Holy Roman Emperor by his brother Matthew in 1606 (189–92).

36. On this point, see Gillies 144–45.
37. As Cox has noted, many postmodern critics see in Prospero's failure to convert Antonio and Sebastian some weakness or falseness in him. But Cox argues that he has done all he could morally do—to force them into some hypocritical show of repentance would be as tyrannical as it would be spiritually pointless; the best he can do is to restrain the pair's villainy and set an example of moral behavior ("Recovering" 49).
38. Greenblatt asserts that Prospero "cannot remake the inner life of everyone" (146)—indeed, can not remake anyone's *inner* life, except perhaps his own.
39. Russ McDonald and others have identified repetition and other kinds of doubling as a general characteristic of the play (McDonald 17). The placement of this particular instance, however, in that most emphatic position, of the last word, cannot but be especially significant.
40. Breight sees this last as part of a continuing effort to control lower class subversion, reminding any potentially unruly groundlings of the Jacobean jailhouses, "not houses of correction but houses of pain" in which "roaring, shrieking, and howling were the results of torture practiced to extract confessions from 'traitors' . . ." (22–23); it might be possible to call the sailors traitors for abandoning the effort to save the king's ship despite the best efforts of the Boatswain to keep them working. Breight does not choose to notice that sailors ashore were notoriously rowdy, especially in groups; these seem to have been unconscious throughout their captivity and hence to have suffered not at all.
41. This interpretation challenges that of some critics who have taken the passage's talk of playing false, and the implicit commodification of playing for 20 kingdoms if not the world, as a sign that the kind of idealized interpretation I am setting up will not cohere. Orgel proposes that the lovers "play out, at chess, a brief game of love and war that seems to foretell in their lives all the ambition, duplicity and cynicism of their elders. . . . In her complicity, Italian *Realpolitik* is already established in the next generation" (29; see also Greenblatt 144). It cannot be denied, however, that he insists he would not betray her for any consideration that can be imagined, and I prefer to find in "Yes, for a score of kingdoms you should wrangle / And I would call it fair play" (5.1.177–78) a statement that she is resolved never to be behind him in forgiveness. I am reminded here of the moment in *Lr.* when Cordelia and Lear, restored to each other and their old, loving relationship, vie with one another in subservience (*TLr.* 5.3.10–11).
42. Materialist critics have tended not to notice that in the absence of any possible subjects (except the marmosets and seamews on whom he is apparently wont to dine), Caliban's claim to kingship is essentially meaningless if the term is to carry instrumental as well as topical force.
43. I do not know if it has been noticed that the book and the staff or rod are ubiquitous emblems of political and religious office in early modern English portraits—items not part of the iconography of mercers or prosperous yeomen, and certainly not of domestic servants, but common in that of courtiers and bishops, and certainly not unique to either the images or the activities of magicians, white or black.

44. Paul Brown notes that Ariel is "paradoxically *bound* in service by this constant reminder of Prospero's gift of *freedom* to him, in releasing him from imprisonment in a tree" (220).

45. Paul Brown argues that the aristocrats are "maddened, then recuperated," while the plebians, "unmastered, are simply punished and held up to ridicule" (222). The summary, however, will not contain a fully repentant and forgiven Caliban, an unrepentant Antonio, or a freely serving and freely liberated Ariel.

46. Paul Brown discerns a similar pattern in Prospero's long initial exposition to Miranda, presenting his history as "a *felix culpa*, a fortunate fall, in which court intrigue becomes reinscribed in the terms of romance, via a shift from the language of courtiership to that of courtship, to a rhetoric of love and charity" (219). But his language really describes the play as a whole.

WORKS CITED

Adelman, Janet. *The Common Liar: An Essay on Antony and Cleopatra*. New York and London: Yale UP, 1973.

Akrigg, G. P. V. *The Jacobean Pageant*. London: Hamish Hamilton, 1962.

———. *Shakespeare and the Earl of Southampton*. London: Hamish Hamilton, 1968.

Althouse, Paul. *The Ethics of Martin Luther*. Trans. Robert C. Schultz. Philadelphia: Fortress Press, 1972.

———. *The Theology of Martin Luther*. Trans. Robert C. Schultz. Philadelphia: Fortress Press, 1966.

Amussen, Susan Dwyer. *An Ordered Society: Gender and Class in Early Modern England*. Oxford: Basil Blackwell, 1988.

Angier, Natalie. "Why We're So Nice: We're Wired to Cooperate." *New York Times* July 23, 2002, D1–D8.

Anglicus, Bartholomeus. See Trevisa.

Anon. *The York Cycle of Mystery Plays: A Complete Version*. Ed. J. S. Purvis. 1st paperback ed. London: SPCK, 1978.

Aquinas, St. Thomas. *Summa Theologica*. 3 vols. London: Thomas Baker, 1918.

Aries, Philippe and Georges Duby, eds. *A History of Private Life*. Vol. I: *From Pagan Rome to Byzantium*. Ed. Paul Veyne. Trans. Arthur Goldhammer. Cambridge, MA and London: Harvard UP, 1987.

Aubrey, John. *Brief Lives*. Ed. Anthony Powell. New York: Charles Scribner's Sons, 1949.

Augustine, Bishop of Hippo. *Commentary on the Sermon on the Mount*. Trans. Denis J. Cavanagh. New York: Fathers of the Church, Inc., 1952.

———. *Opera*. Turnolti: Typographi Brevols, 1954–.

———. *Sermo LXIV*. *Patrologiae Latina* 39.1868–69.

Ayris, Paul and David Selwyn. *Thomas Cranmer, Churchman and Scholar*. Woodbridge: Boydell Press, 1993.

Babington, Gervase. *Certaine Plaine, Briefe, and Comfortable Notes, upon Every Chapter of Genesis*. London: I. E. for Thomas Charde, 1596 [1591].

Baker, J. Robert. "Absence and Subversion: The 'O'erflow' of Gender in Shakespeare's *Antony and Cleopatra*." *Upstart Crow* 12 (1992): 105–26.

Baldwin, T. W. *The Compositional Genetics of Shakspere's Plays*. Urbana: U of Illinois P, 1965.

———. *The Organization and Personnel of the Shakespearean Company*. New York: Russell & Russell, 1961.

———. *William Shakspere's Five-Act Structure*. Urbana: U of Illinois P, 1947.

Baldwin, T. W. *William Shakspere's Smalle Latine and Lesse Greeke.* 2 vols. Urbana: U of Illinois P, 1944.

Barfoot, C. A. "News of the Roman Empire: Hearsay, Soothsay, Myth and History in *Antony and Cleopatra.*" In Hoenselaars 105–28.

Barish, Jonas A. "King John and Oath Breach." In Fabian and von Rosador, 1–18.

———— and Waingrow, Marshall. " 'Service' in *King Lear,*" *Shakespeare Quarterly* 9 (1958): 347–55.

Barker, Francis and Peter Hulme. "Nymphs and Reapers Heavily Vanish: The Discursive Con-Texts of *The Tempest.*" In Drakakis, 191–205.

Barnes, Arthur Dale. "Forms of the Master–Servant Relationship in Shakespeare's Plays." Ph.D. diss., Brandeis U, 1982.

Barnett, Richard C. *Place, Profit, and Power: A Study of the Servants of William Cecil, Elizabethan Statesman.* Chapel Hill: U of North Carolina P, 1969.

Barroll, J. Leeds. *Shakespearean Tragedy: Genre, Tradition, and Change in* Antony and Cleopatra. Washington: Folger Books; London: Associated University Presses, 1984.

Barry, Jonathan and Christopher Brooks. *The Middling Sort of People: Culture, Society and Politics in England, 1550–1800.* London: Macmillan Publishing, 1994.

Baynes, Paul. *An Entire Commentary Upon the Whole Epistle of St. Paul to the Ephesians.* Edinburgh, 1866 [1648; died 1617].

Beier, A. L. *Masterless Men: The Vagrancy Problem in England 1560–1640.* London and New York: Methuen, 1985.

Belloc, Hilaire. *Cranmer: Archbishop of Canterbury 1533–1556.* New York: Haskell House, 1973 (1931).

Belsey, Catherine. "Cleopatra's Seduction." In Hawkes, 38–62.

Benedict, St. *The Holy Rule of St. Benedict.* Trans. Boniface Verheyen, OSB. 1949. http://www.benedictine.edu/abbey/site%202/rule.htm.

————. *Regula Sancti Benedictis.* Pannonholm, Hungary. 1995. http://www.osb.hu/lelki/regula/l_regula/l_rb9.html

Berry, Ralph. *Shakespeare and Social Class.* Atlantic Highlands, NJ: Humanities Press International, 1988.

Bible. *The Geneva Bible, a Facsimile of the 1560 Edition.* Ed. Lloyd E. Berry. Madison: U of Wisconsin P, 1969.

Bishop, T. G. *Shakespeare and the Theatre of Wonder.* Cambridge Studies in Renaissance Literature and Culture 9. Cambridge: Cambridge UP, 1996.

Black, James. "The Latter End of Prospero's Commonwealth." *SSurv.* 43 (1991): 29–41.

Bonfield, Lloyd, Richard M. Smith, and Keith Wrightson, eds. *The World We Have Gained: Histories of Population and Social Structure.* Oxford and New York: Basil Blackwell, 1986.

The Booke of the Common Prayer and Administration of the Sacraments, and Other Rites and Ceremonies of the Churche: After the Use of the Churche of England. 1549.

Boose, Linda. "Scolding Brides and Bridling Scolds: Taming the Woman's Unruly Member." *Shakespeare Quarterly* 42 (1991): 178–213.

Booty, John E., ed. *The Book of Common Prayer 1559: The Elizabethan Prayer Book.* Charlottesville: The UP of Virginia for the Folger Shakespeare Library, 1976.

Bradbrook, M. C. *The Rise of the Common Player: A Study of Actor and Society in Shakespeare's England.* Cambridge, MA: Harvard UP, 1962.

———. *Shakespeare: The Poet in His World.* New York: Columbia University Press, 1978.

Brathwaite, Richard. "Some Rules and Orders for the Government of the House of an Earl." *Miscellanea Antiqua Anglicana.* London, 1816 [from MS, ca. 1605].

Braunmuller, A. R. "King John and Historiography." *ELH* 55 (1988): 309–32.

Bray, Alan. *Homosexuality in Renaissance England.* London: Gay Men's Press, 1982.

Breight, Carl. " 'Treason doth never prosper': *The Tempest* and the Discourse of Treason." *SQ* 41 (1990): 1–28.

Brightman, F. E. *The English Rite, Being a Synopsis of the Sources and Revisions of the Book of Common Prayer.* 2 vols. London, 1915.

Brod, Harry, ed. *The Making of Masculinities.* Boston: Allen and Unwin, Inc., 1987.

Brower, Reuben. *The Fields of Light: An Experiment in Critical Reading.* New York: Oxford UP, 1951.

Brown, Elizabeth A. "Companion Me with My Mistress: Cleopatra, Elizabeth I, and Their Waiting Women." In Frye and Robertson, 131–45.

Brown, John Russell. "The Worst of Shakespeare in the Theater: Cuts in the Last Scene of *King Lear.*" In Charney, 157–65.

Brown, Paul. " 'This Thing of Darkness I Acknowledge Mine': *The Tempest* and the Discourse of Colonialism." In Graff and Phelan, 205–29.

Bruster, Douglas. "Comedy and Control: Shakespeare and the Plautine *Poeta.*" In Davidson et al., 117–31.

Bullough, Geoffrey. *Narrative and Dramatic Sources of Shakespeare.* 8 vols. London: Routledge and Kegan Paul; New York: Columbia UP, 1977.

Burkhardt, Sigurd. *Shakespeare's Meanings.* Princeton, NJ: Princeton UP, 1968.

Burnett, Mark Thornton. "Apprentice Literature and the 'Crisis' of the 1590s." *Yearbook of English Studies* 21 (1991): 27–38.

———. *Masters and Servants in English Renaissance Drama and Culture: Authority and Obedience.* New York: St. Martin's Press, 1997.

———. "Masters and Servants in Moral and Religious Treatises, ca.1580–ca.1642." In Marwick, 48–75.

———. "The Trusty Servant." *Emblematica* 6.2 (1992): 237–53.

Bushman. Marianne. "Representing Cleopatra." In Kehler and Baker, 36–49.

Byfield, Nicholas. *An Exposition Upon the Epistle to the Colossians.* London: William Stansby for Nicholas Butler, 1627 [1615].

Cahn, Susan. *An Industry of Devotion: The Transformation of Women's Work in England, 1550–1660.* New York: Columbia UP.

Calvin, Jean. *Commentaires sur le Nouveau Testament.* 4 vols. Paris, 1854.

Campbell, Lily B. *Shakespeare's Histories: Mirrors of Elizabethan Policy.* London: Methuen, 1964.

Campbell, Mildred. *The English Yeoman Under Elizabeth and the Early Stuarts.* New Haven: Yale UP, 1942.

Chambers, E. K. *The Elizabethan Stage.* 2 vols. Oxford: Clarendon Press, 1923.

Charnes, Linda. "What's Love Got to Do with It: Reading the Liberal Humanist Romance in *Antony and Cleopatra.*" *Textual Practice* 6.1 (1992): 1–16.

Charney, Maurice, ed. *"Bad" Shakespeare: Revaluations of the Shakespeare Canon.* Rutherford, Madison, Teaneck: Fairleigh-Dickinson UP; London and Toronto: Associated UP, 1988.

Chrysostom, St. John. *An Exposition upon the Epistle to the Ephesians.* London: Henry Binneman and Ralph Newberie, 1581.

Clark, John Willis, ed. *The Observances in Use at the Augustinian Priory of St. Giles and St. Andrew at Barnwell, Cambridgeshire.* Cambridge, 1897.

Cle[a]ver, Robert and John Dod. *A Godly Forme of Houshold Government: For the Ordering of Private Families, According to the Direction of God's Word.* 1621.

Coke, Sir Edward. *Reports of Sir Edward Coke, Bart., in Thirteen Parts.* London, 1826.

Cook, Ann Jennalie. *Shakespeare's Privileged Playgoers of Shakespeare's London.* Princeton, NJ: Princeton UP, 1981.

Cook, Carol. "The Fatal Cleopatra." In Garner and Springnether, 241–67.

Cox, John D. "Recovering Something Christian About *The Tempest.*" *Christianity and Literature* 50.1 (2000): 31–51.

———. *Shakespeare and the Dramaturgy of Power.* Princeton, NJ: Princeton UP, 1989.

Cranmer, Thomas. *The Works of Thomas Cranmer.* Ed. J. I. Packer and G. S. Duffield. Applefield, Berks.: Sutton Courtenay Press, 1964.

Cross, Clair, David Loades, and J. J. Scarisbrick, eds. *Law and Government Under the Tudors.* Cambridge: Cambridge UP, 1988.

Curren-Aquino, Deborah T., ed. *King John: New Perspectives.* Newark, DE: U of Delaware P; London and Toronto: Associated UP, 1989.

Danson, Lawrence. "Jonsonian Comedy and the Discovery of the Social Self." *PMLA* 99.2 (1984): 179–93.

[Darell, Walter]. *A Short Discourse of the Life of Serving Men, Plainly Expressing the Way That Is Best to Be Followed, and the Means Whereby They May Lawfully Challenge a Name and Title in that Vocation and Fellowship.* London, 1578.

Davidson, Clifford, Rand Johnson, and John H. Stroupe. *Drama and the Classical Heritage.* New York: AMS Press, Inc., 1993.

Davies, H. Neville. "Jacobean *Antony and Cleopatra.*" *Shakespeare Studies* 17 (1985): 123–58.

Davies, Margaret Gay. *The Enforcement of English Apprenticeship, a Study in Applied Mercantilism 1563–1642.* Cambridge, MA: Harvard UP, 1956.

Dawson, Anthony B. "*Tempest* in a Teapot." In Charney, 61–73.

Dee, John. *The Diaries of John Dee.* Ed. Edward Fenton. Charlesbury: Day Books, 1998.

Delaney, Paul. "*King Lear* and the Decline of Feudalism." *PMLA* 92.3 (1977): 429–40.

Deloney, Thomas. *Novels.* Ed. Merrit E. Lawlis., Bloomington: U of Indiana P, 1961.

Dekker, Thomas. *Dramatic Works*. Ed. Fredson Bowers. 4 vols. Cambridge: Cambridge UP, 1953.

Dekkers, Eligius, ed. *Clavis patrum latinorum: qua in corpus christianorum edendum optimas quasque scriptorum recensiones a Tertulliano ad praeparavit.* 3rd ed. Steenbrugis: Abbatia Sancti Petri, 1995.

Denison, John. *The Sinners acquittance. A checke to Curiositie. The safest Service. Deliuered in Three Sermons at the Court.* 1624.

Dickens, A. G. *The English Reformation.* 2nd ed. London: B. T. Batsford Ltd., 1989.

DiGangi, Mario. "Asses and Wits: The Homoerotics of Mastery in Satiric Comedy." *ELR* 25.2 (1995): 179–208.

Doerksen, Daniel W. and Christopher Hodgkins. *Centered on the Word: Literature, Scripture, and the Tudor-Stuart Middle Way.* Newark, DE: U of Delaware P, 2004.

Dolan, Frances E. "Household Chastisements: Gender, Authority, and 'Domestic Violence'." In Fumerton and Hunt, 204–45.

———. "The Subordinate('s) Plot: Petty Treason and the Forms of Domestic Rebellion." *SQ* 43.3 (l992): 317–40.

Dollimore, Jonathan. *Radical Tragedy.* Chicago: U of Chicago P, 1984.

——— and Alan Sinfield. "History and Ideology: The Case of *Henry V*." In Drakakis, 206–27.

Doran, Madeleine. *Endeavors of Art.* Madison: U of Wisconsin P, 1954.

Downame, George. *A Treastise upon Iohn 8.36, Concerning Christian Libertie. The Chiefe Points whereof were deliuered in a Sermon preached at Pauls Crosse, Nouemb. 6. 1608.* 1609.

Drakakis, John, ed. *Alternative Shakespeares.* London and New York: Methuen, 1985.

Dubrow, Heather and Richard Strier, eds. *The Historical Renaissance: New Essays in Tudor Literature and Culture.* Chicago and London: U of Chicago P, 1988.

Duckworth, George E. *The Nature of Roman Comedy: A Study in Popular Entertainment.* 2nd ed. Norman, OK: U of Oklahoma P, 1994.

Dudley, Martin R., ed. *The Collect in Anglican Ligurgy: Texts and Sources, 1549–1989.* Alcuin Club no. 72. Collegeville, MN: Liturgical Press, 1994.

Dunham, William Huse. *Lord Hastings' Endentured Retainers 1461–1483: The Lawfulness of Livery and Retaining under the Yorkists and Tudors.* London: Archon Books, 1970.

Eagleton, Terry. 1986. *William Shakespeare.* Oxford and New York: Basil Blackwell.

Edelman, Charles. "A Note on the Opening Stage Direction of *Romeo and Juliet*, I.i," *SQ* 39 (1988): 361–62.

Edwards, Philip. *Threshold of a Nation: A Study in English and Irish Drama.* Cambridge: Cambridge UP, 1979.

Elias, Norbert. *The Court Society* [*Die hofische Gesellschaft*, 1975]. Trans. Edmund Jephcott. Oxford: Basil Blackwell, 1983.

Elton, Edward. *An Exposition of the Epistle of St. John to the Colossians, Delivered in Sundry Sermons.* 1615.

Engle, Lars. *Shakespearean Pragmatism: Market of his Time.* Chicago and London: U of Chicago P, 1993.

Erickson, Amy Louis. *Women and Property in Early Modern England.* London and New York: Routledge, 1993.

Erickson, Peter and Coppelia Kahn, eds. *Shakespeare's "Rough Magic": Renaissance Essays in Honor of C. L. Barber.* Newark, DE: U of Delaware P, 1985.

Evans, Robert C. *Ben Jonson and the Poetics of Patronage.* Lewisburg: Bucknell UP; London and Toronto: Associated UP, 1989.

Evett, David. "Luther, Cranmer, Service, and Shakespeare." In Doerksen and Hodgkins, 87–109.

———. " 'Surprising Confrontations': Ideologies of Service in Shakespeare's England." *Renaissance Papers 1990,* 67–78.

———. "Types of King David in Shakespeare's Lancastrian Tetralogy." *Shakespeare Studies* 18 (1981): 139–61.

Fabian, Bernhard and Kurt Tetzel von Rosador, eds. *Shakespeare: Text, Language, Criticism.* Hildesheim, Zurich, and New York: Olms-Weidmann, 1987.

Fehrenbach, R. J., ed. "A Lettere Sent by the Maydens of London." *ELR* 14 (1984): 28–47.

Filmer, Sir Robert. *Patriarcha and Other Political Works.* Ed. Peter Laslett. Oxford: Basil Blackwell, 1949 [1680, written ca. 1635–42].

Fit-John, John. *A Diamond most Precious, Worthy to be Marked: Instructing All Maysters and Servauntes, how They ought to Leade Their Lyves, in that Vocation which is Fruitfull, and Necessary, as well for the Maysters, as also for the Servauntes, Agreeable unto the Holy Scriptures.* London: Hugh Jackson, 1577.

Fleming, P. W. "Household Servants of the Yorkist and Early Tudor Gentry." In D. Williams, 19–36.

Forse, James H. "Romeo and Juliet: A Play for All Seasons, or, How to Please a Patron, Pass the Censor, and Pack the Theatre." *Shakespeare and Renaissance Association of West Virginia: Selected Papers* 16 (1993): 88–117.

Fosset, Thomas. *The Servants Dutie, or the Calling and Condition of Servants. Serving for the Instruction, not only of Servants, but of Masters and Mistresses.* London: G. Eld, 1612.

Foucault, Michel. *Discipline and Punish: The Birth of the Prison.* Trans. Alan Sheridan. New York: Pantheon Books, 1977.

Francis of Assisi, Saint. *Writing of St. Francis of Assisi.* Trans. Paschal Robinson. Philadelphia: Dolphin Press, 1906.

Friedman, Alice T. *House and Household in Elizabethan England: Wollaton Hall and the Willoughby Family.* Chicago and London: U of Chicago P, 1989.

Frye, Susan and Karen Robertson. *Maids and Mistresses, Cousins and Queens: Women's Alliances in Early Modern England.* New York and Oxford: Oxford UP, 1999.

Fumerton, Patricia. *Cultural Aesthetics: Renaissance Literature and the Practice of Social Ornament.* Chicago: U of Chicago P, 1991.

——— and Simon Hunt, ed. *Renaissance Culture and the Everyday.* Philadelphia: U of Pennsylvania P, 1999.

Gabriner, P. J. "Hierarchy, Harmony, and Happiness: Another Look at the Hunting Dogs in the 'Induction' to *The Taming of the Shrew.*" In Hoenselaars, 201–11.

Garner, Shirley Nelson. "Male Bonding and the Myth of Women's Deception in Shakespeare's Plays." In Holland et al., 135–50.

Garner, Shirley Nelson and Madelon Springnether, eds. *Shakespearean Tragedy and Gender*. Bloomington and Indianapolis: U of Indiana P, 1996.

Gillies, John. *Shakespeare and the Geography of Difference*. Cambridge: Cambridge UP, 1994.

Gintis, Herbert, Samuel Bowles, Robert Boyd, and Ernst Fehr. "Explaining Altruistic Behavior in Humans." *Evolution and Human Behavior* 24.3 (2003): 153–72.

Godshalk, William. "Dolabella as Agent Provocateur." *Renaissance Papers* (1977): 69–74.

Goode, Erica. "Women Found to React to Stress by Social Contact Rather than 'Fight or Flight'." *New York Times* May 19, 2000: A22.

Goodman, Christopher. *How Superior Powers Ought to be Obeyd* [Geneva, 1558]. New York: Facsimile Text Society, 1931.

Gouge, William. *An Exposition of Part of the Fift and Sixt Chapters of St. Paules Epistle to the Ephesians*. London: John Bartlett, 1630.

———. *Of Domesticall Duties. Eight Treatises*. 1622.

Grady, Hugh. *Shakespeare's Universal Wolf: Studies in Early Modern Reification*. Oxford: Clarendon Press, 1996.

Graff, Gerald and James Phelan, eds. *William Shakespeare: The Tempest: A Case Study in Critical Controversy*. Boston and New York: Bedford/St. Martin's, 2000.

Greaves, Richard. L. *Society and Religion in Elizabethan England*. Minneapolis: U of Minnesota P, 1981.

Greenblatt, Stephen. *Learning to Curse: Essays in Early Modern Culture*. New York and London: Routledge, 1990.

———. *Marvellous Possessions: The Wonder of the New World*. Chicago: U of Chicago P, 1991.

———. *Renaissance Self-Fashioning from More to Shakespeare*. Chicago and London: U of Chicago P, 1980.

———. *Shakespearean Negotiations*. Berkeley and London: U of California P, 1988.

———. *Will in the World: How Shakespeare Became Shakespeare*. New York and London: W.W. Norton & Co., 2004.

Griffiths, Paul. *Youth and Authority: Formative Experiences in England, 1550–1640*. Oxford: Clarendon Press, 1996.

Gurr, Andrew. *The Shakespearean Stage 1574–1642*. 3rd ed. Cambridge: Cambridge UP, 1992.

Hall, Basil. "Cranmer's Relations with Erasmianism and Lutheranism." In Ayris and Selwyn, 3–37.

Hamer, Mary. "Cleopatra: Housewife." *Textual Practice* 2.2 (1988): 159–79.

Hammond, Dorothy and Alta Jablow. "Gilgamesh and the Sundance Kid: The Myth of Male Friendship." In Harry Brod, 246—69.

Harbage, Alfred. *Shakespeare's Audience*. New York: Columbia UP, 1941.

Harrison, G. B. *The Elizabethan Journals*. 2 vols. New York: Doubleday, 1965.

Hawkes, Terence, ed. *Alternative Shakespeares Volume 2*. London and New York: Routledge, 1996.

Heal, Felicity. "The Idea of Hospitality in Early Modern England." *Past and Present* 102 (1984): 66–93.

———. *Hospitality in Early Modern England.* Oxford: Clarendon Press, 1990.

Heinemann, Margo. " 'God Help the Poor: The Rich Can Shift': The World Upside-Down and the Popular Tradition in the Theatre." In McMullan and Hope, 151–65.

Helms, Lorraine. " 'The High Roman Fashion': Sacrifice, Suicide, and the Shakespearean Stage." *PMLA* 107.3 (1992): 554–65.

Heywood, John. *The Four Prentices of London: A Critical, Old-Spelling Edition.* Ed. Mary Ann Weber Gasior. New York and London: Garland Publishing, Inc., 1980.

Hicks, Edward. *Sir Thomas Malory, His Turbulent Career.* Cambridge, MA: Harvard UP, 1928.

Hillenbrand, Harold Newcomb. *The Child Actors.* University of Illinois Studies in Language and Literature XI, 1–2. 1926.

Hoenselaars, A. J., ed. *Reclamations of Shakespeare: Dutch Quarterly Review Studies in Literature 15.* Amsterdam and Atlanta, GA: Rodopi, 1994.

Hoffman, John. *The Gramscian Challenge: Coercion and Consent in Marxist Political Theory.* Oxford and New York: Basil Blackwell, 1984.

Holland, Norman. *The I.* New Haven and London: Yale UP, 1985.

Holland, Norman N., Sidney Homan, and Bernard J. Paris, eds. *Shakespeare's Personality.* Berkeley: U of California P, 1989.

Holub, Renate. *Antonio Gramsci: Beyond Marxism and Postmodernism.* Routledge: London and New York, 1992

[*Homilies*]. *Certain Sermons or Homilies (1547), and A Homily Against Disobedience and Wilful Rebellion (1570).* Ed. Ronald B. Bond. Toronto, Buffalo, London: U of Toronto P, 1987.

Honigmann, E. A. J. *Shakespeare: The "Lost Years."* 2nd ed. Manchester and New York: Manchester UP, 1998.

Hooker, Richard. *Of the Law of Ecclesiastical Politie. Preface, Books I to IV.* Ed. Georges Edelen and W. Speed Hill. Cambridge: Harvard UP, 1977.

Houlbrooke, Ralph A. *The English Family 1450–1700.* London and New York: Longman, 1984.

Howard, Jean E. *The Stage and Social Struggle in Early Modern England.* London and New York: Routledge, 1994.

Hunt, Maurice. "Slavery, English Servitude, and *The Comedy of Errors.*" *ELR* 27.1 (1997): 31–56.

———. " 'Stir' and Work in Shakespeare's Last Plays." *SEL* 22.2 (1982): 285–304.

Hutchinson, F. F. *Cranmer and the English Revolution.* London: English Universities Press, 1960.

James, Mervyn. *Society, Politics, and Culture: Studies in Early Modern England.* Cambridge: Cambridge UP, 1986.

Jameson, Frederic. *The Political Unconscious.* Ithaca: Cornell UP, 1981.

Jarka, Lois Margaret. "The Perfect Freedom: The Concept of Service in Shakespearean Drama." *DAI* 47.7 (1987): 2596A.

Jones, Ann Rosalind. "Maidservants of London: Sisterhoods of Kinship and Labor." In Frye and Robertson, 21–32.

———— and Peter Stallybrass, eds. *Renaissance Clothing and the Materials of Memory*. Cambridge and New York: Cambridge UP, 2000.

Jones, Jeanne. *Family Life in Shakespeare's England: Stratford-Upon-Avon 1570–1630*. Thrupp: Sutton Publishing, 1996.

Jonson, Ben. *Works*. Ed. G. A. Wilkes. Oxford: Clarendon, 1981.

Kahn, Coppélia. *Roman Shakespeare: Warriors, Wounds, and Women*. London, New York: Routledge, 1997.

Kastan, David Scott. *Shakespeare After Theory*. New York and London: Routledge, 1999.

Kathman, David. "Freemen and Apprentices in the Elizabethan Theater." Forthcoming in *Shakespeare Quarterly* 56 (2005).

Kehler, Dorothy and Susan Baker, eds. *In Another Country: Feminist Perspectives on Renaissance Drama*. Metuchen, NJ, New York, and London: The Scarecrow Press, 1991.

Kernan, Alvin. *Shakespeare, the King's Playwright: Theater in the Stuart Court 1603–1613*. New Haven and London: Yale UP, 1995.

Ketley, Joseph, ed. *The Two Liturgies*, A.D. *1549, and* A.D. *1552: With Other Documents Set Forth by Authority in the Reign of King Edward VI*. Parker Soc. 29. 1894.

Kronenfeld, Judy. King Lear *and the Naked Truth*. Durham and London: Duke UP, 1998.

Kussmaul, Ann. *Servants in Husbandry in Early Modern England*. Cambridge: Cambridge UP, 1981.

LaBoétie, Éstienne de. *De la servitude volontaire*. Ed. Françoise Bayard. Paris: Imprimerie Nationale Éditions, 1992.

Lamb, Mary Ellen. "Tracing a Heterosexual Erotics of Service in *Twelfth Night* and the Autobiographical Writings of Thomas Whythorne and Anne Clifford." *Criticism* 40.1 (1998): 1–15.

Laslett, Peter. "Characteristics of the Western Family Considered Over Time." *Journal of Family History* 2 (1977): 89–116.

————. *The World We Have Lost*. 2nd ed. New York: Scribner, 1973.

Lawrence, Anne. *Women in England 1500–1760*. London: Phoenix Giant, 1994.

Leggatt, Alexander. *Shakespeare's Political Drama: The History Plays and the Roman Plays*. London and New York: Routledge, 1988.

Legge, J. Wickham, ed. *The Sarum Missal Edited from Three Early Manuscripts*. Oxford: Clarendon Press, 1969 [1916].

Lentriccia, Frank. *Criticism and Social Change*. Chicago and London: U of Chicago P, 1983.

Levin, Richard A. "That I Might Hear Thee Call Great Caesar 'Ass Unpolicied'." *Papers on Language and Literature* 33.3 (1997): 244–64.

Lindberg, Carter. "Luther's Critique of the Ecumenical Assumption that Doctrine Divides but Service Unites." *Journal of Ecumenical Studies* 27.4 (1990): 679–96.

Luther, Martin. [Trans. Walter Lynne.] *A Frutefull and Godly Exposition and Declaracion of the Kingdom of Christ, and of the Christen Libertye, made upō the Wordes of the Prophete Jeremye in the xxiii Chapter, with an Exposycyon of the viii. Psalme, in Treatying of the Same Matter*. 1548.

Luther, Martin. *Works*. Ed. Jaroslav Pelikan and others. 55 vols. St. Louis: Concordia Press, 1955–.

M., J. [Gervase Markham?] *A Health to the Gentlemanly Profession of Serving-Men*. 1598.

———. [Facsimile.] Intro. A. V. Judges. London: Oxford UP, 1931.

MacCullough, Diarmid. "Bondmen Under the Tudors." In Cross et al., 91–109.

———. *Thomas Cranmer: A Life*. New Haven and London: Yale UP, 1996.

Macfarlane, Alan. *The Family Life of Ralph Josselin: A Seventeenth-Century Clergyman*. Cambridge: Cambridge UP, 1970.

———. *The Justice and the Mare's Ale: Law and Disorder in Seventeenth-Century England*. New York: Cambridge UP, 1981.

Mahood, M. M. *Bit Parts in Shakespeare's Plays*. Cambridge: Cambridge UP, 1992.

Manheim, Michael. "The Four Voices of the Bastard." In Curren-Aquino, 126–35.

Manning, Roger. *Village Revolts: Social Protest and Popular Disturbance in England, 1509–1640*. Oxford: Clarendon Press, 1988.

Martindale, Charles and Michelle Martindale. *Shakespeare and the Uses of Antiquity*. London and New York: Routledge, 1990.

Marwick, Arthur, ed. *The Arts, Literature, and Society*. London and New York: Routledge, 1990.

Marx, Stephen. "Shakespeare's Pacifism." *Renaissance Quarterly* 45.1 (1992): 49–95.

McClung, William Alexander. *The Country House in English Renaissance Poetry*. Berkeley: U of California P, 1977.

McDonald, Russ. "Reading *The Tempest*." *SSurv* 43 (1991): 15–28.

McEachern, Claire. "Fathering Herself: A Source Study of Shakespeare's Feminism." *Shakespeare Quarterly* 39.3 (1988): 269–90.

McMullan, Gordon. *The Politics of Unease in the Plays of John Fletcher*. Amherst: U of Massachusetts P, 1994.

——— and Jonathan Hope, eds. *The Politics of Tragicomedy: Shakespeare and After*. London and New York: Routledge, 1992.

Melchiori, Giorgio. "Peter, Balthazar, and Shakespeare's Art of Doubling." *MLR* 78.4 (1983): 777–82.

Memmi, Albert. *Dominated Man: Notes Toward a Portrait*. Boston: Beacon Press, 1969.

Middleton, Thomas. *A Chaste Maid in Cheapside*. Ed. Alan Brissenden. 2nd ed. London: A. C. Black; New York: W. W. Norton, 2002.

———. *A Mad World, My Masters*. Ed. Standish Henning. Lincoln: U of Nebraska P, 1965.

Middleton, Thomas and Thomas Dekker. *The Roaring Girl*, Ed. Andrew Gomme. London: Ernest Benn Ltd.; New York.: W. W. Norton, Inc., 1976.

Miola, Robert S. *Shakespeare and Classical Comedy*. Oxford: Clarendon Press; New York: Oxford UP, 1994.

Moisan, Thomas. " 'Knock me here soundly': Comic Misprision and Class Consciousness in Shakespeare." *SQ* 42 (1991): 276–90.

Moore, Barrington. *Injustice: The Social Bases of Obedience and Revolt*. N.p.: Sharpe, 1978.

Neill, Michael. *Putting History to the Question: Power, Politics, and Society in English Renaissance Drama.* New York: Columbia UP, 2000.

Newman, Karen. "Renaissance Family Politics and Shakespeare's *The Taming of the Shrew.*" *ELR* 16.1 (1986): 87–100.

Newton, Arthur Perceval. "Tudor Reforms in the Royal Household." In Seton-Watson, 231–56.

Nietzsche, Friedrich Wilhelm. *On the Genealogy of Morals.* (1887). Compiled from translations by Walter Kaufmann, R. J. Hollingdale, and Ian C. Johnson; text amended in part by The Nietzsche Channel. http://www.geocities.com/thenietzschechannel/onthe.htm.

Norbrook, David. " 'What cares these roarers for the name of king?': Language and Utopia in *The Tempest.*" In McMullan and Hope, 21–54.

North, Thomas. *Plutarch: The Lives of the Noble Grecians and Romans, Compared Together by that Grave and Learned Philosopher and Historiographer Plutarch of Chaeronea.* Trans. Thomas North, from the French of Jacques Amyot. 8 vols. New York: AMS Press, Inc., 1967 [1896].

Ong, Walter J., S.J. *Fighting for Life: Contest, Sexuality, and Consciousness.* Ithaca and London: Cornell UP, 1981.

Patterson, Annabel. *Shakespeare and the Popular Voice.* Cambridge, MA and Oxford: Basil Blackwell, 1989.

Peck, Linda Levy. " 'For a King not to be bountiful were a fault': Perspectives on Court Patronage in Early Stuart England." *Journal of British Studies* 25 (1986): 31–61.

Pembroke, Lady Anne Clifford Herbert, Countess of. *The Diaries of Lady Anne Clifford.* Ed. D. J. H. Clifford. Wolfeboro Falls, NH: Alan Sutton, 1991.

Perkins, William and Ralph Cudworth. *A Commentarie, or Exposition vpon the fiue first Chapters of the Epistle to the Galatians . . . with a Supplement vpon the Sixt Chapter, by Ralph Cudworth Bachelour of Diuinitie.* 1617.

Pierce, Robert. B. "Understanding *The Tempest.*" *NLH* 30.2 (1999): 373–88.

Plautus. *Works.* Trans. Paul Nixon. 5 vols. London: William Heinemann Ltd.; New York: G. P. Putnam's Sons, 1932.

Plutarch. *Lives, with an English Translation by Bernadotte Perrin.* 11 vols. London, William Heinemann, Ltd. and Cambridge, MA: Harvard UP, 1968.

Porter, Joseph A. *Shakespeare's Mercutio: His History and Drama.* Chapel Hill and London: U of North Carolina P, 1988.

Prager, Carolyn. "Heywood's Adaptation of Plautus' *Rudens*: The Problem of Slavery in *The Captives.*" In Davidson et al., 108–16.

A Primer of Boke of Private Prayere most Needful to Be Vsed of all Faithfull Christianss, whiche Boke is Authorysed and Set Fourthe by the Kinges Maiestie to be Taughte, Learned, Redde, and Vsed of All Hys Louynge Subiectes. London, 1553.

Rackin, Phyllis. *Stages of History: Shakespeare's English Chronicles.* Ithaca: Cornell UP, 1990.

Reardon, Bernard M. G. *Religious Thought in the Reformation.* 2nd ed. London and New York: Longman, 1995.

Ridley, Jasper. *Thomas Cranmer.* Oxford: Clarendon, 1962.

Riehle, Wolfgang. *Shakespeare, Plautus, and the Humanist Tradition.* Cambridge: D. S. Brewer, 1990.

Robbins, Bruce. *The Servant's Hand: English Fiction from Below*. New York: Columbia UP, 1986.

Rollock, Robert. *Lectures upon the Epistle of St. Paul to the Colossians*. London: Felix Kyngston, 1603.

Rowse, A. L. *Shakespeare's Southampton, Patron of Virginia*. New York: Harper and Row, 1965.

———. *Simon Forman: Sex and Society in Shakespeare's Age*. London: Weidenfeld and Nicolson, 1974.

Saville, John, ed. *Democracy and the Labour Movement: Essays in Honour of Dona Torr*. London: Lawrence & Wishart, 1954.

Schoenbaum, S[amuel]. *William Shakespeare: A Documentary Life*. New York: Oxford UP, in association with The Scolar Press, 1975.

Sedgewick, Eve Kosovsky. *Between Men: English Literature and Male Homosocial Desire*. New York: Columbia UP, 1985.

Seton-Watson, R. E., ed. *Tudor Studies Presented by the Board of Studies in History in the University of London to Albert Frederick Pollard Being the Work of Twelve of His Colleagues and Pupils*. New York: Russell & Russell, 1970 [1924].

Shakespeare, William. *The Complete Works of William Shakespeare*. Ed. David Bevington. 4th ed. New York: HarperCollins, 1992.

———. *The Complete Works of William Shakespeare*. Ed. Irving Ribner and George Lyman Kittredge. Waltham and Toronto: Ginn and Company, 1971.

———. *Major Plays, and the Sonnets*. Ed. G. B. Harrison. New York and Burlingame: Harcourt, Brace & World, 1948.

———. *The Norton Shakespeare, Based on the Oxford Edition*. Ed. Stephen Greenblatt, Walter Cohen, Jean E. Howard, and Katherine Eisaman Maus. New York and London: W. W. Norton & Company, 1997.

———. *Works. The Riverside Shakespeare*. Ed. G. Blakemore Evans. Boston: Houghton Mifflin, 1974.

———. *All's Well that Ends Well*. Ed. G. K. Hunter. London: Methuen and Co., 1967.

———. *The Comedy of Errors*. Ed. R. A. Foakes (The Arden Shakespeare). London: Methuen and Co., 1962.

———. *Henry VI Part 1*. Ed. Andrew S. Cairncross. (Arden). London: Methuen & Co., 1969.

———. *The First Part of King Henry VI*. Ed. Andrew Cairncross. London: Methuen & Co., Ltd.; Cambridge, MA: Harvard UP, 1962.

———. *King John*. Ed. L. A. Beaurline. Cambridge: Cambridge UP, 1990.

———. *The Life and Death of King John*. Ed. A. R. Braunmuller. Oxford and New York: Oxford UP, 1989.

———. *King John*. Ed. John Dover Wilson. New Shakespeare. Cambridge: Cambridge UP, 1936.

———. *King John*. Ed. E. H. J. Honigmann. (Arden.) London: Methuen & Co. Ltd., 1954.

———. *King John*. Ed. William Matchett. New York: Signet, 1966.

———. *King John*. Ed. R. L. Smallwood. Harmondsworth: Penguin, 1974.

———. *Romeo and Juliet*. Ed. Brian Gibbons. London and New York: Methuen, 1980.

———. *The Taming of the Shrew*. Ed. Brian Morris. London and New York: Methuen, 1981.
———. *The Tempest*. Ed. Frank Kermode, Arden Shakespeare. London: Methuen, 1954.
———. *The Tempest*. Ed. Steven Orgel. Oxford, New York: Oxford UP, 1987.
———. *The Tempest*. Ed. Irving Ribner. Glenville, IL: Scott Foresman, 1984.
———. *The Tempest*. Ed. Anne Righter. Harmondsworth: Penguin, 1974.
Sharpe, Kevin. *Politics and Ideas in Early Stuart England*. London and New York: Pinter Publishers, 1989.
Sheen, Erica. " 'The Agent for his Master': Political Service and Professional Liberty in *Cymbeline*." In McMullan and Hope, 55–76.
Simon, Daphne. "Masters and Servants." In Saville.
Simon, Roger. *Gramsci's Political Thought: An Introduction*. Electric Book, 2001.
Skura, Meredith Ann. "Discourse and the Individual: The Case of Colonialization in *The Tempest*." In Graff and Phelan, 286–327.
Slater, Miriam. *Family Life in the Seventeenth Century: The Verneys of Claydon House*. London: Routledge & Kegan Paul, 1984.
Smith, Abbot Emerson. *Colonists in Bondage: White Servitude and Convict Labor in America 1607–1776*. Chapel Hill: U of North Carolina P, 1947.
Smith, Alan G. R. *Servant of the Cecils: The Life of Sir Michael Hicks, 1543–1612*. London: Jonathan Cape, 1977.
Smith, Bruce R. *Homosexual Desire in Shakespeare's England: A Cultural Poetics*. Chicago and London: U of Chicago P, 1991.
Smith, Henry. *Sermons*. London, 1592.
Smith, Preserved. *The Reformation in Europe*. New York: Collier Books; London: Collier-Macmillan, 1962.
Solomon, Robert C. and Kathleen M. Higgins. *What Nietzsche Really Said*. New York: Schocken Books, 2000.
Sommerville, Margaret. *Sex and Subjection: Attitudes to Women in Early-Modern Society*. London, New York, Sidney, and Auckland: Arnold, 1995.
Stirling, Brents. "Cleopatra's Scene with Seleucus: Plutarch, Daniel, and Shakespeare." *SQ* 15.2 (1964): 299–311.
Stone, Lawrence. *The Crisis of the Aristocracy 1558–1641*. Oxford: Clarendon, 1965.
Stopes, C. C. *The Life of Henry, Third Earl of Southampton, Shakespeare's Patron*. New York: AMS Press, 1969 [1922].
Strier, Richard. "Faithful Servants: Shakespeare's Praise of Disobedience." In Dubrow and Strier, 104–33.
———. *Resistant Structures: Particularity, Radicalism, and Renaissance Texts*. Berkeley, Los Angeles, and London: U of California P, 1995.
Takaki, Ronald. *A Different Mirror: A History of Multicultural America*. Boston, Toronto, and London: Little Brown & Company, 1993.
Taylor, E. P. *The Poverty of Theory and Other Essays*. New York and London: Methuen, 1978.
Theweleit, Klaus. *Male Fantasies*, vol. 2: *Male Bodies: Psychoanalyzing the White Terror*. Trans. Erica Carter, Chris Turner, and Stephen Conway. Minneapolis: U of Minnesota P, 1989.

Thirsk, Joan. "Younger Sons in the Seventeenth Century." *History* 54 (1969): 358–77.

[Topsell, Edward.] *The Reward of Religion. Delivered in Sundry Lectures upon the Book of Ruth*. London: John Windet, 1596.

Touteville [Tuvill], Daniel. *St. Pauls Threefold Cord: Where with are Severally Combined, the Mutual OEconomicall Duties Betwixt Husband. Wife. Parent. Child. Master. Servant*. London: Anne Griffin for Henry Seile, 1635.

Trevisa, John. *On the Properties of Things: John Trevisa's Translation of Bartholomaeus Anglicus De Proprietatibus Rerum*. Ed. M. C. Seymour and others. 2 vols. Oxford: Clarendon Press, 1975.

Vaughan, Virginia Mason and Alden Vaughan, eds. *Critical Essays on* The Tempest. London: Prentice Hall International, 1998.

Velz, John. *Shakespere and the Classical Tradition: A Critical Guide to the Commentary, 1860–1960*. Minneapolis: U of Minnesota P, 1968.

Verkamp, Bernard J. *The Indifferent Mean: Adiophorism in the English Reformation to 1554*. Athens, OH: Ohio UP; Detroit: Wayne State UP, 1977.

Veyne, Paul. *The Roman Empire*. In Aries and Duby, 1–234.

Vickers, Brian. *Shakespeare, Co-Author: A Historical Study of Five Collaborative Plays*. Oxford: Oxford UP, 2002.

Wall, A. "Faction in Local Politics, 1589–1620: Struggles for Supremacy in Wiltshire." *Wiltshire Archaeological and Natural History* 72–73 (1978): 119–33.

Wall, Wendy. *Staging Domesticity: Household Work and English Identity in Early Modern Drama*. Cambridge: Cambridge UP, 2002.

Walton, Izaak. *The Compleat Angler and the Lives of Donne, Wotton, Hooker, Herbert, & Sanderson*. London: Macmillan and Co., 1925.

Weimann, Robert. *Authority and Representation in Early Modern Discourse*. Ed. David Hillman. Baltimore and London: Johns Hopkins UP, 1996.

———. *Author's Pen and Actor's Voice: Playing and Writing in Shakespeare's Theatre*. Cambridge: Cambridge UP, 2000.

———. *Shakespeare and the Popular Tradition in the Theatre*. Ed. R. Schwartz. Baltimore and London: Johns Hopkins UP, 1978.

Weinstock, Horst. "Loyal Service in Shakespeare's Mature Plays." *Studia Neophilologica* 43.2 (1971), 446–73.

Wells, Stanley, and Gary Taylor, with John Jowett and William Montgomery. *William Shakespeare: a Textual Companion*. Oxford: Clarendon Press; New York: Oxford UP, 1987.

Whateley, William. *Prototypes, or the Primarie Presidents out of the Booke of Genesis, Shewing the Good and Bad Things They Did and Had Practically Applied to Our Information and Reformation*. London: G. M. for George Edwards, 1640.

White, Paul Whitefield. "Earning a Living as a Royal Interluder: The King's Men Under Edward VI." Unpublished article submitted to the seminar on service, Shakespeare Association of America annual meeting, 1993.

Whythorne, Thomas. *Autobiography*. Ed. J. M. Osborn. Oxford: Clarendon Press, 1961.

Williams, David, ed. *Early Tudor England: Proceedings of the 1987 Horlaxton Symposium*. Woodbridge: Brydell, 1989.

Williams, Raymond. *Keywords: A Vocabulary of Culture and Society.* New York: Oxford UP, 1976.

———. *Marxism and Literature.* London: Oxford UP, 1977.

Willis, Deborah. "Shakespeare's *Tempest* and the Discourse of Colonialism." In Graff and Phelan, 257–68.

Wilson, Edward O. *Consilience: The Unity of Knowledge.* New York: Alfred Knopf, 1998.

Wilson, H. A., ed. *The Gelasian Sacramentary. Liber sacramentorum romanae ecclesiae.* Oxford, 1894.

Woodbridge, Linda. *Vagrancy, Homelessness, and English Renaissance Literature.* Urbana and Chicago: U of Illinois P, 2001.

Wrangham, Richard and Dale Peterson. *Demonic Males: Apes and the Origins of Human Violence.* Boston and New York: Houghton Mifflin, 1996.

Wright, Robert. *The Moral Animal: The New Science of Evolutionary Psychology.* New York: Pantheon Books, 1994.

Wright, Sue. *Women and Work in Pre-Industrial England.* London: Croom Helm, 1985.

Wright, Thomas. *The Passions of the Minde.* London, 1601.

Wrightson, Keith. *Earthly Necessities: Economic Lives in Early Modern Britain.* New Haven: Yale UP, 2000.

———. *English Society 1580–1680.* London: Hutchinson, 1982.

———. "Estates, Degrees, and Sorts in Tudor and Stuart England." *History Today* 37.1 (1987): 17–22.

———. "The Social Order of Early Modern England: Three Approaches." In Bonfield et al., 177–202.

Wyrick, Deborah Baker. "The Ass Motif in *The Comedy of Errors* and *A Midsummer Night's Dream.*" *SQ* 33 (1982): 432–48.

Yachnin, Paul. "Shakespeare and the Idea of Obedience: Gonzalo in *The Tempest.*" *Mosaic* 24.2 (1991): 1–18.

———. "Shakespeare's Politics of Loyalty: Sovereignty and Subjectivity in *Antony and Cleopatra.*" *SEL* 33.2 (1993): 343–63.

———. *Stage-Wrights: Shakespeare, Jonson, Middleton, and the Making of Theatrical Value.* Philadelphia: U of Pennsylvania P, 1997.

York Cycle. See Anon.

INDEX

Index entries in boldface mark passages of particular thematic importance and extended discussions of particular plays. Individual plays are individually indexed by title; characters are individually listed but grouped under the heading "Shakespeare, individual characters."

actors
  as apprentices, *40*
  as servants, *39, 211*
Akrigg, G. V. P., *83*
Alchemist, The, 133
Althouse, Paul, *13, 14*
Amussen, Susan Dwyer, *13*
Anne of Denmark, household
  of, *163*
Antony and Cleopatra, 15, 58, 124,
  159–81
apprentices, actors as, *40*
Aquinas, *see* Thomas Aquinas, St., *7*
Arden of Feversham, 138
Aristotle, *186*
As You Like It, 104, **152–54,** *169*
Aubrey, John, *84*
Augustine, St., *7–8*

bad conscience, *see* Nietzsche
Barish, Jonas, *244*
Barnes, Arthur Dale, *19, 217*
Barnett, Richard C., *69*
Barroll, J. Leeds, *166, 253*
Baynes, Paul, *14, 110, 239*
beating, *see* violence
Beaumont, Francis, *35*
Beaurline, L. A., *117*
Berger, Harry, *37*

Berry, Ralph, *19, 217*
betrayal, *161*
Bible
  Colossians, 41, 129
  Corinthians, 6
  Ephesians, 123, 129, 139, 140
  Galatians, 7, 9, 123
  Genesis, 10
  Luke, 5
  Mark, 5
Bishop, T. G., *126*
Book of Common Prayer, *1*
Boose, Linda, *87*
Brathwaite, Richard, *110*
Braunmuller, A. R., *114*
Bray, Alan, *237*
Breight, Curtis, *260, 261*
Brooke, Arthur, *233*
Brown, Paul, *262*
Burghley, William Lord, *31, 68*
Burke, Kenneth, *50*
Burnett, Mark Thornton, *17, 20, 21,*
  26, 31, 44, 61, 68, 134, 150,
  153, 216, 217, 219, 221, 246
Byfield, Nicholas, *13*

capitalism
  and the intellectual marketplace, *38*
Case is Altered, The, 64, 239

Cecil, William, *see* Burghley
Changeling, 138
Charnes, Linda, *172*
Christ, *6, 9*
Christianity
  and service, *1*
  and slavery, *21*
Chrysostom, St. John, *6,*
  8, 188
Cleaver, Robert and Dod, John, *43,*
  58, 117, 125
clowns, *58*
Collect for Peace, *2–3, 187*
Comedy of Errors, The, 55,
  57–60
commodity, mode of,
  162, **169**
community, *164*
compliant submission, **30–31**
conscience, and obedience, *109*
Coriolanus, *58, 102*
Cox, John D., *15, 134, 141*
Cranmer, Thomas, *2, 11–13*
  Homilie of Salvation, 12
  and monasticism, *11*
  and obedience, *12*
Cymbeline, 132, **126–32**

Danson, Lawrence, *250*
Danvers, Charles and Henry, **82–85,**
  90, 233
Denison, John, *14*
dependence
  of masters on servants, *43*
  mutual, *79*
DiGangi, Mario, *231*
discourses
  biblical, *33*
  cash-based, **33**
  classical, **33, 56–79**
  household or domestic, **33**
  retaining, **33, 81–108**
  of service, *32*

disobedience, **112–32**
  in *Cymbeline, 131*
  penalties for, *112*
Dolan, Frances E., *21, 46,*
  216, 217
Dollimore, Jonathan, *4*
Doran, Madeleine, *65*
doubling, of characters' names, *241*
Dover Wilson, John, *113*
Downame, George, *14*
Duchess of Malfi, The, 138
Duckworth, George E., *61, 64*
Dunham, William Huse, *87*

Elias, Norbert, *110*
Elizabeth I, household of, *163*
Elton, Edward, *110, 239*
Elton, William, *13*
Engels, Friedrich, *151*
Engle, Lars, *32, 35, 38, 183*
Essex, Earl of, *238*
evolution and human nature,
  36, 257

false consciousness, *see* Nietzsche
familiarity, mode of, **169**
Farrell, Kirby, *89, 94*
Fidelis servus perpetuus asinus, 137
Filmer, Robert, *110*
Fit-John, John, *110, 111*
Fletcher, John, *35*
Fosset, Thomas, *6, 13, 116,*
  129, 187
Foucault, Michel, *17*
Foxe, John, *132*
freedom, in *Tem., 207–11*
Fumerton, Patricia, *21*
Fynch, Roger and disobedient
  fidelity, *109*

Gascoigne, George, *39, 42*
gender, *32,* **159–81**
Gibbons, Brian, *83*

Gouge, William, *14, 43, 111, 112, 116*
grace, and willing service, *201, 202,* **207–11,** *209*
Gramsci, Antonio, *27, 257*
Greenblatt, Stephen, *146, 151, 201*
Gurr, Andrew, *230*

Hammond, Dorothy, *97*
Henry IV Part 1, 81, 170
Henry IV Part 2, 81
Henry V, 81
Henry VI Part 1, 81, 88
Henry VI Part 2, 81, 113
Henry VI Part 3, 81
Herbert, George, *14*
Hoffman, John, *28*
Holland, Norman, *237*
Holles, Sir John, *28*
Homilies, The Book of, 5, 12, 14
Hooker, Richard, *111*
Hop and the Pole, the, *28*
Houlbrooke, Ralph, *21*
household, depersonalization of, *162*
housewifery, *41*
Hubert de Burgh, *114, 123*
Hunt, Maurice, *21, 58, 140, 216*

imitatio Christi, *140*
improvisation, **185**
indenture, *136*
individualism, *28*
invention, *160*

Jablow, Alta, *97*
James, Mervyn, *81, 87, 94, 235, 236*
Jameson, Frederic, *26*
Jonson, Ben, *64, 249*

Kempe, Will, *69, 71*
King John, 85, **113–24**
    textual questions, *114, 240*
    and transaction, *122*

King Lear, 15, 18, 75, **75,** *88–89, 90, 93, 95, 105,* **155–58,** *169*
Kronenfeld, Judy, *239, 250*

Laslett, Peter, *19, 217, 221*
law, divine and human, *109, 116*
Lentriccia, Frank, *51*
locus and platea, 91
Long, Henry and Walter, *82, 90*
Luther, Martin, *10–11*

M., J. [Gervase Markham?], *40, 43, 112, 152*
MacCullough, Diarmid, *12*
Macfarlane, Alan, *86*
Machiavel, the, *102, 144, 193*
Mahood, M. M., *26, 40, 254, 258*
male-bonded group, *86,* **96–103**
Manheim, Michael, *114*
marriage, *180*
Martindale, Charles and Michelle, *231*
Marx, Karl, *17, 46*
Marxism, *28*
masters
    anxieties of, *192*
    dependent on servants, *43, 134*
    and homosexuality, *237*
    responsibilities of, *111*
    things not to do, *111*
    total control of servants, *25*
master–servant relationships in drama, **30–31**
mastery, virtuous, *129, 152*
materialism
    in *Antony and Cleopatra, 162*
    and Caliban, *201*
    and capitalism, *138*
    and determinism, *15*
    evolutionary challenges, *36–37, 257*
    and false consciousness, *151*

materialism—*continued*
  historical challenges, *37*
  and idealism, *17*
  and linguistic determinism, *36–37*
  psychological challenges, *36–37*
  as reductive, *133*
Maydens of London, Letter of, *29*
men, as loners, *164*
Menander, *56*
Merchant of Venice, *70, 160*
messengers, *58*
metaphysics, *139*
methodology, **22**
Milton, John, *140*
Miola, Robert, *69, 232, 255*
modes of service, **168–81**
Moisan, Thomas, *248*
moral over social hierarchy, *132*
Much Ado About Nothing, and retaining, *107*
mutuality and gender, *160, 203, 209*

negotiation, cultural, *38*
Neill, Michael, *17, 19, 20, 21, 58, 75, 131, 134, 138, 139, 216, 218, 219, 221, 261*
New Comedy, *79*
New Way to Pay Old Debts, A, *138*
Nietzsche, Friedrich, *46, 53, 151*

obedience, **112**
  in *Cymbeline,* *127*
  and Iago, *137*
Ong, Walter J., *98*
ordination, mode of, **168**
Orgel, Steven, *210, 262*
Othello, *76, 88,* **134–44**
  domestic vs. military service, *134*
  and lust, *141*
  metaphysical elements, *139*
  and the will, *141*

paradox of service and freedom, *2, 5, 56, 79, 130, 205*
parasite, the, *39, 70–75*
patriarchy, *91, 104, 106, 110*
Pericles, *124*
Perkins, William, *14*
platea, *67*
Plautus, *55, 56, 67*
Plutarch, *166*
Porter, Joseph A., *103, 238*
post-colonial criticism, *201*
potentia humilatatis, *188, see* Cox
Prager, Carolyn, *21, 216*
primacy, *142*

reciprocity, *119, 209*
ressentiment, *17, 28, 46, 51, 58, 147, 157*
retaining, *40,* **81–108***, 156, 161, 177, 200*
  and Essex's rebellion, *94*
  in *Tempest,* *198*
Richard II, *81,* **100–01***, 170*
Richard III, *81, 170*
Ridley, Jasper, *12*
Ridley, Matt, *36*
Robbins, Bruce, *20, 39, 43, 51, 91*
Rollock, Richard, *9*
Romeo and Juliet, *70, 85, 88,* **83–90***, 169*
Rowse, A. L., *83*

Sarum Missal, *2*
Sarum Primer, *2*
sedibus, *67*
self-fashioning, **146–57**
self-sacrifice, *82*
servants
  actors as, *39*
  an asses, *246*
  bad, *154*
  courtly, *193*
  difficult to define, **20–21**

fools, *74*
gentlefolk as, *25*
and household secrets, *44*
indentured, *24, 41*
largely ignored, **20–21**
largely silent, *43*
lena, *69*
loquacity, *64*
loyalty of, *92*
multiple motivations, *133*
New Comic, *56*
not rewarded, *60, 131, 149, 151*
and obedience, *41,* **109–12**
parasites, *70*
and physical abuse, **58–59**
responsibility, *119*
in sexual trades, *231*
in social history, *20–21*
under masters' total control, *25*
vices of, *155*
virtuously disobedient, **113**
wage-earners, *24*
wily, *65, 128*
and women, *160*
service
at accession of Henry VII, *4*
as accident of birth, *129*
and anxiety, *4*
and Augustinian order, *8*
bad, **138**
and Benedictine order, *8*
and capitalism, *45, 159, 162*
and Christianity, *5, 9*
commercial, *40, 43*
competing discourses, **30–31**
concentration on Shakespeare,
    30–31
diabolical, *139*
discourses of, *32*
and display, *42*
divinely ordained, *129*
domestic, *41*
in drama, **30–31**

as dynamic, *1*
and early modern court politics,
    252, 261
faithful disobedience, *127, 156*
and family, *160*
and the family, **30–31**
and forgiveness, **207–11**
and Franciscan order, *8*
as free choice, *133, 143, 150,*
    159, 205
and freedom, *207*
and fun, *160*
and gender, *32,* **159–81**
good, **157**
and grace, **207–11**
household, *41*
in human condition, *140*
as *imitatio Christi,* *140*
ironized, *157*
lack of clear definition, *11*
and love, *150, 203*
and marriage, *180*
modes of, **168–81**
moral, **127**
and morality, **154–58**
mutual, *203*
and natural affection, **120–22,** *150*
necessary to sustain good, *204*
never merely binary, *26*
and Old Testament, *5*
and the papacy, *6*
parody of, *205*
as play, *77*
and political legitimacy, *243*
and power, *17*
range of relationships, *32*
reciprocity in, *130*
retaining, *25, 40,* **81–108,** *177*
as role not status, *56*
and St. Paul, *5*
as theme of *Tempest,* *190*
transactional character of, *122*
troping of, *30*

service—*continued*
  in Tudor period, *4*
  virtuously disobedient, **113**
  and the will, **140**
  willing, *26*, **30–31**, *158, 201*
  willing submission, *17, 188*
Seruingmans Comfort, *24*
servire regnare, *2*
servus callidus (wily servant), *65*
Shakespeare, individual
    characters, *179*
  Aaron, *60, 144*
  Achilles, *73*
  Adam, *152, 169*
  Adrian, *194*
  Alexas, *163, 165*
  Antipholus of Ephesus, *59*
  Antonio (in *Tempest*), *193, 206*
  Antony, *167, 174–75, 177, 178*
  Ariel, *112, 191, 206*
  Arthur, *120–23*
  Aufidius, *102*
  Baptista, *44*
  Bassanio, *70*
  Belarius, *130*
  Biondello, *45*
  Borachio, *107*
  Caesar (in *Ant.*), *171, 173,*
    178, 180, 185
  Caliban, *191, 198–200*
  Camillo, *125*
  Capulet, *92*
  Cassio, *138*
  Charmian, *163, 164, 168*
  Chiron, *61*
  Christopher Sly, *40, 42*
  Cleopatra, *58, 171–73, 179*
  Cloten, *128*
  Conrade, *107*
  Cordelia, *18, 158*
  Cornwall, Duke of, *18*
  Cornwall's servant, *18, 37*
  Costard, *69*

Decretas, *165*
Dogberry, *108*
Dromio, *57, 59*
Edgar, *155–57*
Edmund, *90, 102, 129, 145*
Enobarbus, *58, 165, 167,*
    175–78
Eros, *113, 167*
Fabian, *72*
Falconbridge, *85*
Falstaff, *73–74, 92, 154*
Ferdinand, *203–05*
Feste, *51*
Flavius, *149–51, 249*
Fool (in *Lr.*), *51*
Francisco, *194*
Friar Laurence, *93*
Gloucester, Earl of *18, 101*
Gonzalo, *195–98*
Graziano, *70*
Gregory, *91*
Gremio, *45*
Grumio, *44, 46, 52, 61,*
    62–64, 147
Hastings, William Lord, *85, 114*
Henry V, *24, 92*
Henry VI, *92*
Hortensio, *39–50*
Hotspur, *92, 184*
Hubert, *113–24, 140*
Humphrey of Gloucester, *114*
Iago, *75, 76, 134–44, 185, 232*
Imogen, *127*
Iras, *163, 164, 168*
Jaques, *152*
John, King, *118*
Julia, *76*
Juliet, *93*
Justice Shallow, *81*
Katherine (in *Shrew*), *52, 61, 148*
Kent, Earl of, *15, 25, 85, 90, 96*
Lance, *78*
Lancelot Gobbo, *24, 69, 71*

Lavinia, *61*
Lear, *101*
Lear, King, *18*
Leonine, *124*
Lord (in *Shr.*), *41*
Lucentio, *39, 45, 65*
Macbeth, *102*
Malvolio, *57, 147*
Mardian, *163*
Margaret of Anjou, *92*
Maria, *72*
Menas, *124*
Menenius, *58*
Mercutio, *94, 99, 103*
Miranda, *203–05*
Mistress Quickly, *70*
Montague, *92*
Nurse (*Rom.*), *69*
Orlando, *152, 153*
Oswald, *18, 96, 155*
Othello, *77, 134–44*
Parolles, *72, 74*
Paulina, *125*
Peter (*Rom.*), *69*
Peter Thump (*2H6*), *113*
Petruchio, *45, 46, 52, 61*
Pisanio, *126–31*
Pompey, *70*
Posthumous, *130*
Proculeius, *166*
Prospero, *191, 203–04, 207*
Puck, *149*
Richard III, *145*
Roderigo, *143*
Romeo, *93, 99*
Samson, *91*
Sebastian (in *Tempest*), *193*
Seleucus, *163, 171*
Shylock, *24*
Sir Andrew Aguecheek, *72*
Sir Toby Belch, *72*
Tamora, *61*
Thersites, *73*

Titus Andronicus, *61*
Tranio, *39, 43, 44, 61,
    64–67, 149*
Tybalt, *89, 94*
Valentine, *99*
Vincentio, *65*
Viola, *76*
Shakespeare, William
    and action, *15*
    enactment vs. discussion, *189*
    exposure to classics, *55*
    modifications of Plutarch, *167*
    and responsibility, *116*
    and servants generally, *20–21*
    and tool-villains, *116*
    and willing service, *15*
Sharpe, Kevin, *19, 217*
Simon, Daphne, *23*
Sinfield, Alan, *5*
Skura, Meredith, *201, 202*
slavery, in England, *22*
Smith, Bruce, *99*
Smith, Henry, *111*
Smith, Preserved, *11*
social hierarchy, *132, 134*
Southampton, Henry, Earl of,
    83, 84
St. Paul, *5*
Statute of Labourers/Artificers,
    30–31, 39, 68, 72
Stone, Lawrence, *86*
Strier, Richard, *112, 116, 146,
    157, 239*
subordination, willing, *54*
suicide, and freedom, *168*
Supposes, 39, 42

Taming of the Shrew, The, **38–53***, 58,
    61, 183*
Tempest, The, **189–211**
    all characters masters or
        servants, *189*
    all discourses developed, *189*

Tempest, The—continued
  freedom in, *207–11*
  as heuristic, *209*
Terence, *55, 56, 67*
theater
  as marketplace for ideas, *38*
  social circumstances, *67*
Thompson, E. O., *37, 38*
Tiger, Lionel, *97*
Timon of Athens, **149–51**
Titus Andronicus, *55, 95*
tool-villains, *112, 115, 136*
Topsell, Edward, *129*
Touteville, Daniel, *14, 111, 188*
Troilus and Cressida, *73, 88*
Troublesome Raigne of King John, *117*
Twelfth Night, *76*
Two Gentlemen of Verona, *76, 99*

vagabonds, *200*
violence, *135*
  beating of servants, *58–59*
  and conflict-resolution, *108*
  and gender, *94*
  as punishment for sin, *239*
  and retaining, *84–88*
  in *Tempest*, *192*
  in Wiltshire, *87*

volitional primacy, *7, 27, 79, 134,*
  ***142–48**, *157, 158, 180, 181,*
  183, 204
  in games, *144*
  and improvisation, *184*
  Machiavellian, *193*
  not always rewarded, *184*

Walton, Izaak, *14*
Weimann, Robert, *67, 242, 248*
Weinstock, Horst, *112*
Whately, William, *9*
Whythorne, Thomas, *138*
will
  and faculty psychology, *140*
  and service, *140*
  willing subordination, Ariel's, *191*
Wilson, E. O., *36*
Winter's Tale, **125–26**
women
  and community, *164*
  fidelity of, *161*
Woodbridge, Linda, *157, 250*
Wrangham, Richard, *97, 238*
Wright, Robert, *36*
Wright, Thomas, *141*

Yachnin, Paul, *247*